Mainly About
Lindsay Anderson

Mainly About
Lindsay Anderson

GAVIN LAMBERT

ALFRED A. KNOPF   NEW YORK   2000

THIS IS A BORZOI BOOK
PUBLISHED BY ALFRED A. KNOPF

Copyright © 2000 by Gavin Lambert

All rights reserved under International and Pan-
American Copyright Conventions. Published in the
United States by Alfred A. Knopf, a division of Random
House, Inc., New York, and simultaneously in Canada by
Random House of Canada Limited, Toronto. Distributed
by Random House, Inc., New York.

www.aaknopf.com

Knopf, Borzoi Books, and the colophon are
registered trademarks of Random House, Inc.

ISBN 0-679-44598-6
Library of Congress Card Number: 00-106208

Manufactured in the United States of America
First Edition

To Jocelyn Herbert and Anthony Page, who insisted . . .

Contents

Mainly About
Lindsay Anderson

Old Times

~ Lindsay on Lindsay ~

My father, a Scot and a soldier, was born in North India. My mother was born in Queenstown, South Africa. I was born in Bangalore, a child of Empire. Did these antecedents make for an alienation, long unrecognized?

I remember very well, when my form master at Cheltenham College spoke to me in a very pleasant, polite way, and I think I had been discovered in some peccadillo, and he said to me, "You know, Anderson, if you go on like this, you are going to be persona non grata with a great many people." And I said to him, "You are probably right, sir, but I think it's too late to do anything about it."

Shadow of Empire. Regimental photo, Bangalore, 1922. Captain A. V.
Anderson, Lindsay's father, seated second from the right; Captain C. Sleigh,
Lindsay's future stepfather, seated second from the left.

1

On November 20, 1994, three months after Lindsay Anderson died, a Memorial Celebration was held at the Royal Court Theatre in London. The evening also celebrated almost forty years of English stage and screen history, for it was at the Court that the English Stage Company, founded in 1956 by George Devine with Tony Richardson as his associate, had introduced the London theatre to contemporary life. At the Court Tony directed John Osborne's *Look Back in Anger* and *The Entertainer,* and Lindsay directed several plays by David Storey, including *The Changing Room, The Contractor,* and *Home* with John Gielgud and Ralph Richardson.

As well as David Storey, several other friends and colleagues of Lindsay's onstage that evening had worked at the Court. They included actors Alan Bates, Tom Courtenay, and Albert Finney, designer Jocelyn Herbert, and Anthony Page, Lindsay's assistant before directing plays there himself. And present in spirit was ninety-year-old Gielgud, who sent a letter that David read to the audience: "Dearest Lindsay, I am so very sorry not to be with you this evening, but I am filming early tomorrow and do not think you would want me to be too tired to work. Such happy memories of our work together, you and David Storey, of acting together in *Chariots of Fire,* and your unique friendship. You were always so honest and direct, whether in approval or stricture, and I miss you more than I can say."

Also present onstage were Alan Bennett, with his own wry view of Lindsay being honest and direct when they collaborated on a brilliant TV movie, *The Old Crowd*—"He looks at me enquiringly, then puts a straight line through half a page. 'Boring, don't you think?' "; Richard Harris and Malcolm McDowell, who recalled how *This Sporting Life* and

If . . . had virtually launched their movie careers; Alan Price, who performed the songs he wrote for *O Lucky Man!;* and myself with some memories of a friendship that began during our schooldays. Tony Richardson, who launched Lindsay's career in the theatre by offering him a play to direct at the Court, had died in 1991. But in the audience that evening was Karel Reisz, another major link in the historical chain. The success of *Look Back in Anger* had enabled Tony to form his own film company, Woodfall, which produced Karel's first feature, *Saturday Night and Sunday Morning*—and soon afterward Karel produced Lindsay's first feature, *This Sporting Life.*

"He was a man with a set of values seemingly in place since birth," said David Storey in his introduction to the evening. "They were values by which he observed, scrutinized and judged everything around him, [and he had] an appetite for a world nobler, more charitable, and above all more gracious than the world in which he found himself." But this didn't mean that in person Lindsay was always charitable or gracious, and after noting that he was also "a man of vivid contradictions," David proceeded to list them. "He could be cantankerous and vituperative, he could be obdurate and acerbic, yet he was incorrigibly loyal and unfailingly generous. He was authoritarian, yet unmistakably a liberal. He was a stoic, yet undeniably sentimental. He was a self-confessed atheist, and yet he was imbued with what can only be described as a religious spirit."

Next day I recalled another contradiction. Monty White, the executor of Lindsay's estate, and two of his closest friends, Jocelyn Herbert and Anthony Page, had asked me to write his biography. My first reaction was that I could never be objective enough. But then I thought of Lindsay's book that he called *About John Ford*—which was really about the two of them. A generation separated them, Ford was not an intellectual and Lindsay was not (in the conventional sense) a family man, they grew up and worked in different countries, but at moments each recognized a kindred spirit in the other. Lindsay, like Ford, was at once a rebel and a traditionalist, and in Ford he perceived "a divided man" who could be "gentle and irascible" in equal measure. Ford, when Lindsay remarked that he responded primarily to individuals and detested any form of group discipline, answered at once, "I had the same problem." And perhaps not coincidentally, their movies provoked violent critical disagreement—a sure sign, as Oscar Wilde remarked, that "the artist is in accord with himself."

Alternately personal and objective, *About John Ford* was in part a memoir of a guarded friendship that began in 1950 when Lindsay first met Ford in Ireland, where Ford had just finished location shooting on *The Quiet Man,* and ended in 1973, with a visit to him on his deathbed in Palm Desert; in part a thoroughly researched, critical biography with comments from actors (Henry Fonda, Robert Montgomery) and screenwriters (Dudley Nichols, Nunnally Johnson) who had worked with Ford; and in part a tribute from one director to another, acknowledging Ford as the filmmaker who first alerted Lindsay to "the essence of cinema, the language of style," when he saw *My Darling Clementine* at the age of twenty-three.

About John Ford was also a dual portrait. The man whom Lindsay came to admire as "a poet in the original Greek sense of the word, 'one who makes, a maker, the creator of a poem,' " appears in intimate close-up, distanced medium shot, and point-of-view shot from Fonda and others. Lindsay appears in frequently intercut reaction shots, stunned by Ford's perversity, touched by his moments of warmth, mocked as "some kind of intellectual," and receiving out of the blue a photograph inscribed "with sincere thanks and gratitude for your friendship."

This book is also a dual portrait, but with a difference. Although Lindsay and Ford developed a great regard for each other, they met only six or seven times in twenty-three years. Lindsay and I knew each other for fifty-five years, and interacted far more closely. As contemporaries we lived parallel lives, sharing a past that determined our futures in many ways, and, after I moved to Los Angeles, a continuous present. As well as corresponding fairly regularly, we became each other's first port of call in California and London. So *Mainly About Lindsay Anderson* contains more autobiography than *About John Ford,* and its subtext is one of Lindsay's favorite quotations from E. M. Forster: "Only connect . . ."

We both grew up in England during the late 1930s and early 1940s, and both rebelled against "respectable" families, encrusted with middle-class tradition. But I exiled myself to Los Angeles, where the past was half forgotten although still very young; and Lindsay exiled himself at home, where the past was "a snug refuge," as he later wrote, from the present. And while Lindsay understood why I left England, just as I understood why he preferred to confront it, neither of us could imagine adopting the other's solution.

Unlike Lindsay, I never kept a diary (except for a few weeks during the early 1960s), and was often negligent about preserving my working notes. Lindsay's files proved a rich source for re-creating some of his life and much of his work when I started to write this biographical-autobiographical-monographical memoir; but my own files are comparatively meager, with gaps that only memory can fill. Fortunately my memory is tenacious.

But although my own life, and Lindsay's in the early years of our friendship, came back to me in the form of direct recall, after I left England in 1956 I could recall Lindsay directly only through our subsequent meetings, and the numerous letters he wrote me. The rest of him is a compilation, partly from those extensive files (my letters to him, his diaries, articles, clippings), partly from conversations with his friends and colleagues. So at first the flow of memoir carries Lindsay along, then he passes through the filter of biography.

In Ford's films, with their Whitmanesque view of men as brothers, Lindsay heard "America singing," but when he visited America he heard a different kind of song, and didn't much like it. I never felt at home in Britain, and first heard "America singing" in the seductively bitter romanticism of Scott Fitzgerald, the sardonic human comedy of Ring Lardner, and some indelible Hollywood movies of the 1940s: *Notorious, Sullivan's Travels, The Big Sleep, Remember the Night.* After I came to live in California I heard increasingly darker variations on the same song, from *Touch of Evil* to *Vertigo* to *Casino;* but by the 1990s Scorsese's film was an exception that proved the rule. From the *Lethal Weapon* and *Die Hard* cycles to *The Bridges of Madison County, Titanic,* and *Meet Joe Black,* Hollywood movies have rarely been seductive, least of all when supposed to be romantic. These days America usually sings for me in off-Hollywood movies: Richard Linklater's *Before Sunrise,* Jim Jarmusch's *Dead Man,* Neil LaBute's *Your Friends and Neighbors,* in the novels of Bret Easton Ellis, Armistead Maupin's *Tales of the City,* Cormac McCarthy's *Border Trilogy,* the stories of Rachel Ingalls and Tobias Wolff.

Although Lindsay once described Britain as "this remarkably irritating, paradoxical country" and satirized it with increasing ferocity over the years, he never considered leaving it. The bond of love-hate was too strong, and stimulated his finest work. But by the time we last met, in 1993, the most original British filmmaker of his generation had become a displaced person in his own country, unable to raise money for the movies he wanted to make. "I'm afraid that age, and too much speaking one's mind in the past, have finally caught up with me," he wrote me a few months before he died. "We're not at a time now when dissidence is regarded as a virtue. Once upon a time, I often reflect, people thought highly of the right to fail, but now all that matters is the obligation to succeed." As David Storey pointed out, the man who had so often deplored "the grotesque disparities between talent and recognition," and championed unfashionable artists, finally suffered the "personal pain" of becoming unfashionable himself.

In Europe and the United States Lindsay continued to have a cult following, which often made him feel marginalized and less often gave him great pleasure. That same discouraged letter ended with an account of his recent visit to the European Film College in Denmark, where two of his films were shown. He was particularly happy that the student audience received *Britannia Hospital* "with a lot of laughter and understanding, very different from the scorn and hostility with which it was received in this country. Well, I don't want to go on about Britain—but it really was extraordinary to find how universally that film was derided as 'humourless' and 'undergraduate.' Of course those are the standard epithets with which anything unpleasant or threatening is dismissed."

"It was the differences that kept us close," I once wrote about Lindsay, and the differences have helped me to see him (and perhaps myself) more closely. So have the diaries that he kept from 1942 to 1992. They record in detail another kind of personal pain, something that Lindsay was able to disclose fully only to himself. On separate occasions he allowed David Storey, Anthony Page, and me to catch a glimpse of it, and although we knew that his emotional life was a series of frustrations, did any of us realize how lacerating they were? Pride, and the actor in him, created at least a partial smoke screen. But the ache of repression in his diaries makes an almost Jekyll-and-Hyde contrast with Lindsay at his sharp, humorous, dynamically self-assured and reassuring best. In the same way, a bitterness that he couldn't always control, and that surfaced in flashes of disconcerting cruelty, led Anthony Page to sum up the sum of Lindsay's parts: "Not always likable, but often lovable."

The diaries are a dark mirror. The abrasively unhappy and overly judgmental person who inhabits them reflects all Lindsay's negatives and few of his positives. Some experiences, Nietzsche wrote, either kill a part of you or make you stronger, and in Lindsay's case they did both. The alienated child who perceived himself as an emotional orphan became a young man who sentenced himself, at the age of twenty-one, to grievous psychological stress for life. But by this time, as he later noted, Lindsay had also discovered "a mysterious appetite for drama." He began by responding to movies and the theatre (like me, like millions of others) as a way of escape. Then they awakened a sleeping talent. By directing films and plays, Lindsay was able to work through the feelings he'd locked away, release his imagination, and live out loud as an artist.

Would he have wanted me to draw freely on his diaries? I think so, because if someone wishes this kind of private material to remain a secret forever, he leaves instructions in his will for it to be destroyed or placed off-limits in an archive. Or he may expurgate the most confessional passages and give permission for the rest to be published. But Lindsay's will, very detailed in other respects, simply left all his papers in the hands of his executor. As well as the diaries, handwritten in more than fifty notebooks, the papers included extensive correspondence files. (Lindsay was one of the great letter writers. Soon after he made *This Sporting Life* he began dictating his letters to a secretary, who kept copies—another sign, surely, that he kept an eye on posterity.) One of his friends who understood Lindsay best also gave me a nudge. "His life and work," said David Storey, "were indivisible." And in responding to them indivisibly here, I felt a posthumous nudge from Lindsay himself. Toward the end of that Memorial Celebration, clips from his various TV interviews were projected. " 'Personal,' " he said at one moment, evidently in answer to a question that we didn't hear, "is a very important word."

2

Lindsay and I first met at Cheltenham College sometime during the spring of 1939, six months before the outbreak of World War II, and thirty years before Lindsay returned there to shoot location scenes for *If . . .* Cheltenham was a bit lower down the social ladder than Eton or Harrow, the most exclusive public schools for sons of aristocrats, plutocrats, and diplomats, but had a strong military tradition and specialized in preparing sons of officers for one or other of the Army training colleges, Sandhurst and Woolwich. The most typical and respected Old Cheltonians served the Empire and got together for nostalgic far-flung dinners (black tie and medals) from Nairobi to Bangalore. The most untypical was a great artist, the Australian novelist Patrick White, who hated the school and loved *If . . .* Even though he became the only Old Cheltonian to win a Nobel Prize, White was never officially celebrated—unlike another Australian, the poet Adam Lindsay Gordon. The pauper's Kipling was an alumnus for "Cheltonia's Children" (as the school hymn called us) to feel proud of; and Lindsay's mother was such a great admirer that she named her second son Lindsay Gordon.

Lindsay was sent to Cheltenham because he came from a military family, although unlike his older brother, Murray, who went on to Woolwich, he had no wish for a career in the Army. Neither did I, nor my older brother, and I have no idea why our parents sent us there. We had no military bones, and there had been only one general in the Lambert family three hundred years earlier, a commander in Oliver Cromwell's army who supposedly won an important battle in either the Dutch or the Spanish war.

Cheltenham was a modest spa town until the middle of the eighteenth century, when George III, whose daughters were tormented by constipation and found the waters relieved it, made the pump room fashionable. A few crescents and squares of Neo-Palladian houses reflected an elegant past, but the college buildings were gloomy Victorian Gothic. Lindsay and I boarded at the same house, Cheltondale, and before we finally met I sighted him several times, in the stone corridors that reeked of carbolic acid, in the stark and uncomfortable chapel, and in the dining hall, where we sat on long, worn benches like convicts in a prison movie. He was often in the company of a tall, athletic, handsome boy called David McNeill, whose father was a brigadier general and wrote the Bulldog Drummond novels under the name of "Sapper." Lindsay usually looked like the cat that swallowed the canary when he was with McNeill, who hindsight tells me was one of his first crushes.

Lindsay himself was chunky, with a powerful torso that emphasized the shortness of his legs, and it seems to me now that by 1939 he had almost reached his full height of five feet six inches. But he held himself erect, walked with an almost martial stride, and had a strong, majestic nose and unexpectedly beautiful eyes that sometimes clouded over, like a dreamer's eyes. At Cheltenham we were divided into Toughs and Wets, boys who were good at games and boys who were not. Getting top marks in classical studies, like Lindsay, or in English literature, like me, branded you as the lowest order of human being, an "intellectual." But Lindsay also played an efficient game of rugger, and I came to realize that his posture, briskness, and sometimes aggressive self-confidence were a disguise that enabled him to pass for a Tough. Although I was no good at games, I could make Toughs laugh with a wicked imitation of our pompous headmaster, and the eccentric wife of our housemaster. (Lindsay re-created both characters in *If . . . ,* but I don't think the housemaster's wife ever wandered around nude at night.) This talent for entertaining, as well as a senior Tough who considered me fair sexual game and played the role of protector, saved me from persecution as a Wet.

The school authorities emphatically warned against "unhealthy attachments" between older and younger boys, but had no idea how often they occurred. And I don't remember that any of us "Tarts," as we were called, thought we were committing a criminal offense, or performing "unnatural" acts. We saw ourselves as playing forbidden games, like smoking cigarettes or drinking alcohol. All that mattered was not to get caught. As for the senior Toughs, who were allergic to introspection, they knew it was just a "phase" that "normal" adolescents went through and grew out of. Later, in fact, most of them became husbands and fathers; and so, probably, did most of their Tarts. Apart from myself, I remember only one other Tart at Cheltondale who was already adjusted to a homosexual future.

Blond, blue-eyed, and vacantly beautiful, Rammelkamp had a relaxed contempt for the authorities. "They just don't know what they're missing," he used to say. "Although, when you look at their awful wives, you'd think they *should*." Far more in demand among the Toughs than I, Rammelkamp was an object of gossip and curiosity among the other boys, who occasionally made fun of his name but not his sluttishness. We once compared notes on our sexual initiations, Rammelkamp's at the age of ten with a workman when he was on summer holiday with his parents in Cornwall, mine at the age of eleven with a teacher at my preparatory school, and agreed that we'd felt no shame or fear, only gratitude.

Although in some ways we were sophisticated, in others we were extraordinarily innocent. We had nothing and no one to rely on except our instincts. Homosexual life in Britain was so closeted that we had no idea how many writers, painters, actors, sportsmen, churchmen, members of the House of Lords, and, of course, schoolteachers were queer or bisexual. We had yet to read Proust or Cavafy or Gide, or Bernard Shaw on the peculiar British obsession that equated sexual deviance with moral infirmity. ("A dishonored check," he suggested, "is a safer index to character.") And it was only much later that I realized how powerfully this obsession had affected Lindsay.

Born April 17, 1923, fifteen months my senior and eventually senior prefect at Cheltondale, Lindsay could and did pull rank in the early days of our friendship. I don't remember how we first met, only that our instant bond was a passion for Hollywood movies. Lindsay told me that his favorite stars were Norma Shearer and Robert Montgomery, and was very intrigued to learn that an aunt on my father's side, Claudine West, was a contract screenwriter at MGM. She had worked on the Shearer-Montgomery *Private Lives* as well as several other Shearer movies, including *The Barretts of Wimpole Street* and (Lindsay's favorite) *Smilin' Through*. On a visit to England in the autumn of 1938 she had promised to send me autographed pictures of my favorite MGM stars (except for Garbo, whom she didn't know), and my personally inscribed photos from Norma, Clark Gable, Spencer Tracy, William Powell, and Myrna Loy enabled me to pull a little rank with Lindsay. I also showed him a postcard portrait of Mae West, sent to her c/o Paramount Pictures when I was nine years old and returned with a flamboyant signature in red ink. But this earned me the quizzical look, eyebrows raised and lips clamped together, that Lindsay would become famous for. "Lambert," he said, "sometimes you strike me as quite dangerously sophisticated." First names, of course, were never used at Cheltenham. Anderson and Lambert only became Lindsay and Gavin after Lindsay left the school.

In an autobiographical sketch that Lindsay wrote forty years later, he recalled Cheltenham as "pretty philistine, not in an unpleasant way but in a very English way." I recall it as deeply unpleasant in many ways. The minimal heating in winter, with no radiators in classrooms or dormitories. The metallic tea from a blotched urn, high-fat bacon on fried bread or lumpy porridge for breakfast, ancient mutton or frazzled cod with lumpy mashed potatoes and watery cabbage for lunch, topped off with a dessert of suet, currants, and sugar called Spotted Dick, which earned me another quizzical look from Lindsay when I said the name suggested venereal disease. The decrepit history teacher (nicknamed "Kipper" on account of his strange body odor) who offered to teach me chess and kept groping me under the table, and who used to prowl the toilets, where he finally surprised two boys together and reported them for indecency.

Yet all this proved a valuable guide for the world to come. The mistrust of "intellectuals" or anyone "different" was a foretaste of middle-class pressure to conform, just as unsavory food or persistent winter colds and chilblains signaled its belief in the moral value of discomfort. The teaching staff, almost without exception self-important and hypocritical, prepared me for later encounters with official authority. The chaplain, a creationist before his time, embodied the grotesqueness of official religion when he preached the infallibility of Genesis by pounding the lectern at the end of a sermon and exclaiming, "If this is true, and by God it *is* true, then it *is* true!" (The chaplain was another character drawn from life without exaggeration in *If...*, although Lindsay had forgotten this absurd remark, and later wished I was still in England to remind him of it when he made the film.) The headmaster often referred to himself as "progressive," and announced, on the subject of sex, "I believe in utter frankness about these things." But he encouraged us to associate "these things" with guilt and secrecy when he engaged a school doctor who gave classes in sex education. After projecting various anatomical slides and teaching us new words like "spermatozoa" and "ovum," the good doctor issued all the bad old warnings. Masturbation led to disease and madness, boys who "played with each other" committed a crime against God and nature.

Brought up on this kind of reality, how could Lindsay and I not prefer the illusion of movies, especially the world according to MGM, where the pursuit of happiness and the blessings of liberty were so confidently taken for granted?

In the summer of 1940 the War Office launched a campaign to sign up advance recruits for the British Army from public schools. Germany seemed to be winning the war, but that was no reason to lower the barriers of class; and the powers that be never wavered in their belief that a boy from Cheltenham or Winchester, let alone Eton or Harrow, would make better "officer material" than an upstart from the ranks. And in October, when a colonel from one of the King's Royal Rifle Corps regiments arrived to interview promising Cheltonians, Lindsay was among those he signed up.

By this time, as our headmaster explained to the school, the War Office had launched another campaign. Hitler had ordered his Luftwaffe to cripple the British war machine by saturation bombing of major cities, and his Messerschmitts outnumbered our Spitfire fighters. Without money to build more Spitfires, the Battle of Britain would be lost, and the way left open for invasion by a German army already assembled across the Channel in Nazi-occupied France. Like everyone else, our headmaster said, Cheltonians had a patriotic duty to contribute to the Spitfire Fund, and he asked us each to give *"at the very least five shillings,"* the equivalent then of one dollar.

Next morning, after obligatory chapel service, I approached the headmaster and told him I'd thought of a way to raise more money for the fund. "How very clever of you," he said, insufferably patronizing as usual. "A raffle, I suppose? Or something equally original?"

Without dropping my mask of respect, I smiled to show that I appreciated his wit, then suggested producing a theatrical revue.

Exactly how this idea occurred to me, or exactly what my motives were, I no longer remember. But the lure of show business was certainly stronger than the call of patriotism. To many of us World War II still felt oddly unreal, with no TV to bring images of death and destruction into the home. Radio reported the facts without touching the imagination, newsreel coverage in movie theatres celebrated the excitement of shooting down German bombers but underplayed the terrible damage they did, and Nazis had only just appeared for the first time in a British movie. In *Freedom Radio* (*The Voice in the Night*) they were played by British and Czech actors, with variable accents but the same jackbooted swagger as they tracked down a secret radio station broadcasting anti-Hitler propaganda in German-occupied Holland. The station was run by Clive Brook and Diana Wynyard impersonating Dutch patriots who faced the execution squad in high British stiff-upper-lip style. (In 1941 we began to see more Nazis in British films, notably the secret agent among the English villagers of *Cottage to Let,* played by Alastair Sim, who would be so much more convincing as the headmistress of St. Trinian's; and the survivors of a sunken U-boat in the Powell-Pressburger *49th Parallel*—real enough, but the movie took place in faraway Canada.) As for direct experience, Cheltenham's only air raid warning had been a false alarm; and my parents had left London to stay at my maternal grandmother's country house, where sirens once woke us in the middle of the night. After spending an hour in a large cupboard under the stairs, we heard the faint thud of a very distant bomb just before the "all clear" sounded.

At first my suggestion puzzled the headmaster, who had no idea what a "revue" was. A show with songs and sketches, I explained, and suggested advertising it in store windows and selling tickets to townspeople as well as Cheltonia's children and staff. "Lambert, I never expected such a useful idea from you," the headmaster said. "I'm quite pleasantly surprised." I gave him another appreciative smile and he gave me permission to go ahead.

Lindsay had recently played Feste the clown in a school production of *Twelfth Night.* As well as his performance, I admired the way he sang "With hey ho, the wind and the rain" in a very pure, graceful tenor, and my first move was to ask him to star in the revue. The eyebrows shot up, the mouth puckered. "Just what do you expect me to do?" A very successful revue called *Sweet and Low* was running in London that year,

Cheltenham College, 1940: Lindsay (center) as Feste in *Twelfth Night*

starring Hermione Baddeley and Hermione Gingold. (Both would later become familiar in movies, earthy Baddeley as the barmaid on holiday in *Brighton Rock* and the landlady in *Room at the Top,* astringent Gingold as a witch in *Bell, Book and Candle* and as Maurice Chevalier's improbable old flame in *Gigi.*) "I want us to follow in the footsteps of the two Hermiones," I said, knowing that Lindsay had enjoyed them in *Sweet and Low* as much as I did. "All right, very good," he said briskly. "But I have to be Baddeley."

As well as providing a title, *Good and Proper,* Lindsay discovered a sketch by Noël Coward called "Weatherwise," which became the high point of the show. At Sunday luncheon in her gracious country home, the hostess (Lindsay as the soul of upper-class British normality in tweeds and sensible shoes) entertains a few friends. One of them (myself, wearing a plumed toque) warns another guest, who's never been to the house before, on no account to mention the weather. Any reference to it, I explain, makes the hostess imagine she's a dog. But the guest soon forgets my advice and remarks that the radio has forecast rain. The hostess immediately falls on her knees, then begins to pad on all fours around the table, whining for food and barking for attention. (Lindsay invented some superbly incongruous and vulgar bits of business for this scene, rubbing and snuffling against the guests' legs, lifting a shameless hind leg against a chair.) Like the other guests I pretend not to notice, and we continue to make small talk as if nothing out of the ordinary has happened. Hindsight, of course, makes it clear that when Lindsay chose this sketch he made an unconscious connection with his creative future. Among the characteristics of the British upper class that he satirized in *The Old Crowd* and *Britannia Hospital* was its ability to deny the existence of a disagreeable reality taking place under its nose.

The school audience clearly enjoyed "Weatherwise," unlike the headmaster and all except one of the staff. And in another sketch, Lindsay and I played society ladies discussing the mysterious Count Armand. "They say he undresses women with his eyes," Lindsay remarks, and as if on cue the Count makes a dramatic entrance in a black cloak, his eyes masked by a black-gloved hand. I beg him to lower it, and he asks in a deep, insinuating voice: "You really want me to?" I do, he does, and my dress falls off. Quick blackout, applause and whistles from the school, but authority is not amused.

Only the history teacher congratulated us after the show. (Years later, in his diary, Lindsay referred to Paul Bloomfield as a "humanist" with a gently ironic way of ignoring accepted opinion. He had already ignored it by writing a biography of William Morris, long out of fashion and only "rediscovered" in 1996, the centenary of his death.) "My dear fellows," said Bloomfield that night, "such charming high spirits, and so delightfully obscene." But in chapel next day the headmaster took over the pulpit to announce that the show had filled him with "profound disappointment," and accused me of "wearing a mask of patriotism" to disguise my real motive, "the desire to show off and wallow in bad taste." He was not altogether wrong about the mask, but as I pointed out in an insolent letter that he never answered, *Good and Proper* had earned over £50 ($250) for the Spitfire Fund, and history might remember it for helping to save Britain from a Nazi invasion.

After chapel I asked Lindsay if he'd expected such a violent reaction. "Of course," he said. "Didn't you?" I told him it had astonished me, I thought we were just following in the footsteps of the two Hermiones and wondered why he never warned me. Lindsay gave a long sigh. "Lambert. Sometimes you strike me as quite dangerously naive. If I'd warned you, you'd have started toning everything down, and the show wouldn't have been half as good." It annoyed me to admit that he was right, but pleased me to realize that I'd passed a test. As a rebel. The word was always very important to Lindsay. Several years earlier, on the classroom notice board at his preparatory school, he had written in capital letters, "I REBEL."

In December 1941, in his farewell address to Cheltonians who were leaving the school, the headmaster announced that "Anderson has been awarded a minor scholarship at a university." Was *Good and Proper* still on his mind or was he simply being "philistine in a very English way"? For Lindsay had won a major scholarship in classical studies at Wadham College, Oxford—where he arrived in January 1942 on borrowed time, knowing he could be drafted into the King's Royal Rifles six months later.

Although I spent another year at Cheltenham, our homes were only a few miles apart and we continued to meet during the holidays. No longer able to pull rank as my senior at Cheltondale, Lindsay assumed the role of mentor so naturally that I never questioned his right to it. Some criticisms of my character he kept to his diary, but I remember that he once accused me of being "frivolous." When I said that frivolity didn't necessarily exclude seriousness, the eyebrows shot up. "That *may*, in your case, turn out to be true. But remember, people meeting you for the first time don't know it."

What had I said that marked me as frivolous? It may have been our disagreement over (Tolstoy's, not Garbo's) *Anna Karenina*. "Too much moral heavy weather over adultery," I said, and Lindsay was outraged. For years he held the remark against me, and I held to it. (Still do.) In any case I soon realized that Lindsay's attitude toward sex and his own sexuality, unlike mine, was deeply conflicted. More than fifty years later I read an entry in his diary for January 14, 1942: "There's enough of Mum, and of her sort in me, to warn me off people like Lambert, and yet enough of the other side to make me admire them for their mental achievements." Then, prophetically, Lindsay wondered if "my disapproval and yet feeling at ease with and approval of Lambert [means that] I'm a split personality in a way—the wrong mind in the wrong body."

The same diary entry referred to "the physical question—which I don't feel like discussing here—and my wretched, wretched passions

Bangalore, 1924: Lindsay, aged one, with his brother
Murray, aged four

and inhibitions." Lindsay was not yet ready to call them homosexual, and I feel sure that the main reason was Mum. Born in South Africa, an Army wife in India, she was doubly Colonial, doubly conventional, and singularly unimaginative. A memsahib from her imperial hats to her sensible shoes, she had a robust figure and was three or four inches taller than Lindsay. But when he stood up to her, Mum imploded. The first time I witnessed a row between them, I was puzzled because it erupted suddenly and violently, without apparent cause. Several rows later I discovered a subtext. Lindsay was not Mum's sort, nor she his, but as well as blood relationship they had enough in common— willpower, tenacity, pride, perhaps loneliness—to hope that their basically different natures could be reconciled. Then one of them said something to dash the other's hopes. It was nearly always unimportant, like disagreeing over a movie, or trivial, like arguing over whether to cook roast or mashed potatoes for lunch. The briefest spat could open up the huge intrinsic gap that separated them, but as Mum grew increasingly venomous ("You snooty little bugger!"), Lindsay would shake his head like a father wondering how to deal with the tantrum of a hysterical child—and Mum would admit defeat by stalking out of the room.

Estelle Bell Gasson came from a prosperous South African family, wool merchants on the Gasson side, whiskey on the Bell. Her parents moved to England in the early 1900s, and Estelle met her first husband while on holiday with her mother in Stonehaven, on the northeast coast of Scotland. Stonehaven was the hometown of Captain Alexander Vass Anderson, who happened to be staying with his family on a week's leave during World War I. Immediately after their marriage in 1918 Captain Anderson was posted to India, where he eventually rose to the rank of major general in the Royal Engineers. Lindsay, like his brother Murray, was born in Bangalore; but in 1926 the Andersons separated, and Estelle returned to England with her sons.

Lindsay never talked about his parents' breakup, and I only learned the details of it after his death, when Murray told me a Somerset Maughamesque tale of adultery among Brits in the tropics. Also stationed in Bangalore was Major Cuthbert Sleigh, a close friend of Captain Anderson and a fellow graduate from Woolwich. "He was around so much of the time," as Murray tactfully explained, "that Lindsay and I used to call him Uncle Father." When Estelle left her husband, the major had to remain at his post, but it seems they kept in touch. After Estelle's father died in 1930, she bought a house for her mother and herself in Camberley, Surrey, halfway between London and the Army base of Aldershot, and a favorite country town of military folk. In September 1932 Estelle returned to Bangalore for an attempted reconciliation with her husband. It worked only long enough for her to discover, back in England at the end of the year, that she was pregnant. By the time she gave birth to a third son, Alexander Vass, Major Sleigh had been invalided out of the Army. (He was gassed during World War I and had developed lung disease.) He arrived in Camberley, bought a house called "Cringletie," and in Murray's words, "We all moved in, and after the usual protracted divorce rigmarole—visit to a Brighton hotel and so on," the couple married in 1936.

Lindsay once wrote that his father "was not very keen on his sons," and they never saw him again after his mother remarried. According to Murray, "We saw him off and on when he came back to England on leave," but he was clearly "not very keen" on his sons or their mother. Once, after a gap of several years, he failed to recognize Murray when they met on a train, and later he officially cut them all out of his life. Major General Anderson's entry in *Who's Who* makes no mention of his first wife (he married again in India) or their children.

In his diary Lindsay dismisses his stepfather as "rather a dull bird— but very nice," and he struck me as an almost ghostlike presence at Cringletie. Major Sleigh spoke very seldom and very quietly. His move-

Cringletie, 1941: Mum

England, 1929: Lindsay, aged six

ments were slow, passive, exhausted. No doubt lung disease was partly responsible, but in Mrs. Sleigh's presence he seemed even more diluted, as if about to turn into the Incredible Shrinking Man.

Lindsay sometimes referred to himself ironically as "a child of Empire." But with the father of this child physically absent, and his stepfather spiritually absent, his only active parent was Mum, a formidably conservative Bride of Empire, the source of much of his strength as well as many of his conflicts.

On January 1, 1942, at the age of nineteen, Lindsay began keeping a diary. "Its purpose," he wrote, "is both to remind me in after years of how I felt and what I did, [and] to give me literary exercise." Although he wasn't sure at first whether the diary would be "completely frank," he soon decided that it would: "I can easily expurgate it if necessary." That month he also began to write short stories, one of them based on "the idea that a train disappearing into the distance is a very sad sight." And at the end of January, after wishing that "Mum would take an interest in the stuff I write," he listed some of the books he'd recently read. They included *Pride and Prejudice,* Gibbon's *Autobiography,* and Samuel Butler's *Erewhon.* Among movies, he found Hitchcock's *Rebecca* "well directed and acted, [but] unbelievable. No girl could really be dominated by the dead wife as much as all that, at least I don't think so."

When Lindsay saw *Rebecca,* it was preceded by a newsreel featuring battle scenes from the war against Rommel's army in North Africa. In a striking example of "a set of values seemingly in place since birth," he noted that he had no right to sit watching "a real war, with real gunfire and dead bodies, from a comfortable armchair. If we really want to see such scenes, we should enlist and take part in them ourselves." At the same time he dreaded the prospect of being drafted, and felt distinctly unsettled during his first weeks at Oxford: "What's the use of trying to read the Decline and Fall, starting a film criticism scrapbook, establishing new friends?" But it didn't stop him from becoming "more and more interested in the cinema." Although Lindsay would never lose his early affection for Norma Shearer and *Smilin' Through,* he wrote now of "wanting to make a film of *The Odyssey,* an Eric Ambler spy thriller, and *Hamlet.*" He also compiled a list of "best directors," headed by John

Ford and including Wyler, Hitchcock, Preston Sturges, Fritz Lang, Huston, Capra, Sam Wood, and Anthony Asquith.

This is the first mention of Ford in Lindsay's diaries, and I'm fairly sure it was occasioned by *The Long Voyage Home,* one of the movies we saw together in Camberley. Among our other favorites were *The Lady Eve, The Little Foxes,* and *The Maltese Falcon,* which account for Sturges, Wyler, and Huston. Asquith is probably explained by *Pygmalion,* the only exception to an unexceptional career, and Sam Wood by *Kings Row,* a very classy soap opera with sumptuous theme music by Erich Wolfgang Korngold that Lindsay was still humming fifty years later. If Welles and Lubitsch were not on the list, it was because he hadn't yet seen *Citizen Kane* or *Ninotchka;* and as Britain imported only about half of the new Hollywood movies during the war, with popular appeal and/or propaganda value (as in the case of *Mrs. Miniver*) determining the selection, we had to wait a few years for one of Ernst Lubitsch's finest. *To Be or Not to Be,* unlike Greer Garson, was not considered a shot in the arm for wartime morale.

During his first months at Oxford, Lindsay also began to feel "the desire to create, to perpetuate myself in some way," and wondered how to set about it: "Shall it be a novel, a play, a book on the cinema or a slice of autobiography?" But at the same time he felt there was no point in even thinking about this until the war ended—and after it ended, "stage and films will be packed to overflow. I have no experience and certainly no parental support." His only chance, it seemed, would be "to take some sort of acting job," even though he was "getting very disillusioned about stage and screen" because of rumors that Vivien Leigh and Laurence Olivier were "unpleasant," Diana Wynyard "a bitch," and John Gielgud "a conceited poop." Finally the desire to create won out, and he joined the Oxford Experimental Theatre Club, played a small part in its student production of *The Impresario from Smyrna,* and thought he made the best of "a rather limited opportunity."

As for the part he would soon have to play in World War II, Lindsay now regretted signing up in advance for the King's Rifles, and considered applying to serve in the Intelligence Corps instead. "But I have to reconcile what is right for myself with what is right for the community. Am I morally justified in shirking danger?" His set of values finally allowed that he was, "if the Intelligence job is really important and I am more capable of discharging it efficiently than I am my duties in an infantry regiment."

Then, on June 3, he suddenly announced in his diary: "I am a total wreck." And began to face the deepest conflict of his life. At Cheltenham he had developed a serious crush on "Duff," whom I don't remember, but who made Lindsay understand "the meaning of the expression, 'turned my bosom to water.' The bottom of your stomach falls out and leaves there a gaping, miserable void—that at any rate when he takes no notice of you." They had met again at Oxford, and he found that Duff still gave him "the feeling the woman gets when she's in love." Still taken no notice of, Lindsay "fell behind in work" and was unable to concentrate on anything except the movies. On June 13 he found *Dr. Jekyll and Mr. Hyde* "surprisingly good, S[pencer] Tracy a better actor than I gave him credit for, Ingrid Bergman as good as ever, Lana Turner stooged prettily." But two weeks later, during the Oxford and Cambridge regatta week, he was pitched back into the real world. June 27: "A crew from Trinity Cambridge has been staying in College; one of them, fairhaired, slightly dissolute-looking and extremely good-looking, caused me I am afraid some slight discomfort. It seems then that I am homosexual. Oh God. It really is rather awful and I suppose I shall never get rid of it."

A few weeks later an Oxford friend made it seem even more awful: "My eyes have been firmly opened to the seamier side of life by Gerard, who, an open homosexual himself, is extremely fond of discussing the subject with others. His attitude is, I think, wrong; not only is he tolerant and broadminded but he even encourages conversation about and thus acceptance of it." No details of the seamier side of life, only a reference to Gerard's "revelations" about several famous actors and ballet dancers, which gave Lindsay second thoughts about becoming an actor and made him wonder if he might not be "just as well advised to concentrate on the production and writing side of films."

Although Lindsay never talked about any of this to me, he quickly (too quickly) changed the subject whenever I mentioned any homosexual experience of my own, a habit I soon recognized as a warning signal. Minefield ahead. At the same time I wondered how someone so powerfully intelligent and (as I thought) self-possessed could be living in a sexual straitjacket. His abrupt changes of mood toward me were also puzzling, but Lindsay's 1942 diary reveals that dissatisfaction with himself was spilling over to the world in general.

As well as recording "an increasing hatred" for his roommate at Wadham College, it notes that he felt "very irritated" with his stepfather for giving him a watch: "I have an instinctive dislike of watches. Also it is gold and I much prefer silver." It describes David Vaughan, another Oxford friend, as "decidedly nice in a rather selfish way, but I wonder if he will ever be anything." (In fact he moved to New York, where he became the Merce Cunningham Institute's archivist, and wrote books on Cunningham and Frederick Ashton.) As for me, "for all his faults I like Lambert because I can discuss films and plays with him with the sure knowledge that (a) he's interested and (b) he can understand all the little jokes and innuendos we've by this time built up between us. There's a lot to be said for Old Acquaintance." There was also quite a lot to be said against it, and among my faults listed that year were selfishness, egoism, "lack of consideration" and "prejudicial and unsound judgments."

That year, I remember, we had some edgy disagreements over books and movies. Lindsay greatly admired (Jane Austen's, not MGM's) *Pride and Prejudice,* and when I confessed that I could never get interested in Jane Austen's world, he said, "Not *weird* or *extreme* enough for you, I suppose." When we saw Hitchock's *Foreign Correspondent* together, I found it greatly superior to *Saboteur,* and was put down again with a remark about "at least being consistently true to your own bad taste." But Lindsay always imitated the headmaster at Cheltenham College when he said things like this, as if he didn't expect them to be taken altogether seriously—just seriously enough to remind me that we were still in the mentor and promising-but-erratic-student phase of our relationship.

That year we also decided to collaborate on screenplays. We formed our own "company," Parthenon Films, its name printed in scarlet type on rather elegant buff-colored notepaper, and Claudine West listed (without her permission) as Hollywood representative. Our first effort was a synopsis for a wartime spy thriller, about an attempt by Nazi agents to kidnap the twelve-year-old king of a pro-British Balkan country and install a pro-Nazi government there. According to Lindsay's diary, *Pursuit* was "quite but not outstandingly good." He added that it "took some time to concoct and proved amusing," although once or twice he felt "very annoyed" with me. (Didn't explain why.) I remember *Pursuit* as much livelier than the standard British wartime melodrama, but it was rejected by almost every production company in the land. A hint, which we weren't yet informed enough to take, of the British film industry's closed-door policy toward newcomers.

For our next project we chose *Madame Bovary,* and broke down the novel into scenes which we wrote separately. Lindsay noted that he found it "slow work putting in every shot, every time the camera moves." I only did this when I had an idea for a particular setup or camera movement, as I thought it the director's business to break down scenes into shots. Lindsay disagreed, and by December 23 had begun to suspect that my talent was "more literary than visual." But by December 30 he was "not very satisfied" with his own scenes and thought "perhaps Gavin's will be better." Evidently they were not. January 2, 1943: "I don't think Gavin will ever turn out much on his own. I find I have better ideas than he." We sent the finished screenplay to Alexander Korda at London Film Productions, who rejected it shortly before Lindsay was drafted. And we buried *Madame Bovary* alongside *Pursuit* and Parthenon Films.

"I can understand the mentality of a man who commits suicide," Lindsay wrote in his diary while we were working on *Madame Bovary.* "Sometimes everything seems just too difficult to battle with." After his death this made painful reading—and jolted me into self-examination. (Something, by the way, that Lindsay was very good at in life.) Despair had brought him close to the breaking point, and I never suspected it. Because of my selfishness and egoism?

Partly, I supposed, but partly because Lindsay didn't want me to. The actor in him, who had known how to pass for a Tough at Cheltenham, fooled me with another very effective performance. Three years later Lindsay considered going to a psychiatrist, and noted: "I think I shall consult Gavin about this." But he never did, presumably because he couldn't bring himself to drop his guard: "Even with the friends I have that I value at all, I feel a permanent barrier somehow between us."

It was another feeling that the actor successfully disguised. I was aware of only one barrier between us, which I didn't see as central, and since the subject of homosexuality was Lindsay's mysterious private area, I simply kept out of it. Nothing in his behavior suggested that the mystery was beginning to cast a shadow across his entire life; on the contrary, in our collaborations he seemed to me the leading spirit, quicker to come up with ideas, and what impressed me most strongly about Lindsay at this time was his creativity. Ironically, as he confided to his diary, he felt "the desire to create," but wasn't sure he had the ability.

That Lindsay felt somehow isolated by guilt over his sexuality, and that it led to painful self-doubt, is not in itself surprising. The same thing happened to many others at the time. But it still surprises me that Lindsay, unlike many others, never got over it. Coming from a similar upper-middle-class background, with a deeply conventional father and a mother only marginally less so, I could have grown up equally repressed. Although I never had to contend with Mum power on a Mrs. Sleigh scale, I never felt as Lindsay did that there was "enough of Mum, and of her sort in me," to create conflict and guilt. I simply perceived at an early age that my parents' world was not mine, but didn't resent them for it. On summer holidays my father used to take home movies of family picnics on the beach or in the countryside. One of them showed me, at the age of five, *walking away from everyone else and wandering off on your own, where do you think you're going?"* as my mother used to say—not troubling to ask why and changing the subject before I could answer.

"Character is destiny" was one of Lindsay's favorite quotations, and part of my character and destiny was an innate pragmatism. I never tried "to reconcile what is right for myself with what is right for the community," because I suspected that what was right for the community would almost certainly be wrong for me. But I had to reconcile myself to alienation as a fact of life, and learn not to be surprised or intimidated by the many different ways it was possible to feel (or be made to feel) "different."

Sex, of course, was only one of them. I knew my orientation by the time I was sent to boarding school at the age of eleven, and never questioned it. Probably, as I was already coming to terms with myself as an outsider by then, I would have felt it "abnormal" to be "normal." My personal radar had already sensed a kindred spirit in a male cousin fifteen years my senior. Maurice had declassed himself by working as a movie theatre projectionist in London. He occasionally visited his family, who lived on the same residential country estate as my maternal grandmother, and he seemed to embarrass both houses. My grandmother only invited him to dinner when she needed a fourth at bridge. When we were alone he used to sit me on his knee, and I felt a silent current of understanding and affection flow between us. But my parents said that Maurice was "peculiar," and when he died suddenly in his late twenties, they managed to imply that it was only to be expected—without explaining why.

As I showed an early talent for the piano, my parents decided I was "musical," and like them I was sublimely unaware that the word had a double meaning in the 1930s. Just before my eleventh birthday I won a music scholarship to a preparatory school with a "musical" reputation as well as great snob value. It was situated in the grounds of Windsor Castle and had a royal patron in the person of Princess Marie Louise, a granddaughter of Queen Victoria. At a reception in her honor I remember a stout, dowdy figure not unlike pictures of her grandmother, and an age-mottled hand with grimy fingernails extended for me to kiss.

My parents couldn't know, of course, that St. George's School was also extremely musical in the other sense. Three (that is, half) of the teaching staff were queer, two already had "pets," and the third, who taught music and had awarded the scholarship, chose me as *his* pet. If the headmaster and his wife didn't know what was going on, they were unimaginably naive. In view of what happened later, it seems more likely they followed the example of our neighbors the royal family, turned a blind eye, and hoped for the best.

My teacher-lover made what happened between us seem completely natural, so he must have been experienced as well as handsome and kind. Nothing "wrong" about what we were doing, he explained, but "we have to be careful because some people won't understand." They understood in ancient Greece, he added, and blessed me with the kind of initiation that he held up as an ideal. It not only made me feel superior to the people who wouldn't or couldn't understand. Having to sneak out the dormitory to my teacher's bedroom was exciting, and made him even more attractive.

And soon after falling in love with him, I fell in love with the movies. The headmaster sent the entire school to a matinee of *With Cobham to Kivu*, a documentary about the aviator Sir Alan Cobham's solo flight from England to Rwanda, and we arrived in time to catch the last fifteen minutes of the second feature. *The Man with Two Faces* was played by Edward G. Robinson, but I quickly became more interested in the face of Mary Astor, and glimpses of an excitingly unfamiliar world. Its dark streets and long shadows were standard Warner Brothers low-budget noir, of course, but it made the documentary seem like a home movie.

On Thursday afternoons, when there were no classes, my teacher gratified this new appetite for movies by taking me to see Claudette Colbert in *I Cover the Waterfront,* George Arliss disguised(?) as an Indian rajah in *East Meets West,* and James Mason (with whom I would one day work on a Hollywood movie) rescuing Valerie Hobson from the clutches of a villainous eunuch in *The Secret of Stamboul.* I enjoyed them, and others now forgotten, but nothing quite measured up to that first revelation of Warner Brothers noir. Until *Libeled Lady,* with its wonderful quartet of Myrna Loy, William Powell, Jean Harlow, and Spencer Tracy, introduced me to the bright, voluptuous world of MGM.

The next eighteen months are a series of memory dissolves, from *The Thin Man* to *The Barretts of Wimpole Street* to *Magnificent Obsession* to *The Great Ziegfeld* to *Love on the Run* to *After the Thin Man*—and then to a night in early December 1936, when a radio was brought into the dormitory so we could hear the abdication speech of Edward VIII. The next dissolve is to a letter my parents received during the Christmas holidays. It announced the appointment of a new headmaster at St. George's, and when I returned there in January 1937 my teacher-lover, his two queer colleagues, and one "pet" were also missing. The pet's parents, it turned out, had somehow discovered what was going on and withdrawn him from the school. Under pressure he had informed on the other teachers, but claimed not to know the names of their pets. And like all the other boys questioned by the new headmaster, I claimed never to have heard, seen, or done anything "wrong."

I lied with a clear conscience, and you might say out of love—as well as concealed anger at the new headmaster, who made me feel violated when he spoke of "violation." He had an uncontrollable tendency to spit when he started getting down to details, asking me to swear in the name of God that my music teacher had never "touched" me in any way, then specifying what those ways might have been. (Kissing; hugging; fondling my private parts; asking me to fondle *his* private parts.) The past is said to be another country, but sixty years later that interrogation seems to have taken place on another planet. And it reflected the kind of attitude that could only have intensified the conflicts of someone (like Lindsay) who was already sexually troubled.

In my own case I felt its impact intuitively, of course, and not with the precision that hindsight formulates. But I know it taught me the price that could be paid for being sexually "different," and reminded me never to forget that I had to live in a secret world. By this time I had discovered that my cousin Maurice's death was a suicide, and wondered about the cause. Had he been exposed and lost his job? I also imagined the poor frightened pet being forced out of the closet, reluctantly betraying two other teachers, heroically refusing to implicate his more vulnerable brothers. I compared his situation with the exiled Edward VIII, with whom I now sympathized strongly for being "different" in his own way. Each case was a vivid lesson on the impossibility of reconciling personal needs with the needs of the community, and made me understand more clearly what I was walking away from, as my mother had asked, and where I thought I was going.

I also felt abandoned by my lover-teacher, by then emotionally far more important to me than my parents, who never suspected his existence. But I didn't feel betrayed, only disappointed that he never wrote me a letter—until the other abandoned pet explained it would be too risky. For several years I had fantasies of a passionate reunion when we met again by chance. It never happened. Perhaps he was killed in the war. Just possibly he has survived to read this after turning ninety. In any case he is still remembered, an unfaded photograph in the mind's eye, as my first love and the first love I lost.

Lindsay was not summoned to appear before the draft board at Oxford until January 20, 1943, six months later than he expected. "I was provisionally accepted for the Intelligence Corps, applying for the Navy," he noted, but learned a few weeks later that he would be inducted into the Army. On May 24 he received his induction papers and was sent to an Army base at Wrotham, in the north of England. There he began regular military training, and took a cryptanalysis course in preparation for the work of decoding enemy messages. As well as finding military life in general "physically exhausting and mentally repugnant," he reminded himself that he'd done "nothing creative" since *Madame*

Lindsay at Oxford, 1941

Bovary, and feared that "if in the months to come I am shut off from all congenial companionship, I'm not sure what my mental state will be."

By October 19 Lindsay decided that he had "got over the horror of mentioning homosexuality by name, [but] further development is very necessary." Presumably in the direction of heterosexuality, as he made two resolutions, "to seek congenial female companionship" and "to learn to dance competently." He abandoned both of them a week later, when he met "Alan," a fellow trainee he found "attractive both sexually and mentally." But Alan, like Duff, seemed unresponsive, not even interested in friendship. And on November 27 Lindsay made another resolution, "to beware of *emotional* attachments. I cannot trust myself."

At the same time his attitude toward the Army hardened into "indifference, even contempt," and apparently he didn't try to hide it. On November 30 the colonel reprimanded Lindsay for "a pretty damn bad turnout," and ordered him to get his "quite disgusting" uniform and equipment "smartened up." The result, of course, was to make him despise Army life even more. "Everything is sacrificed to the great God uniformity," he wrote on January 4, 1944, and on January 23 he referred to "the dilemma of the spirit hating the material conditions under which it is forced to live." The same entry defines military discipline as "the habit of unquestioning obedience to the orders of your superior," then echoes the schoolboy who wrote "I REBEL" on the school notice board: "This arouses my most stubborn resistance."

Escaping into movies and books whenever he could, Lindsay was "entertained yet mildly disappointed" by René Clair's *I Married a Witch,* "*very* impressed" by E. M. Forster's *A Passage to India,* the letters of T. E. Lawrence and Keats, Whitman's *Leaves of Grass,* and Virginia Woolf's *To the Lighthouse,* and "*very* disappointed" by Marlowe's *Doctor Faustus,* with its "unsatisfactory central character [who] asks for trouble and gets it."

But although he continued to feel the lack of "congenial companionship," it seems he was not overly popular. The diary notes that fellow trainees often accused him of "conceit," an impression that Lindsay believed he created by trying too hard to disguise his anxieties and his deeply "introspective" and "self-conscious" nature. Over the years, in fact, he will record his amazement that so many people find him arrogant, and no one suspects how insecure he finds himself.

Although Lindsay's last term at Oxford had coincided with my first, we saw less of each other than usual because he disapproved of my close friendship with a fellow student at Magdalen College. Peter Brook, who had instantly attracted me with his self-assurance, flair, and ambition, was planning to direct a 16mm film of Laurence Sterne's *A Sentimental Journey* on a modest budget provided by his family, and in the spring of 1943 he began shooting it: silent, with music and sound effects and a commentary adapted from the novel to be added later on disc. I was his assistant, and also played a bit part—as a drunken slut lolling in the gutter under a street sign, GIN ALLEY. We often went to work together in the eighteenth-century carriage rented for the film, and on the day of the Gin Alley scene, I was already costumed and made up as we rode through the Oxford streets to the location. "You are becoming too *obvious,*" Lindsay warned, and of course he was right.

After Cheltenham, the lack of visible authority at Oxford deceived me into believing I had entered the free world; and I was also influenced by Peter's casual assumption that he could get away with anything. I decided that I could at least get away with skipping tutorials on English literature with C. S. Lewis and not bothering to apologize because I found him so stiff, vain, and condescending. (Also, as I later discovered, homophobic. In 1993 my antipathy was still so strong that I avoided *Shadowlands,* the movie about him.) But when Lewis reported my truancy to the president of Magdalen College, I learned the power of invisible authority.

It had first placed me under surveillance after someone observed me at Oxford station with the notorious black magician Aleister Crowley. Peter knew him, and thought it would be "amusing" to throw a party for him, but work on *A Sentimental Journey* meant that he couldn't meet Crowley's train from London that afternoon. Completely bald, with very dark, very beady eyes, Crowley wore bright green plus fours and carried a cane. When I introduced myself, he grasped my wrist and tried to pull me down with him as he dropped to his knees on the platform. I waited while he intoned a hymn to the sun and a few people watched in amazement. Later, at the party, he boasted that he could invoke Pan, who became extremely amorous when "aroused" by water. We followed Crowley to the riverbank, where he intoned a very long hymn to Pan. Nothing happened, of course, except that it began to rain. Crowley insisted that Pan would still appear if we sacrificed a cat, but by then everyone had had enough.

When the president of Magdalen summoned my parents to inform them that I'd "shamelessly" neglected my studies, the Crowley connection became an additional strike against me. But it was the charge of sexual deviance that horrified them. "It has come to my attention," the president announced, "that your son has brought back American soldiers to his rooms at night." My poor unprepared parents expected me to deny it. Instead, I told the president that his informants exaggerated: "My first week here I picked up *one* GI, in a pub."

My parents seemed to feel the ground give way under their feet, and wanted to send me to a psychiatrist. Back on that other planet, it was a not untypical reaction. As I knew that psychiatrists were supposed to "cure" you, I refused. When I also refused to apologize for anything except wasting my parents' money by neglecting my studies, the result was a painful standoff. I didn't see or even talk to them for more than a year.

With *A Sentimental Journey* in the can, Peter decided to leave Oxford and launch himself as a movie and/or theatre director in London. That summer we went to live there, and by the end of the year the film was ready to be shown. It opened in January 1944 at a very small theatre in Knightsbridge that Peter rented, and we worked the sound discs ourselves (often in far-from-perfect sync) at each nightly performance. Although we had very few reviews, either dismissive or kind but lukewarm, it ran to full houses for three weeks. Lindsay came to see it while he was on leave, and his diary describes it as "technically even worse than I expected," but showing at times "a real feeling for the cinema." I don't remember what he said about it when we met, and my memory of the film is now remote, but I would guess Lindsay got it right. Juvenilia with flashes of talent.

At our first meeting in eight months, Lindsay was extremely interested to learn how I managed to avoid the draft. I told him that when the board summoned me just before I left Oxford, I had originally planned to follow the example of students who pricked a finger and let a drop of blood fall into their urine during the medical test. But friends warned me that the board had become wise to this, and the colonel in charge took sadistic pleasure in rejecting a plea of pacifism from "artistic types" who offered to do farmwork, and sent them straight into the ranks. Homosexuality, of course, was a criminal offense, and I was afraid to admit it to a board of military authorities. So I decided to dress and behave with the utmost normality, except for painting my eyelids gold.

When I entered the room, the colonel was sitting at a table, flanked by two other men in uniform. They stared at me in a silence that felt unnervingly long as well as hostile. Finally the colonel asked, "Why do you put that stuff on your eyelids?" "Because a friend of mine likes it," I said, trying to sound cool and matter-of-fact. A contemptuous order to wait outside, and a few minutes later I was handed a form classifying me 4F, unfit for any kind of military service.

As I still looked on Lindsay as a mentor, and his Army uniform made him even more of an authority figure, I expected at best to be given a stern lecture, at worst to be written off. His first reaction was a long, penetrating stare that reminded me of the colonel and made me nervously defiant. I said something about feeling no guilt or shame at evading military service because I knew I *was* unfit for it, and would be completely useless. "That's right," Lindsay said. Then he smiled. Was he amused at the thought of my uselessness in the Army? "No. That's not amusing at all. You'd have been horribly unhappy." And as he explained that he was trying to imagine the expression on the colonel's face when I walked into the room, I knew why I would always want Lindsay as a best friend.

Years later it was a surprise to discover that he didn't mention this part of our conversation in his diary. Instead: "Gavin was a pleasant surprise when I met him last Friday: far more interesting and individual to talk to. I think he's developing very well." Then he added: "It is amusing that though he talks of homosexuals able to recognize each other, he has not (almost certainly) recognized the same unfortunate trait in me." I had suspected its existence for some time, of course, and knowing the direct approach would never work, looked for a way to cue Lindsay to drop his guard. But he still held back.

Except in his diary. On February 1, back in the Army and the cold north of England during a notably severe winter, Lindsay arrived at a definitive self-analysis: "There are two sides to my character. Masculine/feminine. Conventional/individualist. Hearty/artistic. Inherited/my own. Middlebrow/highbrow. Middle class/intellectual." A few weeks later he met "James," who was attractive enough to banish thoughts of Alan for the moment, but proved totally indifferent. "Starved for love," Lindsay arrived at another definitive conclusion about himself: "I will never be loved as I wish to be, *for myself.*" Then, with a growing sense of isolation, he told himself, "Love is what you haven't got. I wonder if your homosexuality is what cuts you off like this." At the same time he continued to believe that none of his friends suspected his secret, because "I have taken good pains that they should not. You will never perhaps have a friend unless one to whom you can tell such secrets: I hope you find one."

Although mistaken about his "secret," Lindsay at twenty-one summed up his conflicts in a painfully lucid way. The note of finality suggests that he knew they would never be resolved in his personal life, but the diary returns again and again to the idea of another kind of self-fulfillment, "the desire to create," the artist he hopes to become.

Perhaps not coincidentally, he continued reading Forster that spring. *The Longest Journey* was a disappointment after *Howards End* and *A Passage to India,* but left Lindsay still "under his spell." He responded most of all to Forster's theme of "the war against unimagination, against narrowness, against inhumanism. And the struggle for adjustment. Forster is the most *practical* writer I know." But Lindsay's own struggle grew more intense when he learned that he would soon be transferred to India—and that James was being transferred elsewhere within a few days. Their goodbye was "a short embarrassed interchange. A handshake and a smile. And reserve." Afterward, he wondered if James had all along been "interested in Alan. Sex? I once was." Then he added:

LG Anderson, 9th Bn KRRC
ceases to exist
Requiescat in pace.

By June 29 he had come back to life—and Forster: "I feel daily the need to connect. 'Only connect . . .' James, Cringletie, Gavin Lambert, Normandy [this was three weeks after D day], the cinema as an art, The Odyssey, Alan, and the lyrics of contemporary dance tunes. These things are facets of my life. But how to integrate, to relate them? It must be done for life has to be lived."

The transfer to India was postponed until November, and in the first week of October Lindsay came to London again on leave. Although I don't remember what we talked about when we met, I must have disappointed him: "Egoistic and of narrow sympathies, though naturally he really is extremely talented and perhaps will develop." But it seems I wasn't the only disappointment. October 10: "I feel more and more the bankruptcy of my life and of my friendships." Then, in a typical mood swing to the positive, he noted that with Allied forces on the offensive against Germany, the end of the war seemed less far away, likewise release from the Army, and the prospect of travel to satisfy "an intense curiosity about other people, other countries. All things considered, the Passage to India is probably a very good thing."

3

On November 10, the second day of the Passage, Lindsay recorded his shock at an example of British class consciousness. "Lower rank accommodation" on the troopship, he wrote, was "beastly, with the men herded together on the lower decks in great droves of a hundred or so." On November 23, when the ship arrived at Suez, he pondered his total lack of heterosexual instincts: "The thought of taking a woman in my arms and kissing her is as foreign, as abhorrent almost as it would be of the average male to think of embracing a male." A few days later, at Aden, the divided self had a conventional/individual reaction to the singing of "God Save the King" after an Army concert: "It moved me a little; it is difficult to subscribe to and dangerous to scorn."

Bombay, December 4: "My journal is becoming quite a habit with me—an old friend to whom I can turn and talk when idle or depressed or just garrulous. Who else is there to whom I can talk without reservation? I am, it seems, fast becoming my most valued companion." And back in the land of his birth, which he had left at the age of three, too early to retain "any real childhood memories," the child of Empire found India "profoundly depressing." The "squalor and general debility" of the native population reminded him "continuously, if subconsciously, that we are masters here, conquerors, imperialists. And whether our subjects acquiesce or not, it is not a pleasant feeling."

Two weeks later Lindsay had reached his destination, the Wireless Experimental Centre in Delhi: "I am pretty well reconciled to a stooge clerk's job; how can I be anything else when my brain simply will not take in all these details of cryptanalysis? Paragraphs which seem quite clear to others are incomprehensible gibberish to me." By the end of December he was reconciled to the prospect of a "dead end existence" as well. But then, on January 31, 1945: "Am I condemned never to arouse in those I love the sort of emotion I desire, I feel myself?"

The new beloved was "Patrick," and once again proved totally unresponsive. He always called Lindsay either " 'Anderson' or 'Er,' which rather sickens me," and was clearly interested in "Peter," another office colleague. They always left together at the end of the day, a situation that finally became intolerable on May 8, when the three of them heard over the radio that the war in Europe was over. As usual, Patrick ignored Lindsay, and went off with Peter to celebrate.

May 9: "Fuck him! then, that's what I say. Let my emotions run dry. Let me become unconcerned whether he goes or stays, lives or dies."

But he couldn't. And began to fear that sexual frustration, and the moods of violent depression brought on by Army life, "may end in twisting me, incapacitating me as a person or as an artist (if I am an artist.) I feel an increasing need to come out into the open, though that of course is impossible." Lindsay also wondered again whether to consult a psychiatrist: "I need to find out (1) whether I am irredeemably homosexual, (2) whether my instincts can or should be repressed or allowed scope or sublimated (3) how?"

Patrick not only shared with Duff, Alan, and James the "shapeliness, strength and manliness" that particularly appealed to Lindsay, but aroused "a masochistic element in my character, which is excited by thoughts of ill treatment, brutality etc. (probably quite falsely, romanticizing what is in fact sordid and ugly)." At the same time he felt a "great tenderness and affection" for the beloved, and was "tormented by the thought of the waste of so much [that is] potentially good, potentially beautiful."

For the rest of the year, Lindsay was obsessed by "uncommunicable desires," and a diary note in September indicates one reason why he could never see a way out of the situation he analyzed so clearly: "Edmund, I never realized, is a homosexual of the most violently emotional type. I had never realized it because, judging everyone by my own standards, I had envisaged him as homosexually inclined but controlling himself as rigidly as I. He had not got the shoddy, tatty flippancy of the average promiscuous homosexual."

I suppose these images of homosexual life had been created in Lindsay's mind during his first year at Oxford, partly by his friend Gerard's tales of "the seamier side," partly by the small but hardly "average" group of flamboyant undergraduates we used to call "dizzy queens." And Lindsay seems to have been so overwhelmed by his own fears and frustrations that he could only perceive the homosexual world in terms of negative stereotypes.

Fortunately there was another, positive image in his mind, of the artist he hoped to be. "Still resolutely attracted to the cinema," he found *Meet Me in St. Louis,* "a charming comedy of the sentimental-domestic type to which I am always a ready victim," and the most impressive of the movies he saw in Delhi during 1945. Oddly enough, although it alerted him to the talent of Vincente Minnelli, Lindsay made no mention of Judy Garland or the musical numbers. He also saw three movies starring an actress he would direct, forty-two years later, in *The Whales of August* (the last feature film for both of them). He liked Bette Davis best in *Mr. Skeffington,* "an artistic advance on *Now Voyager* and *Old Acquaintance,* with some good adult things in it."

My Learned Friend, starring the former music hall comedian Will Hay, provoked an attack on British comedies as "hopelessly unfunny. They have no idea of visual humor, [and] the verbal humor is appalling." But *My Learned Friend* was Hay at the end of his tether, under contract to Ealing Studios and its layer of gentility. Lindsay and I later discovered his gloriously anarchistic prewar farces, above all *Boys Will Be Boys.* Although Hay's films lacked visual humor, like those of his anarchistic American cousins the Marx Brothers, he created a persona of outrageous but hopelessly ineffectual cunning, and would have been wonderful as Gogol's *The Government Inspector.* In *Boys Will Be Boys* he played a similar character, who forged his own credentials to become headmaster of an English public school run by impostors and thieves; and hindsight suggests this film had a subliminal influence on *If . . .*

As Delhi's public library had more to offer than its movie theatres, Lindsay's reading list for 1945 was extensive. It included *Dr. Thorne, Silas Marner, Esther Waters, Conversations with George Moore,* Tolstoy's *Resurrection, Seducers in Ecuador* by Vita Sackville-West, Thomas Mann's *Tonio Kröger* and *Death in Venice,* poetry by Tennyson, Matthew Arnold, and Christina Rossetti. All these he recorded without comment, but he graded a few others—Graham Greene's *The Power and the Glory* ("good"), Dorothy Parker's *Collected Stories* ("good"), Kipling's *Plain Tales from the Hills* ("quite good"), and a couple of thrillers—Erle Stanley Gardner's *The Case of the Careless Kitten* ("good") and Edgar Wallace's *The Clue of the Twisted Candle* ("poor").

By August 1944 my parents had decided that enough time had passed for them to have forgotten the Oxford episode, which I believe they had convinced themselves had never really happened. In any case, for all our sakes I never tried to disillusion them. As my father had joined the branch of RAF intelligence known as MI5, they were living in a rented house in a London suburb, where I stayed until I got a job a few weeks later and took a flat in Notting Hill Gate.

The job was writing scripts for two-minute film commercials produced by Gaumont-British, and distributed by their theatre chain throughout the country. In the same office, at the same grindstone, were two other writers. Thirtyish William Sansom had recently published his first volume of stories, *Fireman Flower,* which brought him good reviews and important admirers like the Sitwells, but not enough money to live on. Sixtyish Eliot Stannard had scripted several silent movies directed by Hitchcock, including *The Lodger.* His reminiscences of working with Hitchcock were usually complaints, one of which I remember because he made it so often: "Hitchcock took *all* the credit for writing *The Ring,* but *at least* fifty percent of the *most important* ideas were mine."

The two-minute films advertised various detergents, housewares, and cosmetics, from Lux Toilet Soap to Drene Shampoo. Gaumont-British drafted its contract stars to promote Drene, and me to write most of the brief "interviews" in which they revealed the secret of their beautiful hair, and incidentally plugged their forthcoming movies, *The Wicked Lady, The Reluctant Widow, Good Time Girl,* etc. Only the British film industry could have elevated dogged amateurs like Margaret Lockwood, Jean Kent, and Patricia Roc to stardom. Valerie Hobson (*Blanche Fury*) was more interesting, but face-to-face she remained politely, smilingly remote, in contrast to sullen Lockwood, who seemed to nurse a private unhappiness, brisk and ambitious Kent, who seemed to think the assignment beneath her, and perfectly willing, perfectly vacuous Roc.

The last winter of the war in Europe was also the last season of regular German air raids, as well as the first and last of the long-range rockets fired irregularly from Holland. The V2s fell on London without warning, usually during the day, and one just missed the suburban train on which I was traveling to visit my parents. The train shuddered and lurched to a stop, glass shattered, one or two women screamed. Then everyone went back to reading their newspapers after a guard came around to check that there were no casualties, and the train started again. Once you realized there was no way to protect yourself from the V2s, they were no longer frightening. Putting them fatalistically out of mind was preferable to sirens warning that German bombers were on their way and might kill you. And noises off were never allowed to interrupt performances at theatres or movie houses. I remember the thud of a rocket landing not too far away while I sat watching an old, scratched print of Renoir's *La Bête Humaine.*

It also took more than a nearby thud or blast to interrupt life in the bars—or the streets. During World War II London was genuinely cos-

Margaret Lockwood

mopolitan, a city of exiles and not just the goal of foreign tourists it became in the 1990s. The first arrivals were servicemen who escaped from Poland, France, Holland, Belgium, Greece, and Yugoslavia to continue the war, in their own uniforms, against Germany. Then came the Americans. Most of the exiles were lonely, more than a few were randy, and although the streets were unlighted at night, there was plenty of sexual electricity in the air.

Servicemen on the prowl in the blackout had a standard approach: "Got a light?" Then, ostensibly to shield the flame, they cupped their hands over yours. Sometimes, at the moment of contact, an air raid warning sounded; and friends told me stories of running for cover to a dark doorway in an unfrequented side street, then making it with the stranger they'd just met as the first bomb fell. I never did this, not out of caution, and certainly not out of disapproval, but because I was unsuited by nature to instant promiscuity. Before making it with someone, I needed at least to begin to know and like him.

The Café Royal in Piccadilly, a legendary meeting place for High Bohemia since the 1890s, had an upstairs bar which became "mixed" during the war. It was usually full of theatre and movie people, straight and gay, and it was during the last winter of the war in Europe that I first heard the word "gay" from an American serviceman in this bar. (But "queer" was still the usual term when I left England twelve years later.) Like the other gay Americans and queer RAF pilots who frequented the bar, the serviceman was an officer. If you preferred, as I did, to cross the class barrier, you walked north through Soho to the far side of Oxford Street, where Fitzrovia began, and where the Fitzroy Tavern was the center of Low Bohemia—black marketeers and other minor crooks, British sailors on leave, and an occasional AWOL soldier.

The Fitzroy's most picturesque Low Bohemian regular was Nina Hamnett, once a talented painter, friend of Modigliani, and nude model for the French sculptor Henri Gaudier-Brzeska (*Torso of Nina* and *The Dancer*). Now rumpled, pickled, and strapped, she sat at the bar and waited for someone to buy her a drink. "Got any mun [money], dear?" and holding out an empty tobacco tin like a beggar's cup was *her* standard approach. I once bought Nina a gin, and she said, "It's hard, you know." Then she shook her head. "No, you don't. You're too young to know." But the painters who bought Nina drinks, and were only a few years older than I, seemed to know. Most of them were "promising" (but more or less forgotten today), most of them serious alcoholics who constantly stumbled outside to throw up in the gutter, and all of them queer. Did the same conflicts that drove Lindsay to repression drive them to drink? If so, he was luckier than he knew. So many of them died before reaching Nina's age.

Toward the end of 1944, I met a refugee from Germany at the Fitzroy. Wolfgang, who was around thirty-five, broadcast anti-Nazi propaganda for the German Service of the BBC, and wrote for a German-language weekly founded by other refugees. We were soon living together, but he explained at the start that he and his Scots lover, at present in the Army, would get back together after the war ended. Wolfgang was extraordinarily well read and led me to new imaginative worlds, from Cocteau to Ivy Compton-Burnett, Henry Green to Willa Cather, Ring Lardner to Karen Blixen (aka Isak Dinesen). He also gave me a translation, in a beautiful edition (which I still have), of Plato's *Symposium.* At Cheltenham it had been out-of-bounds to anyone who took classes in Latin and Greek, and they fobbed us off with the *Republic.* Reading the *Symposium* for the first time, I was especially moved by Agathon's celebration of pansexuality: "While all the Gods are blessed Gods, Love is the most blessed, the most beautiful and the best. He empties us of all unneighbourliness and fills us with intimacy. In wreck he is a pilot, and in time of dread a shipmate, the best of drinking companions and the noblest champion in debate." It brought to mind my music teacher, and made me realize exactly what he meant by saying "They understood in ancient Greece."

In my spare time from Drene, detergents, and an occasional assignment to script one of the company's sixty-minute instructional films (*Contagious Abortion in Cattle,* etc.), I started writing a novel. William Sansom asked to see it, and was sufficiently impressed by the first hundred pages to recommend me to a committee that awarded grants to "promising" new writers. I didn't get one, in spite of support from Osbert Sitwell. When Wolfgang read the pages, he found them too neo-Kafka (who was very much in the air at the time), and set me on the right road by advising me to write directly from life. Almost at once I wrote a story based on the lives of three of my female cousins, all on the verge of being trapped into spinsterhood by possessive mothers. (In the story, not in life, two of them escaped and ended up with each other.) *Three Sisters,* like several more stories that I wrote during the next few years, was published by one of the literary "little magazines" and anthologies—*The Windmill, New Writing, English Story*—that sprang up during the war.

On the night of May 8, 1945, London streets from Piccadilly Circus to Trafalgar Square were jammed with crowds celebrating the news of Germany's unconditional surrender. Because of the five-hour time difference between England and India, Lindsay would already have been asleep when Wolfgang and I watched people sing, wave flags, embrace, climb Nelson's Column. Streetlights were switched on for the first time since September 3, 1939, but with its gaping bomb sites, vistas of derelict buildings, warped girders, a roof open to the sky, the city looked hardly less drab and battered than in the light of day. In the following months there were few spoils of victory. Oranges and bananas began to reappear in the stores, and I heard children asking what they were. But food rationing continued, and restaurants continued to serve whale, slippery and remotely fishy, or horse, tough but tasty, disguised as steak. Unless you lived in the country, fresh vegetables were still in short supply and you could buy only powdered or chemically preserved eggs, which tasted foul. With the money earned from a couple of stories, I went to Paris for the first time that summer. Unlike London it had endured Nazi occupation, but suffered only minor damage, and almost every kind of food was available if you could afford it. Among the French movies I saw was *L'Eternel Retour,* Cocteau's modern reworking of the Tristan and Iseult legend. A hypnotic blend of the fantastic and the ordinary, with the lovers living everyday lives and yet retaining their mythical quality, it opened my eyes to a new kind of poetic cinema.

Soon after I got back, Wolfgang was reunited with his lover. But we continued to see each other as friends after I went to live on my own again. Around the same time, William Sansom freed himself from Gaumont-British with money earned from his first novel and an advance on his second. But I had to drudge on—like Lindsay, not due to be demobilized from his "stooge clerk's job" in Delhi until the end of the year.

"I arrive at the office at about ten past eight," he noted in June 1945. "It is hot after the night, in contrast with the still cool morning air, and I sweat as I sit at my desk reading a newspaper—probably not even bothering to get out my books and papers and other gadgets (no use to me anyway)." He had developed "an aversion from Patrick" which made for a relatively undisturbed summer, but during September "it seemed unfortunately to be wearing off." Depression followed, and Lindsay ended 1945 on a cryptic note: "The older we get the more we realize that no-one can be blamed for the Evil in the world except God."

By the middle of February 1946 he was out of uniform and back in England. When we met again in a London pub, I gave him a copy of *Winter's Tales* by Isak Dinesen and of *The Windmill,* in which *Three Sisters* had appeared. According to Lindsay's diary my story had "quality and promise despite here and there infelicities of style," and at first he found that *Winter's Tales* "do not interest me very deeply." Later he changed his mind: "Sensitive, poetic and beautifully written."

I don't remember what we talked about at our first meeting in over a year, but Lindsay's diary records that he "almost got around to discussing life—which is of course sex." But he decided not to because "Gavin of course is a sensualist—I mean not predominantly humane, but for all discrepancies and shortcomings I think friendship exists between us, and hope it may remain so." I suppose the split in his own nature created this dichotomy of "sensualist" and "not predominantly humane," for only a few weeks later he noted: "I seem at times to be two people." Lindsay 1 he described as "introspective, repressed, defeatist," Lindsay 2 as "full of ideas about all sorts of things, ambitious, socially conscious." At the time, Lindsay 1 had the upper hand. A family reunion at Cringletie seems to have been partly responsible: "The claustrophobic, utterly *material* atmosphere of the place gets on my nerves. Mum and I get on each other's nerves; to me, at her worst, she seems selfish, inhumane, cynical and lazy—about any but material duties. No doubt there is wrong on both sides, but I feel the chief trouble is the lack of a proper husband to shoulder his proper responsibilities."

Back at Oxford, where he switched from classical studies to English literature, Lindsay discovered that Patrick was also at Wadham College. "My emotions? Quiescent." But not for long. He soon experienced "a sudden resurgence of love or lust," and was also stirred by the sight of German prisoners of war, "virile Nordic louts," on the streets. Not yet repatriated and employed on outlying farms, they came into town on their afternoons off, and Lindsay considered offering "to pay one to go to bed with me." Then he dismissed the idea as "just not conceivable," and doubted that "I should like it if I got it."

When he looked back on 1946 in December, Lindsay decided that playing small parts in Oxford University Dramatic Society productions of *The Cherry Orchard* and *Love's Labours Lost* had brought him "superficial" satisfaction—unlike his "not very good" film reviews for the university magazine, *The Isis*. But a few days after Christmas he saw John Ford's *My Darling Clementine,* which affected him "more powerfully and somehow more intimately" than any other movie he could remember. At the time he didn't explain why, but a few years later wrote that he had sensed "some kind of moral poetry" at the heart of the film—and through *Clementine* had begun to understand "what is, after all, the essence of cinema: the language of style."

The fan letter that Lindsay wrote Ford early in January 1947 has not survived, unlike Ford's reply dated April 18: "It gives one's soul a fillip to hear such intelligent praise. Thank you." An apology followed for sending such a brief typewritten note: "I am as yet unable to write longhand, due to a bathing accident at Omaha Beach." The signature, presumably scrawled with his left hand, was a large and wobbly "Ford."

My Darling Clementine, directed by John Ford

Lindsay saw *Clementine* again several times that spring, twice in the company of a new friend, Peter Ericsson, who was studying for a Politics, Philosophy, and Economics degree, and was also a movie buff. Peter shared Lindsay's admiration for Ford and they decided to coedit a movie magazine. They approached the Oxford Film Society with two requests—for money to publish it, and for permission to call it *Sequence.* This was the name of a magazine previously backed by the society that had fizzled after one issue. Both requests were granted, but before the first Anderson-Ericsson *Sequence* could appear, Lindsay had to pass his examination for an M.A. degree, then give his farewell performance as an actor on the stage.

Kenneth Tynan, whom Lindsay admired somewhat but mistrusted somewhat more, was a highly visible new arrival at Oxford that year. In August he staged a production of *Hamlet* (First Quarto version, playing time three and a half hours), with Lindsay as Horatio and himself as the Ghost. In December he restaged it, with the same cast, at a lecture hall in London. I remember Peter Parker as an intelligent but rather slow, placid Hamlet. (Parker later became chairman of British Rail and was knighted. In 1995 his son Oliver directed a foolish film of *Othello.*) I don't remember who played Gertrude, only that she made her first entrance in a white hoop skirt, leading two wolfhounds on a leash. Even though Horatio had been a student friend of Hamlet's at Heidelberg, Ken "saw" him as a middle-aged pedant with a German accent; and Lindsay, wearing a white pompadour wig and black frock coat, deep lines and wrinkles scored on his face with a makeup pencil, was almost as heavily disguised as Paul Muni playing Zola or Pasteur. Bizarre, like the rest of the production—but, unlike it, intentionally humorous.

The Anderson-Ericsson *Sequence,* with a still from *Clementine* on the cover, appeared during the week that *Hamlet* played in London. It featured a manifesto by Lindsay, "Angles of Approach," which attacked British films for their "dislike of reality" and British critics for their "artistic patriotism" in overpraising the second-rate, typified by that "most handsome of mock-heroic fakes," Noël Coward's *In Which We Serve.* But the reality that Lindsay had in mind was not naturalistic-sociological. Insisting that "poetry, visual as well as verbal, is its own justification," he singled out *Clementine,* Jean Vigo's *Zéro de Conduite* and *L'Atalante,* and *Meet Me in St. Louis* as examples of the kind of poetic reality he admired. This, incidentally, is the critic's premonition of his creative future. By the time of *The White Bus* (1966), and of *If . . .* (1968) with its openly acknowledged debt to *Zéro de Conduite,* Lindsay the director had also absorbed the documentaries of Humphrey Jennings and the "epic theatre" of Bertolt Brecht, and evolved a very personal style from a very individual mix.

"Angles of Approach" ended with a set of imperious critical guidelines: "If you enjoy *L'Eternel Retour,* you may also enjoy *King Kong,* but not *Black Narcissus.* If you enjoy *Black Narcissus,* you cannot enjoy *L'Eternel Retour.* If you think you enjoyed both, you are wrong." This was partly a private reproach to me for enjoying both Cocteau *and* Powell-Pressburger, and finding "poetic reality" in *Colonel Blimp, I Know Where I'm Going,* and much of *The Red Shoes* as well as *Black Narcissus.* But so strong was Lindsay's aversion to Powell-Pressburger that he sneakily amended, on the page proof, one sentence in a survey of British films that he'd asked me to contribute to that issue of *Sequence.* "Michael Powell," I had written, "is the most interesting of British film directors." In the printed article, Powell was demoted to "the most potentially interesting."

The Oxford Film Society declined to finance another Anderson-Ericsson *Sequence* after their first number failed to recoup its costs. But Lindsay's "desire to create" was coming into focus. He decided to continue the magazine as a quarterly, and produced the next few numbers with money from a legacy willed to him by a (Bell's whiskey) aunt. He also decided to leave home, after telling his diary that he found it impossible to go on living at Cringletie with such "ghastly *selfishness*— the obsession with food and material comfort, [and] Mum's unalterable, cowlike stupidity, her refusal to understand the needs, the capacities and limitations of her children. She doesn't try to know what sort of people we are."

Peter Ericsson had also graduated from Oxford, and was working at the Foreign Office, which meant that *Sequence* would have to be edited from London in future. Lindsay had already cast an interested eye on the guest room of my three-room flat in Regent's Park, and offered to rent a space just large enough for his bed, a wardrobe, and an editorial desk. It became *Sequence* HQ from December 1947 to December 1950, and at

Lindsay's request I became a coeditor. As the magazine was produced on a shoestring, I also helped in typing the copy (more than half of which we wrote ourselves), designing the layout, calculating the number of words and the size of stills for each page, correcting proofs, and packaging the orders from bookstores, newsagents, and subscribers.

Four times a year, *Sequence* HQ spilled over from Lindsay's bedroom to the living room, its floor and dining table. For two or three weeks before each issue appeared, we sifted through stills, ordered the blocks, pasted up a dummy of each page, made final corrections. For two or three weeks after publication, the floor was stacked high with copies (rising from two thousand to five thousand over the years), which a few friends helped us dispatch. According to Lindsay's diary, the magazine became "a full-time obsession"—but not for myself or Peter Ericsson, because of our respective jobs at Gaumont-British and the Foreign Office. In an early editorial, Lindsay announced that *Sequence* welcomed (unpaid) contributions "from anyone, on any aspect of the cinema, written from any point of view." In fact we never published anything that we disagreed with, which was why we wrote most of the articles and reviews ourselves. And why Lindsay, with more time and energy to spare, wrote almost as much as Peter and I combined.

The "full-time obsession," in fact, was primarily a creative release. Writing for *Sequence,* Lindsay first discovered the angle at which he stood to the universe. Skeptical but not cynical, he rejected "the ease of non-committal toleration," and declared himself a humanist in the sense that he put his faith (against heavy odds) in this world rather than the next. With an extraordinarily sharp eye for dishonesty and pretension, he also took falseness of any kind as a personal affront; and the films that *Sequence* attacked, as he wrote retrospectively, "hurt us as much as our comments hurt their makers."

"As far as *Sequence* goes," Lindsay informed his diary at the end of the magazine's first year, "I am the leading spirit." His passionate beliefs and his appetite for dissent certainly set the tone, and as well as putting up most of the money, he led the search for additional financing. It was Lindsay's visits to the London offices of the major American film companies that persuaded several of their publicists to buy advertising space. He made equally successful approaches to distributors of foreign movies, and only the British companies turned him down, unsurprisingly in view of the way we dismissed most British movies.

They were even wary of granting our requests for stills, rightly suspecting the use we would make of them. (When Lindsay demolished *Scott of the Antarctic,* I captioned the still that accompanied his review, "The Frozen Limit.") But the American publicists were friendly and generous. Partly because we praised the musicals produced by Arthur Freed, partly because he thought we had "class," our firmest supporter was at MGM. "Everything I have is yours," he used to sing as he pointed to the filing cabinets loaded with stills. Later he underwent surgery at a clinic in Casablanca and came out transsexual.

Each number of *Sequence* was basically the result of seeing films we admired, found overrated, or actively disliked and of separating the genuinely personal (*Louisiana Story*) from the self-consciously "important" (*The Best Years of Our Lives*). We were enthusiasts, not careerists or theorists. Instead of restricting ourselves to the weekly menu of press screenings, we went à la carte and educated our palates in the process. So many movies we hadn't seen, and in the days before video or movies on TV, so few ways to see them.

The British Film Institute was a petrified bureaucracy, and unlike the Cinémathèque in Paris or the Museum of Modern Art Film Library in New York, it never screened films from its archives. There was no National Film Theatre, only the London Film Society, which held monthly screenings of prints borrowed from Paris and New York. (Eye-openers I remember: Stroheim's *The Wedding March,* Buñuel's *L'Age d'Or* and *Los Olvidados,* Pabst's *The Love of Jeanne Ney,* Lubitsch's *So This Is Paris.*) When we could afford it, we took a trip to Paris, then as now the movie buff's paradise. Otherwise we depended on the dozen or so "specialist" theatres that occasionally screened old movies, and an hour's journey by bus or train brought us to some dusty, musty Star or Trocette.

With Lindsay and Peter, the great Ford-hounds, I first saw *Young Mr. Lincoln* and *They Were Expendable.* Other suburban Regals and Granadas introduced me to von Sternberg (*Morocco*), George Cukor (*Holiday*), and James Whale (*The Bride of Frankenstein*). Current American fare was always accessible, of course, but we were usually interested in movies that "serious" reviewers in the national press were disinclined to take seriously. Especially Hollywood noir and MGM musicals, equally disdained by theorists for whom "film" meant only Griffith, Eisenstein, and *The Cabinet of Doctor Caligari.*

We saluted Robert Siodmak for *Cry of the City* and *File on Thelma Jordon,* Joseph H. Lewis for *Gun Crazy,* Jacques Tourneur for *Out of the Past,* Vincente Minnelli for *The Pirate,* Rouben Mamoulian for *Summer Holiday,* Charles Walters, Betty Comden, and Adolph Green for *Good News.* We asked David Vaughan to write "Dance and the Cinema," an homage to Busby Berkeley, Astaire-Rogers, Balanchine's "Slaughter on Tenth Avenue" in *On Your Toes,* Minnelli's *Yolanda and the Thief,* and Gene Kelly's dances in *Cover Girl* (the article came out a month before the arrival of *On the Town*). Most issues featured a study of a director, Lindsay on *"They Were Expendable* and John Ford," Peter on Preston Sturges, myself on Cocteau. We relentlessly knocked British films, the "tasteful" restraint of *Brief Encounter* and *The Winslow Boy,* provoking Lindsay to define "the standard British formula for scenes of emotional tension: 'When emotion threatens, make your characters talk about something else in a little, uncertain, high-pitched voice.' "

Lindsay also wrote a study of Hitchcock, full of detailed enthusiasm for the British movies but dismissing (over my protests) *Notorious* and most of the American work as "stylistic elephantiasis." Later he expressed rather grudging admiration for *Vertigo* and *North by Northwest,* and also retracted his criticism of the *Cahiers du Cinéma* group for their "adulation" of Howard Hawks. But he never forgave the French critic who thought *Red River* better than any of Ford's westerns.

At the screenings known as trade shows, where movies not already booked by the major circuits were on offer to independent theatre owners, I was strongly impressed by a few rejects. I mentioned them to the two critics in the national press (Dilys Powell of the *Sunday Times,* Richard Winnington of the *News Chronicle*) who were sympathetic to *Sequence,* and they arranged a screening for themselves. Our combined reviews persuaded art houses in London and a few other cities to book Ophüls' *Letter from an Unknown Woman,* Polonsky's *Force of Evil,* and—a "discovery" that would have a profound effect on my future—Nicholas Ray's *They Live by Night.*

"They Were Expendable and John Ford" provoked a response from Nunnally Johnson, screenwriter of *The Grapes of Wrath* and *Tobacco Road,* who accused Lindsay of inflating the director's importance. "The contribution of the director [in any movie], in my opinion," he wrote, "is

the least to be proud of." Lindsay responded with "Creative Elements" in the autumn 1948 *Sequence:* "A good film must draw its original inspiration from a script. But it may grow to full creative life through various patterns and degrees of collaboration. And the fact remains that (granted, on his part, the inclination and the capacity) the man most in a position to guide and regulate the expressive resources of the cinema is the director. To that extent it remains, and will remain, the director's medium."

A generation later, MGM musicals and Hollywood noir had become as intellectually fashionable as Ingmar Bergman and Godard; and several critics of the new generation attacked *Sequence* for failing to create a consistent "movie aesthetic," like the auteur theory that François Truffaut propounded in 1954 in *Cahiers du Cinéma.* But for me it remains one of the magazine's virtues that while we wrote about movies as "the director's medium," and made a point of ignoring conventional distinctions between high and low art, we never wrote lunatic fringe articles on the neglect of Hugo Fregonese or the echoes of Murnau in Edgar G. Ulmer's *Daughter of Dr. Jekyll.* In 1975 Truffaut himself admitted that he had "no idea of the real problems a filmmaker faces" when he provoked a barrage of critical crossfire by announcing that "the worst Hawks film is more interesting than the best Huston film." And he went on to explain that "today many of those Hawksians and Hustonians are movie directors" who probably found the whole argument as "ancient" as he did himself.

Unlike Truffaut, Lindsay had some idea of the "real problems" of filmmaking by the time he wrote "Creative Elements." In February 1948 he wrote me from Cringletie, where he was spending a few days with Mum, that he'd had an unexpected visit from a *Sequence* fan he knew and liked. But at first Mrs. Sleigh was reluctant to admit her. Heavy snow was falling when she answered the doorbell to a young woman wearing a fur coat dyed bright orange. Although she couldn't have known that the fur was borrowed, Mum's reaction was fear at first sight, and revealed how little she understood her son. She took Lois Sutcliffe for a whore, come in from the cold to inform Lindsay she was pregnant with his child.

Lois was married to Desmond Sutcliffe, director of a manufacturing company in the coal-mining region of Yorkshire, who wanted to produce a documentary about the company's underground conveyor systems that brought coal from the mines to the pithead. Lois had convinced him that Lindsay should write and direct it, and had come to convince Lindsay of the same thing. "You've got to start somewhere," she said with engaging north-of-England bluntness, after Lindsay protested that he was totally inexperienced and lacked technical knowledge. Finally Lindsay agreed, then wrote to ask if I thought they were both crazy.

"I think you were *absolutely right* to take the offer," I wrote back, "and am really very glad that something has occurred to force a decision on you. Don't for heaven's sake worry, you can do it on your head." As Lindsay had expressed doubts about his ability to grasp the mechanics of underground conveyor systems as well as filmmaking, I made a point of reassuring him: "From my own experience—in having once to write a shooting script on plate glass manufacture—this sort of thing is not nearly as intimidating as it appears. The mechanics are comparatively easy to absorb." It was an encouraging lie. I had found them hellishly difficult.

I also felt that Lindsay and I needed a break from each other. When he moved into my guest room, I had been sharing the flat for several months with a lover, a young assistant director whom Lindsay appeared to dislike almost immediately. There was a silent tension in the air when the three of us were together, and I finally brought the subject up with Lindsay. "I have no feelings one way or the other," he said with a remarkably convincing show of surprise. "I just don't connect with him." Once again he hid the truth in his diary: "My feelings for Bill [Brendon] are not, I'm afraid, in the least amicable. I expect I am unfair to him, but I find him a terrible bore—conceited. Or is there an element of disgust at continuously 'making a third'?"

Or was it also a case of opposites failing to attract? Introspection was simply not part of Bill's nature, and perhaps Lindsay was misled by his emotional innocence. "The innocent," according to Camus, "is a person who never explains anything," and if you're not attracted to that particular innocent, refusal to explain can seem arrogant or dumb (or both). The nearest Bill came to explaining anything to me was after we first made love and told each other we'd fallen in love. Next morning he confessed that for the past few months he'd been involved with a

Wakefield, 1948, first film: On location for *Meet the Pioneers,* coproducer
Desmond Sutcliffe, cameraman-assistant Bill Brendon, Lindsay, and second
cameraman John Jones

girl, and they were planning to spend the following weekend in the
country together. "I can't put it off," he said, "because it wouldn't be
fair to either of you. I need to spend that weekend with *her* to make sure
it's *you* I love."

I knew it was Bill I loved, and that he wasn't being consciously
ruthless, just dealing with the situation in the only way his innocence
allowed. To object would be the likeliest way to lose him, so I spent
most of an increasingly desperate weekend alone in bed. Although the
phone rang a few times, the call I hoped for didn't come until almost
midnight on Sunday, when Bill said that he now felt sure he loved me
and was on his way over.

There is no reference in Lindsay's diary to his change of heart con-
cerning Bill—if it *was* a change of heart. But on the personal level, I
suppose, he must finally have decided that Bill was at least tolerable;
and on the practical one, that his technical knowledge would be
extremely useful on the documentary Lindsay was about to make in
Yorkshire. And much to my surprise, he offered Bill the job of assistant
director. After the shoot Lindsay told me, "I found Bill a great profes-

sional help," and Bill told me, "We're a bit more friendly now, but not really friends." As a director, he added, "Lindsay seemed to learn very quickly."

Meet the Pioneers, which ran forty minutes, took two weeks to shoot and three days to edit during July 1948. Its minimal budget allowed for a minimal unit of cinematographer (working with an unreliable second-hand 16mm camera), Bill as assistant director, and Lois as continuity girl. A local schoolteacher with amateur experience had offered himself as cinematographer, but proved available only on weekends. Fortunately Bill had also worked as an assistant cameraman, and stepped in to shoot most of the film.

"Quite interesting, rather scrappy and also rather too conventional in approach," was Lindsay's verdict in his diary. "As regards a career in films this experience has left me pretty much where I was. I suppose I have gained in self-confidence. Apart from the photography, after all, I did the whole thing myself—editing, writing and speaking the commentary, arranging the music." In fact the film pleased its sponsors, and over the next few years Lindsay was commissioned to make a dozen more documentaries, by the Sutcliffe Company and others.

Preoccupied with *Sequence* and making his first films, Lindsay was also untroubled by an Alan or a Patrick for the next three years. And the satisfactions of work seem to have brought some respite from sexual tension, as his diary refers to it only once during that time. "A celibate life, sexual frustration compensated by friendship, activity, creation?" he wrote on August 31, 1948. "Or sexual release accomplished by lavatory encounters? I have neither the assurance nor the determination to accost, and for the moment the dilemma remains unresolved."

Meanwhile the circulation of *Sequence* steadily increased, and we became minor celebrities when Lee Miller photographed us for British *Vogue,* whose editor supplied a Voguish caption, "Wise, witty and courageous." More spectacularly on his way up as a theatre critic, Ken Tynan took note and invited Lindsay and me to parties at his Mayfair flat. We were always promised Larry and Viv and/or Noël as star guests, but I don't remember seeing any of them there. In fact, I could never understand why Ken expected the Oliviers to appear, since he regularly (and cruelly) attacked Vivien Leigh's performances in the theatre. What I chiefly remember is that Ken's marriage to the American novelist Elaine Dundy (*The Dud Avocado*) was under strain, and they usually exchanged loud insults after a few drinks. A cue for Lindsay and me to retire to the hallway with Jill Bennett, a quirky, witty young actress we both liked very much, and whom Lindsay would later direct in *The Old Crowd* and *Britannia Hospital.*

Eventually Lindsay and Ken had their own exchange of insults, by postcard, after a political meeting at which the Marxist art critic John Berger made a speech. Lindsay heard him out with increasingly loud sighs, then denounced him as pompous, humorless, and doctrinaire. As a result, Ken wrote Lindsay a postcard, accusing him of "betraying the Left" and advising him to "take care you don't degenerate into a scold." Lindsay's reply: "You were always a cunt, take care you don't degenerate into an arsehole." Coolness followed, but after a while they became, and remained, wary allies.

Ken had first been alerted to Bertolt Brecht by Eric Bentley, the theatre critic and translator of *The Caucasian Chalk Circle* and *The Good Woman of Setzuan.* Ken went to see the Berliner Ensemble in East Berlin, was bowled over, and began to use Brecht as a stick to beat the London theatre with—just as Lindsay had found in *Clementine* his touchstone for "the essence of cinema." Each viewed from a different lookout point the strange, dead, culturally isolated landscape of postwar Britain. The Labour Government elected in 1945 had promised a brave new nationalized world, but failed so drastically to deliver it that by 1948 an enormous loan from the United States was needed to bail the economy out. To reduce its dollar and trade deficits, Labour then banned imports of all new American movies, foreign books, and visual art for a year; and when Orwell's *1984* appeared in 1949, Lindsay remarked to me that the Britain it prophesied might come to pass in much less than thirty-six years.

Bread, butter, meat, and paper for books were still severely rationed, but with the same self-righteousness as Cheltenham College overlords, Labour politicians insisted that austerity was morally bracing. With the same hypocrisy, the *News Chronicle* accused Cyril Connolly of betraying Britain's dignity—because, in his dual capacity of editor of *Horizon* and gourmet, he had asked the magazine's American readers to send food parcels to their favorite writers. Orange juice, tomato juice, rice, honey, and tinned meats, he added, were "particularly acceptable to brain workers."

In fact, with the Empire breaking up, unemployment rising, and the pound falling, British "dignity" was in even shorter supply than tomato juice. But rather than face uncomfortable realities in the present, British movies retreated to a heroic past. "Escaping into war" was Lindsay's verdict on a cycle of films that recycled films about World War II. They seemed to arrive at the rate of one a month until the late 1950s, Jack Hawkins in *The Cruel Sea* a stalwart replacement for Noël Coward in *In Which We Serve,* then transposing the same character to the Air Force in *The Malta Story,* while John Mills transposed him to a submarine in *Morning Departure,* then reduplicated his transposed self in *Above Us the Waves . . .* "The British cinema," as Lindsay wrote, "has never recovered from Noël Coward as Captain 'D.' " He was the only critic to point out that all those postwar war movies might have been made while German bombs were still falling, and to understand why their makers allowed themselves to be caught in a time warp: "The world of the armed services is one which perpetuates the traditional social set-up of the country, its distinctions of class and privilege."

"I feel we should start a movement to send the Baroness [Blixen] food parcels," I wrote Lindsay in June 1949, while he was making *Idlers That Work,* his second documentary for the Sutcliffe Company. "She doesn't need them, but I hate to think of all those canned peaches and cured hams piling up for Stephen Spender."

Having recently read *The Angelic Avengers* and written Karen Blixen a fan letter, I was astonished not long afterward to hear a dark, vibrant contralto on the phone: "This is Baroness Blixen. I am in London and would like to meet you." I invited her to lunch at a restaurant in Soho, where she arrived wearing a long black coat and a black toque, hooded eyes ringed with kohl, face powdered ghost-white, a dramatic Woman of Mystery who looked as if she not only traveled but lived on the Orient Express. A spellbinding storyteller in person as well as in print, her most memorable tale that day was set in Berlin not long before World War II, when she was writing articles for a Danish newspaper. As minister of propaganda, Goebbels was delegated to impress the baroness. He showed her Albert Speer's designs for a new chancellery, city hall, and

Führer's Palace, he took her to a Hitler Youth parade, and finally to an open air concert at which Wilhelm Furtwängler conducted Beethoven's Ninth. "I had managed to say very little all that afternoon and evening," the baroness told me, "but Goebbels was impatient to know my opinion of the concert. So I said, 'Yes, very fine, but . . . Beethoven, I mistrust you. You lead to Wagner.' He was not, of course, pleased."

Back in London after completing *Idlers That Work,* Lindsay heard that John Ford was planning to make a film in England. He asked a mutual acquaintance at the Ministry of Information, Jack Beddington, to contact Ford about the possibility of working on it. The reply, according to Lindsay's diary, was "almost embarrassingly sentimental—gushy. But it included an assurance that *if* he comes to England, he'll certainly use me. It is strange how reverential I have come to feel about Ford."

Then second, less reverential thoughts occurred. "References to me as 'the lad' make one fear he may expect me to be something other than I am. Inevitably there are sexual implications. Is Ford homosexual? Viz. the predominantly male cast of his films; his association with [English-Irish film director] Brian Desmond Hurst, a raging pansy, in Beddington's words; certain unspecified hints from Beddington; the effusiveness of his letter. He cannot be homosexual in the feminine way. But his young men are often beautiful and lovingly represented."

By coincidence I had become friendly with Brian Desmond Hurst, a routine director but exuberant and amiable person. He wanted to make a film of *She Stoops to Conquer* and paid me a small advance to adapt it. I spent several weekends at his country home, and Lindsay asked me if "anything went on there." I told him that friendly guardsmen were always in attendance, and he begged me to pump Brian about Ford's private life. "I don't *think* so," Brian said, "but you never *know,* do you?" And we never shall, although I would guess that Ford's homoerotic streak, if it existed, was sublimated in the "lovingly represented" young men of his movies.

She Stoops to Conquer never materialized, like Ford's original plan to shoot the interiors of *The Quiet Man* in an English studio. But in the summer of 1950, before Ford went back to Hollywood after extensive location filming with an American crew in Ireland, Lindsay managed to interview him. In a later issue of *Sequence* he described his first encounter with "a bulky man, craggy as you would expect," eyes invisible behind darkly tinted glasses, dressed in "an old sports coat and a pair of grubby grey flannels, his shirt open at the neck."

It began with Ford living up to his reputation as an interviewer and critic-tease. "It's no use asking me to talk about art," he said—and when Lindsay, "with some trepidation," asked about *My Darling Clementine,* Ford replied abruptly, "I never saw it." Undaunted, Lindsay mentioned another personal favorite, *They Were Expendable,* and "Ford's attitude towards this film so dumbfounded me that a whole tract of conversation was wiped from my memory." All he remembered later was that Ford said, "I just can't believe that film's any good," and claimed he only made it because he was "ordered to," didn't "put a goddamned thing into it, and never saw a goddamned foot of it." Switching tracks, Lindsay asked Ford to name *his* personal favorites. *Young Mr. Lincoln* came first, followed by *How Green Was My Valley, Wagonmaster*—and *Wee Willie Winkie,* because he was "charmed by Shirley Temple, now as then."

By this time Lindsay realized that Ford was "a man who speaks by mood, from impulse rather than reflexion, and without much concern to qualify—he might very well contradict any of his statements the next day." Next morning, in fact, he phoned Lindsay at his Dublin hotel and thanked him "for going to all that trouble to come and see me." Then he promised to make *The Quiet Man* "as good as I possibly can," and to see *Expendable* when he got back to Los Angeles and "let you know what I think."

Lindsay was again dumbfounded, but pleasurably this time. He thought he had failed to break past Ford's "firmly-held position," his dismissal of any attempt to discuss his personal style and convictions as a filmmaker with "I just take a script and I do it." A few weeks later Ford made a second overture, by cable from Los Angeles: HAVE SEEN EXPENDABLE. YOU WERE RIGHT. FORD. "This man who did not like to be known," it seemed, was now prepared to be known, up to a point anyway, by Lindsay. For several years Lindsay carried the cable in his wallet. Then the wallet was stolen. Although the police eventually recovered it, the money it contained was gone, and so was the cable.

By January 1950 the circulation of *Sequence* had risen to five thousand, but production costs had risen as well, and the magazine was still breaking slightly less than even. That same month I received an offer from the new director of the British Film Institute. Denis Forman (later head of Granada TV, later Sir Denis) wanted me to edit the institute's terminally boring magazine, *Sight and Sound,* and bring it back to life. Although the offer promised a way of escape from the need to continue inventing commercials for soaps and shampoos, a reborn film quarterly with money behind it would obviously pose a serious threat to *Sequence.* I told Lindsay that I couldn't accept without his blessing. He gave it unhesitatingly and arranged a celebration dinner. "I can't help feeling this is a triumph for *us,*" he said. "It proves we really started something."

During my first months at the BFI, invisible authority struck again. In an early issue of the new *Sight and Sound* I attacked a recent British movie, *The Blue Lamp,* that had been widely praised. Although it was intended as a tribute to the London police, the chief law-and-order figure was so unbearably smug that I pronounced the young criminal (played by Dirk Bogarde) a rebel hero for shooting him. The review infuriated Michael Balcon, head of the studio that produced the film and a member of the institute's board of governors. He summoned a special meeting of the board to demand that Denis Forman fire me. Trying to make it appear that he was acting on principle, Balcon pointed out that the magazine was part of an organization subsidized by the state, and I had failed in my duty "to speak for British film culture."

Denis was a member of the Establishment who combined strong anti-Establishment instincts with an equally strong talent for diplomacy. He managed not to fire me and at the same time to neutralize Balcon. Ironically, Balcon never knew that I'd become friendly with two of his contract writer-directors at Ealing Studios, both of whom shared my low opinion of *The Blue Lamp.* Alexander Mackendrick, who had a script credit on the film, told me that he was "conscripted" to rewrite a few scenes before starting work on *The Man in the White Suit.* Robert Hamer, whose *Kind Hearts and Coronets* had made Balcon very uneasy until it became a success, gave me dry encouragement: "As for Old Mick [Balcon], I hope you manage to keep up the good work."

With a mandate to establish *Sight and Sound* in the marketplace, I boldly fished for famous names. Among early contributors to the magazine were three directors writing about their own films, von Sternberg with "More Light," Jean Renoir with "Personal Notes," Carl Dreyer with "Thoughts on My Craft"; Michael Redgrave with an article on film acting, "I Am Not a Camera"; Michael Powell with a review of a new history of British cinema; and Ken Tynan with brilliant pieces on Greta Garbo, James Cagney, and W. C. Fields. At the end of the year I asked Cecil Beaton, Benjamin Britten, Agatha Christie, John Gielgud, Trevor Howard, Celia Johnson, Michael Powell, Peter Ustinov, Mai Zetterling, and the romance novelist Ruby M. Ayres to name the films they had most enjoyed. To my surprise everyone responded—and two comedies, the most sophisticated and the most provincial, *La Ronde* and *The Lavender Hill Mob,* tied for first place. The quirkiest entries came from Dame Agatha ("A delightful film about Seals—ungratefully can't now remember the name of it"), and Ruby M. ("Give me Charlie Chaplin every time! He is always so very natural and his every gesture so eloquent. Hoping I shall not have made myself unpopular by this reply to your letter!!!")

Two new friends, and future film directors, became important contributors. Among the notable articles by Tony Richardson, then working for BBC TV, was an homage to Buñuel; among those by Karel Reisz, soon to publish *The Technique of Film Editing,* was a shrewd analysis of *A Place in the Sun* and its glamorous distortion of Dreiser's *An American Tragedy.* In the spring of 1952, Karel replaced Peter Ericsson (by then fully occupied with marriage as well as the Foreign Office) as coeditor of the last issue of *Sequence.* For the rest of that year Lindsay was busy making documentaries, but from 1953 until I left for Los Angeles he wrote several reviews of current movies and two major articles for *Sight and Sound.*

"Only connect" was an homage to the documentaries of Humphrey Jennings, particularly his films about Britain during World War II, *Listen to Britain, Fires Were Started* and *A Diary for Timothy.* I don't remember when either of us first saw them, but it must have been before the accident that caused Jennings's tragically early death (at forty-three) in 1950. In 1949 he came to a party that *Sequence* gave at my flat. Other guests included a visitor from India, Satyajit Ray, who had assisted Renoir in finding locations for *The River* and written "Renoir in Calcutta" for us; most of our few friends in the British film industry, the directors Alexander Mackendrick, Robert Hamer, and Thorold Dickinson, the cameraman Douglas Slocombe (*Dead of Night, The Man in the White Suit*), who had written a study of the cinematographer Gregg Toland for us; and splendid Diana Dors, whom I had described as "the only genuine primitive in the British cinema." Jennings stayed only a short while, and my only contact with him was to ask what he'd like to drink. Lindsay found him "rather cold," but it didn't lessen his admiration for "the only real poet the British cinema has yet produced."

Jennings, he wrote, was unique in his "freedom from the inhibitions of class-consciousness," which allowed him to "range freely over the life of the nation." And because he responded to "the commonplace thing or person that is significant precisely because it is commonplace," he created unforgettable drama out of superficially forgettable, ordinary moments, like the plump factory girl who sings "Yes, My Darling Daughter" as she works on the assembly line, or the two air raid wardens who gaze at distant flames in the night sky while music from a dance hall drifts across the deserted promenade of a seaside town. "He had his theme, which was Britain," Lindsay concluded, "and nothing else could stir him to the same response."

Once again the critic was father to the artist, and "Only Connect" connects Lindsay to his own unborn films with their "theme" of Britain—particularly *O Lucky Man!*, which ranges so freely over British life, and contains such varied and pungent observation of several kinds and classes of people.

Lindsay's second major article was published in the autumn 1956 *Sight and Sound,* the last issue that I edited. It had been commissioned more than a year earlier, when he was again busy making documentaries, and "Stand Up! Stand Up!" finally appeared a few weeks after I left England. It began with an attack on "the kind of philistinism which shrinks from art because art presents a challenge," and opened fire on several film critics in the national press, especially C. A. Lejeune in *The Observer,* who defined movies as "recreation" and asked filmmakers to ignore "the dreadful things that go on around us," and the anonymous reviewer of *The Times* who welcomed *The Rains of Ranchipur:* "This is the cinema as the cinema should rightly be, not concerned with the psychology of drug addicts and prostitutes, but in its choice of subject and treatment, warm, vague, extravagant and sentimental."

Impossible to imagine any reputable theatre or art critic writing that way, as Lindsay commented at the time. And hard to believe, more than forty years later, that a film critic for a reputable newspaper could find *The Rains of Ranchipur* "the cinema as it should rightly be," when

Rear Window, East of Eden, The Night of the Hunter, Buñuel's *Robinson Crusoe,* and Pabst's *The Last Act* were among the movies recently shown in London. But from their earliest days, movies had been regarded as the opium of the lower orders in Britain. In the mid-1920s, quite a few privileged eyebrows shot up when the distinctly upper-crust Anthony Asquith decided to become a film director, and in the mid-1950s condescension was still the prevailing critical attitude.

And condescension, as Lindsay pointed out in "Stand Up! Stand Up!," did positive harm: "By celebrating the merits of the trivial, we lower the prestige of the cinema and, indirectly, make it more difficult for anyone to make a good film." He also took a swipe at Ken Tynan, who had recently written that he saw himself "predominantly as a lock. If the key, which is the work of art, fits snugly into my mechanism of bias and preference, I click and rejoice. If not, I am helpless." Dismissing this as evasive, Lindsay accused Ken of failing to write out of personal conviction, then proceeded to state his own: "I do not believe that humanism is exhausted; nor that we are without rebels capable of defending its cause. Essentially, in fact, there is no such thing as uncommitted criticism, any more than there is such a thing as insignificant art."

In expecting critics, no less than artists, to have a personal vision of the world, Lindsay was really expecting critics to *be* artists. He was right in one sense, of course, for artists from Oscar Wilde to Henry James to Virginia Woolf have been the best literary critics, and from Graham Greene to Lindsay Anderson to François Truffaut, the best film critics. I don't know whether Lindsay had read Wilde's "The Critic as Artist" by the time he wrote "Stand Up! Stand Up!," but his prescription for critics echoed Wilde's: "It is only by intensifying his own personality that the critic can interpret the personality and work of others."

"Stand Up! Stand Up!" made a powerful impact in its day, the critical equivalent of *Look Back in Anger,* which had opened shortly before it appeared. Like John Osborne's play in revival, Lindsay's article has less impact now that it's less topical; but it's still personally revealing in the way it blames the political left even more than the right for the "baffled idealism and emotional fatigue" of the 1950s. The fact that the left "has muffed its chance to capture the imagination and allegiance of the nation," he wrote, "is too obvious to need dwelling on." He never deviated from this "plague on both your houses" attitude, and as a director his disillusion with the spiritual bankruptcy of politics culminated in the no-holds-barred satire of *Britannia Hospital.*

Mismanaged to a surrealist degree, and housed in a building as nineteenth century as the state of mind of its administrators, that hospital was a metaphor for Britain in the 1980s. The movie lampooned an entire society, fossilized royalty and its retinue on the right; self-important, self-serving labor union leaders and their lackeys on the left; and in the middle, scientists with delusions of grandeur, incompetent bureaucrats, mindless strikers, opportunistic media persons, you name it. But the price Lindsay paid for holding up a devastating mirror image to Britain was an equally devastating critical rejection.

"Ford stands apart, an isolated figure," he had written after their first meeting. And by the time of *Britannia Hospital,* so did Lindsay. "I come to believe," he noted in 1982, "that in the end the artist is on his own."

4

As well as writing for *Sight and Sound* during the years that I edited it (1950–56), Lindsay published *Making a Film,* a day-by-day account of the preparation, shooting, and editing of Thorold Dickinson's *Secret People;* directed three documentaries with an increasingly personal profile, and several more routine ones, plus five half-hour episodes of the TV series *Robin Hood,* and commercials for Kellogg's Corn Flakes and Cracker Barrel Cheese; produced and acted in *The Pleasure Garden,* a flimsy whimsy by James Broughton, a San Francisco poet and filmmaker who had moved to London; and under the umbrella title of Free Cinema, organized a series of programs at the National Film Theatre of short films by himself, Karel Reisz, Tony Richardson, and others.

In 1937 Graham Greene was reviewing films for *Night and Day,* and spotted "the very high promise of the direction" in Thorold Dickinson's first film, *The High Command.* But Thorold remained an outsider in the British film industry, with few commercial successes to his name. His 1940 adaptation of Patrick Hamilton's *Gaslight,* with Diana Wynyard and Anton Walbrook, was one of them; and like *The Queen of Spades* (1948, with Edith Evans and Walbrook), it showed a flair for gothic melodrama. But contemporary life was not his strong suit, and *Secret People* was a supposedly realistic story of two young revolutionaries (Serge Reggiani and Valentina Cortesa) from an unnamed totalitarian country, who plan to assassinate a member of its government during his visit to London. Thorold developed his own story in collaboration with several writers, including Joyce Cary (*The Horse's Mouth*), but the screenplay that Lindsay gave me to read was awkwardly plotted, and some of the dialogue sounded close to unplayable. "I know, Thorold has a tin ear," Lindsay said. "And in spite of his visual sense, not much *in*sight." But a new writer was coming in to add "depth" to the main characters, and whatever the final result, he hoped to gain valuable technical experience from watching a feature director at work.

In fact *Secret People* was such a critical and commercial failure that Thorold was able to make only one more film (in Israel). Although Lindsay never anticipated total disaster, he was uncertain of success, and wrote more freely about the technical than the creative side of making this particular film. His book covers a period of eight months, from October 1950 through May 1951, and like a good tour guide leads you through points of interest in every department. But its portrait of Thorold, who had asked Lindsay to write *Making a Film* and arranged for a publisher's commission, was necessarily guarded. And the experience that Lindsay gained was not only technical.

His portrait of the leading actor, twenty-eight-year-old Serge Reggiani, was equally guarded, but for a different reason. Lindsay fell in love with him. A star in France since *La Ronde* and Clouzot's *Manon*, Serge would find his best role opposite Simone Signoret in Jacques Becker's *Casque d'Or*, which he made immediately after *Secret People*. While *Making a Film* concentrates on Serge's professional qualities, his intense self-criticism and nervous energy, Lindsay's diary concentrates on "the ruthlessness, the hardness of the very male. Serge represents to me (sexual attraction apart) a way of living, of organizing life and work and personal relations." He was also the first to play a role that several other actors would later play in Lindsay's life, the heterosexual love object, married with children.

Serge had a "surface fragility," as Signoret once commented, "that concealed an astonishing inner strength." Slight but muscular, neither warm nor cold but somehow armored, he gave the impression of being in control of a life that in reality was a precarious high-wire act. As Lindsay discovered on a visit to Paris a few weeks after shooting on *Secret People* ended, Serge was constantly walking the tightrope between marriage and an ongoing extramarital affair. Lindsay also found that he showed "little interest in my personal feelings." I never saw Serge show much interest in anyone's personal feelings, but Lindsay resolved to "accept the stronger intensity of feeling on my side than on his; and be grateful for a contact which enlivens and illuminates. It is Serge in some extraordinary way who has quickened my desire for expression: which is always the effect of love—the impulse to share, to give."

Serge Reggiani and Simone Signoret in *Casque d'Or*

The only immediate outlet for Lindsay's desire for expression was another industrial documentary sponsored by the Sutcliffe Company. He shot *Three Installations* by day during December 1951, and read *The Idiot* by night, fantasizing a movie adaptation with himself in the title role opposite Serge as Rogozin. Also by night, thoughts of Serge occasionally drove him to cruise the Wakefield public lavatory, "my heart beating faster and perhaps my hands sweating slightly." In a diary note three years earlier, Lindsay had considered finding sexual release in "lavatory encounters," but doubted he had the "assurance" for it. Now his doubts were confirmed, as he invariably retreated whenever a stranger made eye contact, and another door closed.

During 1952, "Thoughts of Serge continue," as well as "fantasies too infantile to be written down. And in the other room Gavin indefatigably works away at his typewriter. To hell with introspection!" And back to expression. Two more documentaries, then producing and making his debut as a screen actor in James Broughton's *The Pleasure Garden,* financed by an Experimental Film Fund that Denis Forman had established at the BFI. Playing a sculptor tormented by his failure to carve a "real" statue of Jill Bennett, Lindsay good-naturedly satirized himself. But the lines he had to speak were embarrassingly unfunny: "Art is *real.* How can I make this more *real?* And can I ever make anything I really *feel?*"

In September he went to Paris again, and became uncomfortably aware of always "making a third"—with Serge and his wife, Serge and his girlfriend, Serge and his circle of friends. "If I withdraw from the viewpoint of love, I see a smaller Serge, temperamental, egotistical, lacking (as he himself told me) in emotional generosity. But the Serge my heart responds to with a leap and a glow, is he *less* real?"

Not for the five years that Lindsay remained in love with him. And although he couldn't disguise his feelings, he never attempted to discuss them with me. Partly, of course, because of the barrier he'd set up with everyone; and partly, perhaps, because we both knew that sexual attraction is imponderable. One man's love is another man's addiction, whether it's the case of a friend made unhappy by unrequited love for someone you wish he'd get over, or a friend with a lover you don't really like.

When Lindsay got back from Paris, Bill Brendon was in Ireland, working as camera operator on a movie shot partly on location there. One afternoon a few days later I was alone in the flat and a phone call came from Dublin. Around seven that evening, as I lay on our bed in the dark, no longer crying, just staring at the ceiling, I heard a knock on the door. I didn't answer. The door opened, and Lindsay asked if something was wrong. I told him that Bill had drowned while filming from a small open boat that capsized in the Irish Sea. After a moment Lindsay sat beside me and put one hand on my shoulder. I reached for his other hand, and held it for perhaps a minute. A scene from a silent movie, in which gesture was everything.

The last of the three documentaries Lindsay made during 1952 was called *Wakefield Express,* after the newspaper that commissioned it. To follow a reporter as he interviewed local people in search of stories; a final sequence of the paper going to press; a running time of thirty minutes—these were the only demands the sponsor made. But Lindsay was working as usual on a tight budget, and was restricted as usual by the technical problems of shooting with a 16mm camera. Sixteen-millimeter image quality remained notably inferior to 35mm, synchronized sound recording had not yet been developed, and recording on tape was at an unreliable early stage. Fortunately the nature of the material allowed Lindsay to spend more time on the individuals who provided the newspaper with stories than on the mechanics of newspaper production.

Apart from a spoken commentary, the soundtrack of *Wakefield Express* is confined, very effectively, to folk songs sung by children, music from a brass band, and the clack of the reporter's typewriter. All these sounds grow out of the material. Children in party dresses sing and dance at a charity performance in the backyard of a working-class home, while their parents watch with solemn pride and distant factory chimneys belch smoke. The brass band plays at a coronation pageant (1952 was the year of Elizabeth II's coronation), and at a ceremony in front of the town's World War II memorial. This is the film's strongest sequence, with an emotive cut from a bugler sounding "The Last Post" to the face of a young widow, clearly remembering the husband she lost as a gust of wind ruffles her hair. A distinctly Fordian moment; but the children singing in the drab backyard, and other scenes of "the significant commonplace" (from the ninety-eight-year-old oldest inhabitant, bedridden but animated, to the bus driver who breeds budgerigars), reflect Lindsay's admiration for Jennings.

A few months later came the opportunity to produce more than talented apprentice work. Guy Brenton, an Oxford acquaintance who had subsequently been employed as assistant director on a few documentaries, invited Lindsay to collaborate on a short film about a school for deaf-mute children. Shot during June 1953, *Thursday's Children* gave Lindsay his first experience of working on 35mm, although on a budget that turned out to be sub-shoestring. There was no money left to complete a soundtrack until World Wide Pictures, a company specializing in documentaries, viewed the footage and agreed to finance postproduction. Then Lindsay introduced himself to Richard Burton, who was appearing with the Old Vic company in London that summer, and asked him to record the commentary without pay. He agreed, but even with Burton's name on the credits, World Wide was unable to sell the picture to any distributor, or even to any London movie theatre.

Pure chance rescued it from the shelf. Without informing World Wide or the filmmakers, the British Office of Information in New York

Thursday's Children

submitted the film to the Motion Picture Academy in Hollywood as an Oscar contender for best short subject. When *Thursday's Children* won, Republic Pictures acquired the distribution rights, and it finally opened in London as curtain raiser to Susan Hayward in *Untamed.*

According to Lindsay's diary, he felt "a certain distance" from the film, mainly because he was exasperated by Guy Brenton's lack of humor and "terrible conviction of moral superiority." But he judged the result a success: "As a project completely his [Brenton's]. After that—I suppose pretty well 50/50 his and mine." Pretty well 35/65, I would say on the evidence of another documentary, made by Brenton on his own, that I saw later. Another study of affliction, it was effective in a way that was not the way of *Thursday's Children*. Brenton's paraplegics were victims, with the emphasis on suffering. *Thursday's Children* are contenders, intensely eager to learn, discover, reach out, understand, connect. Without words, as the commentary (written by Lindsay) explains, there can be no thoughts, only feelings; sounds can only be taught by sight or touch, identified by pictures, received through fingers on a vibrating balloon that the teacher holds to her mouth as she speaks. But the film concentrates less on mechanics than on emotional experience, the hope and brightness of the children's faces, the excitement when they succeed in communicating with their teacher and each other.

"There is a particular quality in deaf people," Lindsay wrote after seeing *Thursday's Children* again in the 1980s. "The sense in which they are cut off from the world gives them a greater desire for contact with others in the hearing world." Was he implying that he'd responded to deafness as a metaphor for his sexual dilemma, and the "permanent barrier" he used to feel between himself and other people? He was certainly no longer aware of "a certain distance" from the film, and seemed to claim it as his own when he found it "interesting, especially in relation to other films I have made."

Not far from the school for *Thursday's Children* was the most popular working-class amusement park in the south of England. "Dreamland" featured the usual roller coaster, gambling machines, fire eaters and squalid little zoo, but when Lindsay first visited it on a Sunday afternoon he was fascinated and repelled by two special sideshow attractions: "Torture Through the Ages" and "Famous Executions." A poster invited him to "See the Electric Chair in which the Atom Spy Rosenberg was Executed," and from a nearby hole in the wall came a lunatic cackling sound. Lindsay peered through the hole and saw a mechanical dummy policeman nodding its head and emitting raucous canned laughter. The effect was memorably ghoulish, and after completing *Thursday's Children* he went back to the park to direct "the first film I made with no other impetus than my own wish to make it." Financing a unit of one (cameraman/sound recordist/assistant) out of his own pocket, he shot *O Dreamland* on 16mm stock left over from *Wakefield Express.*

The dummy's laughter, and Frankie Laine's "I Believe" alternating with Muriel Smith's "Kiss Me, Thrill Me" on a jukebox, form a relentless accompaniment to ten minutes of equally relentless images. Rosenberg shares "Famous Executions" with another dummy victim, a blonde who looks like a 1930s chorus girl but is supposed to represent Joan of Arc at the stake; in the Swiss Beer Garden, puppets twitch and yodel; a lion paces its narrow cage; rows of the overweight inspect rows of greasy food on display in the Happy Family Restaurant; more dummies suffer boiling oil, thumbscrew, and "Death by a Thousand Cuts" in the torture show; and more busloads of the lonely crowd arrive.

The candid camerawork, mainly in close shot, shows faces reacting to everything with the same almost catatonic lack of expression. A child blinks at Rosenberg strapped in the electric chair, a tired elderly woman slurps tea as she stares at an "artistic" nude statue, Bingo players intone the numbers after the caller, like churchgoers mechanically repeating the Lord's Prayer after the minister. The camera also explores other body parts, feet shuffling across ground fouled with litter, tremendous buttocks spilling over counter stools. There is no spoken commentary, only an implied unanswered question: If this is Dreamland, what kind of nightmare is everyday life?

Sometimes the crowd seems as ugly and mindless as the lunatic cackling dummy, sometimes as pathetically trapped as the lion in its cage. Lindsay's ambivalence gives *O Dreamland* its power, and as his first declaration of love-hate for the English, predicts the shape of films to come. But a 16mm documentary only ten minutes long had no commercial possibilities, and the print remained in a suitcase for more than two years, until it became part of the first Free Cinema program at the National Film Theatre.

Unlike his predecessors, Denis Forman believed that the BFI should show films as well as preserve them. A coyly named Telekinema had been built for the 1951 Festival of Britain, then marked for the wrecker's ball. Denis managed to save it, and eighteen months later the remodeled building became the National Film Theatre. In the meantime he arranged to rent another theatre for a series of film programs, and asked me for ideas, and I suggested that we invite any notable foreign director who happened to be visiting London to introduce one or more of his movies.

Among the first to accept were Robert Bresson and James Whale. Bresson loaned a print of his just completed *Journal d'un Curé de Campagne,* which became the first of his films to find commercial distribution in Britain. I remember Bresson as charming but withdrawn. When I admired his previous film, *Les Dames du Bois de Boulogne,* he seemed more surprised than pleased. "You actually saw it? So few people did." And although he agreed that Cocteau's dialogue was brilliant, he couldn't quite repress a shudder when I praised the superb performance of Maria Casarès. "I must tell you," he said, "that after making *Les Dames* I hoped I'd never have to work with professional actors again."

James Whale, who had just directed a play that closed before reaching London, had been unable to find work in Hollywood for ten years. Few movie buffs had yet discovered him, but I knew one of the few, who worked at the London office of Universal Pictures, and who located excellent prints of *The Old Dark House* and *The Bride of Frankenstein.* Their enthusiastic reception gave James a real lift. He remained in Europe for a few more weeks, and we met again several times. Elegant and cool, self-contained on the surface, he claimed at first that he was now more interested in painting than in filmmaking. But one evening in Paris he dropped his guard. We were going out to dinner together, and when I arrived at his hotel suite, James thrust a sheet of paper in my hands. On it he had written a list of all his movies, divided into two columns. "What does that tell you?" he asked. In one column were several movies I hadn't seen, including *The Road Back* and *The Man in the Iron Mask.* In the other, the two *Frankenstein* movies, *The Invisible Man, The Old Dark House, Showboat,* and a few others I would see later, including a ruthlessly original comedy-melodrama, *Remember Last Night?*

"All your best films, or the best of your films I've seen, are in one column," I said. "Correct," said James. "But what does *that* tell you?" I supposed that the movies in the other column suffered from studio interference. "Correct," he said again, with a smile that suddenly vanished as his face flushed with anger. "Bloody god-*damned* producers! Sons of bitches! Unspeakable turds!" Then the bedroom door opened, a young Frenchman appeared, and James quickly recovered himself. "This is Pierre, my—ahem—chauffeur." A typically ironic way of acknowledging his homosexuality and taking mine for granted.

Erich von Stroheim, in London for the premiere of *Sunset Boulevard,* was not feeling well enough to prolong his visit and introduce one of his films to a BFI audience. "In any case, none of the pictures I directed exists in its original form," he told me. "All of them are like corpses that have started to putrefy in their coffins." But Stroheim himself was in memorably original form. During his press conference, he asked for an ashtray in which to stub out his cigarette. "If you're the man you're supposed to be," a giggly male critic said, "you'd stub it out in the palm of my hand." The great man gave him a deadpan look. "If you were a woman, I would."

I first met Abel Gance at the Cannes Film Festival in 1952, when he held a press conference to announce he would shortly begin work on his first film in twelve years, *La Tour de Nesle,* from a novel by Dumas. Noble features and long white hair gave him the look of a biblical prophet, and he sounded like one as well: "I have just returned from the dead, and speak to you with a mouth full of earth." We met again when he came to London to view the first Cinerama program, and introduce a screening of his 1926 *Napoléon.* (Not, of course, the version later fully restored by Kevin Brownlow, but with some of the Polyvision sequences that divided the screen into three panels.) I remember standing with Gance next day outside the Cinerama theatre. Immensely dignified, and at the same time shamelessly theatrical, he exclaimed in a loud voice that startled passersby: "*Mon enfant!*" Then cradled his arms around an imaginary child.

Academic conferences on "film" were something to avoid, but when the BFI sponsored one in Cambridge I went because G. W. Pabst and René Clair had agreed to attend. The buzz when I arrived was that Clair refused to speak to Pabst, who was alleged to have worked as a secret agent for the Nazis when he directed films in France during the 1930s, and later to have supervised a Nazi documentary on the conquest of Poland. Pabst, whose name did not appear on the credits of the documentary, denied both accusations. He insisted that he stayed in Germany during World War II because he was trapped there; just as he'd arranged to leave for New York with his family, the war broke out and all foreign travel was instantly banned. This didn't satisfy Clair, who told me that Pabst had directed two feature films in Germany during the war. But when I asked if he'd seen either of them, Clair admitted rather irritably that he hadn't. (Later I saw both of them: costume pictures devoid of propaganda.) Pabst seemed to me then, and still seems, the most talented German director whose career began in silent movies, and in person I found him as accessible as Clair was remote. I made a point of being friendly, he was grateful for the attention, and we traveled back to London together by train.

When I told Pabst (truthfully, but with an ulterior motive) how much I'd enjoyed *Mademoiselle Docteur,* his espionage thriller made in France in 1937, benevolent eyes suddenly glittered behind rimless glasses. And I remember very precisely the sense if not the exact words of his reply. "That was a film about the three types of spies," he said, and as he smiled to himself rather than to me, proceeded to list them. "The spy who does it for thrills, for adventure. The spy who does it for money. And the spy who does it," he paused as if searching for the right English word, "for *moral* reasons—because he *believes* in the cause he works for. Naturally he's by far the most dangerous. Like all pure men."

Food for thought, but I never dared ask what was on my mind. Instead, as Pabst had told me he was planning to make a film about Hitler's final days in the bunker, I invited him to come back to England when it was finished, and introduce a screening at the National Film Theatre. Although he agreed, *The Last Act* took almost two years to set up, and Pabst had only just finished it when I made a trip from the 1954 Venice Film Festival to see his sumptuously exotic production of *Aïda* in the Verona amphitheatre. When we met after the performance, he told me he was leaving for Berlin in a few days to prepare *The 20th of July,* about the 1944 plot to assassinate Hitler. "I have an interesting idea," he said, and the same glitter appeared in his eyes. "Why not invite me to screen *both* films in London? And after you show them, we will have a discussion. How much better for the world if the plot had succeeded, I will say, and how much less humiliating for Hitler to have died that way."

"It's a date," I said, but soon after he finished shooting *The 20th of July,* Pabst contracted Parkinson's disease. He faded slowly, sadly away, and must have taken many secrets with him to the grave. Yet when I think about our conversation on the train, I can't fit him into any of those three categories. Between 1933 and 1939 Pabst made six movies in France and one in Hollywood, so he didn't need to spy for money. Personally cautious, deliberate in manner, he was not one for adventure or thrills—except on the screen. Neither was he one who believed. Pabst's best films, *Joyless Street* and *The Love of Jeanne Ney,* the two with Louise Brooks and the two about Nazi Germany, share the same dispassionate, camera-eye brilliance. No director ever created more involving drama while remaining fundamentally uninvolved.

Early in January 1954, with "no word from Serge for months," Lindsay went to Paris again. And discovered that Serge was about to appear in his own production of *Hamlet.* Happy to be invited to rehearsals and asked for advice, Lindsay felt frustratingly "third party" away from the theatre. His diary records only one enjoyable evening, when they had dinner with Serge's friend Alexandre Trauner, the set designer who was currently working for Howard Hawks on *Land of the Pharaohs.* He told Lindsay that although the script was officially by William Faulkner and Harry Kurnitz, "Faulkner appeared to have written 1 scene in 3 weeks—a visit by Pharaoh's daughter to one of the Pyramids under construction, with the opening line: 'How's the job going?' "

While Lindsay was in Paris I had a very early morning phone call from Ken Tynan. Our mutual friend the journalist Peter Wildeblood had been arrested, along with Lord Montagu of Beaulieu and his cousin Michael Pitt-Rivers, for "serious offenses" with two young servicemen. I forget how much it cost to free Peter on bail, but remember Ken describing the amount set as "viciously high." He asked me to contribute to a fund for Peter, which I was glad to do; but none of us could do anything to stop a sinister replay of the Oscar Wilde trial. The servicemen were granted immunity from prosecution in exchange for testifying. The defense produced evidence of collusion with the police. A Boy Scout called as witness for a "previous offense" changed his story after a forensic expert pronounced it "impossible." But the judge was convinced that the "peculiarity" of well-born men "consorting" with their social inferiors could mean only one thing. He sentenced the lord to a year in jail, and Peter and Pitt-Rivers, who had no titles, to eighteen months.

It was the climax of a so-called moral crusade against "perverts," headed by churchmen, the police, and the romance novelist Barbara Cartland. "This ridiculous witch-hunt going on all over the country," as Pitt-Rivers called it at the trial, had begun after Guy Burgess and Donald MacLean defected to Soviet Russia three years earlier. As they had both worked at the Foreign Office, homosexuals were branded security risks and potential traitors, as well as "ghouls of perverted sex" (Cartland). And by the time that Peter and his friends were arrested, the crusade had led to almost three thousand prosecutions and a dozen or so suicides.

When Lindsay returned from Paris and I told him about the arrests, he said nothing at first. Then he opened a folder on his desk and handed me a letter, which is quoted directly here, as I found it among Lindsay's papers after his death. Dated May 6, 1952, and headed simply "Hollywood," it was handwritten in a surprisingly elegant script: "Dear Lindsay, Thanks so much for your letter on 'the Quiet Man'—my favorite film. You were charming to write. I tried hard to see you in London—Dick Richards [movie columnist]—Brian [Desmond] Hurst—young Montagu of Beaulieu—all said they knew exactly how to reach you—but—next time . . . Sincerely, John Ford."

"Well," Lindsay said after I read it. "What do you know about Dick Richards?" Nothing, I told him. "Then what do you think about Ford knowing Montagu? Peculiar, isn't it?" No more "peculiar," I said, than Ford imagining that Montagu (whom neither of us had ever met) would know how to contact Lindsay. Perhaps, I suggested, Ford didn't really "know" Montagu, but had been introduced to him by Brian; and as Ford and Brian were both classic Irish boozers, Ford was probably a bit fuddled at the time.

"You could be right," Lindsay said. He seemed much relieved, and I remember thinking that the most "peculiar" thing about all this was Lindsay's anxiety to clear his idol of guilt by association. Some time later I asked Brian about Ford and Montagu. He remembered introducing them, but nothing more. "Were you drunk as a fiddler's bitch?" I asked, quoting one of his favorite phrases for one of his favorite conditions. "As a boiled owl," he answered, quoting another.

After Peter served his sentence, he wrote *Against the Law,* a plea for the decriminalization of homosexuality. I lent the book to Lindsay, saying I found it remarkably brave, but wished Peter hadn't written that he was no more proud of being homosexual than he would be of "having a glass eye or a hare lip." Lindsay asked rather sharply: "Are *you* proud of it?" I said something about being neither proud nor ashamed. He nodded, and as usual changed the subject.

Equating homosexuality with affliction, Peter wrote as a victim of the repressive 1950s who had just spent eighteen months in jail; but in every other way *Against the Law* was boldly ahead of its time. By making the same unhappy equation, Lindsay imprisoned himself; but later, by making films that were ahead of their time, he found release as an artist. Love, he told himself in his diary, is simply "not feasible. Where is the leather-clad motorcyclist who will sweep me away?" In *If . . . ,* love sweeps two schoolboys away, romantic, guiltless, and free.

Although the British film industry showed no interest in employing the codirector of an Oscar-winning short, an enterprising documentary producer called Leon Clore signed Lindsay to make a series of five-minute shorts for the National Society for the Prevention of Cruelty to Children during 1954. He was grateful for the work, but more interested in the possibility of getting a foot in the door of feature films as personal assistant to Thorold Dickinson on *The Mayor of Casterbridge.* After several studios had turned down his adaptation of Hardy's novel, Thorold approached Robin Maugham to write a new script. With his (sometimes) endearing lack of insight, Thorold had never suspected Lindsay's sexual orientation, and warned him as they set out to meet Somerset's nephew: "He's one of *those.*" But Lindsay didn't care for Robin ("a ritzy exponent of the culture machine"), Robin didn't care for the project, and at the end of the year Thorold abandoned it.

In January 1955, at the suggestion of Karel Reisz, who was in charge of programs at the National Film Theatre, Lindsay organized a John Ford retrospective. And in the late spring Hannah Weinstein arrived from Hollywood to produce a British TV series. A tough good-hearted radical, she was a friend of the American directors Joseph Losey and Cy Endfield, who had taken refuge in London after being black-listed as Communists by the House Committee on Un-American Activities. Although Hannah was not blacklisted, Hollywood studio executives had compiled an unofficial gray list, and I believe she came to England because she was on it. She not only helped Losey and End-field pay their bills by signing them to direct episodes of *Robin Hood,* but took Lindsay on board. Typical, he used to say, that he should owe his first chance to work in a British studio to an American.

At their first meeting, when Hannah explained that each half-hour episode had to be shot in five days, and any director who went over schedule would never be employed again, Lindsay recognized an expert at cracking the whip. He responded by singing, "Hardhearted Hannah, the vamp from Savannah." Fortunately, it amused her. Then the executive producer showed him around the main soundstage, where major components of the basic sets—Baronial Hall, Sheriff's Castle, Tavern, Robin's Forest Hideout—were mounted on wheels, so they could be quickly assembled for each change of scene. The star was Richard Greene, an English actor whom Lindsay found "pleasantly uninterest-ing," like the scripts, but *Robin Hood* taught him "a great deal about people" as well as offering a crash course in professionalism. "Consider merely the complications involved in asking the unit to work an extra half-hour on an early night," he wrote later. "The director who worries about the sequence, the assistant who worries about the schedule, the art director who wants to start building tomorrow's set, the camera operator who has backache, the electrician who can do with some overtime, the clapper-boy who has a date, and the actor who was called for seven o'clock in the morning and not used till after lunch . . ." All the same, Lindsay completed his five segments of *Robin Hood* on schedule, and Hannah's recommendation led to an offer to make his first TV commercial, for Lux Toilet Soap.

While Lindsay worked for the first time in a studio, I made my first (and only) film entirely on location. This came about through a chance meeting with an eccentric aristocrat, Sir Aymer Maxwell, who traced his ancestry back to the first duke of Northumberland. Neither his inherited title, nor his ruddy cheeks and bushy mustache, nor his high-bred drawl gave any clue to Aymer's inner self. He was in fact a frustrated impresario, with two very curious unrealized projects. One was the London production of a play by Henri de Montherlant about a love affair between two schoolboys, the other a movie that would take place in his favorite country, Morocco, and cost not more than £25,000 ($75,000). Aymer wanted to involve me in both projects, as translator of the Montherlant play, as writer and director of the movie. When I told him that movies and Morocco interested me more than Montherlant, he suggested we leave as soon as possible for Marrakech. "You'll need to sniff around a bit," he said.

An offer too improbable and exotic to refuse, particularly as it came at a time when I knew that I no longer wanted a career at the BFI, or as a film critic. Like Lindsay at Oxford, I was feeling "the desire to create," without knowing how or what. It didn't feel truly creative to write studies of von Stroheim and Fritz Lang for *Sight and Sound,* and I had stopped writing short stories, and abandoned another novel, because nothing about English life stimulated me. (London, Cyril Connolly announced in *Horizon* at the time, was as "permanently dull" as the sky above it.) In February 1953 Denis Forman had sent me to New York to report on the first Cinerama program, *This Is Cinerama.* I met the company chairman, Louis B. Mayer, who had a dazed expression and a nervous blink, as if he still hadn't recovered from being ousted as head of MGM. "Very good of you to come all this way to see us," he said.

Naturally I didn't explain that my real reason for the journey was to see New York. Or that a roller-coaster trip in virtual reality on a giant curved screen was far less exciting than the energy level of the New World, its optimistic skyline on a clear, sunny winter's day, the Village late at night, bookstores, markets, cafés, bars, jazz spots still open and crowded, the Balanchine-Stravinsky *Orpheus* at City Center, *Guys and Dolls* on Broadway.

Back home, I felt even less at home than before. But when Denis granted me a leave of absence from the BFI, I went with Aymer to Marrakech, where I had my first experience of Otherness—and felt at home. Visually the city was overwhelming, with its sunlight that changed from pale yellow to gold to violet as the day lengthened, its ramparts of red clay, its backdrop of snow-crested mountains. Raucous voices, music, and drums created an equally powerful soundtrack, especially when Sudanese dancers, acrobats, storytellers, and cobra charmers assembled in the city's great open square at dusk. Thousands of fantastically gaudy whores lived in the so-called *quartier réservé,* and the square itself was a pansexual marketplace. After sniffing around for two weeks, then taking a trip across the Atlas mountains to the edge of the Sahara, I told Aymer that it would be interesting to show the country's seductive effect on the most unlikely Western outsider. He asked who that outsider might be, and I suggested a thirtyish, prudish, and still virginal Englishwoman, at first tense and disapproving in the face of Otherness, then devastated to find herself falling in love with a marketplace Moroccan.

Aymer liked the idea, and I went back to London to write the script, as well as to ask Lindsay the same question that he'd asked me before making *Meet the Pioneers.* Was I crazy to attempt a first film with no technical experience? His answer was brisk and clear-sighted: "You won't know till you've done it. But you have to do it. Whatever the result, it's a positive step. Either you'll discover a talent for directing as well as writing, or you'll learn that you'd better stick to writing."

The cameraman on *Another Sky* was Walter Lassally, who had photographed several of Lindsay's documentaries, and would later shoot *A Taste of Honey* and *Tom Jones* for Tony Richardson. Only three actors were brought out from England, and the unit was minimal—like the dialogue, which I'd cut to the bone, knowing our budget would not allow for direct sound on location. The Moroccan cast was recruited on the spot from nonprofessionals, whom I directed in French through a French-speaking interpreter, and the extras for a European party scene from a group of German tourists who fortunately spoke English.

Aymer rented a house in the medina, and invited his friend Elias

Canetti to stay soon after we started shooting. The future Nobel Prize winner watched me direct one of the Moroccan players through an interpreter, then advised me never to learn even a word of Arabic. You will always understand a foreigner more profoundly, he explained, if you don't understand the language he speaks. Later he wrote *Voices of Marrakech* to illustrate this irritating and humorless paradox, but only succeeded in disproving his point.

My greatest technical problem as a novice director was the constant need for improvisation. Although I made a shooting plan for each location scene, we often had to shoot the scene when the sun was too high or too low in the sky for my plan to work. But Lassally was always quick to come to my rescue and suggest alternative setups. That we didn't go over the seven-week shooting schedule was largely due to his technical support. The last third of the film described the English-woman's five-hundred-mile journey across the Atlas Mountains to the Sahara, in search of her lover who had mysteriously disappeared. Her journey began on a ramshackle bus (which Aymer followed in his Bentley), continued on a donkey when there were no more bus routes, and ended on foot when the donkey was stolen. At first Lassally inclined to the same romantic effects that had worked so well in the Marrakech scenes; but when I explained that I wanted to show someone lost in a world that had turned alien and sinister, he devised some powerfully bleak images.

I was equally fortunate in my editor, who understood the style I had aimed for and responded to the material's deliberately slow pace. (Although I didn't always know how to get what I wanted, I knew I wanted it, and earlier that year had seen and admired Antonioni's first feature, *Cronaca di un Amore*.) Vera Campbell began her career as assistant to David Lean in the cutting room. A creative technician with a taste for the offbeat, she had recently edited René Clement's *Monsieur Ripois,* aka *Knave of Hearts.* Lindsay, who had seen my unedited material before viewing Vera's first cut, delivered a bluntly accurate verdict: "No one could have done more to reveal its strengths and disguise its weaknesses."

Another Sky never found a British distributor, but in France Henri Langlois launched its modest art house career (later repeated, even more modestly, in the United States) by inviting Buñuel, Roberto Rossellini, and some of the *Cahiers du Cinéma* group to a screening at the Cinémathèque in Paris. "I like some of it," Rossellini told me afterward. Buñuel, who overheard this, took me aside and said, "I like all of it. It's a very honorable film." Later we had a drink together, and he quoted the Englishwoman's last line: "The people here [Morocco] believe that everything is the will of God. And this I am learning to accept." Then he asked, could I imagine myself ever accepting such a belief? "Absolutely not," I said. "Neither could I," said Buñuel, then smiled. "Thank God."

In late 1955, disappointed by the lack of enthusiasm in Britain for *Another Sky,* Aymer retired to his house on the Greek island of Euboea, where he spent much of the rest of his life. I went back to editing *Sight and Sound,* and a season of internal exile. While I was away, the BFI's Experimental Film Fund had financed two modestly budgeted films, a twenty-minute documentary about a suburban jazz club, and a forty-minute poetic drama about two deaf-mute dockworkers living in London's East End. Both films were by first-time directors, *Momma Don't Allow* a collaboration between Karel Reisz and Tony Richardson, *Together* a solo effort (with some additional shooting and major help in the cutting room from Lindsay) by Lorenza Mazzetti, a young Italian living in London. With no prospect of commercial distribution, they would have gone straight to the film club circuit, but for Lindsay's idea of combining them with *O Dreamland* to make up the first Free Cinema program at the National Film Theatre.

As Tony Richardson later commented, Lindsay was "a sublime and sometimes pugnacious publicist." By claiming that the three films formed a "movement," he not only created one, but became its leader. And the timing was right. Even the critics whom Lindsay had once reproached for "artistic patriotism" were no longer able to beat the drum for British movies. With *Oh Rosalinda,* Powell-Pressburger had begun to lose their way, like Carol Reed with *A Kid for Two Farthings;* with *Summertime,* David Lean had taken his first step along the "international" route and would never make a film in Britain again; Mackendrick was about to leave for America, and Hamer was in alcoholic decline. When Lindsay announced the need for "films of today" with more sense of national realities than *Doctor at Sea,* there was already a gap to be filled. Change, or the possibility of it, was in the air.

The first Free Cinema manifesto, written by Lindsay and signed by Karel Reisz, Tony Richardson, and Lorenza Mazzetti as well as him, was shrewdly calculated to focus on intention rather than achievement:

> As film-makers we believe that
> No film can be too personal.
> The image speaks. Sound amplifies and comments. Size
> is irrelevant.
> Perfection is not an aim.
> An attitude means a style. A style means an attitude.

A second manifesto, signed only by Lindsay, underlined the point: "With a 16mm camera, and minimal resources, you cannot achieve very much—in commercial terms. You cannot make a feature film, and your possibilities of experiment are severely restricted. But you can use your eyes and ears. You can give indications. You can make poetry."

Superficially, all the films had in common was a shoestring budget (all three cost less than a single newsreel), the use of everyday working-class backgrounds, and nonprofessional actors to play "ordinary" people. But the people themselves were as different as their backgrounds: the crowd of *O Dreamland,* passive spectators of horror sideshows at an amusement park; the Teddy Boys and their girls of *Momma Don't Allow,* forgetting their everyday lives while they danced to Chris Barber's band; the solitary deaf-mutes of *Together,* unable to forget their lives, whether sitting in a pub to watch couples dance to music they couldn't hear or being mocked by children when they took a walk along the wasteland left by a World War II German bomb. They were also people and backgrounds that you didn't see in any other British films of the time. They gave "indications."

"You're all making films about life here and now in this country, while I can't wait to get out of it," I remember saying to Lindsay at a reception for the Free Cinema opening in February 1956. "The day you abandon us," Lindsay replied, "you'll be bringing up the rear of a very long line. And if you don't come back, perhaps one day you'll write a book explaining why so many writers have left England for good over the last fifty years." He listed D. H. Lawrence, Somerset Maugham,

Aldous Huxley, Graham Greene, W. H. Auden, Christopher Isherwood, and I added Hitchcock as a filmmaker. But what drove them all away, and made them stay away? Lindsay asked. Didn't most Americans who went to Europe decide to return from exile a few years later? America is not static, I said. When I was in New York, it seemed to me that they perceived change, for better or for worse, as part of the natural order of things. Over here, it's perceived as a threat. This reminded Lindsay of Byron, whose reason for leaving England was that he could no longer endure its apparently unshakable belief that "God is a Tory."

Two years later, when I had decided to settle in California, he sent me a copy of "Declaration," an anthology of protest pieces by the so-called Angry Young Men (Osborne, Tynan, Colin Wilson, etc). Lindsay's contribution, "Get Out and Push," was a sequel to "Stand Up! Stand Up!" and an epilogue to our conversation about leaving England. It returned to the attack on British movies ("emotionally inhibited, wilfully blind to the conditions and problems of the present"), and British political parties (Conservatives "proudly blinkered to the last," Labour crippled by "failure of imagination"). But with the same unique mixture of fantasy and reality that would characterize his best films, Lindsay also created a memorable image of the 1950s Britain that I'd left:

> *Coming back to Britain {from Europe} is, in many*
> *respects, like going back to the nursery. The outside*
> *world, the dangerous world, is shut away; its sounds*
> *muffled. Cretonne curtains are drawn, with a pretty*
> *pattern on them of the Queen and her fairy-tale*
> *Prince, riding to Westminster in a golden coach.*
> *Nanny lights the fire, and sits herself down with a*
> *nice cup of tea and yesterday's* Daily Express, *but*
> *she keeps half an eye on us too, as we bring out our*
> *trophies from abroad, the books and pictures we have*
> *managed to get past the customs. (Nanny has a pair of*
> *scissors handy, to cut out anything it wouldn't be*
> *right for children to see.) The clock ticks on. The*
> *servants are all downstairs, watching TV. Mummy and*
> *Daddy have gone to the new Noel Coward at the Globe.*
> *Sometimes there is a bang from the street outside—*

*backfire, says Nanny. Sometimes there's a scream from
cellar—Nanny's lips tighten, but she doesn't
say anything . . . Is it to be wondered at that, from
time to time, a window is found open, and the family
is diminished by one? We hear of him later sometimes,
living in a penthouse in New York, or a* dacha *near*
Moscow . . .

Back in February 1956, when I told Lindsay that I couldn't wait to get out of England, it seemed that a window had actually begun to open for me. A few weeks earlier, I had gone to a New Year's Eve party given by Leon Clore (the producer for whom Lindsay had made a series of five-minute shorts) and his wife, Miriam. I went to another party first, and arrived only a few minutes before midnight at the Clores, where Miriam greeted me at the door. "There's someone here who's very impatient to meet you," she said, and led me to a far corner of the crowded room, where a man with powerful shoulders, a leonine head, and graying blond hair, very handsome but gloomy, stood alone. By choice, I felt. He seemed to create a circle of isolation around himself.

I recognized Nicholas Ray from photographs, and he guessed who I was, introducing himself before Miriam had time to introduce us. "I am a new director of very remarkable talent," he said, quoting my *Sequence* review of *They Live by Night.* Then it was time for "Auld Lang Syne," and 1956 began with Nick saying, "Let's get out of here." We passed Lindsay, talking to Hannah Weinstein, who stood with her back to us. I wished him a happy new year. He glanced at Nick, then gave me one of his best quizzical looks.

There was a chauffeured limousine waiting outside, and we drove to the Hyde Park Hotel. In the sitting room of Nick's suite we talked for two, maybe three hours. First about *Rebel Without a Cause,* which I'd recently seen and admired, and was due to open in London shortly. Then about James Dean, who had crashed his Porsche and died three months earlier. "You can imagine how I felt," Nick said, and poured himself another vodka on the rocks. "It was . . . ," he began, but left the rest to my imagination by breaking off to ask if I'd liked *In a Lonely Place.* Yes, I said, very much. (The deeper Nick's feelings, I realized later, the less articulate about them he became.) "I had to fight to get the ending I wanted," he said. I told him I liked its ambiguity, the way

86

it left you wondering how the Bogart character was going to spend the rest of his life. "Exactly," Nick said. "Will he become a hopeless drunk, or kill himself, or seek psychiatric help? Those have always been my personal options, by the way."

Before I had time to digest or answer this, he gave one of his startling (because infrequent) smiles, and asked my opinion of *Johnny Guitar.* I said I couldn't understand why the *Cahiers du Cinéma* critics took it seriously. Neither could Nick, who described the making of it as an appalling experience, and Joan Crawford as one of the worst human beings he'd ever encountered. Then he gave me a rather uncertain look, as if wondering how I'd react to what he was going to tell me. "But I talked with one of those critics in Paris recently," he said, "and he almost persuaded me it was a great movie." I told him that I suspected it was the same critic who had recently admired Edgar G. Ulmer's *Babes in Bagdad.* He didn't smile, but said with a trace of disappointment, "You're probably right."

Nick had heard about *Another Sky* in Paris, and asked me to arrange a screening for him next day. "I've got meetings all morning, and a lunch date, so make it three o'clock." Then he got up, riffled through various scripts and papers on a table, and handed me a photocopy of a *New Yorker* article. "I want you to read this and tell me what you think about it at the screening tomorrow." He continued toward the bedroom, stopping for a moment by the door. "How old are you?" Thirty-one, I said. "I'm forty-four," he said. "Not quite old enough to be your father."

What was that supposed to mean? I wondered as Nick disappeared, presumably to the bathroom. Like his opening remark at the party, it seemed to strike a flirtatious note. Or was I fantasizing because I found him extraordinarily attractive? And what was the problem that kept him on the edge of alcoholism, suicide, or consulting a psychiatrist? And was he genuinely desperate, or an expert manipulator? And—ten minutes later—why hadn't he come back from the bathroom?

It was three-thirty in the morning, so perhaps he'd fallen asleep. The bedroom door was not quite closed, and I decided to take a look. As I reached it, the door opened further and I collided with Nick on his way back, naked except for his underpants. He put his arms around me and kissed me on the mouth. An hour or so later he said that he wasn't really homosexual, not really even bisexual, as he'd been to bed with a great many women in his life, but only two or three men.

Nicholas Ray

It was after five in the morning when I got back to the flat at 57
Greencroft Gardens where Lindsay and I were now living—an unfashionable area of London mysteriously called Swiss Cottage, full of immigrants from Central Europe and spacious, gloomy, late Victorian
redbrick houses converted into flats. (Lindsay developed a great affection for the neighborhood, and eventually settled in another flat only
two blocks away.) I slept for three hours, made breakfast, telephoned to
check that the BFI screening room was available, left a message for
Nick (who wasn't taking calls), and left again without seeing Lindsay,
who hadn't stirred.

I remember that while I pretended to work that morning, all I
could think about was the fact that I'd fallen deeply in love with Nick.
(So, as I discovered later, had scores of other people.) I was also afraid
that he might be totally unimpressed by *Another Sky,* and lose interest

in me. But to my enormous relief he liked the film and was astonished to learn how little it had cost. "It's got a strange kind of concentration and the journey to the Sahara really builds," he said. "Even though the scenery didn't look all that unfamiliar to me. It was like parts of California—without Arabs, of course."

Then the limousine took us back to his hotel. On the way we discussed the *New Yorker* article, which I'd read that morning. It was the case history of a schoolteacher, suffering from a degenerative inflammation of the arteries, whose doctor prescribed cortisone. A newly discovered drug at the time, its side effects had not been fully tested; and although it relieved the teacher's pain, it turned him into a manic depressive. "I've signed a contract to make two pictures for Fox," Nick said when we were back in his suite. "This story is going to be the first." He poured himself a vodka on the rocks. "I want you to come out to Hollywood and work with me on it."

He gave me twenty seconds to get over my astonishment and accept, then said he had to catch a plane to Paris in a couple of hours. *Rebel Without a Cause* was due to open there next day, and he was going on to Berlin for the same reason. "I'll be back in a week for the press screening here," he said, gave me a hug, went into the bedroom and closed the door.

Lindsay greeted me with a raised eyebrow when we met that evening. "I presume you got on rather well with Nick, since you spent the night together," he said, adding that he'd heard me come in "not long before dawn." I told him that we'd sat up talking for hours, but not the rest. At first I didn't tell anyone the rest, because there were times when Nick seemed like a visitor from another planet, and I felt like someone hallucinating a romantic encounter with an alien. But next day he called from Paris, and told me that *Rebel* had been very well received by the French critics. "A couple of them compared it to *Johnny Guitar.* Something about inner solitude. I miss you," he said. Then I heard nothing until he was back in London, the night before the press screening. He wanted me to meet him there, then drive with him to the airport, as he had to leave for California the same day.

We sat together in the back of the limousine, and Nick said the British critics had been very polite, but he wondered if they really liked the film. Some of them told me they did, I assured him, but critics over here feel they have to safeguard their integrity by keeping a distance from filmmakers. "A virginity complex," Nick suggested, then said he had already called the studio about arranging for my green card. "I'll make sure the wheels are turning soon as I get back," he promised, "but don't worry if they turn slowly, they always do. In the meantime, go to the American Embassy tomorrow and get your visa application moving."

Then he gave me a lecture on the need to disguise my homosexuality in Hollywood. A butch handshake, he said, is very important, then demonstrated a bone-crushing one, and gave his startling smile. He didn't want me to see him off. "The driver will take you home," he said. A quick goodbye hug, and an afterthought as he got out of the car: "Will you bring me a couple of bottles of Marc de Bourgogne? I can't get it out there."

A week later the phone rang, and a female American voice, briskly friendly, came on the line: "This is Mr. Ray's secretary at Twentieth Century–Fox. He wants you to know we haven't forgotten you, and you'll be hearing from us very soon." The "we" was impressive but disconcertingly impersonal. Two weeks later, when the Free Cinema program opened, I had heard nothing more. But the next day Nick himself came on the line to say the wheels had turned, and *Ten Feet Tall,* as the movie was then called, would start shooting at the end of March. "Officially you belong to Fox, as dialogue director—which means running the lines with actors on the set. Unofficially, you belong to me. The first draft screenplay is very disappointing, and I'll need your help."

"You're sure you really want this?" Lindsay asked. Oh yes, I said. "And you think you can handle it?" I don't know, I said, because I don't really know what I'm getting into. Then he gave me some advice that I found extraordinarily shrewd and (considering Lindsay's own sexual block) empathetic. "It seems pretty obvious to me that you're getting into a rather dangerous area, mixing personal involvement with some kind of creative collaboration. And from what you've told me, I think Nick cares about his work more than anything or anyone else. He seems to expect a lot from you. You'll have to prove yourself."

Early in March I left London for Los Angeles, which seemed far more remote in those presupersonic days, when it took almost eleven hours to fly to New York, and another nine to the West Coast. Lindsay came to see me off, and his final wave before I boarded the plane is another unfaded photograph in the mind's eye. But there is no comment on my departure in his diary, which he had abandoned a year earlier and would not take up again until July 1960.

The last entry before he signed off was a brief note about continuing to miss Serge, and feeling that "I just haven't the will or strength to attack life solely on my own." Once again Lindsay privately underestimated himself, then publicly contradicted himself. Soon after that last entry he brought in five episodes of *Robin Hood* on schedule, without any previous studio experience, and created a vigorous propaganda campaign for Free Cinema. And hindsight suggests that his remarkably accurate reading of Nick was also a reading, perhaps unconscious, of himself. Different in every other respect, they had an energy source in common, and Nick was already what Lindsay would soon become, an artist motorized by secret pain.

"Chance is everywhere," Jung believed, and the day I left England for a completely new life, Lindsay was on the verge of a major breakthrough in his own life. But he had no reason to suspect it, for as he wrote later: "I had never directed in the professional theatre before I did my first production at the Royal Court in 1957."

PART TWO

Sentimental Educations

~ Lindsay on Lindsay ~

You can't love human nature in a sentimental sense. If you truly love human beings, you have to be able to be angry with them.

There are few people in the world who, for good or ill, think and even act in terms of what might be or should be. More people act in terms of what is—i.e., of the situation in which they find themselves. By nature I am strongly possessed by the vision of what might be, what should be.

5

The English Stage Company's first production at the Royal Court opened a month after I left England. But the company itself had been conceived almost three years earlier, and Tony Richardson kept me informed of its difficult pregnancy and delayed birth.

Lindsay and I had both met Tony soon after I began editing *Sight and Sound* in 1950. Imposingly tall and thin, with an inexhaustible appetite for life and (perhaps as a result) inexhaustible energy, his arrival at Oxford in 1948 coincided with the departure of Lindsay and Ken Tynan. He was soon directing plays for the Oxford University Dramatic Society and the Experimental Theatre Club: *King John, Romeo and Juliet, Peer Gynt* (with twenty-two-year-old John Schlesinger as the Troll King), and *The Duchess of Malfi.* Like Gertrude's wolfhounds in the Tynan *Hamlet,* the Duchess's vivid green macaw, which she kept in an elaborate cage, was much talked about at the time. A few very serious-minded members of the audience found it deeply symbolic, but Tony later confided it was just a sign of his passion for exotic birds, especially the parrot genus—a genus that in some ways he resembled. His strong hands and feet seemed designed for grasping and climbing, and to eliminate a north country accent, he had taken speech lessons. They produced a sharp, precisely inflected voice that rose to a squawk when he became convulsed with laughter or indignation.

But most of all Tony reminded me of the young Lucien in Balzac's *Lost Illusions,* who told his "protector," Vautrin, that what he really wanted, more than anything else in the world, was "to be famous and loved." In fact, Tony was loved (and loved in return) before he became famous. During the early fifties he had an affair with a girl who died tragically young of leukemia, then with an American whom he always introduced as his roommate; and for the rest of his life Tony's bisexuality was an open secret to his friends, a locked closet to the world. Coming of professional age when homosexuality was a criminal offense, exposure a threat to the careers of so many people, and police harassment (in the wake of Burgess-Maclean and Montagu-Wildeblood) at its peak, he placed his female lovers center stage and relegated his male lovers to the wings. The media, of course, were far less powerful than they are now—and correspondingly less invasive, unless you crossed the line, like the clergyman accused by the choirboy or the public figure caught "soliciting" in a public toilet. And as a realist, Tony had no hesitation in following the example of Noël Coward, Somerset Maugham, Cecil Beaton, Stephen Spender, Terence Rattigan, Angus Wilson, and all the others who took care never to cross that line.

But the example of Lindsay disturbed Tony. "The price of repression," he used to say, "is extremely high." Although a smoke screen also has its price, I don't know how much it cost Tony. I don't even know if Tony knew. He never discussed it, and as he often said, was "too busy to be introspective." Like Lindsay and Karel Reisz, he became a major contributor to *Sight and Sound,* and like them he wanted to make movies. Unlike them, he was equally determined to work in the London theatre, which was no more encouraging to young outsiders than the British film industry.

An essential part of any talent is a talent for luck, and Tony had that as well. After knocking on various theatrical doors that slammed in his face, he answered a BBC advertisement for trainee TV directors, and was accepted. He completed a training course that he found "absolutely useless," and was allowed to direct several plays for BBC TV, including *Othello* and an adaptation of a story by Chekhov. And in the leading role of Chekhov's broken-down actor who dies onstage during a provincial tour, he decided to cast George Devine, a distinguished actor-director, forty-three to Tony's twenty-five.

Devine had worked with all the established names of the London stage—Gielgud, Olivier, Edith Evans, Ralph Richardson, Peggy Ashcroft—and could have spent the rest of his life in impeccably acted revivals of established classics. But instead of hardening his creative arteries, success had made him impatient with a theatre that resolutely faced the past, and he was so bored with costume drama that he turned Tony down at first, then agreed to meet him for a drink. It was a crucial meeting. As well as agreeing to play the part, the man of great experience and skill and the brilliant novice genuinely liked each other. Tony was astonished and impressed by Devine's openness to new ideas, Devine by Tony's intelligence; and as they both longed for a theatre that would face the present, they realized the mutual advantage of forming a partnership to create it.

A wealthy lady addicted to brandy and flowered kimonos led Tony to believe she would back the project, but suddenly reneged. In the public sphere, Devine contacted various corporations and banks, all of them "interested" but evasive. Meanwhile, another new theatre company had been conceived by Ronald Duncan (author of several verse plays as well as the libretto of Benjamin Britten's *The Rape of Lucretia*) and the earl of Harewood (unique in the House of Windsor for his active interest in the arts). They moved one step ahead of Devine and Tony by acquiring a fund-raiser in the person of Oscar Lewenstein, a member of the Communist Party who was also a shrewd businessman with an interest in promoting anti-Establishment theatre.

When Lewenstein heard that Devine and Tony had similar plans, he proposed a merger. Devine agreed on condition he became the company's artistic director, with Tony as his associate, but he had to accept a counterproposal—that the first season include two new plays by Duncan. "There'll be trouble, of course," Tony said with relish. Like Devine, he was not a Duncan fan, and dismissed him as "part of the blank verse shit tradition of Christopher Fry and T. S. Eliot." But like Devine, he pretended to admire Duncan's work and share his taste, although the only contemporary playwrights they all genuinely admired were Brecht and Beckett. (They tried to acquire the rights to *Waiting for Godot,* but were too late. A West End producer had just paid the asking price of £250.) The next stage of the game, which Tony also relished, was to find a chairman of the new company's board. He was delighted by the choice of Neville Blond, a theatre-struck textile magnate who promised to invest his own money and bring in other investors: "A capitalist, a Communist, a blank verse playwright and a member of the royal family. Can you imagine a more incongruous combination?" Unimaginably, a retired music-hall comedian was added to the combination when Alfred Esdaile, who owned the lease of the Royal Court Theatre, agreed to sublet it.

As well as presenting European plays by writers that the London theatre had ignored (Beckett, Brecht, Ionesco, Genet), Devine and Tony hoped to discover new English playwrights. Their first discovery was John Osborne, whose *Look Back in Anger* had been turned down by every West End producer. I remember Tony expecting trouble from Duncan when they chose it to open the first season, then being unable to suppress the disappointment in his voice when he told me, "He actually *likes* it." But trouble came from the chairman of the board, who pressured them to open with something less controversial.

They eventually settled on Angus Wilson's first and only play, *The Mulberry Bush,* which opened in the spring of 1956, three years after Devine and Tony first met. Like the production that followed, Arthur Miller's *The Crucible,* it received sympathetic but guarded reviews. Lindsay wrote me that although he thought the first "like very minor Shaw" and the second "a worthy bore," at least they were *"about something,"* unlike any other new plays running in London. He also liked what he called "the Royal Court style"—clear, economical, and direct—as opposed to the overrefined, overdressed "West End style." And among the actors who played their first leading roles that first season, he singled out the promise of Alan Bates, Joan Plowright, and Mary Ure.

But the company's tentative start only served to heighten the impact of *Look Back in Anger* later that year. It appalled and excited the critics in about equal measure; played to full houses after BBC TV aired a scene from it; established Tony as a director and the English Stage Company as a theatre with an identity. By the following season, the powers that be had taken note. Sir Laurence Olivier became the first knight of the West End to appear at the Court, in Osborne's *The Entertainer,* and was followed over the next few years by Sir Alec, Sir John, and Sir Ralph.

Early in 1957, Devine and Tony launched a scheme to develop new playwrights and new directors, with Sunday night performances on a minimal budget, no sets, costumes "only indicated," each actor paid £30, each writer and director £50. The second of these productions, Kathleen Sully's *The Waiting of Lester Abbs,* was directed by Lindsay.

Tony sent him the play because he knew Lindsay admired its author. In an article on "New Writers of Promise" commissioned by British *Vogue* shortly before I left England, I had mentioned Sully's first novel, *Canal by Moonlight,* a spare, quirky, poetic account of "ordinary"

John Osborne with Tony Richardson

people in a northern city. Lindsay and Tony liked it as much as I did, and found the same qualities in *Lester Abbs*. "If you didn't know," Lindsay wrote me, "you'd guess who wrote it when the schoolteacher's mother, in the tea party scene, remarks with casual disdain: 'These biscuits are rather dull.' "

I didn't see Lindsay's first stage production, but Tony remembered it, when we met again in California, as "astonishingly professional and wonderfully acted." Lindsay himself attributed its success to the supportive atmosphere of the Court, which didn't expect a director to be "brilliant," or to "*use* a text to show off his own prowess. It was never a director's theatre. The text always came first." But I suspect that Lindsay's rapport with actors was just as important. Alan Bates, whom he later directed several times, was struck by the way "Lindsay kept actors on his side—because he genuinely liked them. He made you laugh, kept you alert, but didn't make you bristle at criticism, which is quite an art."

In the five years between *Lester Abbs* and the start of preparation for *This Sporting Life,* Lindsay worked almost exclusively in the theatre. Tony's intuition had launched Lindsay on a second career, and a lack of film offers consolidated it. Only two came his way during that time, and he turned down one of them. Ken Tynan, who had joined Ealing

Films as script editor, with a mandate to find new stories, persuaded Michael Balcon to option a book about life in the casualty ward of a London hospital and to commission Lindsay to direct his own adaptation of it. But Ken and Balcon found Lindsay's first treatment dramatically weak, too documentary in approach; and even though he wrote a second version that they liked, he withdrew from the project.

However pleasant and sympathetic a producer might appear, Lindsay once wrote me, a first meeting always left him "profoundly skeptical." He'd told John Ford that he instinctively resented authority figures, and for the rest of his life he placed producers at the head of the list. Perhaps it was not a coincidence that the first producer he ever met was Sam Goldwyn, whom he interviewed for *Sequence.* Goldwyn advised Lindsay to increase the magazine's circulation by putting cheesecake on the cover and running a gossip column. When Lindsay replied that if we did that, we would no longer be *Sequence,* Goldwyn told him: "Life is compromise."

This was true, Lindsay the critic wrote in his account of the interview, only for "the lucky ones whose great hearts, shallow and commonplace as bedpans, beat in instinctive tune with the great heart of the public, who laugh as it likes to laugh, weep the sweet and easy tears that it likes to weep." But to Lindsay the director, the voice of compromise spoke for an industry that had the power to muffle his own voice. And although he never began a feature film without an attack of insecurity verging on dread, he put up a front that producers often found arrogant or "too intellectual."

The offer Lindsay accepted in May 1957 was to make another documentary, one of a series sponsored by the Ford Motor Company and coproduced by Karel Reisz and Leon Clore, in which directors could choose their own subjects, free of direct advertising. When Lindsay decided to make a film about the Covent Garden market, the Ford representative had only one request: "If you show any lorries, they mustn't be GM. They must be Ford." Fair enough, yet enough to establish the sponsor as an authority figure in Lindsay's eyes. Karel remembered his quizzical look and mocking reply: "You're such an *enlightened* sponsor, aren't you?"

· · ·

Every Day Except Christmas is a forty-minute impression of the famous market that sold fruit, flowers, and vegetables three hundred and sixty-four days of the year. By 1957 it had been open for more than two hundred years, but within twenty more years it would be replaced by an elaborate gentrified mall of restaurants and boutiques. So the film seems very much a period piece today. The Covent Garden it records has vanished completely, along with the kind of people who worked there, the stray cats, and the scent of apples and roses. Also, as Karel Reisz commented to me, the film itself is "in some ways uncharacteristic of Lindsay. *Reaching* for style, like *This Sporting Life*."

It begins around midnight, with a (Ford) truck driving along a dark, empty country road, and the emphatically upper-class voice of a BBC radio announcer wishing listeners good night. A device typical of Humphrey Jennings, whose effective use of contrasting image and sound Lindsay had noted in "Only Connect," and whose presence is felt behind many of the scenes that follow, with their affectionate and occasionally ironic glimpses of everyday British life. As trucks arrive at the market, workers unload produce and arrange it for display; some time before dawn they take a break in a nearby café; in the early morning, buyers for stores and restaurants arrive; by noon, as unsold produce is wheeled away, it's all over. Until the next midnight.

Although the film is "affectionately dedicated to George and Alice and Bill and Sid and Alan and Derek and Bill" and all the other market workers, Lindsay dedicates his camera most affectionately to handsome young George, who gets the lion's share of footage. And when the workers take their predawn break of tea and sausage sandwiches as they wait for the market to open, John Ford is the unseen presence behind a celebration of male camaraderie (and the folksy musical score). It's skillfully done, but a little too careful and self-conscious, unlike the earlier *Thursday's Children* and *O Dreamland,* and the movies after *This Sporting Life.* The "relaxed and spontaneous" quality that Karel Reisz finds most characteristic of Lindsay is missing, and only appears in a brief scene near the end.

As the market empties, its last customers arrive. Old ladies who have spent most of their lives peddling flowers in the street—superannuated Eliza Doolittles who never found a Professor Higgins—riffle through leftover violets and roses, now on sale at bargain prices.

Every Day Except Christmas. Superannuated Eliza Doolittle

Although shabby and grizzled, there's nothing pathetic about them. They're much too valiant for that, and too busy gossiping, joking, surviving. They would reject any hint of compassion as impatiently as one of them tosses away a bunch of very slightly wilted violets, cheap at the price though it may be. These ladies have their standards and their dignity. But as they hurry off, the commentary strikes a didactic closing note that breaks the spell: "Many things change, but work doesn't change, and we all depend on each other's work as well as our own."

"I want to make people—ordinary people, not just Top People— feel their dignity and their importance," Lindsay remarked at the time. Forty years on, this sounds harmless, but when *Every Day Except Christmas* was entered for the 1957 Venice Film Festival, the British ambassador to Italy tried to have it withdrawn. "It gives a very poor view of British life," he said. Because its view of British life excluded Top People? It's hard to think of any other ambassadorial reason. Fortunately, his request was denied, and the film won the Grand Prix for Best Documentary.

Six months later Lindsay was one of several directors who filmed

First production at the Court: Peter O'Toole (left)
in *The Long and the Short and the Tall*

the 1958 *March to Aldermaston,* which began in central London and
ended at the gates of Britain's largest nuclear power station. Among
the "Ban the Bomb" marchers, nearly all in their early twenties or
younger, was George Devine. Unlike Lindsay, he disliked public
demonstrations but felt, "This one I bloody well have to join." Lindsay
also supervised the editing and wrote the commentary (spoken by
Richard Burton), but no one who worked on the film took a credit. Like
the march itself, it was a collective gesture; and in his own case, as
Lindsay commented ironically many years later, a memorial to a time
when "I still believed, or wanted to believe, that things (society) could
become 'better.' "

In December 1958 Tony offered Lindsay his first production in the
main Court theatre. Willis Hall was another Court discovery, and his
play about an Army patrol unit during World War II was a retort to the
British war films that Lindsay had attacked in *Sequence.* No patriotic
nostalgia and no "Captain 'D' " heroics in *The Disciplines of War,* but a
sharp focus on rank-and-file experience, the tensions created by fear,
danger, and boredom. Lindsay, who once noted that he was "always
drawn by the emotive power of popular songs," had a considerable

repertory of World War II favorites that he liked to sing, from "You'd Be So Nice to Come Home To" to "We'll Meet Again." The play brought to mind another favorite, and he suggested changing its title to *The Long and the Short and the Tall.*

In one of the leading roles he cast a twenty-two-year-old actor from a regional repertory company, who had recently made his first appearance on the London stage in *The Party,* starring Charles Laughton. "You can tell a lot about what England is like today from Albert Finney," Laughton was reported to have said, and the remark aroused Lindsay's curiosity. He went to see the play, and found the first in a line of young actors he would continue to seek out, "unactorish," uncontaminated by "West End style." It was not a coincidence, Lindsay believed, that Finney, Alan Bates, and Malcolm McDowell all came from the north of England, and Richard Harris from Ireland. He always considered the north as "not really English at all," free of "the curse of middle-class inhibitions"—and Ireland, of course, was another country. But during the first week of rehearsal, Finney was taken to hospital with acute appendicitis and replaced by Peter O'Toole. Although O'Toole was Irish, "They didn't get on," according to Anthony Page, who was Lindsay's assistant on the production. And although O'Toole wasn't yet a

Directing Ian Bannen (foreground) and Freda Jackson in *Serjeant Musgrave's Dance*

star, "Lindsay thought him too much of a star performer." In return, O'Toole thought "Lindsay's idea of the working class was 'perfumed shit.' " But O'Toole was "brilliant," and the production transferred to the West End, launching Lindsay's career as a theatre director.

"The Court was like a home waiting for him," said Anthony Page. It would be another year before Free Cinema had any more effect on the British film industry than the March to Aldermaston on production of the atomic bomb; meanwhile, here was Free Theatre in action. And Lindsay realized the extent of that freedom when his next production was a critical and commercial failure. George Devine, who had asked him to direct John Arden's *Serjeant Musgrave's Dance,* showed how little he cared about negative reviews by promptly commissioning Arden's next play. "It's our duty to support writers we believe in," he said, "*especially* when critics and audiences don't."

Serjeant Musgrave's Dance was the first of Lindsay's stage productions that I saw, on a brief visit to London during October 1959. I remember a two-thirds-empty theatre, and the front lights going up on a scrim. Behind it, patches of snow on a vista of mean little houses, crouched under a great pithead, suggested winter and poverty in a late-nineteenth-century mining town. To the accompaniment of some spookily atmospheric music (by Dudley Moore), backlighting made the scrim disappear, and it was raised invisibly to create the effect of a movie dissolve to the scene that followed. The device was repeated to cover each change of scene, and the sets themselves were minimalism (long before the word became current) at its most imaginative. A sinister graveyard materialized out of a few slightly tilted headstones, an iron railing, and a tree with contorted branches; and the same austere yet vivid style contrived a prison cell out of a few iron bars lowered in front of a cube of bare stage surrounded by darkness.

It was the first time Lindsay had worked with Jocelyn Herbert, who would design many of his stage productions and films in the future. "On one level, Jocelyn simply followed Arden's instructions," Lindsay told me later that evening. "On another, she studied each scene and *visualized* its demands in the most original way." The playwright had asked for "sparing" scenery: no decorative touches, everything on the stage, from a door to a chair to the smallest prop, had to be *necessary.* The play itself was an antimilitarist parable, dark and ironic, with a poetically stylized use of language. (Musgrave: "The point being that here we've got a gun that doesn't shoot like: *Bang,* rattle-click-up-the-spout-what-we're-waiting-for-*bang!* But: bang-bang-bang-bang-bang-bang-bang-bang-bang—and there's not a man alive in the whole of this marketplace. Modern times. Progress.") When he first read the play, Lindsay found it "mysteriously impressive," which also sums up his production. But the critic of the *Sunday Times* spoke for the majority when he dismissed play and production as "a frightful ordeal," adding that "it is the duty of the theatre, not to make men better, but to render them harmlessly happy." Words that Lindsay memorized and enjoyed quoting, "as a reminder of everything I'm up against."

Three years before *Musgrave,* Brecht had brought his Berliner Ensemble production of *Mother Courage* to London. For many of the directors and writers working at the Court, it was an indelible experience. *Musgrave* reflected its impact on Arden and Lindsay in several ways: the use of songs to comment on the action, the satirical treatment of authority figures, the conventional structure of the "well-made play" replaced by a fluid, episodic narrative—in Brecht's words, "open" instead of "closed," a way of seeing beyond "the world as it is to the world as it's *becoming.*" Although Lindsay moved away from Brecht and toward a more naturalistic style when he began directing David Storey's plays, Brecht's "epic theatre" had a lasting impact on his films. *0 Lucky Man!* uses songs to comment ironically on the action, and like *If . . .* is loosely divided into "chapters" with headings, an adaptation of Brecht's use of placards that his actors held up to introduce a scene. But "A style means an attitude," and although, in Lindsay's view, *"alienation* is the Brechtian term usually applied to such a style, I have always thought this a very heavy word, and not a very accurate one. The real purpose of such devices is not to *alienate* the audience from the drama, but to *focus* their attention on what the scene is about."

And like Brecht's plays, most of Lindsay's other films (*The White Bus, Britannia Hospital,* the made-for-TV *The Old Crowd,* and *Glory! Glory!*) are neither "political" nor "psychological" in the accepted sense. Through a combination of formal devices and characters as stylized in their own way as Fellini's, they create the world according to Lindsay—and aim to provoke an audience into thinking about it. The stylization may be romantic (the young rebels of *If . . .*) or ruthless to the point of caricature (almost everyone in *The Old Crowd* and *Britannia*

Hospital), but as Lindsay used to tell his actors, with "an essential reality" as its point of departure.

Albert Finney made his first appearance at the Court in Lindsay's next production, which opened its 1960 season. *The Lily White Boys* was a deliberately Brechtian musical in the style of *The Threepenny Opera,* about a group of young working-class East Enders, including a criminal who became a policeman and a whore who became a star. (I never saw it, but at the Memorial Celebration Finney performed one of the songs, Kurt Weill with a cockney accent.) Although Lindsay took Finney to see the Berliner Ensemble in Paris, soon after rehearsals began the actor told George Devine that he was still "not sure what 'Brechtian' means." But according to Lindsay's diary, he learned "astonishingly fast, whether to sing, or to dance, or to play 'objectively' that whole ironic, detached side of the part. Without a talent as outstanding as his, this show would be impossible."

In fact it was well received, and a great personal success for Finney. He worked with Lindsay again in the Willis Hall–Keith Waterhouse *Billy Liar,* which made him a major star in the theatre; and by the end of 1960 *Saturday Night and Sunday Morning* had made him a movie star as well. But a new kind of movie star, as Lindsay wrote, whose style had its origins in "the Court style": "When we auditioned young actors and actresses, we usually had to ask them where they came from, and then to repeat their audition pieces, not in the 'acceptable' accents into which they had been drilled at drama school but in the natural accents of their youth. The results were almost always revelatory." The natural accent of Finney's youth was ideal, of course, for the working-class character he played in Karel Reisz's film; but a leading newspaper, praising it as a one-shot performance, assumed the actor would soon graduate to roles higher up the social scale. Unaware that the tide was running out, it announced a competition to find a new, less "plebeian" name for Albert Finney.

Billy Liar, Lindsay's first production away from the Court, opened in the West End and ran for over a year. When Finney left after six months, he was replaced by another northerner, Tom Courtenay, who also spoke in the natural accent of his youth. Meanwhile, Lindsay's attitude toward Finney had changed. On *The Lily White Boys,* according to his diary, the actor had been "a joy to work with, never a trace of egotism, marvelously sensitive with all his toughness and vitality." And soon after the play opened, Lindsay took a strikingly romantic photograph of Finney in his dressing room. But after *Billy Liar* had been running for a few weeks, his feelings changed: "It's extraordinary how violently I have reacted against him—though not really so, I suppose, in view of the strength of my feeling *for* him for so long. Not that there has been any overt friction between us, but somehow I became more and more conscious of the egoism under the charm."

Once again Lindsay had fallen in and out of love, his "fantasies of working for, living with Albert" gradually dissolving under the pressure of yet another "third party" situation. Living with Albert in reality was Zoe Caldwell, who had recently arrived from Australia and made her first appearance in the London theatre at the Court.

Their relationship was only one of several romantic involvements, triangles, marriages, and/or fatal meetings that occurred among actors and writers during those brilliant early years of the English Stage Company. *The Entertainer* brought Laurence Olivier and Joan Plowright together, a revival of Chekhov's *Platonov* did the same for Rachel Roberts and Rex Harrison. Jill Bennett married Willis Hall, and subsequently John Osborne—who had previously married Mary Ure, who subsequently married Robert Shaw. And after months of working together, George Devine and Jocelyn Herbert, already in love but married to others, decided to break existing ties and live openly together.

There was also professional intrigue behind the scenes, with Tony Richardson at the center of it. In 1958, more eager to direct films than plays, he set up a film company, Woodfall Productions, in partnership with John Osborne. As no British studio would back them, they acquired American finance with the help of a Byzantine operator called Harry Saltzman, reputedly connected to the Hollywood mafia and later the producer of the James Bond films. Tony's first feature, the film of *Look Back in Anger,* was conspicuously underrated by most London critics, and only a modest commercial success. His second, a much less effective adaptation of *The Entertainer,* was a commercial disaster. It led to disagreements with Saltzman, whom Tony managed to jockey out of the company. As a result, he became the sole producer of Woodfall's

The Lily White Boys. Albert Finney photographed by Lindsay
in his dressing room

first major commercial *and* critical success, *Saturday Night and Sunday Morning.*

By this time, as Lindsay's diary for January 1, 1961, suggests, Tony was beginning to find his way around the Byzantine world: "Karel [Reisz] drove me home [from a New Year's Eve party] and we talked about *L'Avventura*—about which I was unable to be as enthusiastic as he. Then he told me there has been unpleasantness about his percentage from *Saturday Night and Sunday Morning*—which has somehow been fiddled so that he would get nothing until the debts on *The Entertainer* had been paid. This is something that occupies and troubles Karel deeply, and has led to shouting matches with Tony." The same entry mentions but doesn't explain Lindsay's own experience with the friend he now referred to as "the abominable Richardson." When I asked Karel if he knew anything about this, he said:

Everything. Lindsay had read and been impressed by David Storey's novel, This Sporting Life. *He took it to Tony at Woodfall as a project for himself. Tony read the novel and said, "It's very good, of course, but not for you." This was because he decided to make a film of it himself. He made an offer for the rights, but was outbid by Julian Wintle and Leslie Parkyn. Their company had a distribution deal with the Rank Organization, and they were acting on behalf of Joe Losey. Then Wintle fell out with Losey and offered* This Sporting Life *to me. But it was Lindsay's project, and I didn't want to direct it anyway, as the material seemed too close in some ways to* Saturday Night. *So I offered to produce it with Lindsay directing, and Wintle agreed.*

The novel was "such a personal piece of work," Lindsay wrote later, "that Karel and I felt that no-one but its author could write the script." Although Lindsay and David Storey eventually became close friends and creative partners, each had misgivings about the other at first. To prepare a story outline, they went to the north of England, where the novel was set. After their return, Lindsay's diary included David among "the cautious, defensive, emotionally ungenerous northerners with whom I seem to have worked so much." (The others were Finney and Willis Hall.) In the past, of course, he had described the southern English in precisely these terms, and found northerners emotionally direct and outgoing. Whatever triggered the reversal, it was not a replay of the situation with Finney, or any extreme differences of opinion on the script; and David found Lindsay "very difficult and puzzling to deal with."

"We had three terrible rows," David remembered, "and I could never quite make out why they erupted." At times Lindsay struck him as "totally irrational." The third and most alarming row erupted in the lounge of their hotel, where they had been talking amicably (or so David thought) after dinner. But when David announced he was going to bed and started to leave, a "scream of rage" made him turn back. He saw other hotel guests staring in astonishment at Lindsay as he

Karel Reisz, with Albert Finney, directing *Saturday Night and Sunday Morning*

screamed again. "Then, white in the face, he shouted at me, 'Come back here, you cunt!' "

As his assistant at the Court, Anthony Page had a similar experience of the "totally irrational" Lindsay: "He was enormously helpful and encouraging, but one day we were walking along the street, something I said annoyed him, and he tried to push me under a bus—or, for a moment at least, it seemed he was going to." For Tony Richardson, moments like this were "the price of repression," and, as Anthony Page recalled,

> *all the gays at the Court were closeted, and*
> *put up different smoke screens, Lindsay by*
> *attacking camp. I'm talking of a time long*
> *before the time of coming out, of course, but*
> *unlike the rest of us, Lindsay could only have*
> *come out in theory. Once, when we were discussing*

his situation, Tony said: "I think we should push
him into a Turkish bath and leave him there."

David Storey soon realized that being under pressure triggered Lindsay's most violent outbursts. The pressure came in two forms, sexual frustration and creative anxiety, and from the start he suffered exceptional anxiety over *This Sporting Life.* He had never directed a feature film before and had chosen to work with a writer who had never written for the screen before; he was smarting over a professional rejection—by Michael Balcon, who had bought the movie rights to *The Long and the Short and the Tall,* and chosen an Ealing Studios workhorse to direct it; and he was not completely recovered from the "emotional problem" with Finney. "It might lead to my having to abandon directing actors," he noted in his diary, "for the strain it involves is too great to tolerate for ever."

All the same, for a while Lindsay visualized Finney as Arthur Machin in *This Sporting Life,* then decided it would involve too much "strain." Meanwhile, he noted in his diary (January 23, 1961) the kind of film he wanted to make:

> *A film about all of us and our lives right now—*
> *of Karel, and Albie {Finney} and Zoe {Caldwell}—*
> *and Jill {Bennett} and Willis {Hall}, and our*
> *aspirations and egoism and unhappiness. This*
> *was obviously the way* L'Avventura *affected Karel—*
> *a film d'auteur, a firsthand work, not a*
> *dramatic construction well directed by somebody—*
> *which is what* Sporting Life *will be unless I can*
> *get inside it and make it a personal allegory.*
> *But it is here that my intuitions and aspirations*
> *have been all too swift and all-at-sea.*

Although Sean Connery was eager to play Arthur Machin, Lindsay agreed with Karel and David that he wasn't right. He finally settled on Richard Harris, whom he had seen a few months previously in the theatre, playing J. P. Donleavy's *The Ginger Man.* But by this time Richard had gone to Hollywood for preliminary work on *Mutiny on the Bounty,* and as the script was not yet ready, Lindsay sent him a copy of David's novel. Richard's reply has apparently not survived, although a diary entry describes it as "a marvelous letter full of enthusiasm." But after sending him the completed script in February, Lindsay heard nothing for ten weeks. He decided to call Richard in Tahiti, where *Mutiny* had been shooting for six months, Lewis Milestone had replaced Carol Reed as director, and nine writers had reworked Eric Ambler's original script. Richard warned there was no end in sight, couldn't say when he might be available, but wanted to talk about the script, and suggested that Lindsay fly out to see him.

Before setting off, Lindsay joined another "Ban the Bomb" demonstration in Trafalgar Square, alongside Anthony Page and other Royal Court colleagues. Both Lindsay and Anthony were among those arrested for refusing to disperse, and spent a night in jail. As well as popular songs, Lindsay had a considerable repertory of hymns, and Anthony remembered his voice in the neighboring cell, ringing out in the small hours with "The Church's One Foundation" and "Abide with Me."

The long journey to Tahiti involved changing planes in New York and Los Angeles, and as Lindsay knew I'd recently bought a house in Santa Monica Canyon, he asked if he might come to stay for a couple of days. Hindsight tells me that the actor gave another fine performance, for when he arrived at the end of May, I found no sign of the "totally irrational" person David Storey had experienced earlier that year. Although Lindsay quickly decided that "Los Angeles could never be for me," he approved the view of the canyon and the Pacific from my living-room. "It's got absolutely *nothing* to remind you of England."

When we talked about *This Sporting Life,* his attitude was ironically detached. "I suspect that Richard Harris has reservations about the script. So do I, but I also have *no idea* what to do about it." "Am I *mad* to be traveling eight thousand miles to see him? Let alone to imagine I'm remotely capable of making this film?" "Why didn't I trust my first instinct, which is *always* to find a reason *not* to do anything I'm offered?" And finally, with a gleam of hope: "Of course, it may never happen."

A wade into the pool of memory reminds me that Lindsay hoped to see John Ford, but Ford was away on location for *Two Rode Together.* And it rescues a few other moments of his visit. Photographing Lindsay in my living room, seated in a wickerwork Hong Kong chair with a fan-tail back. Santa Monica beach on one of those cool, early summer evenings when the world seems to be holding its breath, the air very still and nobody else around. We stand facing the pale, empty Pacific, gaze at the blurred horizon, and after a long silence Lindsay remarks, "I wonder why I don't like it here." Next day I drive him to the airport, and in a replay of his wave as I left London for California, I wave as he boards the plane for Tahiti.

"It was lovely to see you again, in your habitat, instead of as a stranger in England," Lindsay wrote on September 2, soon after his return to London. Our mutual friend the actor-novelist Robert Shaw, he continued, likened the photograph in the Hong Kong chair to a portrait of "a Chinese Aristocrat Two Days before the Outbreak of the Boxer Rebellion." Earlier, while waiting to change planes at Los Angeles Airport on the return trip, he'd phoned to say that Richard Harris had made some very helpful suggestions about the script, and definitely committed to the project. But he said nothing more about this in the letter, only wondered "if you've encountered Richard at all since the *Bounty* returned to Hollywood. If so you'll know we have to postpone the film until next year, since it [the *Bounty*] seems to be going on for ever."

But to his diary Lindsay confided that he'd found Richard "all warmth and ardor—so attractively that I found I responded to him with a whole-heartedness that made me tremble." And as well as the all-too-familiar signs of falling in love, he recognized "the frustration it apparently is bound to involve. As I used to feel about Serge [Reggiani]; Richard has his work, and his wife and children. Is there room for anything else? I am beginning to think this is a mere fantasy: in fact I dare not hope otherwise, except under my breath so to speak."

This Sporting Life is a spare, bleakly powerful first-person novel, set in a bleak north of England city, and narrated in a series of memory flashbacks by a rugby footballer, after an accidental blow has temporarily stunned him and knocked out his front teeth during a game. Fiercely aggressive yet desperately needy, Arthur Machin is more sensitive and more anxious for love than he realizes. He rooms in the house of a widow a few years older than himself, and a mutual attaction develops. But Mrs. Hammond resists it. "Living had turned up so many bad cards for her that she was refusing any more deals. She was withdrawing and lying down. I hated her for it. For not seeing me; how I could help her."

For the first draft screenplay, David Storey and Lindsay had agreed to replace the flashbacks with a straightforward linear narrative. A major mistake, Richard Harris told Lindsay in Tahiti. The screenplay lacked the novel's intensity, he said, particularly in the central relationship between Machin and Mrs. Hammond. Lindsay passed on his comments to David, who wrote a second draft that preserved the novel's original structure, and also changed Machin's first name to Frank, as the character played by Albert Finney in *Saturday Night* was also called Arthur.

In David's case, part of *This Sporting Life* was directly autobiographical. At nineteen he had found himself living two lives, coal miner's son and professional rugby footballer in the north of England, scholarship student at the Slade School of Art in London. On his weekly journey by train from London to the north, he read and reread Wyndham Lewis's autobiography, *Rude Assignment,* and was instinctively drawn to "Lewis's view of the artist as a man isolated in an alien society." Mocked by his family and his teammates for wanting to become a painter, he decided that his only hope of survival was as "an armored protagonist." Then he started to make notes about his situation—and discovered himself as a writer. Two years later he completed his first novel, *This Sporting Life.* Four years and copious rejections later, it was published.

David's view of the "isolated" artist is, of course, very close to Lindsay's belief that "in the end the artist is on his own." And just as Lindsay had analyzed the two sides of his own nature ("Masculine/feminine, Hearty/artistic" etc.) in his diary, David created Machin to externalize what he saw as the conflict in himself between "a self-absorbed, intuitive kind of creature [and] a hard, physical, extroverted character." But by the time *This Sporting Life* was reincarnated as a film, he had married, fathered two children, and found it "terrible to have to go back, poke around in all that stuff. If the people making the film hadn't been such a curious combination of temperaments, I couldn't really have gotten through it."

One result of the combination of temperaments was that in Lindsay's case, part of *This Sporting Life* became indirectly autobiographical. Because of his infatuation with Richard Harris, as David remarked later, "in effect he *was* Mrs. Hammond in the film." One of Lindsay's diary notes (April 23, 1962), made during the shoot, bears this out:

> *From a certain point of view, this is a*
> *personality too big by far for me to cope with.*
> *Emotionally his warmth and wilfulness can*
> *sabotage me in a moment. And of course*
> *instinctively he knows this and exploits it.*
> *I ought to be calm and detached with him.*
> *Instead I am impulsive. We embrace and fight*
> *like lovers. His mixture of tenderness and*
> *sympathy with violence and even cruelty is*
> *astonishing.*

According to Lindsay's diary, the aggression was all on Richard's side: "The storms of his temperament have been fierce and shattering.

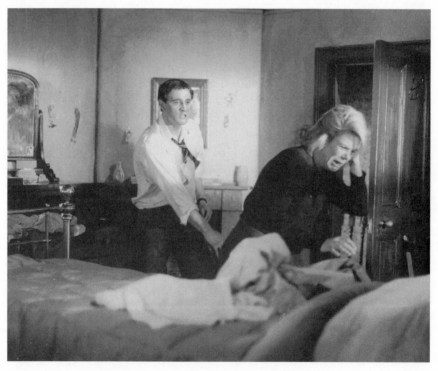

This Sporting Life. Richard Harris and Rachel Roberts

How can I be expected to resist? Whether he is embracing me physically, like some big warm dog, or ordering me to 'heel'—I am at his service completely." According to David, there was aggression on both sides, Lindsay sometimes yelling an insult at Richard for no apparent reason, and apologizing later. Another example, it seems, of his identification with Mrs. Hammond, about whom Machin comments in the novel, "I felt that, in spite of herself, she was always trying to hurt me. Her face seemed to tell me she didn't want to do it, but something prompted her inside, and out these jibes came."

Not surprisingly, the first two weeks of shooting skirted disaster. Karel Reisz: "The situation with Richard, and Lindsay's technical inexperience, created many problems. The camera crew was hostile, particularly the very conservative, old-school operator. Julian Wintle disliked the early rushes and wanted me to take over. I refused, of course." David Storey: "Things didn't go well at first, and being under pressure seemed to trigger paranoia in Lindsay. But he focused it, strangely enough, on Karel—who was doing everything to protect him."

The most equable member of the "curious combination," Karel had arrived in England as an eleven-year-old Czech-Jewish refugee in the late 1930s. He was young enough to learn to speak English with no trace of an accent, and to adopt English manners as if born to them. By the time Lindsay and I met him in 1949, Karel was married and the father of two children; and as David noted, "Lindsay was always enamored of the situation of highly talented men with families. It made him even lonelier, and if he was in love with the person, it fed his appetite for the loved one." But if the married man with children was someone he liked and respected (Karel, or David himself), envy could create ambivalence.

In one of his diary notes on *This Sporting Life,* Lindsay admired Karel's "perfect balance and judgment," then complained in the next sentence of his "reserve and detachment." A few years later he wrote me a letter with a typically barbed aside: "How blessed, I always reflect when I visit him [Karel], it must be to be so happily and intelligently conformist. I'm afraid I shall never learn the trick." In the same letter he expressed hurt that Karel hadn't invited him to a screening of any of his movies since *Isadora.* Had Lindsay forgotten his own behavior at that screening? David Storey, who was present, remembered it very clearly: "When the lights went up he made no comment, but began humming 'Isn't It Romantic' right in front of Karel."

Last to join the "curious combination" was Rachel Roberts, who had won the British Film Academy's Best Actress Award a year earlier for her performance in *Saturday Night and Sunday Morning*. When Lindsay offered her the part of Mrs. Hammond (after Mary Ure turned it down), Rachel and Rex Harrison had been lovers for two years. They were living together in Rome, where Rex was playing Julius Caesar in the Elizabeth Taylor–Richard Burton *Cleopatra*. A star nearing the apex of his stardom, Rex advised Rachel to turn down what he considered a "character" part, but in those days Rachel saw herself as a character actress, not a star. She accepted, and arrived on the set during the third week of shooting, for what Lindsay's diary describes as "the first terrible day of rehearsals [with both Richard and Rachel], which I suppose was Richard's last fling of resistance against playing the part without the protection of his mannerisms."

"But Rachel had a great, bawdy sense of humor as well as a good heart," Karel remembered:

> *She was wonderful about it, and simply laughed*
> *at "the boys doing their stuff." Another time,*
> *another tremendous row went on very long, and*
> *everyone seemed to forget about her. Finally*
> *she said, "When you boys have finished, I'll*
> *be in my dressing room." But by the time Lindsay*
> *and Richard had finished, Rachel was gone. Next*
> *day she told me, "I went to the lavatory, pulled*
> *down my knickers, had a good shit and waited*
> *around until my arse got cold. Then I told*
> *myself, 'No one's going to treat the future Mrs.*
> *Rex Harrison like this,' and went home."*

Halfway through shooting, Rachel had a few days off, flew to Italy, and became the latest (fourth) Mrs. Harrison. By this time Lindsay's "lost, sticky, all-at-sea feeling" had given way to muted confidence: "People now say that the work is good. And I *think* (how can I know?) that Richard's performance is marvelous. Certainly he is acting with a strength and a simplicity that I have never seen from him before." In fact, there was an uncannily close encounter between actor and role. Lindsay could have been making notes on Machin's character when he wrote in his diary about Richard's "mixture of pride and insecurity, insinuating charm and aggressive domination." And as he had never felt "so fatally and thrillingly attracted" by anyone else, he found it a constant struggle to "serve Richard as I really should, conniving at his self-indulgence when I should be calmly, coolly resisting it. Like Karel."

In spite of "the actual moments of hysteria," he succeeded. Partly because, although Lindsay invariably claimed to have no idea what his "methods" were, he had already developed a trial-and-error approach with actors in the theatre. As David described it, Lindsay preferred to "let actors have their heads at first." If the result struck him as "real," he accepted it; if not, he explained what he felt was false, and why.

This instinct for "essential reality," as Lindsay often called it, helped Richard create a dynamic and extraordinarily varied performance, obsessive and ruthless in the football scenes, disturbing in the outbursts of violence he can't control, touching in the moments of loneliness he can't conceal. But the personal relationship was equally

Lonely life: Richard Harris in *This Sporting Life*

responsible. A director in love with his leading actress or actor connects with the beloved on a deep subconscious level, and the visual intimacy of movies always reveals it. Consummation (Pabst with Louise Brooks, von Sternberg with Dietrich, Wyler with Bette Davis) and sublimation (Marcel Carné with Jean Gabin, Hitchcock with Ingrid Bergman, Visconti with Alain Delon) have the same result. The shades of emotion that a director guides his actor to play, from fascination to confrontation, longing to despair, tenderness to cruelty, become extensions of his own, the camera mirrors everything in the beloved that attracts and obsesses him, and in movies for other directors, the actor never reaches quite the same intensity.

But Lindsay's instinct, and his personal situation, served Rachel Roberts less well. A fine actress, she was directed to appear uniformly dour and hostile, without the tellingly vulnerable moments in the novel when "she let herself go a bit," or "she'd almost given in, and she regretted it." Lindsay seems to have underlined Mrs. Hammond's repression so heavily because he identified with it so closely. Kneeling by the fireplace and grimly polishing her dead husband's boots, she might be a not-too-distant relative of the Addams family. And couldn't she have been allowed to lighten up, just a little, just for a moment, after making love?

The miscalculation here undercuts the power of the movie as a whole. Karel Reisz diagnosed the problem as *"reaching* for style," and the style the filmmaker reached for is one that the novelist never attempted. "We tried to make a tragedy," Lindsay told a journalist before the film opened. But by trying too hard, he imposed more weight on the material than it could bear. The novel's compact, precise, "armored" sentences are especially revealing for what they don't reveal. Like the protagonist of a Hemingway short story, or of Camus's *The Stranger,* Machin is only occasionally explicit about his deeper feelings; and by hardening himself up, withdrawing into matter-of-factness or irony at key moments, he suggests how deep they really are. "The dignity of movement of an iceberg," Hemingway wrote, "is due to only one eighth of it being above water." Because of Lindsay's emotional turmoil, the scenes between Machin and Mrs. Hammond are seven eighths above water. Although they have powerfully disturbing moments, the same note of frustration is struck too often, and monotony sets in.

And the same need for less instead of more is felt at the end of the film. As Mrs. Hammond lies dead of a brain hemorrhage in the hospital room, Machin cries, "No! No!" and drives his fist into a (symbolic?) spider on the wall. Then he walks back to her dark, empty house. He prowls around the shadowy rooms, swings from the rafters, and finally collapses to the floor. When Karel saw Lindsay's cut of this sequence, he thought it too long. Lindsay disagreed. "The audience has to be told," he said. But it doesn't have to be lectured.

Apart from Richard's performance, the best of *This Sporting Life* is in its scenes on the rugby field, at the team owner's ghastly Christmas party with its crowd of sycophantic guests, and at an amateur talent night in the local nightclub. The action takes place in a town called Wakedale, and Lindsay filmed the exteriors in Wakefield, where he had made *Wakefield Express* ten years earlier. The footballers play under the same gray, overcast sky as the local amateur team in the documentary; but these are professionals, and their game is feral. The sharp-eyed team owners in their sleek topcoats watch its progress like zoo keepers checking the behavior of caged wild animals, the shabby crowd with alert pinched faces gets a vicarious thrill when play escalates into violence. And in the movie's final flashback, there's an extraordinary moment during a game played under heavy drizzle. As Machin straightens up after a scrum, his clothes dripping black mud and his face smeared with it, he's transformed into a huge, bewildered, apelike apparition.

The nightclub scene opens on a relentlessly cheerful entertainer (blond beehive hairdo, cleavage, black panties) from the world of *O Dreamland.* While she belts out "Walking My Way Back to Happiness," Machin sits with his pals and their girls. Silent and withdrawn, he seems overcome by a sense of isolation, which he can only break out of by aggressively pounding the table and calling for more drinks. Then an MC announces amateur talent night and Machin's pals persuade him to sing. He walks to the spotlit platform and folds his arms in an awkward, defensive gesture. Finally, in a flat, deliberate voice, he sings a refrain of "Here Is My Heart—I'm Alone and So Lonely." Too self-conscious to acknowledge the rowdy applause, he turns quickly, unsmilingly away as the sense of isolation overcomes him again. Masterfully directed and acted, this scene of inarticulate submerged feelings and ironic social observation was invented for the movie; yet it's closer in tone to the novel than many of the scenes adapted more or less directly from it. It also serves as a trailer for Lindsay's later films, with their mixture of private pain and ironic comedy, reflective sympathy and sudden rage.

"It is almost as if his [Richard's] personality has grown with Frank Machin," Lindsay noted after *This Sporting Life* finished shooting. "The admiration and enjoyment of his body, the relish of power, the sudden humorous yet very vital expressions of savagery—as he turns to me with clenched teeth and clenched fist and threateningly jerks out, 'Stop smiling!' 'I'll smile if I wish to.' 'You'll smile when I tell you.' And what is the precise significance of the blows which, towards the end of the picture, landed more and more frequently, and more and more heavily on my arms?"

Lindsay answered his own question by deciding (not surprisingly) "that there is a strange sadomasochistic element in our relationship." On Richard's side, he felt, it was "the obverse of the kindly, generous, sensitive self that is also there." And on his own? " 'Discovery' of masturbation [at the age of forty] has not helped. State of extreme vacillation—absolute inability to think concretely of any project except in terms of Richard Harris."

Among the projects that Lindsay and Richard discussed were a film of *Wuthering Heights* and a season of three plays at the Royal Court, an adaptation of Gogol's *Diary of a Madman, Julius Caesar,* and *Hamlet.* The first of these opened in March 1963, after a rehearsal period that "varied between friendship and creativity on the one hand, and resentment, fear, compulsive talking and nervous bullying on the other." Was there also another close encounter between actor and role? Gogol's Poprishkin is a civil servant whose descent into madness begins with anxiety attacks over his job, and ends with the megalomaniac delusion that he's the king of Spain. "One night," Lindsay's diary records, "I was alone on the stage with Richard, and his booted foot stepped on mine, and his hand grasped me around the throat. A hallucinating moment." Inevitably, perhaps, the reviewers were unanimous in finding the production hysterically melodramatic, and Karel Reisz remembered it as "a disaster."

A month later Lindsay and Richard went to the Cannes Film Festival for the premiere of *This Sporting Life.* It won Richard the prize for best actor as well as the leading role opposite Monica Vitti in Antonioni's *The Red Desert*. As shooting was due to start that summer, the rest of the Court season had to be postponed, but Lindsay still felt unable to focus on any project that didn't involve Richard. He discussed *Wuthering Heights* with David Storey, who began work on a screenplay, but also took a step that he'd often contemplated, and began seeing a psychiatrist. Intrigued at first, doubtful later, he finally called the whole thing off:

> *What amounts from our talks? The probability that*
> *I had suffered traumatically from some early*
> *prohibition against masturbation: that I "couldn't*
> really *be homosexual": that an early emotional*
> *deprivation, which he located in the departure of*
> *Nanny Bullen {nurse employed for Lindsay and his*
> *brother Murray until they left India}, had cut*
> *off my capacity for emotional commitment and*
> *expression. There was something interesting in*
> *his pointing out my inability (or reluctance) to*
> *talk absolutely personally, that I tended simply*
> *to "give the facts." But it seems I need something*
> *different from a psychiatrist, something more*
> *fatherly, more able to pull me along or at*
> *least prod me where I need it.*

Even as late as the 1960s, the majority of psychiatrists agreed with the British Medical Association that homosexuality was a disease in need of a cure. So perhaps Lindsay's psychiatrist couldn't be expected to understand that the disease in need of a cure was intolerance. The law classified homosexuals as criminals, the church condemned them as sinners, politicians accused them of contributing to the decline of the British Empire, and the majority of parents agreed with the medical establishment and the church, if not the politicians; but instead of exploring these multiple pressures, the psychiatrist assured Lindsay that he "couldn't *really* be homosexual." And in other ways he seems to have been just as heartbreakingly obtuse.

The real source of Lindsay's "emotional deprivation" was surely not Nanny Bullen, but the oppressively conventional and selfish mother who refused to understand his needs. (Absent father and remote stepfather are just as surely behind Lindsay's need for "something more fatherly" than a psychiatrist.) Apparently blinded by a Nanny Bullen fixation, the psychiatrist not only decided that the loss of her had deadened Lindsay's "capacity for emotional commitment," but failed to realize he was dealing with a person of intense emotional commitments—and emotional conflicts. Many years earlier Lindsay had noted in his diary, "It seems then that I am homosexual. Oh God," and "I'm a split personality in a way—the wrong mind in the wrong body." Did he fail to talk "absolutely personally" about this, or did the psychiatrist try to reassure him that he "couldn't *really*," etc.? Either way, no problems were resolved.

When Lindsay sent David's first draft of *Wuthering Heights* to United Artists, their first reaction was noncommittal. In spite of favorable notices in both Britain and the United States, *This Sporting Life* had proved a commercial disappointment. But a few months later Richard Harris and Rachel Roberts were nominated for Academy Awards, and by quickly following the *The Red Desert* with two American-financed movies, *Major Dundee* and *The Heroes of Telemark,* Richard became a "bankable" international star. In March 1964, when Lindsay heard from Arthur Krim and Robert Benjamin of United Artists that the company might be interested in *Wuthering Heights* after all, he suspended his visits to the psychiatrist, flew to New York, and made a handshake deal. Then he flew to Mexico, where Richard and his wife, Elizabeth, were on vacation—and where "the game of master and servant" was resumed on the day of his arrival. On his bed in the guest room of their rented house in Cuernavaca, he found a note from Richard: "I am Heathcliff."

Over the next two weeks they did "a bit of work" on the *Wuthering Heights* script and discussed Richard's role of Mark Antony in *Julius Caesar,* now scheduled to open at the Court in November with Lindsay directing. Then Richard left for California to play Cain in John Huston's *The Bible.* The day after returning to London, Lindsay had his hair cut and stared at his reflection in the barber's mirror: "Marks of emotional fatigue clearly showing under the eyes. No wonder . . ." But now there was a concrete project with Richard to concentrate on, he soon felt "fuelled by emotion" again, and decided not to see his psychiatrist anymore.

In September, when Lindsay started to audition actors for *Julius Caesar,* the English Stage Company was nearing the end of the seminal period that began with *Look Back in Anger.* Osborne's latest play, *Inadmissible Evidence,* directed by Anthony Page, with Nicol Williamson, had just opened, and other premieres over the past eight years had included Beckett's *Happy Days,* directed by George Devine; four Ionesco plays, *The Chairs* and *The Lesson,* directed by Tony Richardson, with Joan Plowright and Devine, *Rhinoceros,* directed by Orson Welles, with Laurence Olivier, and *Exit the King,* directed by Devine, with Alec Guinness; Tennessee Williams's *Orpheus Descending,* directed by Tony Richardson, with Isa Miranda; Albee's *The American Dream* and *The Death of Bessie Smith,* directed by Peter Yates; Pinter's *The Room* and *The Dumb Waiter,* directed respectively by Anthony Page and James Roose Evans; and new plays by other young British playwrights, Shelagh Delaney and Arnold Wesker. Tony Richardson also contributed two notable revivals, the Jacobean melodrama *The Changeling,* with Robert Shaw, Mary Ure, and Zoe Caldwell, and *The Seagull,* with Peggy Ashcroft, Peter Finch, and Devine.

But success for *Julius Caesar* was not in the stars, or the star. Two weeks into rehearsal, when Richard still hadn't signed his contract because a few changes demanded by his agent were still under discussion, he was offered a leading role in the movie of James Michener's *Hawaii.* He decided to accept it, withdrew from the play, and was replaced by Nicol Williamson. "Lindsay was already very anguished by the personal situation," Anthony Page recalled. "He had even asked me to drive him past Richard's house one night to see if the lights were on and he was home. And Richard's departure was a really shattering blow—to *Julius Caesar* as well as Lindsay. His heart literally went out of the production and he lost his usual drive."

And for Richard, as Lindsay came to realize, the game was over. The only diary entry about *Julius Caesar* (dated January 1, 1965, a month after the production closed) recalls that Richard's interest in *Wuthering Heights* had cooled since the meeting in Mexico; and Lindsay now believed that "Getting out of Mark Antony" was the real intention behind Richard's contractual disputes with the Court. David Storey had the same impression: "Richard didn't really want to work with

Lindsay again. And it was probably a good thing that *Wuthering Heights* was never made. Could any producer have coped with the two of them?"

Later that month, with no project to detain him in the wake of Richard's departure, Lindsay accepted an invitation to serve on the jury of the Delhi Film Festival and was delighted to meet Satyajit Ray for the first time since the *Sequence* party of 1949. But privately he was "not too impressed" by Ray's festival entry, *Mahanagar* (*The Big City*). Also on the jury was Polish director Andrzej Wajda. Although Lindsay had admired *A Generation* and *Ashes and Diamonds,* he found Wajda disappointing in person, "pleasant but ungiving." In both cases, I suspect, discontent with his own life once again spilled over to other people and their work. I remember telling Lindsay many years later how much I liked *Mahanagar,* and how enthusiastically he agreed it was one of Ray's best films. By that time he'd also become good friends with Wajda, who was a great admirer of Lindsay's work, especially *Britannia Hospital.*

A festival juror always has to sit through an oppressive number of mediocre movies, often at ten a.m., and no doubt this contributed to Lindsay's mood. So did a visit to "huge, sprawling, dirty" Calcutta, where he felt "overcome by ever-present Indian squalor and that strange remoteness behind the effusiveness, the platitudes of respect and affection whose truth one cannot gauge." Finally, his hope of interviewing Mrs. Gandhi was thwarted by the presence of two other guests at dinner, "[Benjamin] Britten and [Peter] Pears on vacation. The unmistakable, musty, old maidish aroma of English good taste—God, how dreary a country it is!" But in spite of Mrs. Gandhi's "nervous preoccupation with the servants dishing out curry," Lindsay had a few good words for her: "Unpretentious and direct, although not really with it."

In February 1965, still without a project, he accepted an invitation to serve on the jury of the Karlovy Vary Festival, then spent a few days in Prague, where Miloš Forman had recently finished shooting his second film, *Loves of a Blonde.* "Full of superb and delicate poetic things," Lindsay noted after a screening at the studio, and also admired the cinematography of Miroslav Ondriček, with whom he began a professional collaboration the following year on *The White Bus.* And ten years later, over dinner with Forman in New York, Lindsay recalled how open and eager Czech technicians seemed in contrast to his English unit on *This*

Sporting Life, and was touched by Forman's reply: "Well, in those days many people from the West came to look at us and talk, but you were the only one who behaved like a human being."

But although he responded to "the vitality of the young Czech cinema," and "the young, ardent, humorous film-makers" he met, the attitude of strangers reminded Lindsay of Kafka's novels: "In the hotel, the maids, the waiters and receptionists *don't look at one*—unless you actually accost them. This can't be just imagination, can it?" No, a journalist assured him. It reflected "the malady of perverted socialism." The country's secretive and impenetrable bureaucracy, he explained, was also Kafkaesque, and so was the attitude it created: "Nobody wants to take responsibility for anything. It's safer to be anonymous."

The same journalist also told Lindsay that the Czech film industry was running into censorship difficulties "with the top men of the Party." Devious enough not to ban a politically incorrect film outright, they had developed a technique of "suppression by delay" in granting a distribution license. Impatient for freedom, Forman would soon leave for Britain, then the United States; but Lindsay, ironically, was stimulated by the gritty constraint of life in Prague—and in Warsaw, when he first visited Poland a few months later. In the authoritarian states of Eastern Europe, he wrote me, the best directors (he mentioned Forman, Wajda, Skolimowski) "somehow manage to make films that recognize only one authority—of passion."

Back in England at the end of April: "It is the morning; the awakening hour that is most dangerous, the idle thoughts that so easily stray to masochistic dreams. Best to get up, but laziness to conquer in the limbs, and inertia in the mind." But a family crisis soon energized limbs and mind. Lindsay's brother Murray had been an RAF pilot during World War II and won the Distinguished Flying Cross. In peacetime, like many other fliers, he found he had no sense of direction on the ground. He went to India, became a civil pilot, and eventually married a young Indian, Mary Tapper. In the summer of 1964 he returned to England with his wife and their two children, Sandy and Jennifer; and the entire family had been staying at Lindsay's flat ever since.

This was the same first-floor flat of the late Victorian Gothic house at 57 Greencroft Gardens that Lindsay and I had shared until I left England: two large studio rooms, kitchen, bathroom. But although four of Lindsay's dependents occupied my former room, overcrowding wasn't the only problem. Murray grew increasingly discontented with his job as instructor at a driving school, and the marriage showed increasing signs of strain. He finally decided to take wife and children back to India, and Lindsay was expecting them to leave a week after his return from Czechoslovakia. But at the last moment Mary became hysterical. She refused to accompany her husband or let him take the children, and Murray went back to India alone, leaving his family without any means of support—except from Lindsay.

"I realize that all this stems from problems not just between you and Mary—but within *yourself*," Lindsay wrote Murray shortly after he left. "And basically I suppose we both of us (with roots no doubt in the disaster of our parents' marriage) find it difficult to accept responsibility." So did Mum: "She just relapses into 'what's going to happen?' " What happened, inevitably, was that Lindsay took charge. "Acting on sense of duty," he noted in his diary, "and hoping that being forced to take on this partial responsibility for the children will be good for me, however much I'd prefer not."

In fact the responsibility was almost total. The children continued to live with their mother at Lindsay's flat, with Lindsay paying the fees for Sandy's day school, and very soon there was another problem besides overcrowding. Mary developed symptoms of manic depression, with a "violent and unexplained change" in her attitude toward Lindsay. Sometimes she refused to speak to him, sometimes she accused him of "incomprehensible misdeeds," of hitting Sandy, "making her his slave," even "indecently assaulting" four-year-old Jennifer. And sometimes "she became so uncontrollable that I had to eject her from my room, whereupon there ensued a screaming and a battering on the door."

Lindsay endured this situation for almost two years, occasionally pleading with Murray to resolve it "instead of just running away from it," while admitting in his diary that in his own life he was as guilty of "vacillation" as his brother: "Undoubtedly there is something blocked in us both." When Murray finally returned to England, he divorced his wife (who went back to India alone), gained custody of their children, and found a job as a civil pilot. In the meantime, partly to escape the "extremely unpleasant atmosphere in the flat," and partly to fill the void created by Richard's absence from his life, Lindsay made four more trips in 1965, to Paris, Madrid, New York, and Warsaw.

About the Paris trip in early May, his diary records only a meeting with Serge Reggiani, who looked "tired under the eyes." At the end of May, a producer at Elstree Studios discovered Thorold Dickinson's adaptation of *The Mayor of Casterbridge* while looking for properties on the shelf. He thought it had "possibilities," and as Thorold had retired from filmmaking, approached Lindsay to direct. Robert Shaw, a star since *From Russia with Love* and currently making a film in Spain, had expressed interest in the project. But when Lindsay went to see him in Madrid, he felt "a lack of rapport," particularly after Shaw's "violent and contemptuous attack on Buñuel's *Viridiana,*" and *The Mayor* died again.

New York in June was to meet with the producer of a play by Athol Fugard. After Bette Davis turned down the leading role, "everything depends on Maureen Stapleton. She arrives scruffy, engaging, in huge pink tent of a dress." Although Lindsay and Stapleton liked each other, she finally decided "she doesn't want to do it," and he felt more relief than disappointment. Fugard's play had appealed to him far less than the chance to get out of England again. Far more appealing was Steve Cochran in *The Big Shot,* which he saw on TV: "Vastly handsome and attractive." Two months later he was saddened to learn of Cochran's death: "Wish I'd met him. Perhaps . . ."

Warsaw in August was at the invitation of Wajda, not so "ungiving" after all. At first Lindsay found the city totally depressing: "At night everything is underlit. In the streets, and many public places, that cold, white strip-lighting serves chiefly to emphasize the darkness round about. Interiors (shops, hotel lobbies, cloakrooms) are made chilly and dingy by this heartless light." And the newsstand in the Grand Hotel sold only Polish and Soviet newspapers. "Warsaw people have a sense of humor, but it's a bitter one," Wajda informed him (in French, the language that Lindsay and most Poles he met had in common). "That's why they don't look happy. Also they are very inhibited. That's why they get drunk so much." Also, according to Lindsay's diary, "As in Prague, Kafkaesque situations are not hard to find. For days everyone has been talking about the Congress of Polish Culture— to celebrate 1000 years of it. Delegates will be arriving from all over the world. Special stamps will be issued. But I have not been able to find a single person who can tell me what the Congress will consist of, what will happen." Refusing to give up, he watched the opening-night ceremony on TV. An audience composed mainly of men in dark suits got to its feet for the national anthem. Halfway through it, Polish TV broke down, and *"we will never know what happened at the Congress."*

Next day he met and was strongly attracted to Tadeusz Lomnicki, the star of Wajda's *A Generation.* Although not as obsessive as the situation with Reggiani and Richard Harris, its basic components were similar. With a girlfriend in the picture, Lindsay found himself once more "making a third," as well as being cast in the role of confidant and listening to her stories of Tadeusz's "monstrous and cruel behavior." Tadeusz shared Wajda's admiration for *This Sporting Life,* and when he suggested to Lindsay that they work together in the theatre, Lindsay proposed *Hamlet.* The play had first acquired romantic associations when he watched Reggiani rehearse it; later, he'd hoped to direct it with Richard Harris. Tadeusz agreed, although film and theatre commitments would keep him busy until May 1966, and Lindsay returned to London feeling "suddenly creative. As David [Storey], with his extraordinary perception, has pointed out—I really do exist, or at least only *act,* by relationship with others."

September in England: "My I Ching has disappeared. I wonder if Mary has pinched it. She just looks glum when I ask her about it." Perhaps Lindsay wanted to consult it about an offer from Tony Richardson, whose duplicity over *This Sporting Life* had been not exactly forgiven or forgotten, but shrugged off. Like almost everyone else, Lindsay realized that Tony's "continual exercise of power" had on the whole done him a power of good. With his flair for "casting" other people's talent, he'd already opened the door to Lindsay's career in the theatre, and was about to open another door for Lindsay the film director.

Triumphantly solvent after *Tom Jones,* Woodfall had several current projects, among them a film of three short stories by Shelagh Delaney, whose *A Taste of Honey* Tony had successfully directed as play and film. He planned to assign a different director to each story, which would run about forty minutes, and told Lindsay *The White Bus* would be "right" for him.

When he read it, Lindsay agreed. Equally important, as he wrote later, was the fact that Woodfall offered him "complete freedom. I have only been any good—if I *have* been any good—when making films entirely freely and in my own way." According to Stephen Frears, who was assistant director on *If . . .* and produced *The Old Crowd,* "Lindsay never felt comfortable with the machinery of filmmaking. Concentrating on the moment took all his energy. He couldn't think ahead to problems of schedule and budget, and needed someone to help him with this. But this incapacity also helped to make his films individual. They were never compromised or diluted by commercial pressures."

On *The White Bus,* Lindsay was also gifted with material that freed him inwardly. Years earlier, writing about Hitchcock's British movies, he found that "their overall realism makes it all the more thrilling when the unexpected occurs. Pretty maids lie to the police without blinking an eyelid, harmless old bird-fanciers are revealed as sabotage agents, old ladies who are playing the harmonium one minute are whipping little revolvers from their handbags the next." Did Delaney's story trigger a memory of this? In working with her on the script, and in a few scenes he added after shooting began, Lindsay certainly took the idea of "the unexpected" a stage further. *The White Bus* is the first of his films to move freely between the real and the surreal world.

6

"Your first Hollywood set," Nick Ray said on my first evening in Los Angeles in March 1956, as we entered a spacious windowless dining room with paneled walls, scarlet leather banquettes, and waiters in formal black and white. One of them walked past us with a silver tray balanced on one hand, like the executioner in *Salome,* but instead of John the Baptist's head the tray bore a pyramid of ice studded with giant shrimp. "House specialty," Nick said. Movie stars were another house specialty at Chasen's, but I didn't see any.

At dinner Nick immediately began talking about *Bigger Than Life,* the final title of *Ten Feet Tall.* James Mason, producer as well as star of the movie, had approved the revised script, but Nick was still dissatisfied with it. He found the relationship between the schoolteacher and his wife very shallow, the medical details presented "with shots of test tubes and microscopes straight out of *The Story of Louis Pasteur,* " and the ending anticlimactic. "You'll see what I mean," he said, "when you read it tonight."

But first we drove to Judy Holliday's house in Beverly Hills. As she led us to the all-white living room, Lotte Lenya singing "Oh show me the way to the next whisky bar" from *Mahagonny* played on the hi-fi. The house felt strangely uninhabited, we seemed to be sitting in a showroom window, and the brilliant comedian was melancholy. She'd just heard over the radio that the U.S.A. was about to test a new type of hydrogen bomb in the Pacific. I don't remember what else they talked about, only that the news disturbed Nick as well. Finally, some time after one o'clock in the morning, they both ran out of angst. I wasn't surprised when Nick told me, as we drove off, that one night during his brief affair with Judy they got very drunk, felt intensely suicidal and walked into the ocean at Santa Monica beach—"so cold that it sobered us up."

By then I had been in California for around ten hours, after spending a night in New York and catching a plane next morning for the eight-hour flight to Los Angeles. Nick had hired a driver to meet me at the airport. His limousine brought me to Bungalow 2 at the Chateau Marmont (living room, dining room, three bedrooms, two baths, poolside patio), carried my luggage into one of the bedrooms, gave me a door key, and said he'd be back to drive me to Chasen's for dinner with Mr. Ray, who was "in meetings" until around eight o'clock.

After we got back to the Marmont that night, Nick put his arms around me. "I'm really glad you're here," he said, then moved away, picked up a copy of *Bigger Than Life,* handed it to me, said he needed to get some sleep, went upstairs to his bedroom, and closed the door. Nick's way of telling me, I supposed, that what had happened once in London might or might not happen again, and it was up to him to decide.

I was not too tired to feel disappointed and confused, but remembered Lindsay's advice and over the next two months was mainly concerned to prove myself to Nick. Before shooting started, James Mason agreed that the domestic scenes could be improved, and I worked with Nick to inject some tension into them. We also paid two late-night visits to Nick's friend Clifford Odets. During the first of them, Odets produced no specific ideas on the script, only a long, mournful aria on "the loss of belief as we all grow older," "the shrinkage of idealism," and "the death of hope." Although it was supposedly a lament for American life in general, to me it sounded more like Odets's song of himself. But on our second visit, when he had taken a sleeping pill and forced himself awake at Nick's insistence, he came up with a brilliant idea for the ending, as the teacher starts to recover from his crack-up.

On the set of *Bigger Than Life* every working day for six weeks, I ran lines with the actors before each scene, told Nick (who watched more closely than he listened) if they changed or omitted something vital during a shot, and supplied a new line or made a cut in an existing scene when he asked me to. It was a crash course in the art and politics of Hollywood moviemaking. Forbidden to make a point verbally, Nick had an extraordinary flair for making it visually. He wanted to add some dialogue about the medical profession's carelessness in prescribing new "wonder drugs" whose side effects had not been thoroughly monitored, but under pressure from the American Medical Association, the studio vetoed the idea. So he cast some tough-looking actors to play the doctors, and shot them nearly always on the move, in dark-suited, gangsterish cabals of two and three. "How I shoot depends on what I want to get away with—to fool the censor, the front office, whoever— or how confident I feel about the scene as written," Nick told me. When he had doubts about a scene, he played it first of all in a master shot, which enabled him to pinpoint its weak moments. Then he conferred with the actors, who sometimes invented a telling piece of business, or asked me to "come up with something" to make a point, or came up with it himself.

Invention on the spur of the moment didn't come easily to me at first. "Think before you speak is criticism's motto," E. M. Forster wrote. "Speak before you think is creation's." Although I had written a few short stories and made *Another Sky,* eight years spent mainly as a film critic had determined my mind-set. Resetting it was only one of the ways that Nick Ray changed my life.

One weekend in Bungalow 2, he woke me around two in the morning, led me without a word to his bedroom, and made love. Almost immediately afterward he fell asleep. Before going back to my room, I tried to identify the mysterious fragrance of Nick's bed linen. I traced it partly to the perfume he sometimes used, and which I could sniff on his body asleep at my side. But there was also something sickly-chemical in the air. Innocent about drugs in those days, I knew Nick took sleeping pills and wondered if they left an aroma. In his bathroom that night I discovered a medicine cabinet crammed with prescriptions, and realized how much he depended on the doctors he criminalized in *Bigger Than Life.*

At breakfast a few days later, I took a sip of Nick's orange juice by mistake and tasted more vodka than orange; and after two or three weeks on the set of *Bigger Than Life* I realized he was an alcoholic. Not the falling-down drunk kind, but some days his usually acute responses were blurred; and once, when he said he needed a vitamin B12 shot, I made an appointment for him with the studio doctor. It seemed to energize him very quickly, and one of the actors told me that the studio doctor was famous for his medical "cocktails," mixing a dash of amphetamine with the B12.

When Nick wasn't on his best form, James Mason reacted with the puzzled, uncertain look that often crossed his face, so different from the strength and occasional menace he conveyed on the screen. But one day he invited me to lunch in the studio commissary, said that he found Nick "a mystery," and wondered why he always seemed "more communicative" with me than with anyone else. "In fact, something about the situation strikes me as very *queer*," he said, looking me straight in the eye. He wasn't hostile, just on a fishing trip. I don't remember my reply, only that it was noncommittal and James looked puzzled again.

In the movie business of the 1950s, of course, queerness was a strictly closeted set. Frank McCarthy, a major executive at Fox and a four-star general who later produced *Patton,* was the lover of a leading publicist to the stars. Invited to the same party, McCarthy and Rupert Allan arrived in separate cars with separate "girlfriends," and drove them home. It was typical that I got to know them separately and, as they lived in separate houses, was at first unaware of their relationship. It was also typical that I learned about it from Rupert. He had come to terms with his sexuality and enjoyed letting down his guard with friends. Unlike McCarthy, who was conflicted and devious, and had no real friends.

Some weekends Nick arranged for a girlfriend to come over in the late afternoon, and asked me to stay out of the bungalow for "a couple of hours." The girlfriend was usually one of several young unknown actresses, very occasionally she was Marilyn Monroe, and in any case she never stayed the night. Although sexually very active with women, Nick was misogynistic. He told me that the only woman he'd ever felt "truly happy with" was his first wife, Jean Evans, a writer he met when they were both living in Greenwich Village during the early 1930s. "I still like and respect her very much," he said. Although sexually attracted to his second wife, Gloria Grahame, he soon came to dislike her, and the same pattern had recurred with many other women. Nick never cared to be questioned further about these personal confidences. Out of the blue he once told me, "I'm afraid that sex destroys intimacy more often than it creates it." A reference to all the women he had never felt truly happy with, or to me? I wondered. But when I asked why he felt that way, he was unwilling or unable to answer.

That summer, as Nick wasn't due to start shooting his second movie for 20th Century–Fox until the fall, I began to explore the multiple worlds of Los Angeles, the only city ever to be built on the edge of a desert facing an ocean that occupies more than one third of the planet. No one, least of all the New Yorkers who always described it as terminally hideous, had prepared me for the dramatic variety of its architecture or the dislocating effect of its imagery. Downtown, I had expected the shadowy bars and grimy residential hotels of Raymond Chandler's novels, but not the Bradbury office building, an outcrop of fantasy as total as an etching by Piranesi, pyramidal glass roof, inner courtyard with a Mexican tiled floor, a series of Art Nouveau balconies above it, and elevators like ornate birdcages moving between the two; or the Art Deco Coca-Cola Bottling Plant shaped like an ocean liner, with porthole windows overlooking Central Avenue; or an eerily abandoned California Gothic mansion of the 1890s, awaiting demolition above a section of abandoned railroad track; or the hugely larger-than-life female limb, advertising a brand of nylon hose, that hung on almost invisible wires above Culver Boulevard.

In the Museum of Science and Industry I played a kind of pinball machine that demonstrated the principles of orbital velocity. And as I tried to discover the minimum speed necessary to place a satellite in orbit around a celestial body, a row of Shirley Temple dolls watched me through the open doorway of an adjoining room. A supreme moment of life imitating surrealism, and a paradigm of Los Angeles as a city of the continuous present. I had another experience of timeless time in the Natural History Museum, where the Los Angeles Man, a human skull estimated at more than 23,000 years old, was on display. A guard told me that after a group of workmen employed on a downtown building project accidentally unearthed it, the homicide squad confiscated the skull on behalf of the county coroner—and ordered a medical report in case he decided to investigate the cause of death.

In Hollywood and Pasadena I saw two Frank Lloyd Wright houses in his design-for-Mayan-living style, and in the San Fernando Valley the streamlined, moated fortress of steel, glass, and stucco that Richard

Neutra created for Josef von Sternberg. (Who had recently sold it to Ayn Rand, who later sold it to developers, who demolished it.) The flatlands of Beverly Hills were full of Tudor, French Provincial, and Cape Cod kitsch, the architecture of exile for homesick movie folk from Europe and the Eastern states; but in the hills above, newcomers who felt less displaced had preferred to re-create the style of the Mexican settlers. In the same street as John Gilbert's imposing Spanish Colonial mansion, recently bought by David Selznick, was the classic hacienda designed for King Vidor by Wallace Neff. And there was a fine example of reverse cross-culturalism in the Hollywood Hills, where the Mexican Ramon Novarro had opted for 1920s American Moderne, a three-storied rectangle of concrete, glass, and copper by Lloyd Wright, son of Frank.

From his rooftop terrace, it was said, Novarro could see (on a clear day) the Pacific. The first day I drove down to the Pacific at Santa Monica it was very clear, and surfboards decorated with bright painted flowers and the word SOUL were scattered on the beach like primitive totems. A few stood immediately below Marion Davies's legendary Ocean House. She had sold it years ago, and after failing as a hotel, the faded-white "Georgian" mansion was closed up. Porticoed entrance, dormer windows, bell tower, row of "Grecian" columns facing the jumbo pool, all awaited the wrecker's ball.

In those days, before too many of its landmarks had been demolished or "remodeled," Los Angeles looked to me like the greatest backlot in the Western world. Its microcosm was the 20th Century–Fox back lot, where I sometimes took a walk along the medieval French village street that led to a Dali landscape, a field of tall dry grass scattered with detritus, a broken spotlight, an oriental archway, a stagecoach with the wheels missing, a flight of stairs leading nowhere. It stirred my imagination in a way that England never did, but always did for Lindsay; and as I write this, I imagine myself standing between that broken spotlight and that flight of steps while Lindsay filmed George and Bill and Sid five thousand miles away in Covent Garden.

When I called James Whale soon after arriving in Los Angeles, he invited me to dinner the following week. A few days later his companion, Pierre, called with the news that James had suffered a stroke. After a partial recovery, he suffered another stroke, and partially recovered again. But not enough to satisfy someone who'd always been a perfectionist. After dressing very carefully for the occasion in suit and bow tie, James flung himself into the shallow end of his swimming pool and shattered his skull. Although he left a suicide note, it was not released to the police or the press, and lurid rumors of murder abounded. I learned about the note from David Lewis, for many years James's lover, and later his closest friend, who quoted its typically lucid and precise last lines: "The future is just old age and pain. I must have peace and this is the only way."

I forget why I never asked David Lewis his reason for concealing the note, but a few weeks later Fritz Lang provided the answer. "We are supposed to be living in paradise here," he said, "so killing yourself is a betrayal of the community image." He gave one of his sardonic smiles, halfway to a sneer and almost as alarming as the African masks on his dining-room wall. "More than one reputation has been ruined by it."

Lang's invitation to dinner came about because he had liked my article on "Fritz Lang's America" in *Sight and Sound.* "But I have one important complaint about it," he told me on the phone, "which I prefer to make face to face." This sounded formidable, and almost immediately after we shook hands in the hallway he gave me an accusing look. "You underrated *Scarlet Street.*" (He was right. Years later I saw it again, and thought it one of his very best films.) Then the sardonic smile. "I forgive you. But I do *not* forgive those critics who praise *The Ministry of Fear* or *Secret Beyond the Door.* When people admire my worst films, I feel insulted. And it becomes meaningless that they admire my best films."

Nick's next film, *The True Story of Jesse James,* was certainly one of his worst. When the studio rejected most of his demands for script changes, he decided to work off his contract and treat it as a potboiler. By then he was drinking heavily, and just before starting the picture, he fell down the stairs of Bungalow 2 and sprained his ankle. For several weeks he hobbled around on a cane, didn't want to drive, and I chauffeured him to the studio and the Fox ranch, where much of the movie was shot under a fiery September sun. One day the earth rumbled and shook under our feet, sending tremors of fear through everyone. But it wasn't the Great Quake, just a missile test in one of the underground sites that ringed the San Gabriel Mountains beyond the ranch.

During this time, when Nick often talked about "getting out of

Hollywood" and "finding freedom" in Europe, he was sent the type-script of *Bitter Victory,* the English translation of *Amère Victoire,* a French novel by René Hardy. The film rights had been bought by Paul Graetz, the Paris-based producer of several international successes, who hoped to secure Nick as director. We both saw possibilities in the story, and Nick's agent worked out a deal that included me as co-scriptwriter.

Hardy, who had joined the Resistance during World War II, was later accused and acquitted of betraying a comrade to the Germans. (Later still, his guilt was established when another collaborator with the Nazis stood trial in France.) Not surprisingly, *Bitter Victory* was a story of betrayal during World War II. After an attack on Rommel's North African headquarters, the mission commander wins a decoration. But he's a false hero, a coward and liar who left a younger officer, the true hero, to die in the desert.

At the end of November 1956, Graetz telephoned his approval of our first draft and Nick left for Paris. I forget the reason I gave for saying I would join him there in two weeks, but it wasn't the real one. I needed time by myself to think about our relationship. Although Nick rarely wanted to make love, he behaved like a possessive lover, expecting me to be always there on call, to talk about projects (he had several he wanted us to work on together), to listen to music together (American folk songs, the blues, Schoenberg's spine-chilling *Erwartung,* a monodrama about a woman stumbling on the dead body of her lover at night), or simply to share one of his long, impenetrable silences, when he seemed to be struggling to confide some deeply buried emotion. At first I used to ask what was wrong, but instead of answering he would get up abruptly and leave the room. Much later I learned that alcoholism was not Nick's only disease. His family had a history of clinical depression.

By this time I had made a few friends of my own in Los Angeles, but as they hardly knew Nick, we could only talk in generalities. ("Do you still love him?" "Yes." "Enough to settle for close companionship?" "No." "Why?" "How can you be a close companion to someone whose central experience is loneliness?") Finally I made a very Southern Californian decision and consulted a psychic.

Plump, fiftyish, with tight blond curls, she wore a Mother Hubbard and operated from a modest bungalow. I told her I was worried about someone I loved and who seemed to love me, but it wasn't working out. Of course she assumed I was talking about a woman, but took it in her stride when I said the person in question was a man. After holding my hand "to get vibrations," she asked for the birthdates of myself and friend, consulted an astrologer's handbook, and shook her head emphatically. "But it *can't* work out! This person is like sandpaper against your skin. Against anyone's skin. So *afflicted.*"

The psychic could have sensed, of course, that I was expecting a negative verdict, but "afflicted" struck me as an uncannily apt word for Nick—and only made me love him more. It clarified his constant struggle with his demons, the almost overpowering need for love and the almost total inability to express it, the sense of isolation he tried to relieve with alcohol. It also made Nick's other qualities intensely touching, the kindness and generosity, the occasional tenderness—and the humor, which you had to dig for, but was very ebullient when it came up for air. And it sharpened my perception of Nick the artist, so inarticulate about his own feelings, yet so openly expressive in creating the love scenes of *They Live by Night* and *Rebel Without a Cause,* so nakedly autobiographical in directing the character played by Bogart ("Will he turn into a hopeless drunk, or kill himself, or seek psychiatric help?") in *In a Lonely Place.*

The plane from Los Angeles landed at Orly around dawn on a misty, rainy December morning, and I saw Nick waiting at the barrier. He stood slightly apart from everyone else, as I had first seen him at the New Year's Eve party in London. The first thing he told me was that Paul Graetz had signed a German actor for the leading role of the British commanding officer. "Box office" was the reason, as Curt Jurgens had become an international star after appearing with Brigitte Bardot in *And God Created Woman.* Nick had protested that an audience would be totally confused by a British officer with a German accent, but Graetz had an answer ready: "Just add a line that he's South African, a Boer."

When Nick threatened to walk off the picture, and Graetz threatened to sue if he did, the psychological duel between the two leading characters of *Bitter Victory* began to play itself out offscreen. Sixtyish, with a baby's pink face, baby-blue eyes, wispy hair, and an agelessly cunning smile, Graetz had a pathological hatred of directors. He couldn't resist tormenting them, even to the detriment of the picture ("I made *Monsieur Ripois* in spite of that monster," René Clément told me), and like any producer who insists on having the last word, he was autocratic with writers. "Please tell Nick I'm concerned about his drinking," he said. Deciding to finesse, I suggested that it was surely up to Graetz, as the producer, to tell Nick himself. "It'll carry more weight coming from you," Graetz said, then gave his terrible smile. "I know *exactly* how much you mean to him, and how upset he'll be if I have to refuse to let you stay on when he starts shooting."

"Son of a bitch," Nick said when I reported back. In the weeks that followed he said it many times, as he realized that Europe would offer no more "freedom" than a major Hollywood studio. He also showed signs of compulsive indecision about the script: "Something's missing, I don't know what it is, but I know it isn't there." He took me to meet with Vladimir Pozner, a blacklisted Hollywood screenwriter living in Paris. Talking through some changes seemed to satisfy Nick for the moment, but Graetz played another wild card before we left to choose locations in Libya. For the role of the commander's British wife, he signed "the important American star" Ruth Roman.

In 1957, when Libya was still a permissive monarchy under King Idris I, there was a casino attached to our hotel in Tripoli. I discovered Nick's addiction to gambling as well as alcohol when he went there every night, seemingly indifferent to the large sums he lost; and I also understood why he understood so well the character of the teacher addicted to cortisone in *Bigger Than Life,* and how (with the help of James Mason's fine performance) he could make the scenes of personality disorder so compelling.

Whether or not we decided to use it, I told Nick, we had to see the ruined Roman city of Leptis Magna. Located on an empty stretch of Mediterranean coast near the Egyptian border, it seemed to exist in a time warp. Two thousand years earlier, a Berber wearing a djellaba must have ridden slowly past on his donkey, just as he did when we arrived, and a wind from the desert must have blown the same sand across arches and temples. In this imperial city, far more extensively preserved than Pompeii, you could still perceive the basic layout, the route from the basilica to the forum, from the baths to a flight of steps leading to the main temple. But for Nick, the huge Roman amphitheatre at nearby Sabratha was even more dramatic. Built at sea level directly facing the Mediterranean, it was a series of curves, semicircular tiers of seats that could accommodate ten thousand spectators, tall archways forming another broad semicircle around the back of the arena, with yellow and blue wildflowers sprouting everywhere through cracks in the stone.

"Do you realize the Romans built in Cinemascope?" Nick said as we looked down from the highest tier. Then he took my arm and hurried me down to the arena, where he began to visualize a production of *Oedipus Rex,* masked and robed figures performing in front of the circle of archways, with the sea as backdrop. Flinging out his arms, he declaimed the last line of Yeats's translation: "Call no man happy till he is dead."

I never saw him happier.

"Is it true Nick got so drunk he didn't even know how much he was losing at the casino?" Graetz asked when we returned to Paris. "What an unreliable informer you must be employing," I said. "Nick will be very amused when I tell him." Graetz thought this over. Then he said, "It's too dangerous for me, as a Jew, to go to Libya. That's why I hoped you'd be on my side. But as you're not, I'm firing you from this picture one week from now." Once again Nick threatened to walk off the picture, once again Graetz threatened to sue him, and once again Nick said, "Son of a bitch."

A few nights later, in a St. Germain des Près bar, he met a girl about eighteen years old who called herself Manon and claimed to be a "Moroccan Sherifian" from a noble family. (Most likely her father was a French colonial who married a Moroccan.) Around two a.m. Nick brought her back to the hotel, found he didn't have enough money to pay the taxi, and woke me up to borrow it. Manon was a heroin addict with dyed blond hair, pale skin, manic eyes, and a violent temper. Nick never discussed their relationship with me, apart from saying he felt sure I would "understand." What I understood was that his impulse to self-destruction had grown too powerful for anyone to deflect.

When I went to Graetz's office to collect the $5,000 he still owed me for the script, he refused to pay it until Nick completed location shooting in Libya. "In the meantime you will remain at the Hotel Raphael for six more weeks at my expense." He knew I couldn't refuse because I needed that $5,000, and the terrible smile told me he was enjoying the power play.

Nick called once or twice a week from Tripoli, to say that he missed me, that Graetz was constantly telexing script changes that he'd signed

Paul Gallico to make, that he was ignoring them but making "quite a few changes" of his own, and felt sure I would approve. "I'm sure I will," I said, sure that it no longer mattered what I said because the film was a lost cause. So, I feared, was Nick. Partly to relieve the sense of loss, and to stop thinking about a situation that couldn't be resolved until I saw him again, I began writing a work of fiction about Southern California. Over the last few months all kinds of images of Los Angeles had been stockpiling in my mind, not just the cityscape, but faces, bodies, voices, lives: movie people, beach people, underside people living in trailers and decrepit clapboard bungalows, worldly-wise European exiles, naive refugees from Oklahoma and Louisiana, pickups in bars, the wealthy and calmly mad young man who called a press conference to announce first that he was about to produce a movie set in outer space, second that he was Jesus Christ reincarnated and returned to earth, the "inner circle" of the late James Dean that Nick introduced me to (the actress who called herself Vampira, the actor Jack Simmons who later did very well in real estate and financed Paul Morrissey's *Madame Wang's*), and the overlapping circle of Samson de Brier. Curtis Harrington, who had made a few short films before becoming assistant to producer Jerry Wald at Fox, introduced me to Samson. He had worked as an extra in Nazimova's *Salome,* liked to dress up as a silent movie star, and held court to all kinds of marginal people—all of them, like himself with Nazimova, surviving on the memory of a single defining moment—the sculptor who had modeled James Dean, the astrologer who had written to Jung and *received a reply.*

Wondering how to shape all this material into a novel, I remembered Christopher Isherwood's *Goodbye to Berlin,* and decided to fragment it into a series of interconnected episodes. I had sketched out a couple of episodes for *The Slide Area* by the time Nick returned from Libya to shoot interior scenes at the Victorine Studios in Nice. Graetz enjoyed another round of power play by forbidding me to join him there, insisting that I remain in Paris until the picture was finished. "Then I'll pay you. But don't try to go to the Victorine, you'll be refused admission." The smile. "Besides, Mademoiselle Manon is there." A month later, he summoned me again. "Nick finished shooting today, and your hotel bill is covered until tomorrow." And he handed me an envelope containing $5,000 in $100 bills.

Back at my hotel I found a message from Nick asking me to meet him at a nightclub near the Champs Elysées the following evening. Manon was there, a frantic, disconnected look on her face, and Nick seemed to have aged ten years in two months. Perhaps I only imagine now that some of the gray in his hair had turned white, but I remember very clearly that he limped and was using a cane again. When I asked if the ankle he'd sprained was giving him trouble, he shook his head. "In Libya this leg began suddenly giving way under me." Then he took me aside to ask if I could lend him some money. "I'm short of cash for a few days because I lost fifty thousand dollars at the casino in Nice," he said, "and Manon needs help right now." I didn't need to ask what kind of help, only how much it would cost. Then I walked back to the Raphael, which was only a few blocks away, took $1,000 from the hotel safe, walked back to the nightclub, gave Nick the money, and left him without a word. He didn't try to stop me.

Sitting on the terrace of a nearby café, tears came to my eyes as I thought how Nick had come into my life at a crucial moment and transformed it irrevocably. I wanted to go back and tell him I would always love him for that. Later I regretted allowing Manon's presence to deter me.

Next day I flew to London, checked into a hotel, and called Lindsay, who had just finished shooting *Every Day Except Christmas*. That evening we met again at the flat we used to share, and almost at once he asked how it felt to be back in England. When I looked around before ringing his doorbell, I said, it felt as if I wasn't really in Greencroft Gardens, but in a not-quite-authentic replica of it on the back lot of a Hollywood studio. "That tells me you've really removed yourself and we've definitely lost you," Lindsay said. Then he wanted to know exactly what had happened the previous evening in Paris, and my account of walking out on Nick at the nightclub produced one of his best quizzical looks. "A bit Joan Crawford, don't you think?"

Back in Los Angeles, I scraped a living over the next two years by writing scripts for TV. By a double coincidence, the first was for Joan Crawford's debut on the small screen, and the offer came when I was working on an episode in *The Slide Area* about a tough, aging, Joan-like movie queen who clung to her throne as fiercely as Joe Louis defended his championship title. Hoping to get and file some impressions of Joan at work, I visited the set. She introduced me to her husband, Alfred Steele, chairman of Pepsi-Cola, and her adopted twin daughters.

Wearing identical white dresses, the girls curtseyed to order, and were abruptly dismissed. "I just hope I can do justice to your wonderful lines," Joan said, huge eyes brimming with sincerity. Later, going through a scene with Steele, she broke off impatiently: "How the fuck does he expect me to say a line like that?" And I remembered Nick saying, "Everything you hear about Joan Crawford is true. If not today, tomorrow."

I also worked briefly for Stanley Kubrick, whom I'd first met in New York in 1953. Two years later, at a trade show in London, I'd "discovered" his second movie, *Killer's Kiss,* which he wrote, directed, photographed, and edited on a shoestring, and had reviewed it in *Sight and Sound.* By 1957, when we met again, Stanley had formed Harris-Kubrick Films with James B. Harris as producer, made *The Killing,* and signed a short-term contract with MGM. He employed me to look for likely material in the studio files, where he'd already discovered Stefan Zweig's novella *The Burning Secret,* acquired in the 1930s and never made into a movie. He commissioned a script from Calder Willingham, but MGM passed on it, and Harris-Kubrick left to make *Paths of Glory,* another project the studio rejected, for United Artists.

When Stanley died, we hadn't seen each other for over thirty years, although we'd occasionally talked on the phone; but hindsight tells me that his progress toward "seclusion" (the media's Pavlovian reflex to his name) was inevitable. In his late twenties he was already self-contained and self-protective to a mysterious degree. His brilliance at chess, that game of patience and concealed aggression, reflected a very astute and tenacious mind; his caustic, sometimes grotesque sense of humor was a front for deep, fearful pessimism about the world. (Years before making *Dr. Strangelove,* he was haunted by the prospect of nuclear warfare.) An intent observer of so many aspects of life while participating in so few of them, had Stanley seen all he wished or needed to see by the time he was thirty-five? Like Proust at the same age, he began to spend more and more time in his own grand equivalent of a cork-lined room, and to follow a creative diet of imagination and memory. As he became the finest American movie talent of his generation, he evidently thrived on it.

The Slide Area was published to good reviews at the end of 1959, just as Jerry Wald was looking for a writer to adapt *Sons and Lovers.* Curtis Harrington arranged an interview with him, it went well, and I began what I look back on now as the most agreeable movie assignment

145

of my life—at least until Jack Cardiff was signed to direct. Jerry was one of those rare producers who genuinely liked writers. He responded intuitively to their work, with results like a gifted psychic's, occasionally off the wall, usually spot on. His production unit at Fox was "independent," but only up to a point, for the studio head considered *Sons and Lovers* a commercial risk, restricted its budget to $800,000, and pressured Jerry to use two of Fox's contract stars. Neither of us objected to casting Dean Stockwell as Paul Morel/D. H. Lawrence, but fortunately James Mason objected to playing his coal-miner father. He knew the part wasn't for him, and we got Trevor Howard, whom we'd wanted from the start. But the studio imposed Cardiff, arguing that he was "economical" because he'd just completed a low-budget movie on schedule in England. This was *Scent of Mystery,* the first and only experiment in Smell-O-Vision, a device supposed to "enhance" dramatic effects by pumping appropriate smells into the theatre.

Cardiff, of course, was a wonderful cameraman. But there was a scent of miscasting about him as our director when he feared that Paul Morel's ambition to become a painter was "not something audiences will sympathize with." Concurrently, the front office sent a memo (which Jerry disregarded) asking us to change the coal-mining background to something less "depressing," and the office of the Hollywood Production Code sent a list of objections (some of which we couldn't disregard) to the "sexual explicitness" of certain scenes.

Somehow *Sons and Lovers* managed not to dishonor Lawrence, although Wendy Hiller (who played Paul's mother) felt there were "too many concessions to Hollywood." She also mocked Dean Stockwell in the usual British way for being too concerned with "motivation," but his performance was no less effective than her own, or Trevor Howard's. (Dorothy Brett, who had accompanied Lawrence and Frieda to New Mexico and was still living there when we met, said that she found Stockwell "uncannily" like the Lawrence she remembered.) Howard, Mary Ure as Paul's lover Clara, Cardiff and I were nominated for Academy Awards, but there was powerful competition from Billy Wilder's *The Apartment,* and I felt sure none of us would win. So did Howard. "We're damn lucky to have got this far," he told me. "Especially Cardiff, considering that Wendy and I directed ourselves in all our scenes." So it was a pleasant surprise when Freddie Francis won the award for best black-and-white cinematography.

To follow *Sons and Lovers,* Jerry offered me *Women in Love* or *The Lost Girl,* both of which he held under option. I chose *The Lost Girl,* but the Writers Guild called a strike just as I was due to start on the script, and a few days after the strike ended, Jerry suffered a fatal heart attack.

Shortly before Jerry's death, I had written Stanley Kubrick in England to congratulate him on *Lolita.* "I am extremely proud of the film," he wrote back, "and feel it is my best work so far. I was sorry to hear about Wald. He was a nice guy and he had that irrational enthusiasm and interest in films. I hope they [Fox] carry on with your project." But "they" didn't, relieved to find an excuse for canceling one of Jerry's "highbrow" productions.

I appreciated him even more after working for the producer of Tennessee Williams's *The Roman Spring of Mrs. Stone.* This was Louis de Rochemont, creator of *The March of Time* and producer of *The House on 92nd Street* and a few other "semidocumentary" melodramas. Tennessee Williams had the contractual right to approve both director and writer, and he asked me to adapt his novel because he'd liked *The Slide Area;* to direct it he chose José Quintero, who had staged *Summer and Smoke* and *Long Day's Journey into Night* so memorably. As Fellini's company had offered to coproduce the movie, exteriors were to be shot on location in Rome, and interiors at Cinecittà studios, but at the last moment de Rochemont made a deal, financially more advantageous to himself, with Warner Brothers. He also gained a substantial tax break by agreeing to spend 80 percent of the production costs in Britain, which meant that many exterior scenes had to be rewritten as interiors, and shot in a British studio.

There were unavoidable losses, of course, but Roger Furse's sets (which included an extraordinarily convincing Roman street) did much to make up for them. And the leading actors were impeccably cast. In a role very close to the bone, Vivien Leigh played the lonely, aging actress with a subtle, elegant, and touching lack of self-pity, and as the young hustler she had the misfortune to fall in love with, Warren Beatty was a seductive fox. For the shifty procuring Countess, José's first thought was of Elisabeth Bergner, who found the character "too dirty." His second choice was Lotte Lenya, whom de Rochemont at first opposed because he'd never heard of her.

Physically, de Rochemont was dinosaurian. He lumbered. He never smiled. And he hated Rome. I asked Tennessee if he knew what had attracted such an unlikely producer to his novel, and why de Rochemont's lips were set in an everlasting pout. "Two words answer both questions," Tennessee replied. " 'Closet queen.' "

At first de Rochemont was surly with Lenya, but, as she wrote me after I'd gone back to Los Angeles, he later became almost agreeable:

> *Even his highness mumbled at a luncheon with José,*
> *"she (meaning me) is marvelous." But I am a notorious*
> *coward and did not go to see the rushes. (I never*
> *listen to my records either—except when I am all*
> *alone.) Nor do I like parties, except one at José's,*
> *but Mrs. Roger Furse drooled all over me in the car*
> *on the way home, with her husband sitting right*
> *next to her. Very embarrassing, but still funny in*
> *a way, because I do like her. But to become a*
> *lesbien {sic} at this stage of my life seems rather*
> *strenuous and not worthwhile for me, as long as*
> *there are other possibilities.*

Tennessee remained especially fond of the movie of *Roman Spring* because it was faithful to his "poetic spirit," and I thought José did some remarkable work under oppressively difficult circumstances. But he never made another film. It's sad although not surprising that a producer whose aura was so powerfully negative, and who grumbled if he went an hour over schedule during the day, sent José running for cover back to the theatre.

Before de Rochemont transferred *Roman Spring* to Britain, José and I had spent two weeks choosing locations in Rome (most of which had to be abandoned). Nick Ray was shooting *King of Kings* in Madrid at the time, and called to ask me to come and see him. I stayed a few days at the house where he was living with his new wife, a young choreographer and dancer called Betty Utey, and their year-old daughter. Nick was essentially undomestic, and every place he lived seemed like a hotel suite, never a home; but although still drinking quite heavily, he appeared more settled, more at peace with himself. Then I watched him at work on the huge exterior set of Pontius Pilate's palace, and realized he was still struggling with the demons of disorder.

King of Kings was an "international" coproduction financed partly by its producer, Samuel Bronston, who had a private conduit to pesetas blocked for export by the Spanish government, and partly by MGM dollars. The cast included Americans (Jeffrey Hunter as JC, Robert Ryan as John the Baptist, Rita Gam as Herodias), Irish (Siobhan McKenna as the Virgin Mary), Swedish (Viveca Lindfors as Pilate's wife), British and Spanish character actors. Jeffrey Hunter, a friend from the days of *The True Story of Jesse James,* told me he was "pissed off" with MGM for insisting that he shave his armpits for the Crucifixion. "And the whole setup is crazy," he said. Bronston, whose pesetas were running out, had not been seen for several days; the screenwriter Philip Yordan, his unofficial surrogate, was no longer on speaking terms with Nick; and Nick and Yordan were working with separate editors to assemble "rival cuts" of the material shot so far.

At opposite ends of the set, in fact, were two widely separated groups, like the headquarters of opposing armies. Yordan commanded one, Nick the other, and they communicated only through their assistants, by walkie-talkie. As usual, Nick was surreptitiously rewriting the script. "Yordan and his people are reporting back to Bronston on every move I make," he assured me. "But I'm sneaking in quite a few changes, and we're so overbudget they daren't make me reshoot."

My last night in Madrid, Nick said he hoped we could resume working together and mentioned a couple of projects he thought would interest me. Although I still loved him, I was no longer in love with him, so it wasn't the prospect of what Lindsay would call "a third party situation" that deterred me. But I'd seen *Bitter Victory* (some powerfully staged scenes, too many others that were muddled or inconclusive, the truth of Richard Burton's performance undermined by the falsity of Jurgens's), and witnessed Nick in his self-created atmosphere of crisis on *King of Kings,* which I felt sure was another lost cause.

I couldn't know, when I equivocated, that I would never see Nick again. (Except on film. Eighteen years later, Wim Wenders recorded him dying of cancer in *Lightning over Water.*) Although we kept in touch and planned to meet several times, the plans went astray. "Sorry I missed you in London and California," he wrote on January 20, 1962, and on August 11, 1965, "I expected to be hearing from you over the telephone from Venice by now. Please plan to come to Belgrade as soon as you are rested." (I don't remember if or why I was actually in Venice at that time.) By then Nick's marriage had broken up. Moving from Madrid to Rome to London to Belgrade, he called me from each city to discuss various projects, but they all evaporated. He also wanted to film one episode from *The Slide Area,* and asked if I'd give him a year's option on it, which I did; but again the financing never came through. In September or October 1965 he called from Belgrade to say Yugoslavia was a wonderful country, he had made a deal to direct several movies there, and would I join him to work on one of them? A few weeks later he called from London to say the deal was off, but he'd get in touch again shortly from the North Sea island of Sylt, off the German coast, where he was planning to create a movie studio.

If the first movie producers hadn't arrived in Los Angeles in 1912 to create "Hollywood," the city would have developed into Middletown-on-the-Pacific, respectable and conformist. Instead, the next wave of immigrants turned it into an enormous self-realization center. Seduced by thousands of movies that concentrated on the pursuit of personal happiness, thousands waited for their own movie to begin.

My first months in Los Angeles had begun in Nick's movie, and I didn't live in my own until I returned from Europe in 1962. When I started to write *The Slide Area* in Paris, I was totally uncertain about the future. If I stayed in Europe, it would only be on account of Nick. Otherwise I would go back to California alone. One part of me didn't want to lose Nick, another part didn't want to lose California. Hindsight tells me that to write more than superficially about both of them, I had to step back, assume the role of observer-outsider. And memory tells me that Nick found the portrait of the movie director "affectionately truthful," but was glad I fictionalized our relationship by involving him exclusively with a young actress.

By the time I began work on *Inside Daisy Clover,* I had lost Nick, left the Old World, and wrote as someone whose future was in the New. The figure of the producer, a response to Graetz, de Rochemont, and the anxious joyless executives at Fox, was partly Old; but Daisy was completely New, a projection of the emerging spirit of the sixties, and the novel (I hoped) would be an ironic fable of conformism versus disobedience in a Hollywood setting.

The sixties had in fact been invented (or prophesied) in the fifties by Allen Ginsberg. "America when will you be angelic? / When will you take off your clothes?" he had asked in *Howl and Other Poems* (1956), and by 1962 the first angelic flower children and hippies had appeared, clothes were beginning to come off, and Ginsberg was on his way to becoming the icon of an era, political activist demonstrating for civil rights and against the Vietnam War, out-of-the-closet Whitmanesque poet, sexual liberationist, Buddhist, adversary of the media ("America . . . Are you going to let your emotional life be run by *Time* magazine?"). And until too many shadows had been cast by too many assassinations (John and Robert Kennedy, Martin Luther King, Jr., Malcolm X), escalating racial violence, and police brutality against antiwar demonstrators, Bob Dylan's "The Times They Are A-Changin'" remained the national anthem of youth.

Today's conservatives dismiss the idealism of the period as naive (what idealism isn't?), but their attacks on affirmative action, abortion, and homosexuality, their demand for censorship of "obscene" art, are really a tribute to the staying power of its beliefs, and to the genuineness of its optimism. This was a time when talk of "universal love" didn't invite mockery, and the boring but beatific drug culture hadn't yet made a connection with organized crime.

In Britain, although there was another "Ban the Bomb" march to Aldermaston, one march didn't make an era. Swinging London was just a fashion show; the musically very gifted Beatles were too amiable to be radical; the less musically gifted Rolling Stones had a streetwise abrasiveness, but unlike Dylan they only sang about themselves. And when Lindsay made *The White Bus* in 1965, he was still waiting for the revolution of "starting to believe in belief" to arrive.

7

Shelagh Delaney's fifteen-page story *The White Bus* is about a young girl living in London who returns for a brief visit to her hometown in the north of England. The girl is unnamed, but easy to identify as Delaney herself when the lord mayor rebukes her for "writing all this sexy stuff about this city [and] giving us a bad reputation in the eyes of the country." (Her reply: "Would you stop feeling my leg, please?") The city is also unnamed, but the mayor is obviously referring to Delaney's hometown of Salford, where Tony Richardson had filmed *A Taste of Honey* on location.

In Lindsay's film the girl is a nameless secretary in a London office. She's first seen working late at night in the typing pool, an isolated figure surrounded by empty desks. Office cleaners vacuum the floor, and in a brief intercut shot the girl has hanged herself from the ceiling, but they pay no attention. This sets the tone of the movie, more disturbing although no less ironic than Delaney's story.

No need to explain why the girl feels suicidal or why the cleaners couldn't care less. The first low-key black-and-white shot of the office, with its Edward Hopperish atmosphere of urban loneliness, says it all. But although loneliness seems to have stunned the girl into passivity, she's really withdrawn and alert at the same time, so used to strange things going on around her that she no longer comments on their strangeness. On the first stage of her journey, walking along a London street to the railway station, she passes a teenager listening to a broadcast of a rugby match on his transistor radio. He reacts with hysterical rage to the news that "his" team has lost, throws the radio to the ground, curses and kicks it. In the station, a young man in a bowler hat hurries after her and proposes marriage. She may be his social inferior, but why should that come between them? "I'll write," she promises, and as the train leaves, he sinks to his knees and sings a farewell serenade to her carriage window.

As the girl gets out of the train at Salford, she's confronted by a group of nuns escorting a man on crutches, and another in an iron lung, to the "Lourdes Special" on the opposite platform. In a deserted street she witnesses two men abduct a woman, drag her into a car, and drive quickly away. A shot of animals herded into a slaughterhouse is followed by a shot of the girl passing a butcher's shop, and there's a sudden, alarming infusion of color as shanks of meat hanging in the window turn blood-red. Then, back in the world of black and white, she walks past a ruined church. Bombed during World War II, it's not the only building still unrepaired twenty years later.

A white "SEE YOUR CITY" tour bus pulls up. She boards it, welcomed by a brisk female guide in military uniform, and joins a Nigerian in ceremonial robes, a Japanese lady in a kimono, several British matrons in elaborate hats, and a group of bowler-hatted businessmen. The lord mayor presides over the tour, assisted by his mace bearer, and both wear full regalia that reflects their self-importance. The bus drives off and the girl's journey continues as it began, in a series of brief, unpredictable, absurd, or sinister episodes. "I was born in this city and proud of it," the lord mayor announces, and as the girl stares out at a stretch of urban wasteland, his hand gropes her knee. As in Delaney's story, she asks him to stop "feeling my leg," but without rancor or surprise. The bus stops at a foundry, the visitors enter it by gangway as the mace bearer solemnly announces, "Money is the root of all progress," and the girl is confronted by pounding machines, roaring flames, and huge discs of molten metal on pulleys. As one of them veers toward her, it turns a violent orange-red. Then the scene reverts to black and white and a close shot of a matron checking her makeup.

"Progress" is the buzzword of the tour, but the visuals undermine it at every stage. At a community center, the lord mayor tells the Nigerian, "This should interest you, coming from an ancient country," and we see a group of men and women making hideous pots. "Successful town planning" cues an overhead shot of the bus dwarfed by enormous and bleak high-rise apartment buildings. In the public library, the mayor quotes an inscription on the ceiling, "LEARNING IS THE PRINCIPAL THING, THEREFORE GET WISDOM," then discourses on the evil of

The White Bus. Tourists, city officials, and tour guide

pornography. "They have some disgusting books in there," he warns
the girl, who doesn't say anything. Throughout, she says very little,
preferring to look or move away in mute, calm protest against whatever
she happens to see, or whatever happens to her, a proposal of marriage
as she boards a train, an abduction in the street, a grope on a bus.

But in a natural history museum, she seems uneasily fascinated by
its collection of stuffed elephants, apes, chimpanzees, and a snarling
tiger; and listening to a painfully amateurish schoolgirl chorus orches-
tra, she has a moment of recall. A brief intercut shot includes her
among the chorus of uniformed girls, then she boards the bus again. It
passes a stretch of desolate parkland and she feels a need for some kind
of escape. Transformed by her imagination, a group of men and women
lounging on the grass are infused with color and imitate the poses of
Manet's famous picnickers in *Le Déjeuner sur l'herbe,* and a child on a
swing suggests a painting by Fragonard. Then there's the sound of a
gun being fired, a shot bird falls to the ground, a hunting dog retrieves
it, and the girl returns to black-and-white reality. Leaves flutter from
trees and the lord mayor remarks unexpectedly: "They say falling leaves
are a sign of death."

The tour climaxes with a civil defense demonstration. "Survival is a matter of preparedness," the mayor informs his visitors, but he's not prepared for what happens next. After a series of simulated battles, mayor, mace bearer, and tourists turn into simulated human beings, dummy replicas of themselves. Only the girl, the only genuine human being around, is spared. She runs away, and in the next shot it's dusk, a few children at play in a square, then an empty street with stores shut down for the night, houses mostly dark. It looks like a street in a ghost town, and although the film doesn't spell it out, the name of the ghost town has to be England. In a house with a dim light in the window, the girl sees an old woman shaving her obviously senile husband, and in a dark alleyway she glimpses a teenager laying siege to a girl ("Go on, let me"). Finally she enters a fish and chips shop, just in time to be served before it closes. In a scene taken directly from Delaney's story, but with a visual metaphor added, the girl sits eating her supper while the owner and his wife stack upended chairs on tables, until they almost surround her. Soon only her face is visible, peering out as she listens to the couple's conversation. He's tired and wants to leave the rest of the work until tomorrow, but she won't allow it. "If we don't do Saturday's work till Sunday," she explains in a singsong voice, "we won't do Sunday's work till Monday, we won't do Monday's work till Tuesday, we won't do Tuesday's work till Wednesday, we won't do Wednesday's work till Thursday, we won't do Thursday's work till Friday, we won't do Friday's work till Saturday and we'll never catch Saturday's work again." Quick fade-out.

Who is this girl? Does she finally get to visit her family? What are they like? And does she go back to her job in London? It's not important. The film has told us all we need to know. First seen surrounded by empty desks in a typing pool, last seen surrounded by upended chairs in a fish-and-chips shop, she's Miss Alienation of 1965. And the young actress Patricia Healey, whom Delaney recommended to Lindsay for the role, has the perfect look for someone adrift in the urban wilderness, pale and fragile, long untidy dark hair, veiled melancholy eyes.

"We aimed at a script without verbal logic," Lindsay said later about his collaboration with Delaney. "You mustn't analyze too much when you're doing it. Once you've worked out the structure, analysis can be dangerous. Intuition and feeling are more important." The scenes at the foundry and the community center, the girl's fantasies in

The White Bus. Fantasy of a picnic on the grass

the parkland, and the simulated battle were all invented at scripting stage. A few others were improvised by Lindsay on the spot, the woman abducted in the street, the stuffed animals confronting the girl in the museum, and a last-minute addition was the shot of the tourists reduced to midgets in silhouette as they walk up the gangway to the enormous, looming foundry ("I saw the opportunity for that image when we were at the location"). The color infusions (to be used again, for different reasons, in *If . . .*) are a deliberately Brechtian device. They focus attention on a dramatic point, connecting the slaughterhouse with the bloody meat in the butcher's window, the bureaucratic progress-speak of the mayor and his mace bearer with the orange flames and black fumes of heavy industry, the girl's bright, lyrical fantasies in the style of Manet and Fragonard with the dismal reality of the city park.

"To some extent the film's a satire on English provincialism," Lindsay remarks in the documentary *About "The White Bus,"* shot by its sound editor John Fletcher (who was also the director's assistant on *O Dreamland*). But later, surveying a classically drab inner-city location, he concedes that "you could make a *White Bus* about almost any place."

This, of course, is what gives an apparently slight forty-minute movie its resonance, just as the freedom of its style, alternating realism and fantasy, satire and sympathy, allusion and directness, creates Free Cinema in a wider sense.

Any film on the making of a film, as Lindsay remarked after seeing *About "The White Bus,"* tells only part of the truth. On camera the director appears unfailingly benign, smiling as he adds a buttonhole to the bowler-hatted Englishman's lapel and adjusts a matron's hat, expressing disapproval with no more than a sigh when he inspects the tour bus, finds its color "a disappointing cream," and asks for it to be repainted. There are no signs of tension, not a single flare-up, even though "my assistant director actually hated me. He had worked on studio-made features, and once he got out onto the streets he didn't know what to do. The art director wasn't much good either. But it *was* great working with Mirek [Czech cameraman Miroslav Ondriček]. We didn't speak each other's language so our communication was excellent."

Today, unfortunately, *The White Bus* is in danger of becoming a lost film. Apart from a very limited distribution many years later in the United States, it was never shown outside Britain, where the negative is unaccounted for and the only extant print is on 16mm, with a few shots missing. The first section of Woodfall's proposed trilogy to be filmed, it decided Tony Richardson and Peter Brook not to compete with Lindsay on Shelagh Delaney territory. Instead, Peter directed a story of his own about a Wagnerian opera singer, played by Zero Mostel, and Tony devised a musical starring Vanessa Redgrave, who performed several songs by the composer of "Le Tourbillon," which Jeanne Moreau sang in *Jules et Jim.* United Artists had agreed to distribute the original package, but according to Lindsay's diary they found *Ride of the Valkyries* and *Red and Blue* "unshowable." And he was not surprised that they remained unshown: "The first (although recut by Peter) remains amateurish and confused, the second was Tony's usual virtuosity, combined with a very flashy TV commercial–style color and a phony, masturbating sensuality."

Robert Benjamin of United Artists liked *The White Bus,* but saw no commercial prospects in distributing a forty-minute movie. He eventually leased the rights to a London art theatre, where it opened on the lower half of a double bill. The upper half was a Czech feature, *Daisies,* which the London critics flayed. The program came off after two weeks, and although Lindsay found the reviews of *The White Bus* "not exactly disappointing," he realized that "except for a few very choice spirits, a film like this can't really *rate* in our society."

Once again he was not surprised. While he was working on the final cut, "Tony [Lord] Snowdon came to photograph Shelagh and myself in the cuttingroom, with an affable ignoramus from *Life.* We played the game, Tony keeping going with a brittle succession of with-it comments, which only made me feel how *un*-with-it is *The White Bus.*"

More than a year before Lindsay began shooting *The White Bus,* George Devine had suffered a minor heart attack. Ordered to rest for three months, he decided to retire as artistic director of the Royal Court, and announced the fact at the theatre's annual New Year luncheon in January 1965. The combined weight of administration, fund-raising, and directing or acting in over thirty plays, had left him "deeply tired," Devine told the assembled guests, who included members of the theatre's advisory board, its regular playwrights and directors, and the

The White Bus. After the civil defense demonstration

leading London theatre critics. A few board members responded with tributes to Devine's achievement that Jocelyn Herbert described as "stiffly conventional," and Anthony Page as "respectful and respectable." As Tony Richardson was in Los Angeles filming *The Loved One*, Jocelyn expected John Osborne to break through the formality. But, like the critics, he remained silent. Then, Anthony Page remembered, Lindsay made "a wonderfully passionate speech. He praised George's energy and vision, his belief in a theatre that encouraged new writers and directors, his political stance and fight against censorship. It brought George alive, and the whole occasion became suddenly alive and real as well."

But in the first week of August 1965 Devine had a far more severe heart attack, stricken in his dressing room at the Royal Court after a performance of John Osborne's latest play, *A Patriot for Me*. The Berliner Ensemble was appearing in London at the time, and Brecht's widow, Helene Weigel, had just paid Devine a visit. "I last saw him with Jill Bennett after a matinee," Lindsay recalled in his diary. "He sailed in in his drag [for the drag ball scene] looking certainly rather splendid, very caustic, complaining that his dresser had drenched him in scent." Two weeks later a stroke paralyzed Devine's left side. Lindsay went with Jocelyn Herbert to visit him in the hospital, and found him "terribly thin, terribly old. Jocelyn was splendid, but then it became too much for her, and she cried off our visit to the Berliner Ensemble together [to see *Saint Joan of the Stockyards*]."

"George Devine died yesterday," Lindsay noted on January 21, 1966. "Only fifty-six." For the rest of the year his diary was mainly occupied with his personal life, and the escalating ferocity of his confrontations with Mum.

Lindsay's younger brother Alexander Vass, a junior officer in the Navy, had died in 1958 at the age of twenty-three, after contracting a polio virus that paralyzed his brain. ("It's not just his youth that makes it so sad," Lindsay commented to me. "He was the opposite of Murray and myself. So well-adjusted. No clouds in his sky.") The Sleighs sold Cringletie and moved to Fuchsia Cottage, Rustington, on the Sussex coast. A year later, the major died there. And after many "typical" weekend visits to Mum, it seemed to Lindsay that grief had only hardened her disposition: "Her absolute need to create a scene. She works herself up, tells me she's getting old, finally bursts out, 'You *bugger!* You never think about anything except yourself—you won't care when you see me shoved into the crematorium—you're just waiting for me to die so you can get your claws on my money.' "

Although all is not quiet on Lindsay's own emotional front, his attitude is more ironic and reflective:

"I feel I should be going round buying some clothes. It is certainly true—I wonder where I read it—that clothes and the buying of clothes represents a sexual urge. Significant, I suppose, must be the way I tend to stop short of actually buying *anything*."

"Thinking of Richard again."

"Perhaps I should try to become a dignified father figure with some reserve to younger actors like Anthony Hopkins." (Two years before he became famous at the National Theatre, twenty-eight-year-old Hopkins had impressed Lindsay at an audition. He played small parts in *Julius Caesar* and *The White Bus*.)

"Still trying to set up *Hamlet* in Warsaw with Tadeusz."

"That funny Saturday afternoon feeling—nothing really to do except wander around Smith's [bookstore] a bit, buy *Life* and *Slimming*, and some food at the supermarket. I am rather randy right now; I suppose I'm lucky to have a play to direct."

The play was *The Cherry Orchard*, which opened August 25, 1966, at the Chichester Festival, with Celia Johnson as Ranevskaya. "Celia is 'divine' as they say," Lindsay noted during the first week of rehearsal, "genuinely charming and witty and with a most sensitive intuition." But he feared the performance would remain too genteel. Anthony Page remembered it as "very touching at moments, although her costumes were a bit drab. But the high point of the production was Tom Courtenay as Trofimov." Star and director received generally good notices, and Lindsay was "pleased"—but infuriated by "the obsession with class" of a few critics who complained of Courtenay's regional accent: "He's playing a student from the provinces. Why should he sound like a Romanov?"

A few days after the opening, Tadeusz Lomnicki asked Lindsay to direct him in Osborne's *Inadmissible Evidence* at the Polish Contemporary Theatre. He left immediately for Warsaw, but a brief diary note on the experience suggests that Tadeusz's appeal had begun to wane: "I wonder about Tadeusz, Serge and Richard as I first knew them. Did they change? Or did I lose my illusions?" In any case, there was no more talk of Lindsay directing Tadeusz in *Hamlet.* Instead, after *Inadmissible Evidence* opened, he made a short film at the invitation of the director of the Warsaw Documentary Studio: "Very generous, but also intimidating, as I didn't really know Poland." But he found a subject when he visited the Dramatic Academy, watched a class of musical theatre students perform a variety of songs, and was charmed by their innocence and enthusiasm. His first thought was simply to make a film about the class, his second that "it would be a good idea to go outside and shoot in the streets of Warsaw, so that the film could be a sort of montage of scenes contrasting the class and the life outside."

An opening title describes *The Singing Lesson* as "a sketchbook or poem," and explains that "the words of the songs are not important, only their themes, the images and memories they evoke." And the opening shot, a slate with the film's title and director's name written in chalk, is a Brechtian device to let the audience know it's watching a director's film, not cinéma vérité footage with the camera recording whatever happens in front of it—even though the images are designed to *look* immediate and unstaged.

The first song, a ballad about Poland "buffeted by the winds of history," is a prelude to images of war and privation. But there are no obvious effects, no newsreel-style battle scenes, air raids, dead babies, terrified or starving children. Instead, intercut with the boy singing, the students and their professor listening, are shots of a memorial inscribed with the names of the fallen, a shattered building, people crowding onto a train to escape the city, an empty plate on a kitchen table, a photograph of a young man with a black border around the frame.

Next, as a young girl sings "A Lullaby—For Those Who Wait," to a room of faces as alert and expressive as her own, other faces are intercut from the separate world of the city. Tired shabby patient women wait to be served in stores, another gazes longingly at a window display, an old man nods off to sleep on a station bench as he waits for a train. Then the scene and the reality level shift again, with a boy and girl rocking to "big beat." To the same beat, Warsovites hurry along rainy streets, almost invisible under umbrellas that advance, retreat, collide, and change direction like mobiles suspended in the air. The final folk song, performed by a boy and girl in folk costumes, sets everyone dancing. While the music continues, the scene changes from joy in the classroom to weary rush hour crowds in the city; and the camera holds a parting shot of a woman staring blankly ahead as she clutches a single daffodil.

"Perhaps I was thinking of a subtext of innocence and experience," Lindsay said later. Also, perhaps unconsciously, of the "father figure" role that he'd been considering for himself? *The Singing Lesson* makes a point of showing the professor in this role, encouraging, criticizing (he interrupts the last song to show the boy a livelier, faster way of performing it), and sharing his students' enthusiasm when he leads the final dance. And in the contrasting moods of classroom and city, there's a hint of parental concern. By the end of the film, the audience shares it. What will happen to these students when they leave the world of the classroom, and cross the line from innocence to experience?

The Singing Lesson was never distributed commercially outside Poland, although BBC TV aired it many years later, and in 1985 Film Forum in New York screened it as part of its "Early Documentaries of Lindsay Anderson" program. (The others were *Thursday's Children* and *Every Day Except Christmas*.) At only twenty minutes, the film runs half the length of *The White Bus* and is lighter in tone. But the lightness is deceptive, and another, darker subtext emerges. The appeal of Poland as well as of Tadeusz has waned, with Soviet-style communism making everyday life in Warsaw a mirror image of everyday life in the drab, anonymous city of *The White Bus.* When *The Singing Lesson* was screened at the Warsaw Documentary Studio, the director commented that nobody in the street ever smiled. "But this had nothing to do with me saying to them, 'look alienated,' " Lindsay noted. "It was just an example of the social alienation evident in Poland." And in a letter written from the Hotel Europejski, he described Poland as "a sluggish, drab, egocentric place, strangled in bureaucratic red-tape. . . . Everything takes an age; no one is paid enough."

Lindsay wrote this letter to the coauthor of a first-draft screenplay about an English public school. David Sherwin and John Howlett had collaborated on *Crusaders* in 1960, when they were both undergraduates at Oxford. Over the next few years they submitted it to various British producers, one of whom told them it was "evil and perverted," another that they should be horsewhipped. They also sent it to Nick Ray in California, sensing a kindred spirit in the director of *Rebel Without a Cause.* But although Nick liked it, he thought the film should be directed by an Englishman. Finally Sherwin and Howlett submitted *Crusaders* to Seth Holt at Ealing Studios, a friend of both Lindsay's and mine, and a talented second-generation Ealing director. (*Nowhere to Go,* written with Ken Tynan, was a rare hybrid, Hollywood-style film noir transposed to a genuinely realistic British setting.) Seth also liked *Crusaders,* but thought the film needed a director with a public school background, and offered to produce it with Lindsay directing.

At first Lindsay was doubtful. He told Seth that he responded to "something authentically adolescent and rebellious" in the screenplay, but found it disorganized, too sentimental, and short on humor. "Outline, characters, relationships remain appallingly fluid," he added in his diary. All the same, he met with Sherwin and Howlett a week before leaving for Warsaw, liked them, agreed to work with them on a second draft, then confided the usual self-doubt to his diary: "I'm afraid I'm too subjective to be a writer; and I don't trust myself. Their problem is opposing me with enough confidence."

Lindsay, of course, was not easy to oppose. Concealing self-doubt by laying down the law, he told Sherwin and Howlett that *Crusaders* "had to be taken to pieces," and needed "new characters, incidents, relationships." After Sherwin sent him some notes for these, Lindsay replied from Warsaw: "You have (excuse me for writing like a school report) a fecundity of imagination, but it seems to operate rather without organic sense. Sometimes a whole idea is valuable, sometimes a couple of lines, sometimes nothing." And then, in a moment of breakthrough, the letter summed up what Lindsay believed *Crusaders* should be about. The British public school, he wrote, is "a strange sub-world, with its own peculiar laws, distortions, brutalities, loves, [and] its special relationship to a perhaps outdated conception of British society."

Soon there was no "perhaps" about it. "I feel the story, even the style is shaping," he noted on January 5, 1967, after another meeting with Sherwin and Howlett on his return to London. "But I find myself very confused between epic, fantasist, liberal protest (an initial danger)." A few weeks later, both Seth and Howlett bowed out. "They didn't really like the direction the script was taking," according to Lindsay, who had begun to feel personally involved with *Crusaders,* and proposed to Sherwin that he and Lindsay continue on their own, "with no thought of pleasing anyone but ourselves."

No thought, either, of accepting the first of many improbable Hollywood offers that came Lindsay's way—to direct a film of Lawrence Durrell's *Justine,* which was eventually made by George Cukor. Instead, to put a little money in both their pockets, Lindsay directed a commercial for Kellogg's Corn Flakes, and another for a new brand of carpet sweeper, casting Sherwin as the salesman who demonstrated it. Then, having discovered a mutual admiration for Jean Vigo, they saw *Zéro de Conduite* again, "not for its anarchistic spirit—we had plenty of our own—[but for] Vigo's poetic method, episodic, fragmentary, charged." The film also gave Lindsay an idea for the finale of *Crusaders,* but a finale very different in tone. Vigo's schoolboys are mischievous children who pelt teachers and governors celebrating Alumni Day with tin cans and old shoes. Lindsay's are lethally angry adolescents who open fire with stolen machine guns on teachers and dignitaries celebrating Founders Day.

It didn't take long for the screenplay to move beyond "liberal protest," and as director and writer exchanged memories of public school life, appalled by its cruelties and delighted by its absurdities, Lindsay no longer felt confused between "epic" and "fantasist." The new draft fused them, and fused the ideas that emerged from an almost daily collaboration that began in the second week of March. Their working routine, which Lindsay established, was to agree on a general outline of each scene, and discuss it in detail before Sherwin wrote it. After Lindsay read the scene, he made further suggestions, and Sherwin rewrote it. Although prolific with ideas for scenes, Sherwin needed Lindsay's help to develop them (when he didn't reject them); and although he sketched out many of the characters, Lindsay needed Sherwin to invent dialogue for them.

Their codependency became more than professional when Sherwin's unresolved wife-versus-girlfriend problems sometimes reduced him to tears or sent him off on an alcoholic binge. Then Lindsay played personal adviser and scold, as well as sternly monitoring Sherwin's consumption of barley wine, and they finished the draft during the second week of May.

At the end of August, after every major production and distribution company in Britain had turned it down, a chance meeting with Albert Finney rescued the project. A share of the enormously profitable

Tom Jones had enabled Finney to set up his own company, Memorial Enterprises, and he'd just finished directing his first film, *Charlie Bubbles,* from a script by Shelagh Delaney. Finney offered to show *Crusaders* to his partner, Michael Medwin, who liked it, offered to coproduce it, and set about raising American finance:

> *I knew that Charles Bludhorn, who was running*
> *Paramount at the time, was star-struck and a*
> *great Albert Finney fan. I had to go to New York,*
> *and I used Albert's name to get to Bludhorn. He*
> *didn't know that Paramount's London office had*
> *turned the project down, and asked me about*
> *budget. I told him, $600,000. Bludhorn didn't*
> *read the script (people like that never do), but*
> *sent it to Paramount's New York script department*
> *and got an enthusiastic reaction. Then he sent it*
> *on to Paramount in London, who realized it was*
> *now Bludhorn's baby, pretended they'd never read*
> *it and reacted enthusiastically. So Bludhorn gave*
> *us the green light.*

Lindsay had always wanted to shoot as much of the film as possible on location at his alma mater; and to gain permission from the current headmaster of Cheltenham College, he thought it prudent to submit a laundered script. Sherwin prepared one, but as it needed a less subversive title than *Crusaders,* Lindsay pinned an appeal for suggestions on the notice board outside Michael Medwin's office. Daphne Hunter, formerly my secretary at the British Film Institute, and a longtime friend of both Lindsay's and mine, was then working as Medwin's secretary. And after Sherwin completed the "official" version, he asked if she could think of "something very oldfashioned, corny, and patriotic":

> *"Like Kipling," he said. This set me off. And I*
> *began reciting, "If you can keep your head while*
> *all about you / Are losing theirs and blaming it on*
> *you / You'll be a man, my son." And then I said,*
> *"What about If as a title?" David liked it, so I*
> *wrote it on the notice board. Lindsay came in*

later, saw it, added three dots, and decided it
it would make a better title for the real *script*
than Crusaders.

If . . . opens with a long shot of Cheltenham College chapel, and the sound of schoolboy voices singing a hymn. Their voices dissolve first to laughter and chatter after the hymn ends and they leave the chapel, then to the deep bass chanting, drumbeats, and rattling gourds of the African *Missa Luba.* Traditional hymns, and a pagan mass with its hint of disruptive forces in the wings, are one of the devices used to comment throughout on the action of the film. Another, equally Brechtian, is the series of intertitles that serve as chapter headings. The first of these, "College House—Return," appears as the main credits end. It introduces the leading character, Mick Travis (Malcolm McDowell), who makes a conspiratorial entrance wearing a black slouch hat, black scarf across the lower half of his face, and long black topcoat. Like his two friends, Wallace and Johnny, he's a romantic at heart. Unlike them, he's also a Byronic-ironic self-dramatizer who talks in militant slogans: "Violence and revolution are the only pure acts," and "One man can change the world with a bullet in the right place." Mick's vanity and his sexual fantasies strike similar chords. "My face is a source of never-ending wonder to me," he remarks to the mirror, and to a photograph of a Vogueish model: "There's only one thing you can do with a girl like that—walk naked into the sea with her as the sun sets, make love once—and then die."

But in spite of his talk of revolution, and the battle photographs pinned to the notice board of his study, Mick is not really "political." His protest is youth's outcry against a repressive adult world. "When do we live?" he asks Wallace and Johnny. "That's what I want to know." In the late 1960s, almost 70 percent of the British Establishment—politicians, generals, Church of England bishops, directors of major companies, including the Bank of England—were products of "the strange sub-world" of the public school. And in the next chapter of *If . . . ,* headed "Discipline," the adult world emerges as an Establishment of headmaster, staff, chaplain, and the prefects known as Whips, all guardians of an empire on which the sun must never set, apostles of Duty, Tradition, and the Importance of Winning.

The rebels: David Wood, Richard Warwick, and Malcolm McDowell in *If. . .*

When I first saw *If . . . ,* it wasn't difficult to identify the headmaster that Lindsay and I knew at Cheltenham College with the glib, self-satisfied authority figure who tells Mick and his friends: "You're too *intelligent* to be rebels." The math teacher, fondling and pinching a favorite student, was clearly inspired by "Kipper" of the mysteriously fishy smell, and I felt a shiver of recognition at the chaplain's genial smile and chilling belief in original sin. "We are all corrupt," he tells the boys assembled in chapel, "and we all deserve to be punished." Later, during a military exercise, he rides horseback in uniform and clerical collar, and reminds the boys preparing for a mock battle: "Jesus Christ is our commanding officer."

Fractionally less absurd but far more disturbing are the betrayers of their own generation, the Whips. In keeping with Lindsay's decision not to make schoolboy costumes (or slang) literally contemporary, the Whips wear black tailcoats, starched white collars, carry elegant canes, and even recline in bathtubs, sipping tea served by juniors known as

Scum. Arrogant and "frigid," as Mick calls them, intent on preserving "the stability of the school," they seem even more contemporary thirty years later. Persisting human types, the Whips have mutated into Yuppies, Young Tories, Young Republicans, or members of the Christian Right. And like all the characters in *If . . .*, they exist on a level of reality, in a Zen phrase that Lindsay often quoted, "two inches off the ground."

During the first week of shooting, the film's reality moved an extra half inch off the ground. Its modest budget allowed for a fairly limited range of lighting equipment, and after making a few tests, cameraman Miroslav Ondriček told Lindsay that he couldn't guarantee color consistency in the chapel scenes. "Then let's shoot them in black and white," Lindsay said. "I really love black and white." At first the idea made Mirek uneasy, and he wondered how Lindsay could explain it away. (Stephen Frears, assistant director on the film, remembered Mirek as "a bit literal-minded. He came out of the Miloš Forman–Ivan Passer Czech school, with its more candid camera style.") But Lindsay insisted that he didn't have to "explain it away. I'll just shoot a few other scenes in black and white when I feel like it."

Although playing for time when he said this, Lindsay proceeded to "explain it away" after he saw dailies of the first chapel scene. Its atmosphere of bleak uniformity, he decided, would have been less effective in color. In the black-and-white *The White Bus* he had used color for a reverse effect, and now he rationalized that "if you shoot a film entirely in monochrome or entirely in color, you don't disrupt the audience in any way." There are many other ways of disrupting an audience, of course, and what matters here is the creative instinct that turned a limitation to advantage. But Lindsay always had what he called a "pedagogic side," not always beneficial to him as an artist, although in this case it helped him to see that black and white could intensify the bleakness of other scenes, the ugly roadside café, and the grim attic where the assistant housemaster was lodged.

In fact there's only one moment in the film when Lindsay "disrupts" the audience according to his theory. It occurs during the fencing match between Mick and Johnny, which begins in monochrome, then switches to color as they move from the gymnasium to the walkway outside, where Johnny's sword accidentally pricks Mick's hand, and Mick is entranced by the sight of a red blob on one finger: "Real blood!"

But the film contains a few other, quite different uses of black and white. Softly lit monochrome underlines the romantic episode when Phillips, the pretty junior, admires Wallace exercising at the gymnasium bar, Wallace responds with some show-off acrobatics, and the current that starts to flow between them is shown in subliminal slow motion, with the *Missa Luba* heard very quietly offscreen. One of the most lyrical homoerotic episodes in any movie, it suggests that Lindsay was working unusually close to his subconscious. So does the roadside café scene, which becomes a fantasy of passionate liberation. It opens in

Malcolm McDowell and Lindsay at work on the fencing scene in *If* . . .

If . . . , on the rooftop: Christine Noonan and Malcolm McDowell

If . . . , Founders Day: Attack and counterattack

deliberately harsh black and white as Mick and Christine meet, then start to play the mating game. "Look at my eyes, I've eyes like a tiger, I like tigers," Christine says. Mick snarls, she snarls back, they paw, growl, pretend to cuff and claw each other, finally tumble to the floor. A quick cut, and they're both naked at the moment of orgasm. Another quick cut, to a landscape flooded with color as Mick rides a motorbike across a vividly green field, Christine standing on the passenger seat behind him, resting her hands on his shoulders, and then, as the bike gathers speed, triumphantly flinging out both arms.

Back in the world of "Discipline," Mick and his friends are increasingly penalized by the Whips for their "general attitude," sentenced to long cold showers, and later the savage beatings that lead to "Resistance." This section opens with Wallace and Johnny watching as Mick fires a popgun at various authority images, notably Elizabeth R in her coronation coach, among the photographs on his study wall. Then the three of them swear blood brotherhood and exchange battle cries, "Death to tyrants!" and "England, awake!"

Ironically, their next punishment (for attacking the chaplain during a military exercise) supplies them with the weapons they need for rebellion. Ordered to clean out the basement of the college lecture hall, they sift through all kinds of junk, including a rotted Union Jack, an upside-down map of the British Empire, and a stunted fetus preserved in a jar. (The film wears its symbols of outdated tradition and repression with a casual elegance.) Finally they discover a stockpile of light machine guns and ammunition cases from World War II.

"Crusaders," the final chapter, begins in the lecture hall on Founders Day. Boys, parents, and staff listen to a speech by former Cheltonian and "national hero" General Denison. On the stage with him are the headmaster and two picturesque former Cheltonians, a visiting bishop in ceremonial miter and robes, and an ancient baronet in medieval knight's armor. "Today it's fashionable to belittle tradition," the general opens his speech, and as he proceeds to defend "privilege" and "the habit of obedience," smoke begins to drift through the floorboards near the bishop's chair. It grows dense, the audience coughs and splutters, then the headmaster announces the building is on fire, and everyone hurries to the quadrangle outside. Cut to a low-angle shot of Mick on a nearby rooftop, wearing a combat jacket. He opens fire with a machine gun on the crowd below, and is joined almost immediately by Christine, Wallace, Phillips, and Johnny, all armed, all wearing combat jackets. The general organizes resistance by calling for weapons from the college armory, the bishop topples over clutching his pastoral staff, a bullet hits the headmaster between the eyes, and a ferocious mother (with a passing resemblance to Mrs. Sleigh) yells "Bastards! Bastards!" as she returns the rebels' fire. The last shot, close on a determined, vengeful Mick as he continues to fire, is followed by a repeat of the main title, *If . . .* , in blood-red letters.

"Emotionally the film is revolutionary—but intellectually, I don't know," Lindsay said later. "The massed fire power of the Establishment is ranged against Mick." And the three dots after the title seem deliberately ambiguous. Is this a film about what *might* happen? Or is it saying that a rebellion of this kind is not the most likely to succeed—but if only it *could*? Or, most probably, all of the above?

Wish fulfillment was certainly a part of one former Cheltonian's reaction. Patrick White found "the smallest part perfectly cast and acted, the direction what I dream of. The buildings of my old school added to the horror of the story: the revolution part of it seems to have been simmering in me all these years, and I was on the roof with the other sten-gunners."

It was simmering elsewhere as well. As Lindsay and Sherwin finished the script of *If . . .* , Students for a Democratic Society staged a mass demonstration in Chicago, and other protests erupted at Columbia University in New York and the Sorbonne in Paris. But Lindsay was determined to avoid any exploitation of current events, which is why the Cheltonians don't wear literally contemporary costumes or use contemporary student slang, why the "revolutionary" photographs on the wall of Mick's study are generalized (no Che Guevara or Bobby Seale or Chicago Seven), why no one performs or listens to any contemporary popular music, and even the jukebox in the roadside café scene plays the *Missa Luba.* And, of course, the film was never intended to be naturalistic. In *If . . .* reality is negotiable. It coexists with fantasy, and there's no dividing line.

Does the housemaster's wife really wander around naked at night, or play the recorder to her husband in bed? Does the history teacher really arrive in the classroom on a bicycle, singing a hymn? When the headmaster orders Mick to apologize to the chaplain for attacking him, he opens the drawer of a massive wardrobe to reveal the chaplain lying there. In hiding? Or where he properly belongs? It's negotiable, like the railroad train steaming out of a fireplace in Magritte's painting—or the last shot of Mick Travis desperately firing his machine gun from the rooftop. Will he be killed, arrested and sent to jail, or escape? Can any revolution succeed without violence? Or if these rebels succeed against all odds, will they create a new Establishment, as repressive as the one they overthrew?

Although *If . . .* gives the impression of moving freely between reality and fantasy, and color and black and white, to create what Lindsay called "an atmosphere of poetic license," every camera setup and movement was worked out beforehand. The same control extended to the cutting room, where his editor, David Gladwell, remembered that "no cut satisfied him [Lindsay] until all the possible arrangement of shots, or alternative frames on which to cut, had been fully considered." In the same way, the direction of the young unknown actors playing the rebels (Malcolm McDowell, Richard Warwick, David Wood) was detailed yet flexible. At the Memorial Celebration almost twenty-five years later, Malcolm McDowell demonstrated a telling moment of business that Lindsay invented for the scene of Mick's beating. Confronting the Whip who's going to administer it, Mick is cool and insolent. Then he bends over, the Whip brings down his cane for the first blow, and he manages not to wince. But as the beating grows increasingly vicious, the camera stays behind Mick or on the Whip. We don't see Mick's face again until it's over. Shot from behind, he makes the gesture of wiping a tear from his eye, then turns to camera with the same defiant expression as before.

When *If . . .* began shooting, Malcolm was twenty-four, but he looked no older than the actual sixteen-year-old Cheltonians surrounding him in the chapel. Neither did Richard Warwick or David Wood, who were approximately Malcolm's age. "Youth," Lindsay concluded, "is a matter of spirit, attitude and feeling," and at forty-five drew on his own youth to make a film with a strong international appeal to the young. But the executives of Paramount's London office were dubious about its commercial prospects, and planned to delay its release. Then *Barbarella* (for which the same executives had predicted a great hit) flopped disastrously at the company's London theatre, the Plaza; and

Paramount's only immediately available replacement was *If . . .* , which opened in December 1968 and drew the crowds that had failed to show up for Jane Fonda's striptease.

Outside London *If . . .* was less successful, but drew large audiences in the United States, then in France—where Graham Greene, who "liked it enormously," noted with astonishment that it was taken very seriously as a "realistic portrait" of English public school life. The film also won the Palme d'Or at the 1969 Cannes Festival, although the British ambassador to France (part of that 70 percent of the Establishment with a public school education) called it "an insult to the nation" and tried to have it withdrawn.

For Malcolm, *If . . .* led not only to the starring role in Kubrick's *A Clockwork Orange,* but to one of the most important friendships of his life. Cast as Mick after he auditioned the café scene (the budget didn't allow for any filmed tests), he arrived at 57 Greencroft Gardens "on a cold January morning" to discuss the part:

> *I rang the bell. Nobody answered. I knocked. Still
> no answer. Then, some way down the street, I saw
> this figure carrying two large shopping bags. "Sorry
> I'm late," he said. I offered to carry one bag. It
> was very heavy. Like the other, it contained a can of
> kerosene. The flat had no central heating and there
> were only those oldfashioned oil-burning contraptions.*

Lindsay always lived very modestly, and after the success of *If . . .* his only concession to fame was to employ a secretary one day a week. He never learned to drive. (In California, I persuaded him to take lessons, but he soon abandoned them. "Like Los Angeles, driving is not in the bloodstream.") During the early 1970s his diary often refers to evenings spent alone with TV and a "home-cooked meal." Sample entry: "Back to the flat, where I watch 15 appalling minutes of *Esther Costello* (Joan Crawford), then cook myself a tin of mince, a tin of carrots and 2 poached eggs." Sometimes stewed steak or baked beans replace mince, but apart from the eggs, the home-cooked meal consists of canned fare.

· · ·

In retrospect, it seemed to Malcolm, "*If . . .* was the happiest time of Lindsay's life." Until 1973, in fact, he was untroubled by unrequited love, although he developed a minor crush on Jon Voight. "An immensely attractive character," he noted after their first meeting. "And I suppose this says something about me. Dangerous?" But when they met again, Voight first suggested collaborating on "*Peer Gynt* as a musical on Broadway," then told Lindsay that he might give up acting to become "a pop singer, like Joe Cocker." And the danger passed along with the crush, leaving Lindsay free to create his own, alternative "family."

As well as becoming a "father figure" to Malcolm, he began to assemble an unofficial repertory company from the actors in *If . . .* Among those who would often work with him again, in theatre as well as movies, were Graham Crowden (the history teacher), Arthur Lowe (the housemaster), Mary MacLeod (the housemaster's wife), Peter Jeffrey (the headmaster) and Mona Washbourne (the matron who cheerfully points a flashlight at the boys' genitals, looking for signs of infection). And to a pair of exceptionally gifted but disturbed actresses, Rachel Roberts and Jill Bennett, he became confidant and adviser.

Since *This Sporting Life* and her marriage to Rex Harrison, Rachel had spent much of her time in New York and Los Angeles. I first met her in 1963, when Rex was making the film of *My Fair Lady.* As a movie star by association after her marriage to Rex, she tasted enough honey to imagine herself as Elizabeth Taylor, even though she knew she didn't have movie star looks. She also imagined herself as Zoe Caldwell, with a distinguished career in the theatre, even though (quite irrationally) she lacked confidence in herself as a stage actress. There was a parallel conflict in Rachel's personal life, between self-image as a sex symbol and as a devoted wife and homemaker. By the time I met her, the marriage with Rex was precarious. (Sexual incompatibility, she confided, was a major problem.) By the time Lindsay made *If . . . ,* they had separated, and in 1969 Rachel went back to London to appear in a play at the Royal Court. Both Lindsay and Anthony Page were alarmed by her condition, and on Christmas Eve Lindsay phoned Anthony to tell him "to get over to St. George's Hospital as quick as you can. Rachel's there with a stomach pump down her."

It was her first suicide attempt, and when Rachel came around, she asked a nurse to call Lindsay. It was not the first or last time that he ministered to her. During a visit to London a year later, I arrived at Lindsay's flat just after he'd finished a long conversation with Rachel, who'd called him from California. "She's back with Rex," he said. "She wants to kill him." A sigh. "She doesn't want to kill him." Another sigh. "She just wants to be Rachel Roberts." He poured us each a glass of wine. "You think she knows who Rachel Roberts is?" I said, and he shook his head. "They've never met. That's the whole problem."

As another child of Empire, impatiently nonconformist but a strong believer in discipline, Jill Bennett felt a special bond with Lindsay. With a more self-sufficient public image than Rachel, she was almost as insecure in private, outwardly playful but inwardly turbulent. Rachel knew that her best chance of getting through a three-o'clock-in-the-morning-of-the-soul was in the spare bedroom at Greencroft Gardens. Jill preferred to get through it at home, but after the painful breakup of her marriage to John Osborne, she said to me: "Whatever else happens, I feel my life will be possible as long as Lindsay's *there.*" Jill never became fashionable in the London theatre. This created another bond with Lindsay, always sympathetic to talent that he felt was underrated, and always doing what he could to encourage it, even when away from London or busy making a film. "Your talents are a great deal too good to waste," he once wrote Jill, who was involved in an unhappy love affair and discouraged by lack of progress in her career. "Just Look Forward!"

"How consistently and constructively kind he was," Alan Bennett wrote after Lindsay died, "shouldering other people's burdens (albeit with a sigh), housing the homeless, his flat in Swiss Cottage always sheltering someone down on their luck." Like Vladimir Pucholt, a leading Czech actor whom Lindsay met during his 1965 visit to Prague. Impressed by Lindsay's "kindness and intelligence," Pucholt felt instinctively that he was "someone I can trust, and talk to without fear of being betrayed." Three years later, on June 16, 1968, Lindsay noted in his diary: "Chance meeting in London street with Vladimir." Who put his first impression to the test. "Lindsay," he said simply, "I have escaped."

They took a walk together, and Pucholt told him in halting English that life in Czechoslovakia had become "impossible. What the communists want is not to make happiness. It is power." Pucholt also confided that he wanted to give up acting, go to medical school, and become a doctor. Lindsay's diary records only that "I bought him a copy of *Animal Farm,*" but in fact he did a great deal more. As Pucholt had little money and few connections, Lindsay invited him to stay at Greencroft Gardens, gave him English lessons, and paid most of his medical school fees.

"I know he was famous in Prague, but who exactly is he?" Malcolm McDowell inquired after meeting Pucholt at Greencroft Gardens later that month. "Vladimir Pucholt is the Tom Courtenay of Czechoslovakia," Lindsay replied. A quizzical look. "Where there is no Albert Finney."

In the spring of 1969 Lindsay was back at work in the theatre. His production of David Storey's *In Celebration* opened at the Royal Court on April 22, launching a theatrical partnership that continued for more than twenty years. *The Contractor,* the first Storey play that I saw, followed on October 20. It convinced me, as I told Lindsay afterward, that writer and director had contracted a perfect marriage. He agreed. But when I added that Storey belonged with Joe Orton and Harold Pinter as the most talented of post–World War II English playwrights, he responded with a long pause and an incredulous *"Pinter?!"*

Storey once claimed that he and Lindsay had "nothing in common." Certainly they were personal opposites, David thoughtful and deliberate, Lindsay emphatic and sometimes explosive. They also came from different backgrounds; David's father was a Yorkshire coal miner, Lindsay's a pillar of Empire, which prejudiced Lindsay in favor of the working class and left David disillusioned by it. ("Suspicious, parochial and conservative," he once called it.) And as artists, according to David, they worked from different viewpoints, Lindsay's "a total picture of what you're doing, an overall conception," his own "starting off from a detail and working up toward a complete picture."

Yet the "total" and the "complete" picture, however arrived at, became very similar in the theatre: a nation in decline. The invisible background to their collaboration is a period when Britain had the highest unemployment rate of any major European country, and an economic growth among the lowest. Factories and mines were closing down, poverty and racial tensions causing riots in northern cities. Lindsay's films make this background visible, Storey's plays subtly infer it.

When they focus on a collective event, family reunions in *In Celebration* and *The March on Russia,* the erection of a marquee for a wedding reception in *The Contractor,* prologue and epilogue to a rugby match in *The Changing Room,* a life class at an art school in *Life Class,* getting together never becomes an occasion for solidarity. Fathers and sons grow even more estranged, long-married couples protest their respectability but turn out to protest too much, hostilities disrupt the superficial friendliness of the workmen and the members of the rugby team.

Although I was unable to see *In Celebration* in London, Lindsay made a film of it in 1974, with the original cast, for Ely Landau's American Film Theatre. (He also re-created his production of *Home* for WNET's Playhouse New York—and often pointed out that, like *If . . .* and *O Lucky Man!,* the only records of his work with Storey in the theatre owed their existence to American finance.) The film of *In Celebration* is intentionally more David Storey than Lindsay Anderson, and more theatre than film. But Alan Bates, who played the leading role, felt that by discreetly paring the dialogue, and adding "a highly

Parents and alienated children in *In Celebration* (1969 stage production). Left to right: Brian Cox, Alan Bates, James Bolam, Gabrielle Daye, Constance Chapman, and Bill Owen

cinematic flair," Lindsay was able "to bridge the difference [between theatre and film] almost better than anyone I know."

After a few strongly atmospheric exteriors of Storey country, a wheel turning at the pithead of a Yorkshire mine, rows of ugly cloned houses in the gray town, children playing in the street, the film stays mostly within the setting of the play: the house of a miner and his wife on the day of their fortieth wedding anniversary, which their three sons briefly return home to celebrate with them. The actual celebration occurs offstage (like the wedding in *The Contractor* and the rugby match in *The Changing Room*), and the family reunion turns into no celebration at all. Gulfs of misunderstanding open up, a hurtful secret comes to light, but although both sides chafe at the bond of family, it proves unbreakable. Storey writes plays of situation rather than plot, and this was a situation that struck a personal chord for Lindsay, bound to his own family by ties of ambivalence.

"Here, let's have a look at you," says Mrs. Shaw to her son Steven (Brian Cox) in *In Celebration.* "You've put on a lot of weight. Or taken it off. I can't remember." She laughs, then Steven says, "I forgot myself." Classic Storey dialogue, with conversations on parallel lines that never quite meet, the speakers disconnected from themselves as well as each other. But Storey also writes poetic arias in which the soloist's personal history becomes a metaphor for the state of things. "I've had a good life," says Mr. Shaw, the miner father. "Can't ask for anything more." He could, of course, as he implies when he describes the town beyond the living-room window: "Miles of nothing, this place. Always has been, always will be. The only thing that ever came out of here was coal. And when that's gone, as it will be, there'll be even less. Row after row of empty houses. It's starting . . . I pass them on the way to work . . . Holes in the roof, doors gone, windows . . ." And the past haunts the future as he remembers: "All this was moorland a hundred years ago. Sheep. And a bit of wood . . . When they come in a thousand years and dig it up, they'll wonder what we made such a mess of it for."

Did Lindsay read Stanislavsky before starting to rehearse the original production? A diary note on "realistic theatre," dated April 4, 1969, echoes the System: "Realism is not just a matter of words. It applies to everything that is done on the stage. Every naturalistic detail should fulfill a function: if not poetic or psychological, then rhythmic." And the performances in the film, especially Alan Bates's as the ironic, rebellious Andrew, and Brian Cox as the deeply troubled Steven, are rich in these kinds of detail. Alan, who worked with Lindsay for the first time when he played the same role in the play, found that "as well as loving the author as much as the interpreter," he understood each actor as an individual:

The Changing Room. Sport theater

The Contractor. Work theater

> *He had a different approach to different people,*
> *and helped you do it* your *way. So many directors*
> *want you to do it* their *way. He also knew how*
> *to help you find confidence in your role and*
> *be able to take suggestions and criticism.*
> *When he wasn't satisfied with a scene, and*
> *wanted to try a new approach, he didn't*
> *interrupt it but cleared his throat very loudly.*
> *It made the actors look up and interrupt*
> *themselves. He also made very effective use*
> *of The Sigh—and when an actor began moving*
> *around too much, he refocused the performance*
> *simply by saying, "Steady, Joe."*

At the start of *The Contractor,* workmen are erecting a tent for a wedding reception that will occur offstage (like the rugby match and the family celebrations). They joke, complain, quarrel; glimpses of the bridal couple imply that they're not particularly well matched, and like the tent, their marriage may not be built to last; and Ewbank, the contractor and father of the bride, is revealed as prosperous but insecure, alienated from his son, confused by "the modern world." After the workmen have dismantled the tent, he stares at a few bare poles left behind, then turns to his wife. "What's to become of us, you reckon?" She smiles, shakes her head, they exit together, and the lights fade on an empty stage, loneliness, and uncertainty.

On the surface, a naturalistic play; but the ending, as so often with Storey, has a finely understated poetry. And like several of his plays, *The Contractor* demands extraordinary technical skill from actors and director. During the first two acts, at moments in the action very precisely indicated in the text, a marquee has to be set up, and a dance floor laid. During the third, everything's dismantled with the same attention to dramatic timing. Under Lindsay's direction, physical labor was transformed into beautiful and exciting spectacle, like a high-wire act or an Olympic contest. No less strikingly, his actors mastered every occupational demand of the text along with their roles. A year later, playing footballers in *The Changing Room,* they had to take off street clothes, change into rugby outfits, and strap on pads, then perform the same actions in reverse, as well as horse around while they showered.

In the plays by Storey that I managed to see, Lindsay solved the technical problems with unobtrusive skill, as well as submerging his own personality in the text. His films, like Buñuel's, are gauntlets thrown down to the audience, but Storey's plays are as understated as Chekhov's. Coincidentally, both writers made contact with a wide variety of "ordinary" people early in their careers, Chekhov as a doctor in Moscow and a country village, Storey as footballer, workman for a contractor, art student, farm laborer, and teacher. Lindsay's experience was narrower, but while making his early documentaries, he developed a rapport with working-class people, and his later work reflected it. So, at times, did his everyday life. Anthony Page recalled having lunch with Lindsay at a New York deli: "When the waitress came to take our order, he discovered she was Polish, sang her a Polish folk song he'd learned in Warsaw—and moved her to tears."

The next play, *Home,* which opened at the Court on June 17, 1970, was a departure for both writer and director. It was Storey's first step toward a more abstract, minimal style that culminated in *Stages,* the last of his plays that Lindsay directed; and it was Lindsay's first experience of working with two great actors of an older generation, John Gielgud and Ralph Richardson, in a contemporary play.

When Storey began writing *Home,* he assumed that the conversation he'd invented between "the two increasingly eccentric gentlemen" was taking place in a resort hotel. Halfway through the first scene, he realized they were inmates of a mental home, and it takes the audience the same amount of time to realize it. No doctors or nurses appear, and Jocelyn Herbert's set never suggests an institution. In a fine example of less as more, a bare stage frames an isolated world containing only one white metalwork table and two metalwork chairs. Harry (Gielgud) and Jack (Richardson), the two well-dressed gentlemen who open the play, are not obviously mad. In another departure for Storey, they belong to the upper-middle class, but he portrays them with the same authority as the working-class inmates, Marjorie, Kathleen, and Alfred.

"It is the nature of things, I believe," Jack says, "that, on the whole, one fails." He speaks for the others as well, casualties of circumstance and as Harry says (echoing Ewbank in *The Contractor*), "the modern world." They're not "dangerous," except possibly to themselves, and they may not even be clinically insane, just too estranged from reality to be capable of looking after themselves. Rejected by their families, who don't want to be responsible for them, their only "home" is an asylum—which makes *Home* a doubly ironic title for a play about the metaphorically homeless. An asylum is also a sanctuary, and where else can this class without social distinctions feel "at home" in its madness?

"Opening night. Cracklingly good. The knights are just marvelous. Malcolm [McDowell] genuinely moved," Lindsay noted in his diary. "Gavin plainly cool (nice about direction)." In fact I said that I was fascinated but mystified by the play, and wanted to see it again. (On opening night, anything except unreserved praise translates as "he didn't really like it.") When I went back a few nights later, *Home* seemed as despairingly funny and as despairingly human as *Waiting for Godot.* As it did twenty-five years later, when I watched the video production.

No one in *Home* is waiting for anything, or under the illusion there's a Godot who can "save" them; and although Beckett's outcasts are adrift in the world while Storey's are shut away from it, illusions and the lack of them prove equally confining, equally perplexing. "Get nothing if you don't try, girl. Get nothing if you do, either," Kathleen tells Marjorie. "This little island," Jack says to Harry. "Shan't see its like," Harry says to Jack. "The sun has set." Then, as they gaze at clouds in the sky, Jack: "Shadows." Harry (tears forming in his eyes for no reason at all, except his whole life): "Yes." Jack: "Another day." Harry: "Ah, yes."

As Kathleen and Marjorie, Lindsay cast two sublime character actresses: Mona Washbourne, already part of his stock company, and Dandy Nichols, whom he would use again in *O Lucky Man!* and *Britannia Hospital.* Working with Gielgud and Richardson, he fused two traditions, the old guard of the Old Vic and the avant-garde of the Royal Court. Probably no one else could have brought it off. "Conservatism was the flip side of Lindsay the rebel—and for a rebel, conservatism becomes an act of rebellion. And Lindsay was alone in his generation," Helen Mirren realized when he directed her scenes with Richardson in *O Lucky Man!,* "in venerating and truly loving the older generation of actors."

"I haven't the slightest idea what I'm doing, I don't understand a word of it, I'm so frightened they [the audience] will get terribly bored with me sitting here saying Oh yes, Oh yes." Lindsay's diary recorded this outburst from Gielgud during the first week of rehearsal. And Storey, who was present at many rehearsals, recalled a dialogue that might have come from the play itself. Gielgud: "It isn't possible for an actor to sit on a stage without moving for twenty-five minutes." Lindsay: "Move, in that case, if you feel like it." Gielgud: "It's strange, but once sitting here, I don't feel I want to move." Lindsay: "In that case, don't." Gielgud: "I shan't."

Richardson had "much more of a method of approach, however eccentric or misguided," according to Lindsay, and his diary makes a telling comparison:

> *John can produce the most sensitive, apparently deep vibrations, with apparently a minimum of* thought. *Likewise he is weak at concretely imagining—creating for us the clouds, the church in the distance, the dust on the table— or rather not weak (since he can do it brilliantly, magnetically) but just* negligent. *Such is his relationship, I suppose, with the world outside him. Ralph's a brilliantly contrasting talent. He thinks*

> *a great deal, but often tortuously, creating and*
> *sticking to an idea which is eccentric and quite*
> *wrong.*

When they acted together, Lindsay also noted, "each found it difficult to look at the actor he's playing with. It's a solidarity lyricism." (But ideal for the play.) In life, he found, their relationship had an element of distance, "friendly and touching and somehow formal," with Richardson amused by the fact that "Gielgud could never bear to talk of anything that doesn't spring from or impinge on the Profession," and confiding to Lindsay: "Sometimes I talk about diesel engines, just to see the horrified look in his eyes." But Lindsay always enjoyed Gielgud's "charming gossip about Peggy [Ashcroft], Edith [Evans] etc. Strange to realize that in spite of all the work together throughout the years, the relationships of these people are friendly rather than close":

> *"I was disappointed in Peggy's Ranevskaya and*
> *Arkadina," says John blithely. "She seems to*
> *have lost her way. Of course she's always had*
> *a very hectic sex life, and now that's over,*

Rehearsing *Home:* Ralph Richardson, Dandy Nichols, Warren Clarke, John Gielgud, and Mona Washbourne

I expect she misses it. She doesn't enjoy
being successful very much—spending money
on dresses and getting her hair done."

Sometimes Gielgud irritated Richardson with his "itchy desire to change moves for no very good reason," and sometimes Richardson's refusal to consider changing a move irritated Lindsay. On one occasion he started to lecture Richardson, who interrupted him: "I don't like being addressed like a schoolboy," the actor said in his most precise, deliberate manner. "I don't like this fucking headmaster act." Then he walked offstage, leaving Lindsay devastated, almost in tears. Storey went to look for Richardson, and found him hiding in the wings. "Did I go too far?" he asked. "Do you think I shouldn't have done that?"

They reconciled, of course, and Lindsay became friends with both knights for life. "Enormously sympathetic and exciting," was Gielgud's verdict on the experience of *Home.* "You have introduced me and have helped me in every step that we have taken in this venture—thank you," Richardson wrote Lindsay. "Affection to you for EVER."

Home transferred to the West End in late July, and after the opening Lindsay and Jocelyn Herbert went to stay at Tony Richardson's estate in the South of France. "Peculiar atmosphere," Lindsay reported to his diary. "Completely homosexual in a charming, unforced, well-mannered way. Tony is very democratic. The cook and major domo join other guests at meals." The other guests at Le Nid du Duc were "a chunky, blond American ex-marine, another American, solidly built but campy," and a French actor: "I am touched like a schoolgirl by handsome young boyish virility."

Compared to his own way of living at Greencroft Gardens, Lindsay found "the life that Tony has constructed for himself is so extraordinary—fantastic, spending *certainly* on a millionaire's level: the house in London—apartments in Paris and Rome—the simple paradise of Nid du Duc." Yet Tony was so "casual" about it that "you could almost forget how much it cost, the swimming pool that has to be continuously heated, the champagne that is opened every morning, the cars (a new Mercedes just delivered), the total hospitality of open house."

Back in London, he found that the success of *Home,* and the news that it would move to Broadway in December, was responsible for a new wave of improbable offers from Hollywood. "At Columbia," he wrote me, "Peter Guber wants me to do a picture about corruption in the American unions. Miles away from me, though, and not even a script or original to start from. How strange these people are." Jon Voigt's agent called him about a movie of *The Leatherstocking Tales,* "but I'm a bit scared about James Fenimore Cooper's deeply conservative race feelings." Arthur Miller's agent sent him the playwright's adaptation of *After the Fall,* "but I never got through the script. It was one of those *very* heavy ones." He wasn't surprised, having met Miller a year earlier at a party given by Ken Tynan: "Let's face it, a bore. Says some quite interesting things but at such length one can't be bothered to listen."

Far more appealing was the idea of making a documentary about Alan Price, a young composer-singer-bandleader who had composed the effective incidental music for *Home.* Attracted to his talent and looks, and his northerner's directness, Lindsay accompanied Price and his band on a tour, a romantic experience in the company of "the only true vagabonds left. Out of their fast cars, or their minibuses, they lumber their cases through pokey back doors, along passages into dressingrooms where they change, tune up, get ready." And at a recording session he noted "the rapt, sensuous commitment of his [Price's] whole self, body and mind, as the music plays back and he jigs to its rhythm."

Unfortunately, copyright difficulties over some of the songs forced Lindsay to abandon the project, and in November he left for New York, with an idea of "crossing the U.S.A. by Greyhound bus" after restaging *Home:* "I do think Hollywood is a fantasy—since I am pretty sure I will find the dynamic there (even at its least bullshitty) too naive. But it might reconcile me to Britain."

Dandy Nichols, committed to a TV series, had to leave the Broadway production after a month, and Jessica Tandy replaced her. "Not really a natural for the part," according to Lindsay's diary. "Humor, I'd say, is not her strong point." But although he thought "she did pretty well" at her first performance, "Ralph [Richardson] looked at me stonily and whispered into my ear, 'It's like drinking very thin, *tinned* soup.' "

Filming the production for WNET before Dandy Nichols left it, then rehearsing Tandy, had prolonged Lindsay's New York stay, and he abandoned the idea of a trip to Hollywood. Instead, he began going to Hollywood movies: *Where's Poppa*, "ponderous and unfunny," *Catch-22*, *Five Easy Pieces* (no comment on these), and Paul Morrissey's *Trash*, "by far the most impressive." On TV, he responded to Shirley Temple's "astonishing charm" in *Little Miss Marker:* "In those early pictures she enjoyed showing off, and it was fun to see her doing it before professionalism took over." *Man's Castle* made him reflect on "the innocent poetry movies had then (about 1933, I think), and with a director like [Frank] Borzage, the genuine survival of silent film imagery." A long way from innocent poetry was a screening of *Hollywood Blue*, clips from porno movies allegedly featuring various stars early in their careers: "More repugnant than exciting, although the encounter of marine and sailor, with appearances attributed to Burt Lancaster and/or Chuck Connors, is wistfully attractive."

At the screening Lindsay met "Kate Hepburn's hairdresser," who proved as lively a gossip as Gielgud:

> He used to do Constance Bennett's hair and every hair had to be individually dyed. When she went into **Mame**, *and looked* 100 *years old, she had to be followed everywhere with a pink spot, and* 13 *spotmen were fired for losing her. Finally she decided to have her face lifted in Switzerland. came back looking radiantly youthful, was on all the talk shows and a year later dropped dead at a dinner party.*

Another item of gossip from the hairdresser was colored a lighter shade of Hollywood Blue:

> *Janet Gaynor and Margaret Lindsay were discovered in some passionate embrace on Santa Monica beach. The studio got it hushed up, but told them they'd both have to get married. Janet Gaynor married Adrian and even managed to get pregnant and nearly*

lost the baby—and when they told Adrian he said,
"Oh, don't tell me I have to go through all that
again." But the baby lived after all.

While Lindsay was in New York, Malcolm McDowell and David Sherwin started to collaborate on a screenplay called *Coffee Man.* The original idea came from Malcolm, who'd worked as a coffee salesman in the north of England after leaving school. Back in London, Lindsay read the first twenty pages: "Not very good, is it? Too cozy, like an Ealing comedy. But keep going, and *make it more epic."*

A few weeks and discussions later, Malcolm started filming *A Clockwork Orange* and had no time to spare on *Coffee Man.* But Lindsay had begun to feel personally involved with the project, and decided to continue working on it with David Sherwin. Exactly the development Malcolm had hoped for: "I suggested *Coffee Man* chiefly to get Lindsay to make another film with me. And I knew he needed to feel an idea growing up around him before he could feel really confident about working on it." But as Lindsay didn't want to approach a studio or distributor for financing until the script was complete, he and Malcolm paid Sherwin "enough money to live on" for the duration.

Writer-director collaboration continued as it had begun on *If . . .* So did their codependency. Lindsay's diary records Sherwin's ongoing domestic crises, "his tonsillitis and bronchitis; his cups of black coffee laced with Guinness left around the flat," as well as the need, on several occasions, to give him "a fairly intensive blasting." And once again the film's definitive title came about by chance. "The hero's lucky, isn't he? Everything he touches somehow brings him luck," Malcolm said to Sherwin one day, a remark that gave both of them the same idea at the same time. As Lindsay recalled later: "Malcolm came to me, very excitedly, and said, 'Your new film is going to be called *Lucky Man.'* I thought for a moment and then said, '*O Lucky Man!*' "

PART THREE

The Middle Years

~ Lindsay on Lindsay ~

If you want a continuity of theme, I think this is one: a mistrust of institutions and an anarchistic belief in the importance of the individual to make his or her decisions about life—rather than simply to accept tradition and the institutional philosophy.

8

The first twenty pages of *Coffee Man* were based on Malcolm's own experiences, first as an apprentice salesman, then on the road, where the hero has a brief sexual episode with a landlady, is invited to a party at which local city officials and businessmen watch blue movies, and gets arrested as a spy after stopping his car near a secret government research station. To make these early scenes (and the rest of the film) "more epic," Lindsay recommended Sherwin to think *Pilgrim's Progress, Candide,* and Kafka's *Amerika,* with the protagonist "journeying through a lot of adventures and encountering a lot of characters. It's a form which hasn't been attempted very much recently—middle-class artists lack the confidence for it."

The protagonist himself, Lindsay suggested, should be a naive innocent who never questions the success-worship of the world he was born into. But the more he reaches for success, the more he's corrupted without realizing it—until he lands in jail. Although he comes out sincerely reformed, he proves no more successful in his naive attempts to lead the Good Life. So the first part of the film would satirize corruption in the form of big business, politics, the law, the police, and whatever else came to mind; and the second part would puncture do-goodism, from sentimental liberals to religious fanatics. How would it end? As yet Lindsay had no idea, and trusted that instinct would lead him, like the protagonist, to some kind of resolution.

Progress on the script was slow, partly because, as Lindsay noted on August 7, 1971, "a different style was necessary when working on this material than on *If*—if only because that film was based on a world we both knew intimately, and this has all to be created." And partly because of David Sherwin, increasingly disoriented as he continued to

193

shuttle between wife and girlfriend. For a while, Lindsay pressured him successfully: "He's a writer who absolutely needs to be bullied, and I find that is a stimulus for me to come up with ideas." But later that month David's girlfriend left him for her previous boyfriend in Australia, his wife left him for *her* previous boyfriend, and he became temporarily blocked. "I still respect David's intuition greatly—but his invention is lagging," Lindsay noted on August 24. "For the moment, anyway, he's a dead duck. The script is even more of a shambles, a disappointing nothing, than I had expected."

Two weeks later, Sherwin's girlfriend promised to return as soon as her boyfriend promised not to commit suicide if she did. It unblocked him, at least temporarily. Meanwhile Lindsay had come up with an idea that radically affected the movie as a whole. He decided to use songs to comment on the story at various moments, chose Alan Price to compose and record them, and took Sherwin to meet with him in the north of England, where the band was on tour. They all drove to a concert in the band's minibus, and the journey gave Lindsay another idea. As well as creating the musical commentary, Price would appear in the film as a character that the hero encountered on the road.

The idea, of course, was consciously Brechtian. But Lindsay only realized later that Brecht was in his subconscious as well, and the role he conceived for Price had its origins in the Street Singer of *The Threepenny Opera*. Each song was written after Lindsay explained where he planned to use it in the script, and the idea he wanted it to reflect. Then, according to his notes on their collaboration, he asked Price to interpret the idea "in terms of his own feelings and attitudes, which were sufficiently different from mine to be creative, and sufficiently the same for it to work."

For Lindsay, in fact, Price became a Kurt Weill who wrote his own cheerfully disillusioned, streetwise-poetic lyrics. But his music was never imitative, only so apt that *O Lucky Man!* becomes as unimaginable without it as *The Threepenny Opera* without Weill. Like one of his best songs, "Everyone's Goin' Through Changes," the tone of Price's music goes through its own dramatic changes—from pop to pastoral, folk to reworked hymn tune, jazz to ballad—as it reflects the changing tones of Mick's adventures.

A first-draft script of *O Lucky Man!* was completed by October 10. "Full of holes," Lindsay commented in his diary, but cabled Sherwin's ex-girlfriend, still in Australia, that it was "BRILLIANT STOP DAVID LOVES YOU AND NEEDS YOU PLEASE RETURN." Then he suspended further work on the project to start rehearsing David Storey's *The Changing Room.* Play and production opened at the Royal Court on November 9 to excellent reviews, and transferred to the West End, where business was only fair at first, Lindsay wrote me, "then picked up after Prince Charles came to see it."

Ten days after receiving Lindsay's cable, Sherwin's ex-girlfriend had come back to him, but on Christmas Eve she decided to leave him again. He made a drunken suicide attempt with an overdose of sleeping pills, and was rushed to hospital. Diagnosed as manic depressive, he was prescribed lithium and remained under psychiatric care for a week. "The lack of a creative writing collaborator" caused Lindsay to reflect on "the enormous strain" of trying to combine two worlds, " 'personal' (auteur if you like) cinema, and popular, commercially viable entertainment":

> *Anglo-American cinema is essentially organized for the production of pre-planned narrative cinema, and anyone who takes on the risk of personal, poetic, changing and developing film-making, exposes himself to enormous problems. This is true of Kubrick and Schlesinger and even Peckinpah as well as myself.*

It was also true of Nick Ray, of course. In 1978 Jim Jarmusch was a film student at New York University, where Nick conducted a workshop. They became friends, and Jarmusch later recalled that he learned "more from Nick's character than about the specifics of directing, or even anything to do with film." He also learned "what kind of backbone it takes to stand up to all the confusing problems in film production." It influenced Jarmusch's decision to work outside the mainstream; and fortunately, unlike Nick or Lindsay, he wanted to make the kind of films that required only very modest financing.

In spite of misgivings about the first draft of *O Lucky Man!*, Lindsay had shown it to actor-producer Michael Medwin. Medwin liked it well enough to offer to coproduce the movie, and suggested they submit the project to Warner Brothers. Warners agreed to finance it, but on the plane to New York to clinch the deal, Lindsay confided to his diary: "What an ordeal lies before me, what an orgy of posturing and play acting. It really does make the whole business of film-making repugnant." In the event, he agreed to Warners' budget ($1,500,000) and financial terms (10 percent of the gross up to $350,000, followed by a cutoff at $15,000,000 until the movie paid for itself), but "Warners will not accept the idea of taking my name off the picture in the event of distributors finally making cuts of which I disapprove."

Warners' cutoff figure of $15,000,000 "until the picture paid for itself" was remarkably high, and its budget remarkably low for a movie estimated to run at least two and a half hours (the reason why Lindsay feared distributors' cuts). To relieve the strain of trying to combine two worlds, he planned to surround himself with collaborators from *If. . . ,* Jocelyn Herbert, David Gladwell, and Miroslav Ondriček. But to persuade the Czech government to allow Mirek to leave the country, he had to fly to Prague and plead his case to the bureaucrat in charge of exit permits. He was successful, although the bureaucrat kept him waiting around for days; and back in London on January 4, 1972, he found himself under additional pressure. Two days earlier, Mum had developed severe stomach pains and entered a London hospital for tests. Diagnosis: gallstones and hepatitis.

From a diary entry for January 5, 1972: "I visit Mum at King Edward VII [hospital]. She seems quite philosophic, though scared. I fight my fatalism, wish there were prayers to say. We watch a bad TV film with Robert Wagner, devastatingly attractive." But although he worried that Mum looked suddenly much older, and for the first time weak and frail, she survived the operation for removal of her gallbladder fairly well: "Mum looks not too bad, but she has little interest in the outside world. 'I seem to have forgotten who I am.' "

At the end of January, Lindsay began goading Sherwin, reunited (temporarily, at least) with his wife, to plug various holes in the script: "The only way we can work is to talk, for him to write, to talk again, to write again, for me to rewrite." And bullying his writer stimulated Lindsay to come up with another radical idea. "I said to David Sherwin one day, 'Graham Crowden could play this part.' And David said, 'No, we already decided he's going to play another character.' And I said, 'Well, he can play both parts.' "

Like his decision to shoot the chapel scenes of *If . . .* in black and white, it came on the spur of the moment. Then he realized: "Each of our characters might have been somebody else, if his luck had been different." And with Graham Crowden cast as two different research scientists, one deranged by ambition and the other by failure, the final "epic" idea fell into place beside *Pilgrim's Progress/Candide/Amerika* and *The Threepenny Opera.* Other actors given dual or triple roles included Ralph Richardson, eccentric resident of a provincial hotel and supremely unscrupulous multimillionaire; Rachel Roberts, public relations manager of the coffee factory, mistress of a black dictator, and suicidal woman living in a London tenement (a disturbingly true performance if you see *O Lucky Man!* again today); and Mona Washbourne, her neighbor in the tenement as well as chief nurse at Dr. Millar's clinic and dominatrix to a judge.

During the casting process, Lindsay wondered if his own life might have taken a different turn, and decided it was impossible. When an agent submitted a photograph of a handsome young actor for a small part, he asked his diary: "Were I honest and courageous, would I arrange to meet the boy? Would I attempt to seduce him? Such a thing is somehow just not conceivable in terms of what I am, in terms of what I (apparently inevitably) have become."

The only important role that Lindsay found difficult to cast was Patricia, the multimillionaire's daughter. He hesitated between Fiona Lewis (from Polanski's *The Fearless Vampire Killers*) and Helen Mirren (from Michael Powell's *The Age of Consent*), and finally decided that Lewis would be "more authentically upper class." According to Helen Mirren, "he also thought I was too fat." Then, as Malcolm McDowell remembered, "Lindsay fired Fiona after the first few days of working with her, offered the part to Vanessa Redgrave, who rightly thought she was wrong for it, and cast Helen, whom I'd favored from the start."

On March 17, three days before the first day of shooting, Mum became the latest occupant of the spare room at Greencroft Gardens. Before she arrived, Lindsay set about cleaning the kitchen and bathroom, and was tackling the fireplace in Mum's room when the studio driver arrived:

> *Thinks: at 48, turning 49, this leading British*
> *director on his knees at a dirty grate with a*
> *plastic bucket and detergent. Possibly from the*

*outside this looks admirably humble and
determinedly individual. To me it feels just a
desperate rearguard action. Nobody realizes what
a mess of loneliness and inadequacy I am inside.*

But as usual he didn't want anybody to realize it, especially when
about to undertake the most ambitious project of his career.

O Lucky Man! opens with a pre-credits intertitle, "ONCE UPON A TIME,"
accompanied by the whir of a silent movie projector, and followed by a
sepia-tinted silent movie sequence that parodies Eisenstein-style montage. Watched by brutish-looking colonial guards, Mexican peasants
pick beans on a coffee plantation, and one of them (Malcolm McDowell
in brownface) is caught stealing a few beans. "UNLUCKY!" the next
intertitle comments, and "JUSTICE" precedes a shot of a machete chop-
ping off his hands. An abrupt cut to "NOW," then to a recording studio,
where the credits begin as Alan Price and his band perform the title
song, and in a briefly held shot, Lindsay listens to it: "If you have a

O Lucky Man! Lindsay (second from left) and Alan Price (right, singing
title song) in the recording studio scene

O Lucky Man! Mysterious hotel resident (Ralph Richardson) gives
Mick Travis (Malcolm McDowell) his lucky gold suit

friend on whom you think you can rely / You are a lucky man! / If you've found the reason to live on and not to die / You are a lucky man!"

The Singing Lesson established a dialectic between the actual and the filmed world with its opening title chalked on a studio slate. *O Lucky Man!* takes the idea a stage further. Price is at once a part of the action and apart from the action, and as the story develops, his songs imply a knowledge of life that the hero spends the movie searching for. In the same way, the opening scene wants us to know that we're watching a movie, but a movie whose world is as real as our own.

Like the schoolboy from *If . . .* , the hero of *O Lucky Man!* is called Mick Travis, and ten years later Mick Travis reappears as a successful photojournalist in *Britannia Hospital.* But he's not the same person in all three films. The name is a metaphor for a prototypical hero: adolescent rebel in a "strange sub-world," naive young man out in the real world, not-so-naive-or-young man corrupted by success. And in *O Lucky Man!*, as in *If. . .* , reality is negotiable. Early in the film, when Mick turns on his car radio, he characteristically pays no attention to a program that (improbably) follows the weather forecast and the news: a talk on Zen Buddhism and its teaching of sudden, irrational enlightenment, the unexpected route to discovering one's true nature and the nature of the world.

Just how unexpected Mick's route will be is foreshadowed at a hotel where he spends the night. A mysterious, eccentric resident gives him a "lucky" suit made of gold thread, then says: "Try not to die like a dog." But Mick almost does exactly that after he's arrested (wearing his gold suit) outside the government research station, and interrogated by two icy young bureaucrats while they sip afternoon tea. Tortured into making a "confession," although his accusers refuse to say what offense he's committed, Mick is rescued—for the time being—by a violent explosion at the station. It hurtles him down a steep, blasted hillside to a

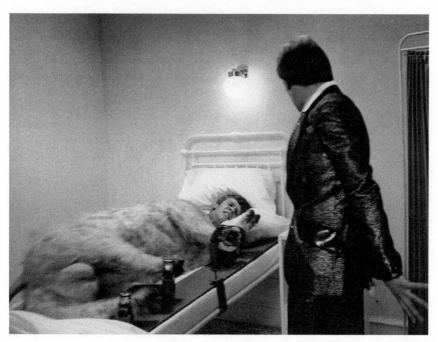

O Lucky Man! Mick Travis discovers the mad doctor's victim

pastoral valley where a harvest festival's in progress at a church. "No, that's God's food," a pregnant woman says when she surprises Mick hungrily eyeing the vegetables, and breastfeeds him instead.

"Go south—there's nothing in the north for a boy like you," the woman advises Mick (the north of England is evidently still the urban wasteland of *The White Bus*). Then she adds: "The children will show you the way." A momentary lapse into heavy-handedness, the line strains for a mythical element that the images convey beautifully on their own. Two children lead Mick across sunlit fields and through a shadowy forest to an ugly, busy highway—where they leave him to his next misadventure. A Rolls-Royce pulls up, he happily but unwisely accepts the offer of a ride, is taken to a medical clinic, and signs up as a paid guinea pig for a medical scientist's latest "experiment."

"Both Lindsay and myself were obsessed with so-called scientific advances and kept newspaper cuttings about them," David Sherwin remembered, an obsession that led them to create an episode alarmingly prophetic of the age of cloning and genetic technology. Dr. Millar believes that the DNA of the dinosaur, the only species to have survived for more than a hundred million years, is the key to human longevity. But the result of his "experiment" is a dazed, whimpering young man whose head has been grafted onto the body of a large, vaguely piglike quadruped. Mick catches a glimpse of the creature, manages to escape from the clinic, and lands back on the highway, where the actual and the filmed world coincide. When Mick thumbs another ride, he strikes lucky again. The minibus that stops for him is carrying Alan Price and his band back to London after their tour of the north.

Also in the minibus is Patricia (Helen Mirren), rich, High Bohemian, and a Buddhist, who's "studying" the band. She has an affair with Mick but soon drops him, more interested in amusing herself than in committing herself, and dismissing his success-worship as "old-fashioned." But Mick manages to gain a foothold in the world of the superrich as personal assistant to Patricia's multimillionaire father, a man she describes as "absolutely ruthless." Mick discounts her warning, of course, believes he's made it at last, and becomes the fall guy in an investment scam. In exchange for the right to build resort hotels (with forced native labor) along the coast of an undeveloped African country, the Western tycoon agrees to supply its black dictator with napalm (code name, "honey") to liquidate a rebel army in the interior. The scene is as chillingly (and topically) funny as the episode of Dr. Millar's clinic, but this time Mick's luck turns again. As Alan Price sings "Don't forget, look over your shoulder / 'Cos there's always someone coming after you," he's arrested for smuggling chemical weapons out of Britain.

"Society is based on good faith," the self-righteous judge reminds Mick before sentencing him. "I only tried to do my best," Mick protests. The judge gives him an accusing look: *"And you failed!"* Failure, he implies, is Mick's real crime, and condemns him to five years in jail. The law gets a further satirical whipping when the judge returns to his chambers, strips off gown (but not wig), and lies down to be flagellated by his clerk. Another authority figure, the prison governor, is dealt with more leniently. Five years later, he gives Mick an ambiguously fond farewell hug, then asks: "Did anyone ever tell you you have eyes like Steve McQueen?"

Determined to be "good," Mick gets no encouragement from a Salvation Army major, who rejects his modest gift of money as a guilt offering from a sinner. He also fails to convince a desperate mother of two children living in a tenement slum not to commit suicide; encounters Patricia and one of her boyfriends, the duke of Belminster, now down on *their* luck as they huddle among a group of derelict meth drinkers; endures some rough handling by a policeman; and when a formidably cheerful soup-kitchen lady delegates Mick to feed a group of the homeless, he learns that the poor can be just as mean as the rich. Mistaking Mick's nervous politeness for superiority, they pelt him with stones and throw him into a garbage dump. Finally, reduced to point zero, he wanders into an open audition for the star role in a movie called *O Lucky Man!*

As well as completing the circle of dialectic between the actual and the filmed world, the end of Mick's story aims to show him arriving at the beginning of wisdom. The movie director, played by Lindsay, tells him to smile. "What's there to smile at? I can't smile without a reason," Mick objects. Lindsay's answer is to hit him over the head with the script. A blow that stuns him at first, then literally knocks some sense into him. In a moment of Zen-like revelation, Mick gives a broad smile—and there's a quick cut to all the characters of *O Lucky Man!* dancing together, as if they're at an end-of-shooting party, with bal-

O Lucky Man! Judge (Anthony Nicholls) and the dominatrix (Mona Washbourne)

loons floating above Mick in his lucky gold suit and Alan Price singing the title song again.

"This so-called world is like a juggler's act or a picture show. To be happy, look at it that way." Like the Zen koan, the idea behind the final scene of *O Lucky Man!* is basically very simple, and Alan Price echoes it ironically when he sings: "Someone's got to win in the human race / If it isn't you then it has to be me. / So smile while you're making it / Laugh while you're taking it / Even though you're faking it / Nobody's gonna know." But in the realization of the scene, something went wrong. Mainly because Lindsay was the only actor in the film who needed stronger direction.

Eleanor Fazan, who choreographed the dance and appears as Lindsay's assistant at the audition, remembers him as "very nervous" about playing himself: "I tried to relax him, told him just to concentrate on the moment with Malcolm—but he remained tense." Thirty years earlier, Lindsay had noted that by trying too hard to disguise his anxieties, he created the impression of standoffishness and conceit. In *O Lucky Man!* the same effort makes him appear arrogant instead of friendly, cold instead of genial, and negates the surprise when he clouts Mick over the head. (You'd expect no less, and probably more, if you dared to argue with such an imperious personage.) So the scene isn't funny or surprising or outrageous enough as the climax of an almost continuously funny or surprising or outrageous movie.

Another, less obvious problem: *O Lucky Man!*, unlike *If . . . ,* was emphatically not "the happiest time of Lindsay's life." Soon after shooting began, Michael Medwin recalled, it became clear that "the film was under-prepared. There were an enormous number of locations, from London and the south of England through the north to the Scottish border. At one point production actually had to close down for a week's hiatus. Lindsay realized he'd embarked on a long and arduous journey, and was often extremely peppery."

In his diary notes on the production, Lindsay peppers cameraman Mirek with complaints: "He never looks at the script [and] has no instinct for what we are doing. He's continually just off the beam *dramatically*—obsessed by 'composition' and 'photographic quality.' " During the last month of shooting, Mirek was on Valium, and throughout it Sherwin was "on 4 Equanil and 2 something else." On the bottle as well, as Malcolm remembered: "Some of the scenes he was supposed to have rewritten were only sketched. Lindsay fleshed them out, dictating to a secretary, with some assist from me." Also from David Storey: "Lindsay appealed to me for help several times."

With his cinematographer, and especially his writer, Lindsay had reason to be peppery. The need for constant repairs to the script added to the pressures of underpreparation and a very tight budget. But for a very minor reason (disappointment with a location she'd chosen), Lindsay's production designer became his chief target. Michael Medwin: "On every film Lindsay had to have a whipping boy. On this one it was Jocelyn Herbert. At one point he was so rude to her that she walked off the picture." Malcolm: "To get her back, I had to persuade Lindsay to apologize. And it took some persuading." Jocelyn: "I came to realize that Lindsay treated all his favorites that way. Abuse was a kind of affection." David Storey: "Lindsay was always testing the love of others, and one time or another they failed the test. But I thought Lindsay's test of Jocelyn really excessive, and wrote him a letter about it. A coolness developed for a while, then we mended fences."

An undated diary note, made after a day's location work in the south of England, shows Lindsay equally unsparing with himself: "The country location reminded me of Camberley, home, family kindness, and a childhood I was somehow never able to enjoy. And now 50, and alone, and no-one to love, and every day an increasing impatience and intolerance with those who surround me." Another negative factor was the diet he didn't begin to correct until too many years later. After a day of location work in London, another undated note records that he's grown "disgustingly fat," and another that he woke up with a queasy stomach, "having consumed 3 slices of brown bread, 2 slices of smoked salmon, 1 tin of stewed steak, 1 tin of carrots, 2 digestive biscuits, glasses of wine and a cup of tea while watching TV the previous night."

Part of the "enormous" strain of film production is that schedule and budget commit a director to be on his best form every working day. When fatigue or anxiety show through, he can seldom afford, unlike a writer, composer, or painter, to retake the day's work. And during the last two weeks of shooting, Lindsay was battling creative fatigue: "The sheer *mass* of it. And the isolation. As Jocelyn said last night, 'If you died tonight, this film could never be finished.' " Less exhausted, would Lindsay have been more consistently inventive in directing the still underwritten last thirty minutes of the movie? And would his own performance in the final scene have been more relaxed?

In the first case, very likely. The final scene was still less than a sketch when Lindsay heard the words and music ("Around and round / and round and round and round we go / Round the world in circles turning / earning what we can / While others dance away") that Alan Price wrote for it. Lindsay said later that it gave him "the whole idea at the end," and it also influenced Malcolm's approach to the dance, "where my character is reaching for the balloons and is understood to be forever reaching up for something in life. That just happened because of the music." But there wasn't enough time for "the whole idea" to take coherent shape, and the dance looks hastily shot.

As for Lindsay's performance: his scene with John Gielgud in *Chariots of Fire* (1981), where they played a couple of ultraconservative anti-Semitic Oxford dons, is assured and camera-comfortable. But although it was shot under less strained circumstances, Lindsay may also have been released by not playing himself.

Its uneven last thirty minutes make *O Lucky Man!* a less perfectly real-
ized movie than *If . . . ,* but its rewards are in some ways greater. Only
Michael Powell and Emeric Pressburger, in their brilliant *The Life and
Death of Colonel Blimp* (1943), had previously attempted a film about
Britain on such a panoramic scale. But its focus was narrower, upper-
and middle-class characters sharply defined, working-class characters
strictly background figures. Still immediate and contemporary in style,
Colonel Blimp has become a gorgeous period piece in its social attitudes.
By contrast, the world of *O Lucky Man!* is still very much with us, the
cult of success, the search for longevity, corrupt big business and
police, the various and secret corridors of power, the destitute and
homeless—whose plight, according to several British reviewers at the
time, the movie "greatly exaggerated."

"Some comedy!" Lindsay wrote me in March 1973, after approving the
final cut, which ran just under three hours. "A strange and individual
monument, less romantic than anything I've done before. I really
would love to know what you think of it. Karel [Reisz] thinks my cutting style is too conventional." .

By then, of course, the rapid post-*Breathless* editing style had
become fashionable, and the deliberately paced *O Lucky Man!* struck not
a few people as conventional or old-fashioned. Today, the post-*Breathless*
style has mutated to the frantic post-MTV style, yesterday's innovation
to a cliché, and *O Lucky Man!* seems defiantly personal and reflective.
"Straightforward, rather middle-distance," Lindsay described its style in
a letter to me, "and no doubt influenced by poor old Brecht's ideas of
influencing an audience, trying to make them think, instead of forcibly
absorbing them."

In this story of a search, during which the audience has no idea
what the hero will find along the way or at the end of it, the characters
he meets provide most of the surprises. Richly varied, from the highest
to the lowest walks of life, they are "real but not realistic," as Malcolm
McDowell pointed out. "Lindsay demands a certain kind of playing
which is very clear and very simple—but heightened in a way that says,
'We're making a movie.' "

O Lucky Man! Mick Travis and Patricia, the multimillionaire's daughter (Helen Mirren)

The challenge for Malcolm as Mick Travis in *O Lucky Man!*, which the actor solved brilliantly, was to find enough variations on the single theme of innocence. He found them, Lindsay noted, "in a very stylish performance, though with the kind of style that hardly shows." At first he worried that "Malcolm resists 'talking about'—which may be a strength but can also be a weakness in rejecting the idea of *designing* a performance." But he soon realized that Malcolm had his own way of designing it, and left him alone, "except when he fell back on mere behavior. When he did, it never rang true, and we had to stop and start again."

The challenge of Patricia was how to complete an incompletely written character. Although David Sherwin had written several drafts of Helen Mirren's first important scene (drinking champagne with Mick on the rooftop of a London house), "it was still a difficult scene and seemed to go off in too many directions," she remembered. "But Lindsay was enormously patient with me. He made a few simple suggestions while feeding me champagne, and got me quite drunk. I thought I was terrible. But it worked."

This "different approach to different people," as Alan Bates described it, worked with more than fifty actors, many in dual or triple roles, differentiating their characters with a minimum of external disguise, but so clearly that at first you may not recognize Graham Crowden transformed from egomaniac Dr. Millar to desperate Professor Stewart, or Philip Stone, from sinister bureaucrat to Salvation Army major.

Leading, supporting, and cameo, every performance has the physical expressiveness of silent-movie acting at its best (Chaplin, Garbo, Louise Brooks, Lillian Gish, Lon Chaney, Charles Laughton in *Piccadilly,* ZaSu Pitts in *Greed*). However much larger than life, no character is less than recognizably human. And the film itself reinvents a traditional genre. Its sense of adventure, combined with disrespect for the established order, makes *O Lucky Man!* the ultimate road movie.

A few days after Lindsay viewed his final cut, Mum's stomach pains recurred and she went back into hospital for tests. Diagnosis: colon cancer. A week later, on March 20, she died. In her will she left Lindsay and Murray around $15,000 each, and bequeathed Fuchsia Cottage to Lindsay. He never informed me of his mother's death, which I first heard about from our mutual friend Daphne Hunter on my next visit to London. As Eleanor Fazan commented: "A veil was always drawn over certain aspects of Lindsay's life. He never talked about his childhood or his family. Or, of course, about his deepest emotional experiences."

And Mum's death was certainly one of them. Lindsay became very attached to Fuchsia Cottage, often spent weekends there alone, and kept everything exactly as it had been before Mrs. Sleigh died. A typical contradiction in someone whose diary was so full of angry complaints about her.

"Has life still any surprises to hold?" Lindsay wondered when his film was chosen as the official British entry at the Cannes Festival in May. "Will *O Lucky Man!* sweep me out into the world? O FANTASIES." According to Michael Medwin, "it was not too well received, in spite of Lindsay's drumbeating and complaints about Warners' inept publicity." The ineptness that particularly enraged him was a beach party for several hundred people, at which the head of publicity announced that

Alan Price would perform songs from the film, then discovered that his department had forgotten to order a microphone.

Still rankled when he arrived for the showing of *O Lucky Man!* that evening, Lindsay found his entrance to the Palais blocked by a starlet posturing for the paparazzi. He accused her of "degrading" the festival, gave her a slap on the buttocks, and loudly ordered her to "either get out of the way or go inside and see the film." And before returning to London, he sent me a peppery postcard that dismissed Pasolini's *Canterbury Tales* as "amateurish balderdash," and signed off with a jab at Bertolucci: "Am rather enjoying not seeing *Last Tango in Paris.*"

In Sydney, at a dinner party, Patrick White called *O Lucky Man!* "a work of genius." In London, the reviews were about evenly divided between positive and negative, and in New York they were mainly enthusiastic. For the American release, Warners decided to trim twenty minutes from Mick's attempts to lead the Good Life, including the Salvation Army scene and the tenement suicide of Mrs. Richards, but Lindsay managed to get the cuts restored for the New York run, although not for general distribution. He also responded firmly to complaints from British reviewers that *O Lucky Man!* was cynical and reactionary in depicting poor people as vicious. "The poor were not beastly to their fellow-men only because they're poor," he told David Robinson, film critic of *The Times.* "They're beastly to them because they're human beings." But the idea of "man's inhumanity to man," he added, "is something that socialists consider reactionary, and I expect my progressive friends to attack me."

In the same interview, Lindsay described himself as "becoming less radical." No coincidence, he suggested, that Mick Travis walks past a wall with the graffito REVOLUTION IS THE OPIUM OF THE INTELLECTUALS. (A phrase borrowed from Jerzy Petekiowicz, a Polish writer Lindsay had met in Warsaw.) And finally he made a plea for "healthy laughter." Twenty years ago, it was acceptable to make "a serious, sentimental film" about the poor, but in 1973 even the hydrogen bomb was an impossible subject for a serious film, as Kubrick discovered when *Dr. Strangelove* turned itself into a comedy: "The follies you read about every day when you open the paper are so absurd that the only way to comment on them is through laughing at them, because if you try to be serious about them, they dwarf you."

. . .

In August Lindsay began casting David Storey's new play, *The Farm.* A return to the "family" style of *In Celebration,* its central event was an engagement party instead of a wedding anniversary. "Things with David Storey are not the same," Lindsay noted in his diary. "With my usual malicious wit I say, He's no longer a modest man who is also an important writer, he's now an important writer who is also a modest man." Evidently David's letter about Jocelyn Herbert was still on his mind, but they also disagreed over the casting of a young Irish actor called Frank Grimes.

Two years earlier, Lindsay had noticed Grimes in Charles Wood's *Veterans,* a comedy about the filming of Tony Richardson's *Charge of the Light Brigade.* "Is he good or bad?" he wondered in his diary. "A somehow *attractive,* narcissistic performance." At his audition for *The Farm,* Grimes seemed unmistakably "good," and had "moments of magic." But the magic escaped David Storey, who recalled later: "I knew something was going on when Lindsay called Frank Grimes back three times to audition. This was the real 'scene behind the scenes,' and he didn't know how to control it."

Grimes's "rather thin, harsh voice" worried Lindsay, but not enough to shake his confidence: "I feel sure of my judgment, although somewhat shy of the extremely personal implications of it." As well as the role in *The Farm,* he gave Grimes a copy of Isak Dinesen's *Seven Gothic Tales,* and (always a gesture of love) looked forward to directing him in *Hamlet.*

David Storey saw Grimes as "a more malleable version of Richard Harris." He was also the last in a series of actors, married or living with a girlfriend, to become the object of Lindsay's unrequited affection. Fatally attracted to the new beloved for all the old reasons, toughness combined with sensitivity, egoism with charm, Lindsay also perceived in him the necessary "hard" or "mean" streak that excited his own masochistic streak. But like all the others, Grimes was unattainable.

"England doesn't change," Lindsay wrote me (more than once) after I moved to Southern California. But in Los Angeles it seemed that almost everything was changing almost all the time. If my first impressions focused on the surface, it was because the dreamscape architecture and convergence of mountains, desert, and ocean appeared so dramatically seductive. Not that the mountains were beautiful, scrubby in winter, arid in summer, and not that the coastline was appealing, with its jagged lurching cliffs and rows of squat beach bungalows. But the constantly changing light transformed everything, and the light owed its transformations to a violently changeable climate. Intense purple and gold sunsets, the only positive photoelectric side effect of a day's smog, made the often anemically pale Pacific turn midnight blue. The light became spectral and blurred when early-morning or late-afternoon fog rolled in from the ocean, glaring and brittle while the desert winds lasted, London gray when clouds massed for the winter storms that toppled trees and flooded streets.

The city itself had begun to change irreversibly during World War II, when industrial growth led to a vast increase in population and real estate development. By the time I arrived in Los Angeles, the San Fernando Valley ranchlands had turned into Main Street, more than a few landmarks of the past had been destroyed to make way for the future, and not a few landmarks of the future took the form of instant surrealism, like the offshore oil derricks disguised as islands by palm trees that appeared to be growing out of the ocean. And as the population continued to increase, it was predicted that Mexican, Asian, and Afro-American immigrants would soon outnumber Southerners and Middle Westerners.

Because its huge space surplus had made Los Angeles a horizontal automotive city, it seemed natural for these immigrants to settle in self-contained communities, mainly on the Eastside with its lower land values. Separated by distance as well as income from the white neighborhoods of Hollywood, Beverly Hills, and Santa Monica, the newcomers were seldom encountered on the Westside except as gardeners and servants. But as a white person you found yourself in the minority when you went downtown or visited the Watts Towers. Fantastic mixed-media creations (stone, steel, colored glass, bottle caps) personally built over a period of twenty-five years by an Italian settler, the Towers stood on the edge of an anonymous African American suburb. It looked clean enough, decent enough, but curiously lifeless and isolated, like an exterior set left standing on a studio back lot over the years. The atmosphere of marooned stillness, I realized, was due to a comparative lack of street traffic. Then I noticed how few cars were parked in front of the houses, and supposed that for people living in an automotive city who couldn't afford a car, Watts was in effect a ghetto.

Downtown, a major tourist attraction that also looked like a standing set was Olvera Street. Mariachi musicians, waitresses in the cantinas, and assistants in the souvenir shops all wore ethnic costumes and might have been extras rented for a south-of-the-border movie. But at night, after the tourists had bought sombreros, mirrors, and silverware and grabbed a few enchiladas, the local color went home to run-down frame houses or murky tenements. Los Angeles newspapers, all of them ultraconservative, rumbled from time to time about Mexican juvenile delinquency, but failed to recognize early warning signals of the racial anger that exploded in the 1965 Watts riots.

So did I, succumbing for a while to the optimism of the counterculture, and of Los Angeles itself, although alarmed by the polar extremes of the city, the sanitized theme park of Disneyland, with its fantasy of life untouched by anxiety or doubt, and Forest Lawn, the Disneyland of death. But I recognized (and later often recalled) another early warning signal from director Robert Aldrich, when he talked about the future of the movies. "Until a few years ago," he said one evening, "everybody thought everything was going to last forever." But since the antitrust suit that deprived the major studios of security in the form of guaranteed distribution outlets, "Nobody really has any idea what's going to happen anymore." When I asked Aldrich if *he* had any idea what was going to happen, he said: "For a long time, nothing much. Rome didn't fall in a day. When you have all that concentration of established power, and established money, it dies hard. It changes its name, its presidents, its investors, its accounting methods—but it's still there."

True, of course, not only about the movies, but the world of corporate and political power.

The music in the California air in those days was "Go Where You Wanna Go," from the Mamas and the Papas, and (a great favorite of Lindsay's) "Good Vibrations" from the Beach Boys. Too sweet and hopeful for Aldrich, whose view of established power, in the Pentagon as well as Hollywood, hadn't changed since he made *Kiss Me Deadly* and

The Big Knife. To go where he wanted to go, he had set up his own production company, but by 1964 was already uncertain how long it could survive. Only until the early seventies, as it turned out. After making several movies that lost money, he tried to recoup with a series of potboilers.

By 1964 I had done time in the world of *The Big Knife,* working for Hal Wallis at Paramount, and for Pandro Berman a few months later at MGM. Both producers seemed wedded for life to the conventions of forties movies, and I felt more relief than pain when both projects were shelved. But I was involved in a briefly intense and intensely frustrating love affair while working at Paramount, in another while at MGM, and in both cases felt only pain when *I* was shelved. For a while, my only wakeup calls were depression or anxiety. I started a new novel, abandoned it as unpromising after a few weeks. Hoping (but failing) to enlighten myself about myself, I started to keep a diary:

> *I feel lazy, remote, disorganized, and enjoy*
> *getting drunk. A couple of sexual adventures*
> *leave me depressed. I'm deeply sick of*
> *cruising, although for the moment there's no*
> *alternative.*
>
> *For most of my life I have lived with someone.*
> *Not always a lover—Lindsay, for example—*
> *but with someone with a shoulder that*
> *could at times be leaned upon. Yes, even N's*
> *{Nick's} shoulder, much bigger than mine*
> *though more apt to give way, had its steady*
> *moments. Now for the first time in my life*
> *I feel extreme loneliness.*
>
> *Raffish bar on the Venice waterfront. An*
> *attractive very drunk boy called David put*
> *his arms around me and kissed me a lot,*
> *then said I scared him because I was so*
> *"classy." Then (fortunately) changed his*
> *mind.*

The parallels between Balzac's Paris and
L.A. Desire and pursuit of sex and money
and success. Is my idea of doing something
loosely and very modestly Balzacian about
this place—kind of Human Comedy—worthwhile?
Or is S.Cal in the end too narrow?
But can I write well about anything else?

Strange dream last night. I'd come back to
England for a visit, then found I didn't
have enough money to pay my fare back here.
Woke up in absolute panic.

Visit to Samson de Brier. Sly eyes flashing
up at me, he quickly brought up two names,
waiting for their effect: J.E. and M. {lost
lovers}. I didn't mind. He's not really
malicious, just can't resist little
barbs at everybody.

It's autumn, which is always poignant to me:
the heavier clouds in the sky at sunset,
the chill in the air at the end of the day.
I have this periodic sentimental (?)
recurrence of yearning for a solid shoulder,
and distaste for cruising. And still think
about J.E. too much. It's ridiculous.

But calling it ridiculous didn't stop me, as I noted several times, from continuing to think about him. I don't remember what decided me to start reading Krishnamurti's *Commentaries on Living,* only that his commentaries on anxiety struck a resoundingly deep chord. You will only free yourself from anxiety when you stop resisting it, he wrote, and "the mind is quiet." My own unquiet mind wanted to know more, and I asked Christopher Isherwood to introduce me to Krishnamurti.

In 1909 Jiddu Krishnamurti was the fourteen-year-old minimally educated and undernourished son of a clerk at the international headquarters of the Theosophical Society in Madras. Charles Leadbeater, an official of the society who believed himself to be clairvoyant, saw the boy walking on the beach with his brother Nitya, and "discovered" the next incarnation of the Lord Maitreya, the World Teacher. Annie Besant, the society's president, evidently trusted her colleague's powers. She brought Krishnamurti to England, and after supervising his education there, took him along on her worldwide lecture tours. In 1925 she bought him a house on six acres of land in Ojai, California, and in 1927 arranged for him to visit the set of DeMille's *The King of Kings,* then held a press conference to proclaim him the World Teacher. Two years later, while on a lecture tour of Europe, he renounced the title in her presence, and told a crowd of several thousand: "I do not want you to follow me."

Ironically, the Pavlovian reaction to Krishnamurti's name is still "guru," the role he refused to go on playing. Many years later, clearly remembering the terrible headaches he endured when people bowed and knelt to him as the World Teacher, he described personal worship of another human being as "inhuman." But when I first met him, I understood why people might want to worship Krishnamurti. In his late sixties, youthfully slim, with a thatch of white hair and pitch-black eyes, he had an aura of power and grace, energy and calm, and a nobility that seemed extraordinary in light of his humble origins. But there was nothing assumed about it. It was innate, like the elegance with which he wore an open white shirt and blue jeans.

That summer he was staying at the Malibu house of his friend and patron Mary Zimbalist, widow of Sam Zimbalist, producer of *Ben-Hur;* and he held Sunday morning seminars in one of its rooms overlooking the Pacific. There were only six of us, and "no guru, no teacher, no pupil, only ourselves," as Krishnamurti insisted before picking a subject for "dialogue." He introduced "belief" by telling us he was not a believer in it, because every kind of religious or political belief was destructive, and created conflict. I soon recognized a few key phrases that he used, as each seemed to lead to the next: "Learning not to accept things as they are" to "a way of living differently" to "a transformation of the mind." Although I needed no encouragement not to accept things as they were, a way of living differently was another matter. Of the "dialogues" that cleared my mind of various toxins, some occurred at a seminar, some in private after we became friendly and occasionally lunched together. And still clear in my mind is the nub if not the exact phrasing of what he said, his precise fluent English, his distinct emphatic voice and flashes of impatience.

The quiet mind, he told us one Sunday morning, was a free mind, and I asked what he meant by free. "Freedom from what—?" I began, but he cut me off. "No, sir. Real freedom is not freedom *from* anything. It is freedom to question everything." To one of us who asked if he believed in life after death, he answered at once: "That's not the point. The point is to avoid a living death *now.*"

To another who asked his opinion of psychoanalysis: "If you're prepared to wait seven years to find out whether something *might* work, by all means try it." And to a question about his attitude to meditation as practiced by California Vedantists and followers of the Maharishi: "Fixing the mind on a mantra and excluding every other thought, is just spiritual Valium. True meditation has nothing to do with routine, which tries to control the mind. It means setting the mind free and totally aware, then following it wherever it takes you."

"Anything respectable is immoral," he told me over lunch one day, then clapped a hand over his mouth like a naughty schoolboy. And when I asked if I should feel guilty for accepting a movie assignment not because I believed in it, but to earn some money, he shook his head emphatically. "You should only feel guilty if you deceive yourself that you believe in it." Then, very firmly: "The kind of people you work for have more money than they need or deserve. *Soak them.*"

But it was after I explained the reason for my loneliness that Krishnamurti pointed the way to "living differently." Just because your relationship with someone has come to an end, he said, don't imagine that your relationship with the world has come to an end. "It's only when you isolate yourself from the world through a single relationship that you feel so terribly lonely when it ends." "I think I see," I said, and he shook his head. "No. Don't think about it. *Look* at your loneliness." Look at it without any thoughts or feeling at all, he said, no regret, no blame, no hope of curing it, and see it for what it *is.* "Otherwise you'll never understand it. And until you understand it, you'll never be free of it."

Then Krishnamurti mentioned the inner struggle he had to endure before he could renounce his "mission" according to the Theosopical Society. Intense headache pain, he said, finally relieved by a sense of "revelation" when he understood that organized religion could never create a religious mind. But this understanding came from "perception" and "attentiveness," not "thought," he said. The only diary note I made about Krishnamurti reminds me that I must have asked him to explain more fully what he meant by this kind of understanding, and how you "see" or "look at" something without "thinking" about it:

> *K's example. Thought is only one part of the*
> *brain. When you look at the ocean—a landscape—*
> *moonlight on a lake—you don't really see it*
> *unless the rest of your brain, your senses and*
> *nerves, are fully awake. If you think at the*
> *same time, it distracts you and you see only*
> *partially. The two states, seeing and*
> *thinking, are completely different.*

"For me, Krishnamurti is the real satori," I wrote Lindsay later. Certain that he would appreciate the idea of "freedom to question everything," I recommended him to read or at least look into *Commentaries on Living*. It didn't take. Next time we met in London, he told me that he'd "nibbled at" the book, and as far as he could make out, Krishnamurti seemed to believe that conflicts in the external world resulted from conflicts within ourselves, and would never be settled until we settled our own personal accounts. "That's right," I said. "You seriously think it's practical?" Lindsay asked. "If it's not," I said, "what do you seriously think *is* practical?" Pause for an eyebrow to raise. "Nothing, probably."

And over the years, Lindsay persisted in claiming that he couldn't "really understand what Krishnamurti was about." In April 1986, a few weeks after Krishnamurti died, he wrote me that "I saw him just about a year ago in Washington, when I went with Frank [Grimes] and [Frank's second wife] Ginette to one of his lectures. A really bizarre occasion, packed with respectful middle-class Americans expecting I don't know what. Krishnamurti himself, frail and elegant, communicating with great clarity ideas that I personally couldn't make head or tail of. I seemed to be the only person there who couldn't."

And evidently preferred an idea that recurs in his diary. It involved an exchange of roles and the sudden appearance of a Zen master, who would effect for Lindsay the transformation he'd imagined for Mick Travis at the end of *O Lucky Man!*

During the exceptionally cold London winter of 1947, when coal, gas, and electric power were in short supply, Lindsay and I lunched one day at a Soho restaurant that served above-average whale steak. At a table toward the opposite end of the fairly small room, an English voice over-laid with an American accent was suddenly raised. "Yeah," it said, "he's a terribly sweet guy." Looking up, Lindsay and I recognized Christo-pher Isherwood, although not his lunch companions. And we heard nothing more, because he didn't raise his voice again.

Ten years later, when I met Christopher for the first time, he was living in Santa Monica Canyon with Don Bachardy. I asked who the terribly sweet guy might have been, but not surprisingly he couldn't remember. "After all," he said with a smile, "I've known quite a few." A few years later we had become good friends, although not without diffi-culty on both sides at first. Christopher always wanted to know a good deal about you before he decided you were worth knowing, and in those days I was more reticent than now. His genuine curiosity struck me as inquisitorial, and my response to it struck Christopher as evasive. But by the time I asked him to introduce me to Krishnamurti, my self-described "foul-weather friend" knew I was unhappy, and agreed at once.

Vedantists never attempt to "convert" others, and Christopher never suggested that I might find his religion helpful. In fact he only talked about it when asked, and I'd previously asked him enough about Vedanta to feel it could never offer the kind of help I needed. Mainly because it seemed as distanced from the everyday processes of living as the Christian churches, and in spite of its claims to the contrary, basi-cally as organized as every other religion, with its own set of beliefs and sacred texts, temples and rituals, even training centers for monks.

Christopher often said that he owed his extraordinary happiness to his religion, and his deep irrevocable love for Don Bachardy. He cer-tainly seemed as happy as any artist in the second half of the twentieth century could expect to be, although not quite as overwhelmed by bliss as he claimed. Otherwise, I wondered, why did he get drunk so often? We all drank then more than we do now, but Christopher's drinking could be epic, could reduce him to a kind of self-obliteration. And it also puzzled me that Don, an artist who excelled at mapping the human face and surely knew Christopher better than anyone else, made so many portraits of him looking preoccupied, stern, even grim.

Every creative artist is full of personal contradictions, which he tries to resolve into a central myth about himself, and at first Christopher the novelist brilliantly concealed a powerful and sometimes ruthless ego by inventing the "I Am a Camera" persona. In the later autobiographical books about his family, the swami who initiated him into Vedanta, and his years in Berlin, he began to shed the persona. Perhaps, if he'd lived, he'd have gone even further, and shown the reality behind another vital part of his myth. The public image of himself and Don Bachardy that Christopher projected was always a bit too cozy. Although a partnership of more than thirty years is certainly remarkable, the truth is even more impressive. Their partnership was not "ideal," but often acutely problematic. They not only endured conflicts, tensions, and separations that would have torn most couples apart, but loved each other to the end.

Performance was a basic ingredient of Christopher's character, and in private his human insights, emotionally precise or devastatingly funny or both, were always heightened by the way he delivered them. In public, his instinctive sense of theatre could always hold an audience, as I learned when I heard him lecture, or watched him on Oscar Levant's TV show. Unlike the later Carsons and Lettermans, whom you interrupted at your peril, Levant wanted his guests to do most of the talking. The result was a literate, disorderly, charming hour of TV that seems unimaginable today. On a typical evening, Levant cracked a joke or two about his neuroses and medications, played a piece or two by Gershwin or Ravel on the piano, then cued Christopher to recite poetry, tell stories about Auden, Thomas Mann, Virginia Woolf, Berlin, and Hollywood. Sometimes I'd heard one of the stories before, but the telling was so virtuoso that sometimes I didn't realize it until Christopher was halfway through.

When I asked George Cukor if he'd met Krishnamurti, he said: "Oh yes, I found him very impressive, but I'm afraid he found me too worldly." In fact they had a similar energy and awareness, and a different kind of grace. George was sixty-five when I came to know him well, and like most directors his age, facing the prospect of displacement.

But he was never bitter about this, never jealous of the younger generation. In a ruthlessly competitive world, he had never been corroded by ambition; and as one of those fortunate movie artists, like Lubitsch and Hitchcock, who didn't have to compromise to make popular movies, he could find creative fulfillment within the studio system. Like them, of course, he made a few movies disfigured by studio interference, and a few others to work off a contract, but "integrity" in this context is meaningless. Balzac and Trollope are no more diminished as novelists because they wrote a few potboilers to pay their bills than the director of *David Copperfield, Camille, Holiday, The Philadelphia Story, The Marrying Kind, Pat and Mike, A Star Is Born,* because he also turned out *Wild Is the Wind* and *A Life of Her Own.*

It was the "new" supposedly independent Hollywood, not the old one, supposedly rigid and mogul-dominated, that refused George's most enterprising later projects: a movie about Victoria Woodhull, and an adaptation of Lesley Blanch's novel of "low behavior in high places," *The Nine-Tiger Man.* The situation struck him as deeply ironic, but he followed his own advice to others. "It's important not to panic or wilt and not ape the times when you feel you're not part of them," he said during one of our conversations for the book *On Cukor.* "Just try to understand them and continue to stand on your own feet."

By the time I came to know him well, George had reached a point, after being obliged to live a closeted life for so many years, when he realized that he had nothing to lose by talking about his sexuality. But not for publication, as he made clear when we began *On Cukor.* Later he wanted me to write his biography, but I declined when he set very definite limits on what he would reveal about his personal life. Was it so important to tell everything? he asked. Not in the tabloid sense, I said, but can you separate an artist's sexuality from his creativity? "It's so good of you to consider me an artist," George said with an ambiguous smile, and an edge to his voice that I recognized as his way of closing the subject.

But sometimes I reopened it. He answered very freely when I asked about the Hustlers Only parties he used to throw for himself and friends. The guests were procured by "a most discreet and reliable person" who acted as their agent, and sometimes "one boy would ask if he might bring a friend next time, like an actor recommending a friend for a part in a movie." Contrary to any rumors I might have heard,

George also told me, the parties were not "orgies" but "auditions." Around the pool, of course. "That way you could see everything, or almost everything, you were getting. And make an appointment for later."

"During all those years in the closet," I asked, "did you suffer very much when you realized that you could never have a complete, out-in-the-open love affair?" After thinking this over, George supposed that "many of us suffered." But when there's no choice, he pointed out, you either make the best of it or suffer even more. And during any affair, out-in-the-open or secret for whatever reason, same or opposite sex, didn't lovers *always* suffer? "I certainly hope so," George said with the same deflecting smile. "After all, it's what many of my pictures that you like so much are about."

Another time I asked George if he thought James Whale became unemployable because he lived openly with his producer-friend, David Lewis. "I don't really know," George said, then suddenly bristled. "But if it's true, it was his own damn fault. I wasn't the only one to find something arrogant in the way he behaved. That kind of flamboyance was no help to any of us."

Like his good friends Somerset Maugham and Noël Coward, George was a pragmatist who took care not to cross the line; and like them, he balanced personal cost against professional gain. If he didn't care to dwell on the personal cost, it was because he'd made up his mind long ago to bear it with grace and discretion, and not allow himself to be crippled by it. Unlike most directors of his generation, he continued to work until less than two years before he died at eighty-three. His last movies, *The Bluebird, The Corn Is Green* (for TV) and *Rich and Famous,* were not the ones he hoped to make, and not the ones he'll be remembered for. But after years of being mislabeled "essentially theatrical" and a "woman's director," he was very touched to learn that young movie buffs were discovering how much more there was to him. And unlike Fritz Lang, he thought it "rather sweet when they praised my worst pictures."

Josef von Sternberg, unlike Cukor, peaked very early. After making his last movie of any distinction (the hypnotically weird 1941 *The Shanghai Gesture*) at the age of forty-six, he worked for Howard Hughes, who ordered both *Jet Pilot* and *Macao* partly reshot; and his final movie, the 1953 *The Saga of Anatahan,* made for a Japanese company, was weird but not hypnotic. In my occasional diary of the early sixties, I recorded our first encounter:

> *Yesterday evening Curtis {Harrington} took me to*
> *meet von Sternberg. He lives in the penthouse of*
> *a large, solid, old-fashioned Hollywood apartment*
> *building. A small, white-haired, rather stocky*
> *man with a benign expression opens the door for*
> *us. But the surface mellowness turns out to be*
> *deceptive. In conversation he contradicts you*
> *sharply, gratuitously, often without explanation.*
> *If you do not admit his superior knowledge—on*
> *practically every subject under the sun—you*
> *won't get very far.*

The subjects von Sternberg began by discussing were his fine collection of Chinese and Sumerian pottery in the living room, the British royal family, whom he admired, and the "script-graph" of *Anatahan.* He was very proud of this colored scroll-chart, where each character in the movie had a separate "lifeline" and changed color according to the mood of the scene: "Yellow for nostalgia, scarlet for rage, and so on," he explained. "And the cross at the end of a line means the character dies. My own invention, the first of its kind."

Then, watching my face keenly for a sign of disappointment, von Sternberg warned me not to expect any further discussion of the movies. "Solving little artistic problems is of no importance beside the great problems facing us today." It seemed that the von Sternberg who directed some of the most visually seductive movies ever made, *Underworld, The Last Command, Docks of New York, Morocco, The Scarlet Empress, The Devil Is a Woman,* was a distinguished man of the past. The equally distinguished man of the present, he implied, was von Sternberg the oracle, who talked about the Soviet persecution of Boris Pasternak after *Doctor Zhivago* ("I expected it"), the need for reforming education ("not of our children, but of the ones who really need it, their parents"), and his affection for England ("I feel sure you'll regret leaving such a beautiful country"). He also showed us an illustrated catalogue of the art collection he auctioned after selling his Neutra house: Picasso, Braque, the German Expressionists, the inevitable Chagall.

Then, unexpectedly, he steered the talk back to movies. It turned out that he still went to them, and his favorite movie of the last few years was *Damn Yankees.* He disagreed with me that the size of the screen was important. "CinemaScope or Panavision or the old shape, it makes no difference at all." He disagreed with me again when he asked if I knew why he stopped making movies, and I supposed he couldn't tolerate increasing studio interference with his work. "Not at all. I could always handle that. But there was nothing I could do when producers stopped *respecting* creative artists." When he made *The Scarlet Empress,* von Sternberg continued, the producer never dared to come on the set without asking permission first. But when he made *Jet Pilot* at RKO, "I encountered nothing but incompetence, bad manners, and effrontery." Again on *Macao,* I supposed, and this time he agreed. "Of course. I'm sure you know that your friend Mr. Nicholas Ray was called in to reshoot some of it. He made a better job of imitating my style, by the way, than he ever did of creating a style of his own."

By the late 1960s von Sternberg had apparently overcome his indifference to solving little artistic problems, and was teaching a cinema class at UCLA. One evening he invited me to join the class for a screening of *The Scarlet Empress.* Afterward I told him, "It's one of those movies that gets better and better every time you see it." He acknowledged this as a simple statement of fact, not a compliment, and gave me a very direct, almost severe look. "Yes," he said. "That is true." Then his eyes flickered, and he shook my hand and turned abruptly away.

A few years earlier, Jerry Wald had told me that when 20th Century–Fox announced plans to remake *The Blue Angel,* von Sternberg wrote the studio to offer his services as director, and his letter was not even acknowledged. But although I'd guessed from the first that his arrogance was a smoke screen, I wondered if it would ever lift. Finally, in those few seconds as his eyes flickered before he turned away, he permitted an unforgettable glimpse of the wound beneath the pride.

Whenever I left his penthouse apartment after a visit, von Sternberg always insisted, with a formal old-fashioned courtesy, on accompanying me to my car. And another image has stayed in my mind: his figure in the rearview mirror as I drove away, standing alone in that quiet, underlit street where almost nothing had changed since the 1920s.

"The man most in a position to guide and regulate the expressive resources of the cinema," Lindsay wrote in an early issue of *Sequence,* "is the director." As a screenwriter, I never expected to be allowed the last word, or the freedom Lindsay himself later needed as a filmmaker. But apart from Jack Cardiff on *Sons and Lovers,* I was fortunate in working with directors (and on *Inside Daisy Clover,* with the producer-director team of Alan Pakula and Robert Mulligan) who had considerable expressive resources of their own.

As the first half of the novel took place in the early 1950s, a difficult period to establish visually less than fifteen years later, Mulligan and/or Pakula (I don't remember which) wanted to set the entire story back in the 1930s. I agreed, realizing that a period look would also help to establish the story as a fable. We also agreed on a second change, involving the movie star that Daisy falls in love with and marries. In 1965, the idea of a romantic icon who's a closeted gay was unacceptable to general audiences as well as the Production Code. (Unless, of course, he killed himself.) Pakula and/or Mulligan (I don't remember which) suggested making Wade Lewis bisexual, functioning openly with women and secretly with men. When I thought this over, I decided we could create an interesting portrait of a glamorous, intelligent, beloved, and narcissistic movie star who led a successful double life.

But after solving the censorship problem, second thoughts in the form of self-censorship appeared while the film was shooting. Pakula and/or Mulligan decided that the revelation of Wade's sexuality in the script was too explicit and cut several lines. (As a result, the scene became almost unintelligible, and some but not enough of the lines had to be post-synched back.) They also removed a scene in which Wade gave Daisy a veiled, ironic warning about himself, and an expressive visual comment when he visited Daisy during her breakdown: in the script, the figure of a young man waited outside on the veranda.

As usual, self-censorship proved self-defeating, and the movie was indifferently received at the time. Later, more sophisticated audiences saw it on TV, then on video, read between the absent lines and appreciated its very real qualities, Natalie Wood's performance, and the way

Mulligan conveyed the disorienting strangeness of coming of age in a movie studio instead of the outside world. "It doesn't really work," Lindsay said when he first saw the movie in Britain, where the distributors cut almost fifteen minutes. "It almost works, but not really," he said when he saw it again in Los Angeles. Fair enough. *Inside Daisy Clover* was probably as good an adaptation of the novel as it was possible to make in 1965.

"She was often underrated because she was so beautiful," Cukor said about Vivien Leigh. Equally true of Natalie Wood, a beloved friend who died much too early, when she had so much left, as human being and actress, to give. Child stars seldom become adult stars, let alone adults, but Natalie became both. In a world strewn with casualties, she kept her head. (She also lost it a few times, but, as Daisy sang in the movie, "Wouldn't you?") Not by coincidence, she was ferociously determined to play the part, identifying with Daisy's wary humor and precarious sense of balance, her wild streak often at odds with her instinct for self-preservation. As a contract movie star from childhood, Natalie had experienced the same resentment at living a dictated life, and the same fear of losing touch with herself after so many years of "just becoming" the roles she was ordered to play.

She found personal happiness, after several false starts, in a typically original way—when she married Robert Wagner for the *second* time. ("What went wrong the first time?" I once asked her. "I guess we hadn't found out who we really were," she said, then laughed. "So how could we know who each other was?") She gave birth to a daughter, and found motherhood so fulfilling that she decided to retire from the screen. Then she saw no reason not to have the best of both worlds, refusing to bury her talent but determined never to allow it to take over her personal life. And after becoming so completely herself, shrewd, humorous, caring, Natalie became an even more remarkable actress. Like every original, she found too few good roles, but when she found them, she was riveting. Her Maggie in the TV movie *Cat on a Hot Tin Roof* was seductively feline, with an amorous purr and a dangerous claw; and as a disturbed housewife in another TV movie, *The Cracker Factory,* she explored her own dark places and played unnervingly close to the edge.

During the months before I began work on the movie of *Inside Daisy Clover* and the months after it finished shooting, I had two major disappointments. At Tennessee Williams's suggestion, producer Ray Stark assigned me to adapt *Night of the Iguana,* and Alexander Mackendrick to direct it. Sandy and I had left England at the same time, and his American career began brilliantly with *Sweet Smell of Success.* But a run of bad luck followed. He was replaced on *The Devil's Disciple* after disagreements with the producers, then wrote a script about Mary, Queen of Scots, for which promises of finance kept melting like snow in the hand.

After I wrote a first-draft screenplay of *Night of the Iguana,* which both Sandy and Tennessee liked, we heard only silence from Ray Stark's office. Peculiar for the first two weeks, then ominous. "Something's up," I said to Sandy when his phone calls were not returned, and neither of us could imagine why, if Stark disliked the script, he didn't say so. The reason, it turned out, was that his good friend John Huston had become interested in directing the movie. "If Huston's in, it's a takeover and I'm out as well," I told Sandy. So it proved. He read my script, told Stark it had too much sex, told me "it would make a nice little art film," and collaborated with another writer on a new adaptation with (over Tennessee's protests) a new, "happy" ending.

For me it was a loss not only of another association with Tennessee, but also of the chance of working with Sandy, whose run of bad luck continued. Four years later, financing for *Mary, Queen of Scots* seemed in place at last, only to be withdrawn two weeks before shooting was due to start. Profoundly discouraged, Sandy decided to direct a film school instead of more films. Although he was greatly admired as a teacher at the California Institute of the Arts, it was sad to realize there would be no more Mackendrick movies. And to suppose, if he'd made *Night of the Iguana* and it had turned out well, that there almost certainly would have been.

Over the next few years, Tennessee wrote some remarkable plays (*The Gnädiges Fräulein, The Two-Character Play, In the Bar of a Tokyo Hotel*) that the reviewers annihilated. Personal loss, the death of his lover, Frank Merlo, and a series of professional failures left him very disturbed. During that period, when I hadn't seen Tennessee for some months, he called from New York to say he'd found a backer for a low-budget movie of his story *One Arm,* and wanted me to write it. Contracts were signed, but a few days before I expected to finish the screenplay, a call from Tennessee made me realize to what extent amphetamines, booze, and sedation had taken their toll.

"Baby," he said, "I have just visited our so-called producer in his apartment. On my way to the bathroom, I had to pass through his bedroom, and you cannot imagine what I discovered there. A suit of medieval armor hanging from the ceiling! We must have nothing more to do with a man like that. Stop work immediately, and if he asks to see any pages, *don't send them.*"

This put me on the spot, I told him, because the producer could sue me for breach of contract. Then I remembered that Tennessee's contract gave him script approval. "Why don't I finish the script," I suggested, "then you can say you don't approve it, and the project's off." After a long pause Tennessee said in a strange voice, "Okay, if that's the way you want to play it," and hung up. The way I played it was the way it played, but Tennessee told many people that I'd conspired to betray him. For several years he refused to speak to me, even turned his back when we happened to meet at a Hollywood party. Finally, in 1972, I was in New York during the run of *Small Craft Warnings,* and wanted to see it, especially as Tennessee and Candy Darling had taken over two of the leading roles. On my way out after the performance, I saw Tennessee at the theatre bar. At the same moment, he spotted me, hurried over, and gave me a hug. "Baby! Where have you *been* all this time?" And insisted on taking me out to dinner.

Exuberant and lucid throughout the evening, he never mentioned *One Arm* and, no doubt because he was still under fairly heavy medication, had entirely forgotten the incident (even though, in the meantime, he'd written his own screenplay of the story, which never found a producer). We remained friends for the rest of his life, during which Tennessee never lost his capacity for laughter and pain, or his will to create. He added some adventurous, fiercely poetic plays to the canon, and endured with stubborn grace the critics who continued to annihilate them: "They flay us, but we learn how to grow new skins."

As well as money, I earned time to write more novels by occasional movie work, and while Lindsay confronted England in *If . . .* and *O Lucky Man!,* I continued to explore the city-state of Los Angeles. Unlike

Lindsay, I focused on individual lives, but in *A Case for the Angels* (1968) and *The Goodby People* (1971), lives that incidentally reflected the lengthening shadow cast by the war in Vietnam. Optimistic and rebellious in the early 1960s, the young had grown alienated and indifferent by the end of the decade. The characters in both novels dropped out, withdrew into drugs and the occult, found an escape from involvement in sexual promiscuity, and in *The Goodby People* a deranged outsider (called Godson, and suggested by Charles Manson) headed a band of extreme casualties:

> *It used to be much simpler. Either you withdrew*
> *passively to simple hills and lived in peace*
> *the way nature is supposed to, or you chose*
> *militancy, staying in the world to protest*
> *against it, making noise and trouble. Now,*
> *withdrawal itself seemed to be turning militant.*
> *According to Godson, anyone who stayed in the*
> *world was weak, passive, a dupe. The true*
> *strength and the only action were up here in*
> *the mountains, protected by guards.*

Compared to Waco and Oklahoma City, the Manson gang's spaced-out murder frolic, which shook Los Angeles like an earthquake 8.0 on the Richter scale, seems now no more than a minitremor. At the time, when a movie producer optioned the rights to *The Goodby People,* we agreed that the screenplay should concentrate on the young draft dodger's story, his progress from rebellion to total disillusion, and from simultaneous affairs with a former movie actress and a writer ("I" in the novel) to Godson's "family" in the hills. But no studio was ready for a nonjudgmental, taken-for-granted treatment of bisexuality *and* draft evasion. One major executive, whom I'd never met before, even introduced himself at a party to tell me: "I thought your script one of the most disgusting things I ever read, and I hope it never gets made."

It didn't, and when I heard later that the executive in question was a closet case, it seemed almost too banal to be true.

.   .   .

The draft dodger of *The Goodby People,* with his blond shoulder-length hair, buckskin jacket, bleached Levi's and desert boots, and his desire for ice cream after sex, entered my life for only a few months. The photographer of *A Case for the Angels* ("pale face and fiercely blue eyes") entered it for a few years. In the nonfiction world he was Clinton Kimbrough, an actor I first met in New York in 1960, when he was playing Kilroy in José Quintero's revival of *Camino Real.* Two years earlier, Clinton told me, he'd fled Hollywood in panic, having made *Hot Spell* for Paramount and rejected the studio's offer of a contract: "I don't know why. Just couldn't handle the whole situation." By 1963 he was back in Hollywood, involved with an actress and hoping he could handle a movie career after all. But nothing worked out, he broke up with the actress, and called me, in panic again, to ask to borrow airfare back to New York.

I gave him the money, and signals were exchanged, but over the next two years Clinton worked mainly in regional theatre, and we didn't meet again until he called to say he was being paid to drive someone's car from New York to Los Angeles, wanted to make one more attempt at a movie career, and hoped to stay at my house until he "got settled."

"I've often thought how great it would be if we got a thing going," Clinton said when he arrived, and I told him I'd often thought the same thing. But then he issued a warning: "I seem to give the other person a pretty difficult time whenever I get involved. If you're not ready for that, we'd better just stay friends." I told him I was prepared to take the risk, and we had dinner at a restaurant on Santa Monica pier. "Candlelight, ocean view, how romantic," he commented ironically, then we went back to my house and got a thing going.

"I love you, but you're in love with me," Clinton remarked after we'd lived together for a few weeks. "That means you're the one who'll get hurt." Although he turned out to be right, there was another problem: Clinton's reluctance to accept his sexuality. Sometimes he expressed it by warning me "not to ask too much" or "not to try and get too close," sometimes by a disappearing act, lasting several days, for a marijuana fest or an "unimportant" brief encounter. I knew I risked losing him by making a scene, but finally made one after learning, from a girl who was briefly the object of his affection, that Clinton had said we were close friends, not lovers. "Why be so dishonest?" I asked, and he seemed genuinely surprised. "Why do you want me to complicate things?"

It was "the new morality," of course, and plausible in its way because Clinton was often loving, humorous, good company, and intelligent about everything except himself. For a few months he got no work as an actor, then became one of two finalists for the role of Dick Hickock in the movie of *In Cold Blood*. Before shooting the test scene, he played it brilliantly for me, but he lost the part to Scott Wilson and it was a terrible psychic blow. Slowly enough for neither of us to recognize it at first, our relationship began to deteriorate.

During its final year, the marijuana haze thickened, the disappearing acts lengthened, and our loving moments dwindled. One day the idea of *A Case for the Angels* suddenly clicked into place, and hindsight tells me it was due partly to a subconscious nudge from Krishnamurti. (You mustn't isolate yourself in a relationship, he had said, and writing about it was one way to avoid isolation.) When I told Clinton what I was going to do, he liked the idea of appearing in a novel and "finding out what you really think of me," but hoped I would turn our situation into a heterosexual thing.

As it happened, the situation had already been turned. A couple I knew, an Englishwoman and her American husband, were in a relationship curiously similar to mine with Clinton. And something that occurred between them had suggested the novel's point of departure, as well as a sentence in its opening chapter: "There are people who declare a war of nerves when they feel the beginning of an involvement." And when I transformed Clinton and myself into a fictional married couple, it was not to disguise an actual relationship that I'd never tried to disguise, but to distance myself on the page from a deep involvement in my life.

If I stayed too close to my nonfiction life, I couldn't release my imagination; and as comedy can be just as cathartic as tragedy, I also decided to make my predicament comic. In the character of an Englishwoman trying to adjust to the anything-goes California scene, I saw an opportunity to satirize aspects of myself in love, gamely resolved to get as with it as my lover and, behind a mask of amused indulgence, not as emancipated from convention as I thought.

Clinton read the finished typescript, approved the portrait of himself, and provided a telling line of dialogue for the final scene. In the fictional world of *A Case for the Angels,* the couple decide to stay together for a typically cooled-out reason: "You don't want to let me go, not because you can't live without me—when the chips are down you can live without anybody," the Englishwoman says. "But you don't want the personal failure of losing me. So neither of us can break out of our situation, and it makes no difference at all what we do." Thanks to Clinton, the husband answers, "But you make us sound just like other people."

In the nonfiction world, unlike other people, we broke out of the situation a few months later. If we stayed in it, I told Clinton, we'd end up neither lovers nor friends, so we parted as loving friends; and for a while I felt very sensible and very miserable.

9

"More and more conscious of my feeling for him, and the fascination of his personality," Lindsay noted three weeks after Frank Grimes entered his life. "No one has affected me in this way since Richard [Harris]." A week later, on September 26, 1973, when *The Farm* opened at the Royal Court, he noted "a cool audience reception" but made no further comment; and for the next three years Lindsay's diary was concerned almost exclusively with his new friend.

October 28: "Frank's conversation is easy, charming, lively, humorous and sensitive. A lovely person." But Eleanor Fazan quickly formed the impression that "Frank knew exactly how to handle the situation, how to 'play' Lindsay." Although I had the same impression when I saw them together, I supposed that as an entirely heterosexual young actor with whom an important director had fallen in love, he found himself in a situation that had to be played. Particularly as the director believed that Frank had the talent and personality to become a star.

To most of Lindsay's friends, including me, Frank at his best (in David Storey's *Life Class* and Lindsay's TV movie of Alan Bennett's *The Old Crowd*) was an effective supporting actor. And Lindsay's diary suggests that he responded most deeply to Frank's touch of black Irish, not on the Richard Harris scale but strong enough to arouse similar fantasies. December 1: "Frank gets aggressive when drunk. And of course I don't mind being kicked; half, I react with the mildness that turns away wrath, and half with a certain masochistic pleasure. Frank did kick me; and we even wrestled; and I hit him quite hard on the arm. Strange goings-on."

As the strange goings-on continued, Lindsay's response alternated between "secret masochistic fantasies" and "tenderness and concern."

After inviting him to meet his (first) wife, Michele, Frank confided that "the marriage is on the rocks," and also that his mother, who was "psychic," had recently predicted her son would meet "a middle-aged man with gray hair, stocky, who would be very influential in his life." On another occasion he talked about the Bhagavad-Gita and the transmigration of souls, "which he seems to have adopted as a belief." And when Frank added, "I hope you'll come back as my dog," Lindsay rose to the bait: "I said, 'If I do, you'll feel my teeth sinking into your calf.' "

At his new friend's request, Lindsay demonstrated how to consult the I Ching, and "Frank (dear God) asks whether he should leave Michele." And as Frank was "into transcendental meditation," Lindsay thought they might grow closer if he got into it himself. On February 3, 1974, the diary records that he left his flat "carrying the red leather grip that belonged to Mum" packed with gifts for the ceremony: peaches, a pot of violets, and an Irish linen handkerchief "in homage to Frank." At the center in East London where Frank received his initiation, Lindsay sat "facing a sideboard on which is a dish of rice, a bowl with water, the violets, the peaches and the handkerchief, some incense sticks" and a portrait of the Maharishi, "pudgy faced, crudely colored." Given his mantra and told to meditate on it, he found "no great difficulty in sustaining the quiescence, in holding the mantra, [but] I don't experience any results; nor do I expect them."

But he clearly expected a great deal from Frank, and left the center feeling "very glad he's around, living and breathing in this world, and determined to do my best to help." As with Richard and Tadeusz, one way Lindsay planned to help was by starring Frank in a production of *Hamlet.* This time the project eventually materialized, and meanwhile fired Lindsay to make his only work note for 1974:

> *To find the greatest psychological consistency*
> *possible—but bearing in mind always that that*
> *tradition Shakespeare was working in was not*
> *psychological in the Ibsen sense. In addition*
> *it seems to me that Shakespeare did write in*
> *empirical fashion—which means he didn't always*
> *follow or fulfil his own leads. Thus how far are*
> *characters like Ophelia, Claudius, Polonius,*

even Hamlet, wholly consistent? And how far are
certain apparent inconsistencies explicable in
terms of character and motive—and how far are
they just to be accepted and "played"?

By then he was rehearsing *Life Class,* which opened April 9 at the Court. Like *The Contractor,* it's a play of collective event, a day in the life of an art school class, but with a single character in the foreground. A talented painter whose creativity has run dry, Allott is still a fountain of aesthetic theory as a teacher. His armor against a failed marriage and a failing career is a sardonic, self-deprecating wit, and he explains the blank pages of his sketchbook by describing himself as "a purveyor of the invisible event, so far ahead of his time you never see it."

But most of his students seem less interested in art than in Stella, the nude female model; and at the play's strange, disturbing climax, when two of them apparently rape her, Allott makes no attempt to restrain them. He withdraws first of all into silence, as if trying to distance himself from the scene, and when the students reveal, between bursts of laughter, that the rape was only a pretense, he retreats into aesthetic theory. The human condition is essentially "ambivalent" and "indefinable," he tells the class, then suggests that everyone "return to the job in hand." And Stella, apparently so used to brutish behavior that she can shrug it off, calmly resumes her pose.

Among the students, only self-righteous and humorless Saunders (Frank Grimes) is offended by Allott's attitude. Believing that "if life itself is degenerate, then art should set ideals," he reports his teacher to the school principal for failing to maintain discipline; and *Life Class* ends on a note as ironic as its title, with Allott dismissed for tolerating an "invisible" event, something that never really happened.

In *The Contractor* the interplay among workmen erecting a tent made theatre out of work, and in *The Changing Room* the footballers' changing moods made theatre out of sport. *Life Class* made theatre out of art school, which Lindsay staged with the same inventive detail and eloquent timing, effects so perfectly and invisibly calculated that they seemed spontaneous: the students eyeing Stella as she disrobes, sitting or standing, whistling or belching, while they sketch her, and Allott, in a virtuoso performance by Alan Bates, always isolated and apart as he circles the room or observes his class from the doorway.

After working with Storey and Alan Bates again on the film of *In Celebration* during the summer of 1974, Lindsay concentrated on theatre for the next five years. Necessity, not choice, was responsible. Hoping to make a movie about Germany's Baader-Meinhoff gang, he had started a collection of newspaper clippings about youthful terrorists in the United States and Europe and made notes on them. But he was unable to find backing for the project, or for a new version of Patrick Hamilton's *Hangover Square,* first produced by Fox in 1945 and retaining hardly anything of the novel except its title.

In April 1975 the Royal Court's festival of plays by Joe Orton opened with Malcolm McDowell in *Entertaining Mr. Sloane.* Although the reviews were mostly favorable and a star name ensured good audiences, Malcolm was dissatisfied with the production and refused to transfer it to the West End unless Lindsay redirected it. This he did, uncredited, not only to help a friend but because he felt a strong affinity with Orton's exuberant assault on English middle-class life.

By encouraging the actors to play for easy laughs, the original director diluted Orton's subtext. By staging *Sloane* "perfectly seriously," as Orton had wished, Lindsay exposed it; and Malcolm found the result "truer *and* funnier." The same thing happened with *What the Butler Saw.* When Orton's final comedy premiered in 1969, two years after his death, the director was uncomfortable with its travesties of religion, psychiatry, the police, marriage, and accepted ideas of sexual identity. (Mrs. Prentice to her husband: "Have you taken up transvestism? I'd no idea our marriage teetered on the brink of fashion.") But cautiousness had a reverse effect, like razor-sharp jokes bluntly told. It provoked cries of "Filth!" from the gallery, and whimpers of "Revolting" from the majority of reviewers. On July 16, 1975, Lindsay's production opened to great acclaim at the theatre where George Devine had insisted that "the text always came first," and *What the Butler Saw* was revalued (in some cases by the same reviewers) as Orton's most brilliant play.

But it was Lindsay's last production at the Court. Since 1969 it had been run by a triumvirate of artistic directors, Anthony Page, William Gaskill from the National Theatre, and Lindsay himself. When Gaskill resigned in 1972, Oscar Lewenstein, one of the company's original founders and previously chairman of the board, became its sole artistic director. Although Lindsay and Anthony agreed to stay on as associates, in Lindsay's case the Court began to seem increasingly less like "home."

Its main focus had always been on contemporary work, but the Court also presented one or two revivals of classic plays every year. During Lewenstein's reign this policy changed, and apart from Joe Orton, who didn't become a classic until the Court revived him, Lewenstein focused exclusively on living playwrights. Ironically, Lindsay had to approach a "commercial" West End producer to back his revival of *The Seagull,* which became the first of two plays he directed at the Lyric Theatre with a company headed by Joan Plowright, and including Helen Mirren and Frank Grimes.

Helen, who played Nina, found Lindsay a much less "gentle" director in the theatre: "At times he was abrasive, and very tough—not on me but on Joan, whom he made cry more than once. One problem was that Laurence Olivier [her husband] would sometimes watch rehearsals from the wings, then give Joan notes at home that night. Next day, when her performance changed, Lindsay would ask loudly, 'What the hell do you think you're doing?' "

Alan Bates and students (including Frank Grimes, center, in glasses) in *Life Class*

I saw *The Seagull* three weeks after it opened at the Lyric Theatre on October 28, expecting to disagree with the majority of reviewers, whom Lindsay had told me were "cool." But Joan Plowright, always at her best when sturdily earthbound, seemed miscast as the airy, volatile Arkadina, and Lindsay equally miscast as a director of Chekhov. His approach was too literal and solid, like the sets that Helen later described as "an example of Lindsay being so anti-trendy that he became old-fashioned." The only exception to a disappointing evening was her Nina. As well as capturing the "look of angelic purity" that captured both Trigorin and Konstantin, she brought an undercurrent of ambition and eroticism to the character. Nina's famous monologue in the last scene is usually played for tragic vulnerability, but life in Chekhov's plays is never that simple (or tragic). Helen's performance implied that Nina, in spite of her hopeless obsession with Trigorin, was sustained by her belief that she could become a great actress. And you were no longer sure it was an illusion.

The second play, although British, took place in a country far from the Britain of Lindsay's films, or from Storeyland. During the 1920s and '30s Ben Travers wrote several enormously popular farces, in which misunderstanding piled on misunderstanding, misadventure on misadventure, people rang the wrong bells and ended up in the wrong beds. Like the Will Hay movies, and the kinky *Old Mother Riley* series, with Arthur Lucan as an Irish washerwoman and his offscreen wife (Kitty McShane) as his onscreen daughter, Travers's farces were absurdist before the fact. Both Hay and Lucan died soon after the end of World War II, and the genre mutated into the rowdy, slapsticky *Carry On . . .* movies. By the time Anthony Page directed a revival of *A Cuckoo in the Nest* at the Court in 1974, Travers had been out of fashion for more than twenty years. Its success prompted him, at the age of eighty-eight, to write *The Bed Before Yesterday.*

Although he set his farce in 1930, Travers devised a situation that would never have passed the censor at the time. "A woman of young middle age and ample means," as he described his heroine, has been brought up "in the aftermath of the Victorian age," ignorant and fearful of sex. A disastrous wedding night turns her into a celibate prude, but many years later, she reluctantly allows herself to be seduced, "discovers the delights of the orgasm and is driven to the verge of nymphomania."

The charm of the play, which opened December 9, lay in its treat-

Entertaining Mr. Sloane. Beryl Reid
and Malcolm McDowell

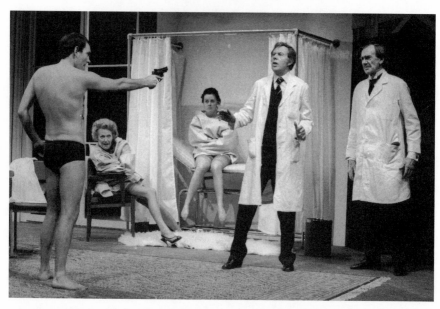

Just another day in a private clinic: Kevin Lloyd, Betty Marsden, Jane
Carr, and Valentine Dyall in *What the Butler Saw*

ment of a "permissive" subject without recourse, in Travers's words, to "smut for the sake of smut": no fashionable nudity (*Oh! Calcutta!* was then in its second year) and no four-letter words. And as well as providing a superb role for Joan Plowright, sweetly believable before her "conversion" to sex and exuberantly funny after it, *The Bed Before Yesterday* sent Lindsay on vacation from the world of "follies that you read about every day when you open the paper." To evoke the superficially innocent and profoundly genteel era in which he (and I) grew up, Jack Buchanan was heard offstage before the curtain rose singing "Everything Stops for Tea," and other 1930s songs bridged the intervals between scenes.

Sitting in on rehearsals, Travers noted Lindsay's "appreciation, or rather judgment, of values—the value of an inflection, of a pause, of the movement or reaction of a character at the right moment." And Helen Mirren, delicious in a platinum-blond wig as a "fast" girl of the period, saw his admiration for Travers as another example of the "flip side of Lindsay the rebel." In the sense that nostalgia is not for rebels, it was; but he also understood that a Travers farce, with its tight and ingenious plotting, its characters on but not over the edge of caricature, was as subtle as it was broad.

"I admire and enjoy him [Lindsay] onstage and off, this side idolatry," Travers wrote later. And Lindsay was fascinated to discover that a writer from a conservative older generation had his flip side as a rebel, who listed Nabokov and Graham Greene among his favorite novelists, and told the director of *If . . .* that the first time he saw it, he was so impressed that he went to see it again next day.

By the end of the Lyric Theatre season, Lewenstein had decided not to renew his contract as artistic director of the Court, and Lindsay, who never enjoyed administrative work, had declined an offer to replace him. Instead, he accepted an offer of a college lecture tour in the United States. During March and April 1976 he screened *This Sporting Life* and *If . . .* on various campuses, as well as talking about John Ford and making notes for the book that became *About John Ford.* "These colleges with film departments really put you through it," he wrote me before leaving for New York to discuss the Broadway production of *The Bed Before Yesterday.* Carol Channing had invited Lindsay to direct with herself as star. In his next letter, written after their first meeting, he described her as "truly weird." But he doubted that a production "in the London style" would be successful on Broadway, and hoped that working with Channing would be "something of an adventure."

Before it turned into something of a disaster, Lindsay flew to Hollywood to audition actors for the production. During his week there he saw two movies, *Shampoo* and *The Hospital,* "polished and expert in the recognizable American style of the moment, the camera too close to the actors, and performances of self-conscious self-absorption." At Republic Studios he watched Rachel Roberts tape a segment of *The Tony Randall Show,* "getting her laughs like a trouper" and hoping it would run two years, so she could buy a house in Connecticut. The show itself, he noted, had the "brisk, hygienic, predictable proficiency of a cellophane-wrapped MacDonald's hamburger," and the studio where "Orson Welles shot *Macbeth,* Nicholas Ray produced his camp classic *Johnny Guitar,* and most memorably, John Ford made for Republic release *Rio Grande, The Quiet Man* and *The Sun Shines Bright,*" was now a TV factory.

By that time I had taken a leave of absence from Los Angeles, so we didn't meet, but soon after Lindsay began rehearsing *The Bed Before Yesterday* in New York, he wrote me that Carol Channing had become "a prisoner of her own myth [and] was no longer an actress but an act." He soon gave up trying to rescue the prisoner, and the play closed after its pre-Broadway tour. Lindsay told me later that with nerves fraying and failure looming at the end of the road, Channing saw him take a nip of scotch from a hip flask one night, and accused him of being a drunk.

No comment on the Channing experience in his diary, but an amused note on a New York sadomasochistic bar, as described by his gay theatre assistant: "Have you heard about a new place called The Toilet? They say it's the last word in decadence. A lot of people running around naked, and a wall with holes in it you can stand up against. I must go there, I think you should experience *everything.*"

On the plane to London he read a paperback, *The Mob in Show Business,* about "the murderous plotters behind the [Hollywood] studio bosses," and wondered how much of it was true. In any case, he concluded, behind all these stories lay "dark, indubitable truths: the amoral, irresistible, ugly power-force of American capitalism. No wonder Hollywood, founded and powered by energy of this kind, swept the world. What chance has the poor little suburban English cinema ever had against a dynamic of this kind?"

The poor little suburban English cinema also showed no interest in

The Bed Before Yesterday. Frank Grimes, Helen Mirren, John Moffat,
and Joan Plowright as the sexually unawakened Alma

a new project that Lindsay hoped to develop, about the 1857 Indian
Mutiny against British rule. But as he thought it might be interested
in something less ambitious, he wrote to ask if I had any ideas for "a
not too demanding but reasonably intelligent story" we might work on
together. I suggested Arnold Bennett's *The Grand Babylon Hotel.* Written in 1900, it was the model for Vicki Baum's 1929 *Grand Hotel,* and
had a rich variety of tongue-in-cheek stereotypes, gullible American
millionaire and his beautiful wide-eyed-about-Europe daughter,
romantic Balkan crown prince, French "adventuress," and assorted
international spies, including a timid spinsterish secretary. By transposing the action to 1914, I thought we could create an enjoyable
melodrama of political and financial intrigue in a luxury hotel on the
eve of World War I.

Although Lindsay liked the idea, it failed to generate any enthusiasm in Britain. Turning once more to America, he managed to set up a
development deal with Stanley Jaffe, an "independent" producer at
Columbia. In December I went to London to work on a scene-by-scene
story outline with Lindsay, who proved a demanding yet genial
taskmaster. After a long sigh, sometimes mutating to a groan, when he

didn't like one of my ideas: "You can't be serious." After a raised eye-brow when I criticized one of his suggestions: "Then come up with something better, *if* you can." And after I hesitated for more than ten seconds: "I am waiting." But although our collaboration was less explosive than Lindsay's with David Sherwin, disagreement was clearly his stimulant of choice.

Lindsay had recently moved to a new and considerably larger flat two blocks away, at Stirling Mansions, another converted late-Victorian house. I recognized several comfortable, old-fashioned pieces of furniture from Greencroft Gardens, and others from Cringletie. On one wall a photograph of Murray at Cheltenham College hung next to a poster for *If . . . ,* on another a photograph of Mum was neighbor to a signed photograph of John Ford. I remember thinking, when I looked around at all the lares and penates, Lindsay's sacred household possessions, that although he rebelled against tradition (especially as represented by Mum), it remained an emotional stronghold.

The flat's operational base was a spacious kitchen, with its round table at which we worked and its notice board of newspaper and magazine clippings. By this time the board had acquired a permanent cast: Rachel Roberts and Jill Bennett photographed side by side in fur coats, John Wayne in Monument Valley, Elizabeth R with crown on head and spectacles on end of nose, and Queen Mother with the smile that seemed permanently stamped on her face, like Conrad Veidt's in *The Man Who Laughs.* And the royals' significant neighbors that year were headlines about young terrorist gangs.

During the first two months of 1977 I wrote a first-draft screenplay of *The Grand Babylon Hotel* at the house I'd rented in Tangier. Then I went to London again to discuss it with Lindsay. "Good but could be better," he said, and came up with several ideas that proved his point. When I finished the revisions, Lindsay sent the screenplay to Stanley Jaffe in Los Angeles. For a long time he heard nothing at all, then Jaffe made a brief call to say he'd found it "disappointing," and canceled the project.

He gave no reason, but Lindsay discovered it a few weeks later. Columbia had a new head of production who not only thought our project would be too expensive, but planned to discontinue the studio's policy of financing movies made in Britain:

This corresponds to our instinct that change
of management would involve a jettisoning of
previous subjects, just for the sake of
change. Stanley did indeed have the grace to
be a bit embarrassed—but of course no less
decisive in wielding the axe. And within 24
hours of this turndown I received a script
being developed by Jon Peters (the Barbra
Streisand one) whom Stanley described as "my
dearest friend in Hollywood." The biggest
mishmash of pseudo-sophisticated rubbish I
have ever read.

But *Eyes of Laura Mars* got made, and Lindsay returned to the theatre. Although I'd hoped we could interest another studio in *The Grand*
Babylon Hotel, he became discouraged when his agent warned that it
would be difficult, as recent movies set in Britain had not done well at
the box office in America. "I have always had a horror," Lindsay wrote
me, "of that film director's life which consists in endless meetings with
producers, distributors, lunches, telegrams and international phone
calls, and am now inclined to look around for something new."

As it turned out, he had no choice. Columbia refused to part with
the rights to our script, even though they had no intention of producing it; and with no movie offers at hand (apart from *Eyes of Laura Mars*),
Lindsay agreed to direct Ralph Richardson and Celia Johnson in *The*
Kingfisher, a sentimental comedy by William Douglas Home about two
septuagenarians in love. This was partly out of affection for the stars,
and partly because he thought "a West End success would do me no
harm." The play itself, he wrote me, was "so insubstantial (polite word
for thin)" that it depended on the skill of its stars to bring it off. Evidently they succeeded, and *The Kingfisher* opened at the Lyric on May 8
to reviews that Lindsay found "surprisingly indulgent" under the circumstances:

A power failure on the afternoon of the opening
night, throngs of public and critics having to
be penned in the half-lit foyer and bar for

Directing Celia Johnson in *The Kingfisher*

about an hour and a half, before anyone could
say that the performance would definitely take
place. The actors had spent a miserable time in
their cold dressing rooms, Ralph huddled mournfully
over a book and Celia playing patience by candlelight.

"The liberal-intellectual critics," he noted, "seemed surprised that I should lower myself to directing a play that might make some money. Their conception of themselves as the moralistic guardians of everybody's conscience never fails to astound me." But it didn't deter him from agreeing to direct *The Kingfisher* again in New York, where it opened in February 1978 and another star couple, Rex Harrison and Claudette Colbert, made it a Broadway success. As usual, Lindsay enjoyed working with enormously skillful professionals of the old school, although "Rex has a measure of insecurity which can account for his often very bad temper. But he is blessed with the most extraordinary charm and the capacity to forget from one day to the next how odious he's been."

London again in March, and an offer from a British producer that seemed promising; but financing for an adaptation of Evelyn Waugh's *Vile Bodies* fell through. ("I don't need to tell you that things are very dismal here.") Then, during the summer, another offer resulted in Lindsay's third film of the 1970s, and his first for TV. *The Old Crowd* was originally conceived as one of six hour-long scripts by Alan Bennett that Stephen Frears would produce for the BBC. "But when BBC TV turned the whole lot down," Alan remembered, "Stephen offered *The Old Crowd* to London Weekend TV with Lindsay as director, and they took it over."

George and Betty, an upper-crust married couple who have just moved into a new house in London, are giving a housewarming party; but a moving company has misrouted their belongings, and apart from a piano, a trestle table, a set of gilt chairs, and a mirror rented for the occasion, the house is without furniture. Lindsay liked the "bizarre" undercurrents of the situation in Alan's first draft, and admired much of the dialogue, "the way it so precisely catches the poignancy as well as the comedy of existence," trivial party conversation becoming somehow grotesque, even disturbing in an incongruous setting. But the script as a whole, he told Alan, needed to be "harsher." "And we can get away with it," he added, "because the British public adores you."

As London was the target of IRA terrorist bombs at the time, Lindsay suggested the party "should take place during a situation of civil unrest, violence, upheaval and so on, with the guests going out—gallantly, of course, and unperturbed—into a night full of offscreen explosions and whistles and running feet." But they decided not to politicize the situation, and set the party in a London of the near future, where gangs terrorized the streets at night.

Like his idea for an outrageous erotic episode under the dinner table, this was an homage to Buñuel and *The Exterminating Angel,* and it encouraged Alan to develop the "mysterious suggestions of catastrophe and threat" that Lindsay found in the subtext of the first draft:

> *Lindsay had a way of making you think, "I*
> *don't have to do what I always do, I can*
> *take risks." Some people who worked with him*
> *resented this, but I found it a relief to have*
> *someone push me in a different direction.*
> *Lindsay brought out the best in you, like the*
> *best sort of schoolmaster.*

Another of Lindsay's ideas came from the memory of watching live TV dramas, and being fascinated by accidental glimpses of the camera crew and sound equipment on the screen. "Without quite knowing why," he suggested incorporating these glimpses throughout the film, and Alan agreed because he knew why: "It gave the whole story an extra dimension, like watching through a hole in the wall, and seeing the near future as only a slight exaggeration of the present."

Witnessing Lindsay at work with actors for the first time, Alan was struck by "the sheer pleasure he took in rehearsals, his provocativeness, and a mutual enjoyment." Friends and/or colleagues comprised most of the cast—Rachel Roberts, Jill Bennett, Frank Grimes, John Moffatt, Isabel Dean, Philip Stone, and a famous actress of the older generation, Cathleen Nesbitt, who played a character invented by Lindsay: Betty's mother, glued to a TV set in an otherwise empty room upstairs, and ignoring anyone who spoke to her.

The Old Crowd began shooting in the last week of November, at a pace slower than usual for a TV movie, mainly because Lindsay declined to follow the usual practice of directing from the control room. To communicate with actors through an earphoned assistant, he believed, would reduce the director to "a depersonalized voice," and he spent most of his time on the set while Stephen Frears called the shots from the control room. Completing the film on schedule sometimes involved shooting until three a.m. (four a.m. on the last day), but Stephen remembered *The Old Crowd* as "a very happy experience, with no outbursts of anger from Lindsay." And like almost everyone connected with it, he was astonished by the outbursts of anger the film provoked from almost every critic.

It opens with a favorite device, as an assistant director's voice calls "Take One," and a slate appears on the screen, with "6 ALAN BENNETT PLAYS NO 3" written in chalk beside a timer moving toward zero hour. Next, over a low-angle shot of a section of freshly painted white ceiling, the main title appears. An ominous offscreen thud accompanies THE OLD CROWD, and is followed by a grating sound like fabric being torn apart as the ceiling develops a crack, then releases a handful of dust. Camera moves away, past a naked electric bulb dangling from a wire, as we hear a single note insistently repeated on a piano. Across an empty hallway, the open door to another room reveals a piano tuner with his back to camera, and a reverse angle reveals that he's blind, gazing ahead through dark glasses while his guide dog lies nearby.

An empty upstairs corridor, another open door, and another room with a solitary piece of furniture, this time a makeshift bed. Tuxedoed George (John Moffatt) polishes a shoe while Betty (Isabel Dean), in evening gown, casually informs him that their friend Totty is fatally ill and has been given three months to live. (George: "Three months? That'll put us in Scotland." Betty: "I'm not sure I feel like Scotland this year.") A doorbell chimes and George goes downstairs to admit a strange pair carrying suitcases, one (Philip Stone) middle-aged and rather grand, the other (Frank Grimes) young and unshaven. Waiters from the catering service, they claim to be out-of-work actors who specialize in playing policemen, but the way the older one handles a large kitchen knife and the younger one uses a heavy flashlight for bludgeon practice suggests they moonlight in more sinister occupations.

Tuxedoed and gowned, the guests always emerge from total darkness, the front door quickly unbolted to admit them, and quickly bolted again. Pauline (Rachel Roberts) admires the house's "uncluttered" look before she learns the reason for it; Stella (Jill Bennett) exchanges a quick signal with the young waiter when he takes her coat; her elderly escort, a financial wizard, wanders off listening to world news (a series of disasters) on his transistor radio; upstairs, the old lady concentrates on her TV program (close shot of a surgeon's knife about to descend on a wildly rolling eye) while the guests pass through on a tour of the house; and nobody notices when another crack develops in another ceiling. Later, over champagne cocktails, they deplore the state of the country: street lighting blacked out by a power failure, public telephones out of order, "vandals" roaming the streets, where "holes keep appearing everywhere," and of course the impossibility of finding good servants.

For "the old crowd," social decay means personal inconvenience, nothing more. And when the camera crew is glimpsed recording this scene through a gap in one wall of the set, its intrusion has the effect of an ironic comment by the filmed world on the actual world, its absurd, instinctive selfishness.

Dinner is served at the long trestle table, and as the older waiter lifts the lid of a silver casserole dish, he spots a purple plastic glove among the pieces of meat, and deftly pockets it. Stella "accidentally" drops her napkin, and the young waiter crawls under the table ostensibly to retrieve it, in fact to remove one of her shoes, slit her stocking and lick her toe. Later, while a refined female singer entertains the other guests with "We'll Gather Lilacs," Stella and the waiter make love in the room where Betty's mother watches TV. She glances at them for a moment, mildly irritated, then stares at the TV screen again, riveted by a shot of African tribesmen paddling a canoe.

By the time a slightly disheveled Stella rejoins the party, Pauline has developed a crush on Betty's sweet and vapid young nephew. "Isn't he pretty?" she asks, laments the passing of her own youth, and suddenly gives an animal wail, like a dog baying at the moon. (Alan Bennett: "Lindsay's idea, and typical of his personal ways with actors. One of Rachel's party turns, after she'd had a few drinks, was to go 'woof woof' on all fours.") Then, as George announces the evening's final entertainment, a slide show of "family" pictures, the doorbell chimes again.

An imposing figure, regal as Britannia and accompanied by Elgarian music, emerges from darkness, and Totty (Elspeth March) graciously informs her old friends that not even fatal illness can keep her from joining the party. With an expectant smile she settles in a chair, the room darkens, and George projects the first in a series of slides as incongruous or sinister as the TV images upstairs. Like the old lady, the guests appear to find them perfectly ordinary. Stella identifies a shot of a black bear as "Boris," and a close-up of a snarling mouth with yellowed teeth provokes excited discussion. Is it "Angela," or "Percival," or perhaps "Auntie Clare"?

Then the lights go up to reveal Totty slumped motionless in her chair. A heart no longer beats and a pulse no longer throbs in that splendid, maternal, benign figure, but the guests are unable to come to terms with a dead Totty. Two of them carry her to the table, then notice a heavy mirror on the wall. They take it down, start to carry it to the table, and like an uncanny reminder that another world is watching, the mirror catches the camera crew's reflection in the glass. But when they hold it close to Totty's mouth, hoping her breath will mist it, the glass remains clear and Oscar the artist (Valentine Dyall) delivers a solemn verdict: "But one does die. That's what one does. Die."

Now the camera rises to an overhead shot, to include studio lights, the control room with monitor panels, Stephen Frears calling "Start your pan here," while the guests sing "Goodnight, ladies" to the motionless figure on the table. With row after row of monitor panels recording the scene, the filmed and the actual world merge and "the old crowd" seems to be mourning, in the person of Totty, Britannia herself.

Later that night in the actual world, Totty still lying in state after the guests have gone, George and Betty go down to the kitchen and discover that the waiters have also left. But they haven't been paid, and the older man has left his carving knife behind. "They'll be back," George tells Betty, and as they exchange uneasy glances, her mother cries out in alarm. They hurry upstairs and find the old lady frantic because her TV's on the blink. After George tries unsuccessfully to fix it, the camera moves in close until the blank screen, jittering and growling with static, fills the actual screen, and the final credits roll.

Unfurnished house with cracks that keep appearing in its ceilings and three out of four toilets inoperative, weird images that erupt on TV and slide-show screens, plastic glove floating among the meat in a silver casserole, servants who may be planning to murder their masters, communications increasingly cut in the dark and lawless world outside—every metaphor in *The Old Crowd* is charged with menace, but the treatment is consistently light. The actors make the most of Alan Bennett's sharp throwaway wit by underplaying it in sophisticated deadpan style, and the direction has the kind of personal authority and detail usually found only on the larger screen.

Early in the film, an unerringly timed sequence shows Betty and George taking their guests on a tour of the house, each stark empty room and bare uninviting corridor the object of languid admiration. And near the end of it Lindsay employs another favorite device, switching to black and white for a couple of shots that transform the guests into ghostly relics as they pair off to dance with each other before going home.

"Drivel," "rubbish," "meaningless," "crass stupidity" and "pretentious load of old cabbage" were among the critical verdicts on *The Old Crowd* when BBC TV aired it in February 1979; and there was a note of gratuitous personal hostility in *The Spectator,* with its reference to "tiny, conceited Lindsay Anderson."

Alan Bennett attributed the violent backlash in part to the bitter mood of the country at the time—"the film was aired during the so-called Winter of Discontent, when all public services went on strike"—and in part to "too much favorable prepublicity." Stephen Frears agreed about the prepublicity, citing a newspaper article with the unfortunate heading "THE MASTER AT WORK." But Lindsay detected "a sense of affront" and wounded national pride behind the insults and outrage:

> *The English like to think they like to laugh*
> *at themselves. This may have been true once,*
> *when there was no apprehension that the Sun*
> *might one day Set. But it is not true today.*
> *The good ship Britannia is waterlogged in a*
> *shark-infested sea. Don't rock the boat!*

One reason to suppose Lindsay right is that the only dissenter among the national critics was an American journalist working for the *Daily Mail.* "*The Old Crowd,*" Herbert Kretzmer wrote, "reflects with superb skill and timing [Britain's] current mood of impotent rage and despair." Another is that the Finnish director Jörn Donner, who was also president of the Swedish Film Institute, admired *The Old Crowd* so much ("a beautiful, funny and ripely theatrical parable") that he offered to raise money for an expanded feature film version. Alan Bennett wrote a screenplay with a brilliant new scene: the party interrupted by a squad of "health police," who insist on stripping all the guests to search for bodily signs of a "mysterious virus" that has started to sweep Europe. But financing collapsed a few weeks before shooting was due to start, and the film became yet another of Lindsay's unrealized projects.

Was it more than unlucky coincidence that *The Old Crowd* aired when its ironic portrayal of Britain in the near future seemed uncomfortably close to the actual present? Or was it another example of imagination moving a step ahead of reality? Six years earlier, *O Lucky Man!* opened during "Heath's Dark Age," as the British prime minister's opponents labeled a period of miners' strikes, power cuts, high unemployment, and high visibility of the homeless, and was accused of "exaggeration." Three years later, the opening of *Britannia Hospital* would synchronize with Mrs. Thatcher's ordering an army to the Falkland Islands as a patriotic diversion from labor troubles, cuts in social services, and an unemployment rate that had caused riots in northern cities. This time the film's satirical portrait of Britain as a misgoverned hospital, with venal administrators at odds with venal union leaders and workers on strike demanding "equal sickness for all," was accused of being "petty" and even "wilfully blind to the conditions and problems of the present."

Two months after *The Old Crowd* aired in Britain, I saw it in Los Angeles. Lindsay had arrived there to discuss a development deal with Orion Pictures, brought a videocassette with him, and was "very curious to know what you think. Am I mad, or are the critics insane?" He was relieved when I certified the critics, but in disguising the depth of his feelings, the actor was less successful than usual.

He seemed to have aged several years in the year since I had last seen him, and I remarked that he looked tired. "Well, I'm beginning to feel more and more isolated, and isolation *is* tiring, you know." Then he shrugged it off. "I've also had an exhausting time with Rachel Roberts in Australia."

Rachel was "fine," he told me, on *The Old Crowd:* "Work is the only thing that pulls her together; she always rises to a professional challenge." But right after filming ended, she relapsed into alcoholism and a bout of suicidal depression. As the sleep cure had never really helped Rachel, Lindsay put his faith in the work cure, and offered her the leading role in *The Bed Before Yesterday,* which he'd been invited to direct in Australia. This time she failed to rise to the challenge, and had trouble memorizing her lines on opening night in Sydney. Reviews were cool, the producers canceled the tour that was supposed to follow, and "Rachel flew back to L.A. hoping yet again to reconcile with Rex. It didn't happen, of course, and now she's in Bali or Hong Kong with Darren."

This was Darren Ramirez, a bisexual fashion stylist twenty years her junior, with whom Rachel had become involved after taking up and breaking up with a black hustler. But in spite of his genuine affection, she was still obsessed with Rex Harrison, continued to drink too much, alternated between outbursts of rage and mute withdrawal. "Darren is simply not as strong as Rachel's will to self-destruct," Lindsay said. "And I'm beginning to fear that nobody is."

The Old Crowd. The married couple (Peter
Jeffrey and Rachel Roberts)

The Old Crowd. Stella (Jill Bennett), young waiter (Frank Grimes),
and Oscar the artist (Valentine Dyall)

For different reasons he was worried about Frank Grimes, who had talked about following Malcolm McDowell's example and making a career move to New York. "But I'm not sure he really means it," Lindsay added too quickly, as if trying to reassure himself. "And as for *my* next career move, Orion are interested in a remake of *In a Lonely Place.*" To remake one of Nick Ray's best movies struck me as an unpromising idea, but Lindsay insisted that he wanted "to go back to the original novel," which Nick had used only as a point of departure. "Besides, nobody's offered to back the film I *really* want to make."

The idea for *Memorial Hospital,* he told me, had occurred after he read a news story about a labor union official who organized a strike to protest the admission of private paying patients at a nationalized London hospital. "Pickets actually refused to admit ambulances with emergency cases, or delivery vans with medications that the lives of some patients depended on. Nice idea for a comedy, don't you think? I see Arab sheiks thrown out the windows by union members, and floating in slow motion from the twentieth floor, with life-support machines attached to their beds."

A few days later he told me that Orion was prepared to go ahead with *In a Lonely Place,* but " 'they have to look into the figures first,' to quote one of their ghastly expressions, which means there's still hope the deal will be called off." Hope was quickly and unexpectedly rewarded when Lindsay's agent phoned from London with the news that financing had "definitely" been found for *Memorial Hospital* after all. Leaving the deal with Orion "up in the air," and regretfully declining an offer to play "the Prince of Darkness (or some such) in *The Empire Strikes Back,*" he returned to London. A week later, financing for the film Lindsay *really* wanted to make fell through, and the following week he learned that Orion found "the figures" for *In a Lonely Place* too high: "I'm a *hopeless* careerist, aren't I?" And in the absence of any immediate prospects, he spent the rest of 1979 working on his book about John Ford and ministering to his dysfunctional "family."

By this time his flat had become a hospice for the mildly or seriously desperate. As well as caring about and for them, Lindsay found a temporary escape from his own needs in being needed. The outer circle, writers and actors struggling for recognition, came for lunch (which Lindsay cooked) or scotch and sympathy, but the inner circle demanded more intensive care. Lindsay's nephew Sandy, soon to be diagnosed as manic depressive, was a more or less permanent occupant of one spare bedroom at Stirling Mansions; Patricia Healey, star of *The White Bus,* who had never completely recovered from a breakdown in the late 1960s, was a more or less permanent occupant of another. After a frustrating, paranoia-inducing season in Hollywood, David Sherwin needed assurance that his phone wasn't tapped and encouragement to finish a novel he'd started; and at least once a week there was a call from Rachel Roberts in New York or Los Angeles, about loving and not loving Rex, leaving Darren and going back to him, enrolling in Alcoholics Anonymous and consulting psychoanalysts but never staying the course, and insisting "*You* are my only strength" when Lindsay reproached her.

"Life at home has its stresses," Lindsay wrote me with surprising understatement in December, and in the next play he directed, the stresses of a dysfunctional family took center stage. By then he had severed all ties with the Court, and David Storey's *Early Days* opened at the National Theatre on April 22, 1980, starring Ralph Richardson as Kitchen, an elderly retired politician in the sensory twilight zone. Paranoid fantasies trigger the obscene anonymous phone calls that Kitchen makes to his son-in-law's office, and a fractured memory impedes his attempts to write an autobiography. His daughter agrees to help with this, but while Kitchen hopes to lay some troubling ghosts, she has scores to settle and keeps summoning them. Family tensions and generational conflicts are familiar Storey themes or obsessions, but the style of *Early Days* was a departure: nonlinear, past and present intermingled, like time and experience viewed through a kaleidoscope, patterns of memory shifting, colliding, and reshaping themselves. But my own memory of the play remains fixed: Storey's disturbing insight into a mind at the end of its tether, the invisible authority of Lindsay's direction, and a mesmerizing performance by Richardson.

Shortly after *Early Days* opened, Lindsay's friend Sandy Lieberson was appointed head of production at 20th Century–Fox and offered him a development deal for *Memorial Hospital;* and at the cottage in Rustington inherited from his mother, he began work on the script with David Sherwin, who had abandoned his novel and was no longer paranoid, although sleepwalking from time to time. As usual, Lindsay found it necessary to reduce Sherwin to "a state of neurotic impotence" by shouting at him, then holding him at emotional gunpoint until

Conferring with David Storey on *Early Days*

Directing Ralph Richardson in *Early Days*

they somehow managed to solve a problematic scene together. But in July there was a change of management at Fox, and the new executives turned down their first draft. Fortunately Lindsay had learned the lesson of Columbia and *The Grand Babylon Hotel,* and his contract specified that if Fox decided not to go ahead with the project, the script remained his property.

With a new and "more epic" title, *Britannia Hospital* eventually found a producer, but not before Rachel Roberts had left Darren again, made another unsuccessful suicide attempt, and arrived unexpectedly at Lindsay's flat. Fortunately there was a spare bed available, as Sandy had left to study photography at the polytechnic in Oxford, tuition and living expenses paid by Lindsay. Unfortunately Rachel seemed beyond help. She tried one clinic recommended by Lindsay, another recommended by Eleanor Fazan, another recommended by Jill Bennett, then asked for sanctuary again at Stirling Mansions. Hoping that work could still prove Rachel's salvation, Lindsay offered her the role of Gertrude in a production of *Hamlet* that he'd started to plan with Frank Grimes. The idea seemed to revive her, and she read the part ("brilliantly," according to Lindsay) with Frank. Then, without saying yes or no, she left for Los Angeles as suddenly as she'd arrived. But with a hoard of Nembutals in her luggage, saved up from various doctors and clinics.

She swallowed most of them soon after returning to California and Darren, was rescued once more by stomach pump, tried once more to reconcile with Rex, then drank an entire bottle of lye on November 3, 1980, and endured brief but intense physical agony before she died.

From Jill Bennett and other mutual friends in London, I heard that Rachel's death had affected Lindsay very deeply, and he was characteristically reticent in talking about it. Three months later, in February 1981, we met in Los Angeles, and when I said that I'd seen Rachel only two or three days before she killed herself, his first response was a shrug. Then: "The angry or the self-pitying or the I-don't-care-if-I-never-act-again or the all-I-care-about-is-Rex Rachel?" None of the above, I said. Just someone so damaged that I could only feel happy when she achieved what she so desperately wanted, and had tried so often to get, although I wished she hadn't chosen such a horribly painful way to make sure of getting it. "Yes," Lindsay said, dropping his guard for a moment. "I miss her very much." Then, ironic-defensive: "But it's a relief not to have to see her again."

(Later he told me that he'd written a note to Rex, and showed me Rex's letter in reply. It revealed a surprisingly dark side to the professional charmer who was starring at the time in a highly successful revival of *My Fair Lady.* After thanking Lindsay "for what you tried to do for Rachel" and supposing that "her wish to go" was too great for anyone to succeed in changing her mind, the letter continued: "Meanwhile we miserable survivors go on living our own particular hell on earth. The only time I can stand being alive is when I'm on the stage. Not a very promising sign at 72 because sooner or later—?")

Lindsay had arrived by way of New York, where he directed a TV version of *Look Back in Anger* starring Malcolm McDowell, whose career move had brought him success on Broadway in a revival of Osborne's play. He continued to Los Angeles on a career move of his own, to discuss an offer to direct another film that he didn't really want to make. *Dress Gray* (a project that mutated to a TV series several years later) had been adapted by Gore Vidal from a novel about homosexuality and (of course) murder at West Point. With *Britannia Hospital* still unfunded, Lindsay played for time, prolonging the discussions by suggesting a number of script changes, and hoping all the while for the "reprieve" that a phone call from London might bring.

It came in the first week of April, from Clive Parsons, an enterprising young producer who had been trying to set up *Britannia Hospital* for almost a year. With his partner, Davina Belling, he'd finally succeeded. But the executives at EMI who agreed to finance the film were not particularly impressed by the script. The company had £3,000,000 (at that time about $7,000,000) on hand, which for tax purposes it needed to spend before the end of 1981, and the deal specified that principal photography had to start not later than August 10. In theory this allowed Lindsay just over four months for preparation, casting, and assembling a production unit. In practice it allowed him considerably less, as he refused to consider breaking a commitment to open *Hamlet* with Frank Grimes at Theatre Royal, Stratford East, on May 28.

In that labor of love, love's labors were at least partly lost. Of the critics who covered the production, several found it a "*Hamlet* without the prince." But David Storey found it "fascinating in spite of Grimes. Lindsay put the text together as a kind of once-upon-a-time narrative, a myth, and I'd never seen it done that way before."

By the time *Hamlet* opened, Lindsay had decided that he wanted "a new look" for *Britannia Hospital,* as stylized and broadly outlined as the characters. He found it in TV commercials, specifically the work of Norris Spencer, a young black designer, and Mike Fash, a young Australian cameraman. After engaging both of them, he took Sherwin to Rustington to finalize the script. He had supplied the original idea and most of the story construction when they worked together on the first draft and, bearing in mind the Ben Travers rules for farce—the need for briskness, concision, and an acceptable motive for even the most extravagant situation—had compressed the action into a single day and devised four simultaneous, intersecting plot lines.

Even though some of its workers are on strike, the hospital prepares for a visit by "HRH" (aka the Queen Mother) to celebrate the opening of its new wing; a union leader threatens to hold up the royal party at the picket line, and triggers frantic last-minute negotiations to let them through; meanwhile Dr. Millar (the genetic research scientist from *O Lucky Man!*) prepares to unveil his latest invention, an artificial brain, at the ceremony; and Mick Travis, a successful photojournalist, investigates rumors that the mad doctor is continuing to make horrific experiments in secret.

The final script contained no basic changes, only finishing touches. Dissatisfied with the opening scene, Lindsay asked Sherwin to replace it with something "totally outrageous" that would set the tone of the whole film and prepare audiences for the satirical onslaught to come. And in the original newspaper accounts of the actual strike, Sherwin found an item that needed only a light frosting of exaggeration for reality to become totally outrageous. An ambulance with an emergency case is allowed through the picket line, but hospital porters insist on taking their tea break and leave the patient to die in the lobby.

The first reading of the script was held in the ballroom of a hotel near the budget-priced Wembley Park Studios, which Clive Parsons had selected for shooting interiors. "This is a comedy, but it's also serious," Lindsay began by informing his cast of more than seventy-five speaking parts. Every character, however absurd, he added, had to be played with "total conviction." The advice on performance style was probably for the benefit of newcomers to Lindsay's "repertory company," for the actors included many favorite colleagues, Malcolm McDowell and Graham Crowden repeating their roles from *O Lucky Man!*, Jill Bennett as Millar's assistant and lover, Joan Plowright as a senior union official, Dandy Nichols as the hospital cook, and Alan Bates in an unpaid cameo as one of the mad doctor's victims.

To expose human folly, Lindsay continued, and to issue "a cautionary word to the human species," you have to make people laugh. Otherwise they won't pay attention, and "to this extent, what we are doing is a serious venture as well as an extravaganza." A year later, when Andrzej Wajda saw *Britannia Hospital* in Warsaw, he wrote Lindsay that it was "the best Polish film I've seen in a long time." When censorship was very strict in Poland, he explained, Polish directors always included as many subversive elements as possible in their movies, knowing that some were bound to be cut out; but *Britannia Hospital* was full of subversive elements, and none of them had been censored.

Although savagely funny, the film is never intolerant or unfair. Even its most unscrupulous characters have their own integrity, a total belief in themselves and their goals, and the Brechtian in Lindsay implies that social processes have made them what they are. The ruling class, from hospital administrators to royal advisers, has been brought up to assert its natural superiority, and the working class naturally resents it. So every aggressor is to some extent a victim of circumstance, and a victim of circumstance may be provoked to turn aggressor.

The same even-handedness extends to Mick Travis, no longer a hero or an innocent. When he found Britain a land of no opportunity, he emigrated to America and was corrupted by success there. Openly cynical about his motive for exposing Dr. Millar, he simply wants to be the first with a sensational story, and has no concern for the victims. Ironically, he ends up as one of them. In a way he asked for it, but Malcolm McDowell has carried over the "lucky man" persona of Mick's previous incarnation, and his horribly unlucky death calls for at least a twinge of sympathy.

Millar himself, although even more electrifyingly mad than before, genuinely believes that every human problem can be solved by the pure, computerized intelligence of an artificial brain. At the same time, his experiments have become even more reckless and bizarre. Among the collection of body parts in his laboratory is the head of a decapitated victim. Stored on a tray in the freezer, it starts to rot when the strikers create a temporary power failure. The capture of Mick Travis provides a replacement, but when the doctor grafts it onto a reassembled body, the creature viciously attacks his creator. In the struggle that follows, the creature literally loses his head and spatters everyone with blood, but still manages to strangle Dr. Millar's assistant before expiring.

Although a great deal of blood flows in the laboratory scenes, the direction is spare and restrained, no frantic cutting and no literal details in gloating close-up. The combination of Lindsay's discreet "middle-distance" style and Norris Spencer's fantasy setting—black walls, harsh overhead surgical lights, cabinets with trays of decapitated heads and dismembered limbs behind frosted glass doors—creates a dual satire: on genetic science out of control and on the B-movie "mad doctor" sci-fi genre, from *Doctor X* to the Frankenstein series recycled by Hammer Films.

In contrast to the ironically sinister laboratory, the hospital boardroom is ironically respectable, a fantasy of English clubland, with heavily framed portraits of founders and patrons on paneled walls, where the powers that be negotiate with union officials. One of the latter, aggressively working-class-and-proud-of-it, determines to make no concessions, then agrees to admit the catering van with the royal lunch after he's promised an OBE in the Queen's list of New Year honors. The other agrees to let the kitchen staff serve the lunch after she's invited to sit at HRH's table. A closet royalist, she immediately starts practicing her curtsy. In both cases, self-interest proves the deciding factor in breaking down barriers of political affiliation as well as class.

Smuggled past the picket line, HRH emerges calmly from an ambulance, followed by a mace bearer. Wearing a dress and floppy hat of peculiarly repulsive electric blue, she extends a gloved hand to be kissed. Although her arrival is the cue for chaos to escalate, nothing can wipe the royal smile from the royal face. It doesn't waver when the key to the door of the new wing jams in the lock, or even when a violent battle between demonstrators and police erupts beyond the gates. And like the smile, the military band that continues to play the national

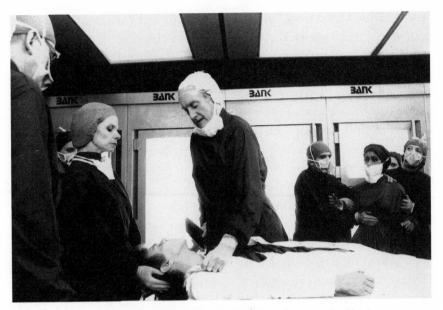

Britannia Hospital. Mad doctor (Graham Crowden, center) still at it
with assistant (Jill Bennett, left)

anthem suggests that authority is confident of emerging, as usual, the
winner.

In the final scene Dr. Millar stands on the stage of a lecture theatre.
Beside him, a small, dark, opaque pyramid. His speech to the royal
party and hospital staff begins with a plausible analysis of the absurd
and dangerous state of the world. "A motion picture entertainer of
North America," he points out, "will receive as much money in a
month as would feed a starving South American tribe for a hundred
years." At the same time, wars proliferate and the manufacture of
destructive weapons increases daily. How can humanity be saved from
annihilating itself? According to Millar, only by the creation of a "new"
and "pure" intelligence: "Those without it will perish, washed up on
the shores of the future." And he turns to the pyramid that contains
"Genesis," the miracle device he's labored for years to perfect.

The doctor presses a switch, a light gleams from the interior, and in
a precise robotic voice Genesis begins to recite a soliloquy from *Hamlet:*
"What a piece of work is a man." But after reaching "In apprehension
how like a God," the new intelligence hesitates. Then it continues to

repeat "How like a God," like a phonograph needle stuck in a groove. Fade-out, intentionally abrupt, and the end titles roll.

Knowing that the apparently wise man is really a lunatic, and world problems will never be solved by electronic intelligence, does HRH still smile? We never see her reaction, but British audiences didn't laugh, and when *Britannia Hospital* was shown at the Cannes Festival (during the Falkland Islands War), the British delegation staged a walkout. "You haven't left us much hope, have you?" a critic from a London newspaper said to Lindsay, who interpreted her reaction as "this desperate middle-class craving to cling to some—even fictitious—idea of hope, rather than be invigorated by the truth."

With moral intelligence still in shorter supply than technological and acquisitive skill, the truth as Lindsay saw it remains undeniable. "I had the odd idea that *everyone* knew how crazy the world had become," Lindsay wrote me in September 1982, "and how apparently vowed to destruction is the human race. But no, they crave the Turkish Delight of *Chariots of Fire* and *E.T.*"

Although there were lines around the block for *Britannia Hospital* in Buenos Aires, and the film was generally well reviewed in Europe

Britannia Hospital. The last of the old guard, as private patients are evicted

Britannia Hospital. Union leader (Joan Plowright, second from right)
watches Lady Felicity and Sir Anthony demonstrate royal protocol

and the United States, it failed to show a profit. Searching for reasons,
Lindsay recalled George Kaufman's warning that "satire is what closes
Saturday night," and Wajda's comment that the film was perhaps "*too*
Polish" and aimed at too many targets. Perhaps, Lindsay thought,
Wajda was right: "When many years go by without a chance to make a
film, when you're finally able to make one, you put into it everything
you can." But the way *Britannia Hospital* sets no limits for itself seems
to me one of its strengths.

   Its occasional weakness is a failure to hit a target squarely; and in
the underwritten, overplayed episodes with Mick Travis's assistants
(Frank Grimes and Mark Hamill) in the TV truck, there isn't really a
target. Instead of staying in contact with Mick while he stalks Dr. Millar in the hospital, they get high on "holy mushrooms" and ignore his
call for help when he's captured. But exactly how they could have
helped him is left vague, and the only apparent point of the scenes (the
stupidity of giggling at stupid TV programs when you're high) seems
hardly worth making. They provided a role for Frank, of course,

although the camera did him no favor by favoring him, only showed him overplaying more often than Hamill.

The film scores a bull's-eye with the nonspeaking but eternally smiling role of HRH, but just misses another with her advisers on royal protocol. Sir Anthony is played by a midget, Lady Felicity by a man in drag, a promising idea that misfired in the casting. Lindsay first offered Sir Anthony to the president of the Small People's Society, but he was booked to attend a conference in Canada. The actor finally chosen for the part had an authentically self-important air, but lacked the necessary overbred, upper-class speech. So did Lady Felicity, who muffed what should have been her finest comic hour, when she shrieked "Arse-holes!" with unladylike fury at the picketers.

These are only incidental flaws in an intellectually uncompromising movie that Derek Jarman prophesied "would finish Lindsay in the British film industry." A few years later Jarman made the emotionally just as uncompromising *The Last of England,* at no risk to his career because he never depended on mainstream financing. But Lindsay, who did, never made another feature film in his native country, and, in spite of his experience with *The Old Crowd,* was totally unprepared for the hostile reaction to his idea of a besieged and incompetent hospital as a metaphor for Britain.

A symptom of what David Storey perceived as his "schizophrenic element," or the naiveté of an idealist? Perhaps both. As a ferocious critic of British films (and film critics), verbally as well as in print, Lindsay had made quite a few enemies in the movie world, and as an associate artistic director of the Royal Court, his outspoken antipathy to several emerging playwrights (Christopher Hampton, David Hare, for two) had made quite a few more in the theatre. Now he was being paid back in kind with ferocious attacks on his own work, although a few more years would pass before Lindsay made the connection between cause and effect.

Less surprisingly, he was disappointed by the general misunder-standing that greeted *Britannia Hospital.* "Mary Poppins Anderson is not" typified the facetious critical reaction; "embittered" and "mean-minded" and "misanthropic" the angry snubs. But by satirizing every kind of institutionalized power, political and scientific, labor and the media, the film comes down emphatically on the side of individual power, and it's hard to see the meanness or bitterness in asserting, like Krishnamurti, that only human intelligence can create a wiser world.

At moments, in fact, the film even "catches the poignancy as well as the comedy of existence." As it proved technically too ambitious to show the strikers hurling Arab sheiks on life-support devices out of windows, Lindsay devised a sequence that made the hospital's private patients a bargaining chip in settling the strike. A Middle Eastern potentate and his entourage are among the evicted, but the emphasis is on a group of elderly true-blue Britishers, who retain a touching, bewildered dignity as they're escorted to a bus amid jeers from picketers and demonstrators. Later, during the battle between police and demonstrators, a woman walks up to a policeman and offers him a flower. Sentimental? Not really, just piercingly real. Her reward is a blow in the face.

Shortly after *Britannia Hospital* opened in London, an event occurred that gave its director minor satisfaction. For a reason he never discovered but attributed to an ironic mistake, Lindsay received an invitation to a royal luncheon at Buckingham Palace. The guest of honor, he wrote me, was "the president of Iceland, who had aroused great interest as a divorcee with an adopted child," and the occasion was "an extraordinary experience, all the falsely unassuming charm of the English establishment on parade." Although the Queen gave Lindsay a welcoming smile when he was introduced, she made "not the slightest effort to conceal the fact she hadn't the slightest idea who I was—and didn't care."

Unlike one of her aides, whom Lindsay recognized as a noted Tough from Cheltenham College. Although the aide didn't recognize Lindsay, and apparently hadn't seen his latest film, it became clear he'd seen an earlier one when Lindsay identified himself as a fellow Cheltonian: "He danced instantly away. I suppose *If . . .* has branded me forever as a Mole. I left the Palace extremely glad to have made *Britannia Hospital*."

10

"People in Hollywood *always* think one is arriving out there soon," Lindsay once wrote me. "In fact they can't imagine how one can survive without *not* arriving there soon." Even more unimaginable, to my agent and various colleagues in the movie industry, was the idea of leaving Hollywood. "It's the end of your career," they warned, but I never thought of myself as having a career in that sense; I read *Variety* only two or three times a year (in my doctor's waiting room), and never saw *Ben Hur* or *The Longest Day.* One reason I decided to go to Europe for a while was the last-minute collapse of financing for another project that I cared about, an adaptation of D. H. Lawrence's *The Woman Who Rode Away.* I never learned exactly why the producer who'd commissioned my script and his backers fell out, only that it had something to do with "percentages."

Another reason for leaving, as I explained to a journalist who interviewed me in June 1972 for a (long since defunct) magazine called *The Movies,* was the industry's financial and creative slump:

> *In the movie business it feels like graveyard*
> *time, and a kind of creeping Nixonism is*
> *overtaking America as a whole. I'm not*
> *particularly politically motivated, but when*
> *the country is being governed in a certain way*
> *and continuing to commit crimes like Vietnam,*
> *it does seep into life. The youth movement has*
> *run its course, they couldn't stop something*
> *much stronger than they were, and I miss the*
> *activity and hope of a few years ago.*

Maybe I was rationalizing disappointment, the journalist suggested. Maybe so, I agreed, but what else did he expect me to do with it? A couple of script rewrites (uncredited by request) and the sale of my house left me financially secure for the next four or five years. But as it turned out, I spent only a few months in Europe, mainly in Rome, where I began writing *The Dangerous Edge,* a study of several novelists and one filmmaker whose work reflected an obsession with criminal life. Not the mechanical puzzles of the Agatha Christie school, but the creative puzzle of the criminal himself, his world of guilt and betrayal, fear and suspense. A remark by Hitchcock had given me the idea. "If you create the fear, you've got to relieve it," he said in an interview, and I wondered why he wanted to create the fear in the first place. I began reading the works of various "crime artists," as I eventually called them, then researched all the biographical material I could find, and a pattern of cause and effect emerged. According to Raymond Chandler, melodrama was "an exaggeration of violence and fear beyond what one normally experiences." But all these artists (including Wilkie Collins, Conan Doyle, Graham Greene, Eric Ambler, Georges Simenon, and Chandler himself) had experienced supernormal fear in childhood or adolescence, and threads of secret autobiography ran through their fiction. And what Chandler defined as "exaggeration" in the 1940s had become part of the normal melodrama of everyday life thirty years later.

The crime artist's imagination, in fact, often moved disturbingly ahead of reality, or current perceptions of it. As early as 1860, Wilkie Collins created a twentieth-century archetype, Count Fosco in *The Woman in White,* who celebrated murder, terrorism, and fraud as a protest against "society" and the increasing limitations it imposed on personal freedom. A few years later, in *The Moonstone,* Collins foresaw the role that recovered memory ("every sensory impression which has once been recognized by the perceptive consciousness and registered, so to speak, in the brain") could play in solving a crime. In 1915 John Buchan became the first conspiracy theorist when he warned in *The Thirty-nine Steps:* "Away behind all the Governments and the armies was a big subterranean movement going on, engineered by very dangerous people." And a 1946 article by Eric Ambler forecast the post-Watergate world of secret taping and listening devices: "In most human beings the ideas of spying and being spied upon touch fantasy systems at deep and sensitive levels of the mind."

. . .

A reference to Tangier in Ambler's *Dirty Story* prompted me to recover a memory of Paul Bowles, whom I'd met five years earlier, when he came to Los Angeles on a visiting professorship at San Fernando State College. He found nothing to like or admire in the city and couldn't imagine why I lived there. "If you ever decide to live somewhere else," he said, "you should consider Tangier." An idea that seemed remote in 1968, but took up residence in my subconscious. By the time I read *Dirty Story,* I knew that I didn't want to live in Rome, and like a window suddenly blown open, Tangier came to mind.

I arrived there in May 1973, and stayed at a hotel opposite the beach with sand as pale and fine as the beach at Santa Monica. The view from my bedroom window, in fact, was déjà vu: palm trees, bougainvillea, a road running parallel to the beach, like the Pacific Coast Highway with fewer lanes and much less traffic. Five minutes' walk away, the main boulevard of the European town looked like an exterior set for a 1930s French movie with Jean Gabin. But a set left standing too long in the sun, with missing letters on neon signs that flashed cryptic messages: HARP, LIPS, HELL; peeling movie billboards, with actors' faces missing an eye or a jaw; a few houses, abandoned halfway through construction because the money ran out, sinking into ruin before they were finished; and, like reminders that time was on suspension here, public clocks that had stopped at different hours.

In the 1970s, most American exports to Morocco were dreck, TV series, CIA agents, and (because Moroccans have even sweeter teeth than Americans) Coca-Cola with extra sugar content. The only exceptions were blue jeans and a unique experiment in multicultural education, the American School of Tangier, whose students also included French, Spaniards, Italians, and Moroccans. Soviet Russia exported cold war personnel in the shape of engineers and so-called military advisers. The English had contributed a church and two cemeteries, one for their dead, one for their dead pets. But France and Spain had their cultural centers with libraries, occasional art shows, and movie programs.

Not long after I arrived, the French center presented a season of movies by the (still) underrated Julien Duvivier, including two elegant and bitter comedies, *La Fin du Jour,* set in a home for retired actors, and

L'Homme du Jour, about an electrician who donates his blood to save the life of an actress and becomes famous for a day. And it was a curious experience to see *Pépé le Moko* again, with its superb studio reconstruction of the Casbah and medina in Algiers, then to walk through the real thing in Tangier, where the harsh, mournful music from café radios sounded no different than in Duvivier's 1937 movie, and the shadowy alleys with secretive barred windows looked very similar. But signs of Westernization had sprung up almost everywhere—an advertisement for Coca-Cola on the wall opposite a mosque, a barrel of local honey below a shelf of Kellogg's Corn Flakes in a grocery store.

Tangier, according to Paul Bowles, was deteriorating more slowly than most other places, but by Western standards deterioration translated into progress: more hotels, more cars, more TV. I asked a young Moroccan whom I'd recently met, and who became my lover for twelve years, what he felt about this. Mohammed Cherrat was seven years old when his family moved from a nearby fishing village on the Atlantic coast to Tangier. He had never seen "a real city" before, he said, and "nobody ever tell me the world can change." Then, after thinking this over: "But change is okay as long as most things stay the same."

"Nowadays most things don't," I said. Cherrat shook his head, and told me a story in his fluent, ungrammatical English:

> *A long time ago a traveler pass through a big*
> *empty desert. Five hundred years later he come*
> *back and find it a great city. "How long this*
> *city here?" he ask a man in the street. "Always,"*
> *the man say. "You never find nobody who remember*
> *no time when it wasn't here." Five hundred years*
> *later this traveler come back again, and find*
> *a big ocean where the city was. "What happen to*
> *the city?" he ask a fisherman. "What city?" the*
> *fisherman ask him. "Nobody here remember a city.*
> *Always nothing but ocean here." Five hundred years*
> *later this traveler come back again and he find no*
> *ocean, just the same desert he cross in the first*
> *place. And now he understand. If you wait long*
> *enough, nothing change. Not really.*

In retrospect, this seems true of my fifteen years in Tangier. The international colony had dwindled by the early 1970s, and I kept hearing that I'd arrived twenty years too late. (But I'd kept hearing the same thing about Los Angeles.) In July 1973 Tennessee came for a visit and cut it short, saying the town had changed so much that it reminded him of what people said about Tallulah Bankhead in her last phase: "You should have seen her in her prime." But a few years later he returned and found Tangier "almost the same" as his original memory of it. In fact the place was slowly reinventing itself. Once famous as a social and sexual funfair attraction for café society and High Bohemia, and a tax shelter for "import-export" businessmen, it had become part of an independent Morocco. But as the country was still economically dependent, it continued to stand between two cultures: its own, which had so few material resources, and the West, which had so many.

Cherrat, who learned to speak practical English and French from encounters with tourists, had the looks and accomplishments for a highly successful career as a gigolo. But not the temperament. Shortly before we met, he'd caught the eye of Malcolm Forbes, who took him to New York and Los Angeles. By the end of the trip he decided that he didn't really like Forbes, a "colonial" who treated him as an inferior, and although he liked California, he didn't want to live in the United States. He dreamed of setting up his own small business in Tangier, either "a little factory" that produced handmade carpets, or a bakery. I helped him first with the factory, but it failed. So did the bakery. Then Cherrat needed help to evade the draft. He couldn't claim that he supported his family because his father was dead, his mother had married again, and he'd quarreled with his stepfather, who turned him out of the house. But he knew of a colonel in Rabat who would "give him a paper" for $500. This at least was a success. Cherrat returned with a certificate of exemption, and a message from the colonel: if I had any other Moroccan friends who didn't want to join the army, he would "make a price" for three or more.

Like most affairs between a Westerner and a Moroccan, my relationship with Cherrat had an element of power struggle, a half-serious game played in the same spirit as Moroccans played cards in cafés, or bargained in the souks. The big losers in the game were Westerners who couldn't accept or enjoy it, the vain or the vainly romantic who believed that Mustafa or Abdelsam "really" loved them, and would love them if they had no money at all, or who reopened old colonial wounds by employing their lovers as servants. Unlike pleasure, mutual need, attraction, and reward, "love" in the Western sense was not part of Cherrat's emotional vocabulary, except for dramatic effect. A custom of the country that you had to understand or come to grief.

At the end of 1973 I found a house to rent in the hills above Tangier. Although Cherrat wanted to move in with me, I offered to pay his rent on a flat in the town instead. This was partly because I didn't want to increase his sense of dependency, and partly because I couldn't expect him to understand the amount of solitude I needed as a writer. Speaking the same language didn't always mean speaking the same cultural language, and my work was never quite real to Cherrat. Although not illiterate, he looked incredulous when I explained that movie actors had to learn their lines from a script, then wondered why I bothered to write books if I earned more money on screenplays.

From Cherrat's point of view, my refusal to surrender an important bargaining chip was a challenge, and he never gave up hope of persuading me to change my mind. From my own, our affair seemed more likely to last if we didn't spend too much time together. But there were periods of separation when I went to Los Angeles for movie work, leaving him enough money to live on and keeping in touch by phone. Each call became an occasion for Cherrat to insist we renew our vows of fidelity. I kept my vow, and so did he, at least on the emotional level. Three years into our affair, I came back from Los Angeles and learned that he'd recently got married. "It only happen because she do magic on me," he said very apologetically, and gave a dramatic account of the black medicine, rotted tooth, dried spider, ashes, and menstrual blood that the girl had put in a plastic bag and slipped under his mattress. "But now you come back, I never see her again."

Like Morocco itself, Cherrat stood between two cultures, working out at a gym, drinking scotch, yet retaining his country family's belief in magic. (He once told me that he didn't share his mother's fear of djinns in the toilet, but knew it was "dangerous" to bake bread at night.) Convinced his wife would never try more magic while I was in Tangier, he told her he wanted a divorce. "When she refuse, I tell her I never see her again anyway. And now I think, maybe it's good, divorce very expensive for you." A few weeks later, a rather beautiful, obviously pregnant girl came up to us in the street and delivered a rapid verbal assault on Cherrat in Arabic. It was so angry that a few passing Moroccans stopped to listen, smiling and whispering to each other. "She say I am the father and if I don't come back to her I must pay child support," Cherrat explained. "If I don't pay, she tell me, I go to jail." I had never seen fear in his eyes before, knew the threat must be real, and agreed to help out with another small business.

"You are my lover, my father, my mother, my brother, and you will always be my only wife," Cherrat said that night. He gave me a long, intense, almost searing look that I knew was rehearsed, for I'd often caught him trying out various expressions and poses in front of a mirror. Then a single tear rolled down his cheek, because for Cherrat the dividing line between theatre and life was always thin. He could start by trying to convince me of something, and end by convincing himself.

When he heard that his wife had given birth to a son, Cherrat suddenly became a proud father. He still wanted nothing to do with the mother, who retained custody of the child, but as soon as Cherrat junior was old enough, he took him for walks in the town. One day he asked me to accompany them, and Cherrat junior immediately placed himself between us and we joined hands. I thought it strange that he accepted the situation so unquestioningly, but Cherrat merely shrugged. "Why shouldn't he?" "He doesn't know who I am," I pointed out, and this time the answer was an intent, mysterious look. Cherrat was an occasional Moslem; he might suddenly fall to his knees in my living room when he heard the muezzin call, or decide that we mustn't make love during Ramadan, and he had an attack of devoutness as the three of us walked together that day. "I told my son," he said with a fine throb in his voice, "that God had willed you and I to meet."

Would Cherrat junior be very disconcerted when he learned that his father and I were lovers? At the time I thought not. Today I wonder. Until recently, bisexuality in Morocco was a fact, not a category. Just one color in the sexual spectrum. But the West has gradually infected middle-class Moroccans with its sexual prejudices, and even the young of all classes, exposed to the sexual stereotypes portrayed on American TV, worry about something that never occurred to them before. Being "normal."

. . .

I always had the impression, although he was much too tactful to say so directly, that Paul Bowles found Cherrat too Westernized, and less interesting than that rare and endangered species, the "natural" Moroccan. But "other people's solutions are for other people's lives," as he once remarked, and he indirectly encouraged the affair when I asked if he thought a relationship between a Westerner and a Moroccan was necessarily limited. I see it not as a question of limits, he said, but of differences.

"The outsider always *sees* more than the man in the crowd," Paul said at our first meeting. We were talking about exile, and he told me that he'd felt like a displaced person in America for as long as he could remember. Later he came to think of himself as an exile no matter where he happened to be living. England had given me a similar experience of displacement, and I remember wondering, after our conversation, if I'd completely escaped an early sense of internal exile by moving to another, more congenial country. Then I moved to another other country, and knew that I hadn't and never would; and as I came to know Paul well in Morocco, I realized that one reason I'd found him so immediately sympathetic was his solitude of the heart. Why had it taken me so long to accept the same condition in myself? Because Paul was the first person, I supposed, to make me understand that it wasn't the kind of condition that needed a cure.

Exile creates a degree of distance from the world, and received wisdom has classified Paul as a "distant" person. But distance is not the same as innate reserve, any more than his stories are "cruel" because some of them describe acts of cruelty. It's the extreme clarity of Paul's writing that confuses some of his critics. For although he never allows a point of view to intrude in his writing, a consistently far-seeing eye operates behind the scenes. Whatever the event, the marvelous stillness of the desert or a brutal castration, he describes it with the same exact, objective reality. The result is a mysteriously complete view from every angle, like the Campbell soup cans and silk-screened Marilyn Monroes that acquired an extra dimension when Andy Warhol depicted them with such noncommittal precision.

Another source of confusion: Paul's indifference to moral judgments, which he once dismissed as "nonexistent save as a social attitude," and his belief that you have to "accept" whatever the day brings. It has caused him to be misidentified as passive, when (like Warhol again) he became one of the most subtle of passive-aggressives long before the term was invented. And perhaps not coincidentally, in view of Paul's fascination with them, Moroccans fall into the same category. Whatever happens, they believe, God willed it. But although this prepares them for the worst, they also believe God willed them to do all they can to make sure that everything happens as far as possible for the best. At once resigned and alert, they pin their hopes on human adaptability, a subject that once produced some memorably terse and loaded Bowlesian sentences. Alarmed by what he perceived as the rise of intolerance in America, Ned Rorem wrote to ask: "Do you think this is the beginning of the end?" Paul's reply: "You speak about the end. Yes, but of what? Something is always ending. Now it seems to be a case of 'life as we know it.' Then it will be life as we don't know it."

In his later years, Paul began to encounter life as he didn't expect it. Sciatica and a blocked artery in his leg made it difficult and sometimes painful to walk more than a short distance; then his eyesight began to fail. Although no longer able to read, he could discern the outlines of a movie on video by peering closely at the screen. But in every other way his vision remained extraordinarily sharp. When I first knew Paul, I was struck by his ability to keep in touch with the outside world while spending so much of his time inside a dimly lit apartment without a telephone. Then one day he remarked that he'd always relied a great deal on his unconscious; and I thought, perhaps it was the place he kept most closely in touch with, and he'd acquired a kind of second sight.

In any case, when physical frailty compelled him to spend even more time there, and he saw the apartment as even darker than it was, and he recognized friends by their voices instead of their faces, his friends recognized Paul by the distinguishing marks he always retained: the curiosity that led him to explore so many countries, the memory that made him a vivid storyteller, the sense of humor and talent for vocal impersonation (of Truman Capote, a parrot he once knew, a deranged fan), and the long experience of human absurdity and cruelty that made it impossible to surprise him with even the most fantastic tale of deception or violence: "But what else did you expect?"

.   .   .

One result of basing myself in Tangier was that I saw more of Lindsay, as London was only three hours away by plane. He had started cooking for his friends, and specialized in what he called "simple but I hope satisfying fare," roast chicken or baked fish with roast potatoes and brussels sprouts. Dinner was served in the kitchen, whose notice board often contained a new item each time I visited, most memorably a tabloid's alarming close-up of Margaret Thatcher captioned "WHY WE NEED THE BOMB."

On a shelf in Lindsay's office stood a swank shopping bag with a Gianni Versace logo. It contained a gift-wrapped box, which contained the ashes of Rachel Roberts. Darren Ramirez had brought them to the flat, Lindsay explained, "because he thought I was the best person to decide what to do with them." Rachel's ashes remained on the shelf for over ten years.

Sometimes Lindsay's nephew, Sandy, joined us at dinner, but sometimes I learned that "poor old Sandy is back in the hospital for therapy." (The same hospital, Lindsay commented wryly, that served as the exterior of *Britannia Hospital.* "One of life's little ironies, I suppose.") Out of hospital, Sandy was an amiable, subdued presence, and, as Eleanor Fazan recalled, "There was a genuine affection between the two of them. It wasn't easy for Sandy to be dependent, and live in the shadow of a famous uncle, but he was never ungrateful, never mean." And Lindsay seemed to grow increasingly comfortable with his role of "dignified father figure."

Although his other live-in dependent, Patricia Healey, very occasionally played a small part in a movie (including a walk-on in *Britannia Hospital*), she spiraled into depression whenever he encouraged her to resume a professional career. Convinced that Patsy would never take her place in the world again while she continued to regard Stirling Mansions as her permanent refuge from it, Lindsay asked the local housing authorities to find her a council flat: "Although I explained that she was sometimes suicidally depressed, the only one they offered her was on the top floor of a new high-rise, ideal for plunging to your death." So Patsy kept to her refuge, Miss Alienation of the 1980s now, with the same affectingly withdrawn look on her face.

In the summer of 1982, Frank Grimes moved to New York, where he had a contact at the Roundabout Theatre. When the Roundabout expressed interest in his idea of producing *The Playboy of the Western*

World, with himself as star and Lindsay as director, Lindsay flew to New York for discussions. But by the time he arrived, the theatre had offered Frank a role in its next production, *The Holly and the Ivy.* "A cosy, sentimental, well-fabricated middle-class play," Lindsay wrote me on October 29, 1982. "The director ran away from it, and they asked me to 'doctor' the thing." It opened to mildly favorable reviews, overshadowed by "the dramatic sensation" created by another British import, David Hare's *Plenty,*

> *which I saw half of at the National Theatre {in London} two or three years ago, a shallow, humorless and very theoretical condemnation of postwar values etc. The cold, ruthlessly ambitious Kate Nelligan—Canada's answer to Faye Dunaway—is universally acclaimed.*

Then the Roundabout decided to postpone *The Playboy* "indefinitely," and Lindsay returned to Stirling Mansions. "It doesn't get any easier," he concluded, and by the summer of 1983 it hadn't got any easier for Frank, who moved back to London when Lindsay offered him the role of Trofimov in *The Cherry Orchard.*

Lindsay's second production of a play by Chekhov opened at the Haymarket Theatre on September 12, with Joan Plowright as Ranevskaya. I didn't see it, but David Storey later described it as very similar to *The Seagull,* "with a realistic approach that simply didn't work." He also remembered that while *The Cherry Orchard* was in rehearsal, Lindsay asked him "to talk to Frank about his role." Although surprised and puzzled by Lindsay's unwillingness to talk to Frank himself, David reluctantly agreed. But Frank only wanted to talk about his "tortured" relationship with Lindsay, confessed that he'd "exploited" him, "hated himself" for doing it, and was particularly disturbed by the fact that Lindsay had loaned him "a considerable sum of money," which Frank had no prospect of repaying. Finally he asked David, "very disingenuously, in my opinion, if I thought Lindsay was homosexual."

Next day, in a "really painful talk about Frank," Lindsay gave David the impression of "trying to persuade himself that his relationship with Frank was normal," while admitting that he felt "in deep water":

> *I advised Lindsay to renegotiate the terms*
> *of the relationship by telling Frank not to*
> *worry about the loan, because it was meant*
> *as a gift. Lindsay took the advice, with*
> *the result that Frank felt released from a*
> *financial burden and Lindsay no longer felt*
> *he had a hold on Frank.*

But Frank still had a hold on Lindsay, because Lindsay was still in love with him.

In the spring of 1984 Lindsay turned down an offer to direct *Gorky Park* ("They tell me 'Dustin is interested,' but I'm not"), then managed to set up a production of *The Playboy of the Western World,* with Frank and Nichola McAuliffe. After a pre-London tour, it opened at the Riverside Studios in Hammersmith for a six-week run beginning August 9. It was "well received and drawing good houses," Lindsay wrote me, and McAuliffe's performance made him realize that Siobhan McKenna, who had starred in the play several years earlier, "really did the play a damage by the sentimental pseudo-lyrical manner she adopted."

He cast Frank again, as the troubled younger brother in an off-Broadway revival of *In Celebration,* which opened at the Manhattan Theatre Club on October 28, with Malcolm McDowell in the role created by Alan Bates. Less successfully, Lindsay restaged his production of *Hamlet,* with Frank of course, at the Folger Theatre in Washington. It opened February 21, 1985, and was coolly received. In a notably testy letter, Lindsay dismissed the Folger company as "a collection of jaded repertory hacks," and Washington as a place of "insufferable provincial complacency":

> *If I was here for long (I mean anywhere in the*
> *U.S.) I'm sure I'd be as savage about the*
> *Americans as I am about the English. Partly,*
> *perhaps, this mood is induced by looking at*
> *too much TV in an hotel room. These morning*
> *{talk show} programs make a fascinating*
> *comparison with the cosy English article.*
> *The bullshit is so much more professional,*
> *so confident, so dynamic, where the English*

are self-deprecatory, tentative, unassuming.
But both cultures equally shallow, equally
reductive of everything to a banal conformist
norm.

"I know," he added, "these are observations of someone no longer in love with the human race."

"Energy without depth" had been Lindsay's verdict on the United States for some time, and I used to reply that although creeping Reaganism might be even worse than creeping Nixonism, it was still better than Britain's lack of energy *and* depth. But Lindsay's verdict on himself as "no longer in love with the human race" was new and surprising, and I suspected that more than an overdose of American TV and the failure of *Hamlet* lay behind it.

Next time I saw Lindsay in London, he said that he'd written the letter in a mood of exasperation, after a trip to New York to discuss a movie project in New York with a *producer.* (He always italicized this word, as if referring to a strange and menacing species.) Any discussion with a *producer,* he explained, involved "endless dealing" and left him feeling that he lived "in an age of non-communication." Then, after a moment: "But the *real* reason I'm depressed is that I still haven't recovered from seeing *Gandhi* two years ago." Richard Attenborough was the director Lindsay held personally responsible for the conventional middlebrow tone of mainstream British cinema, and he never missed an opportunity for a jab. "If you'd seen Little Richard's Nursery History of India," he said, "you'd understand."

We had moved away from the human race, and never got back to it, but hindsight tells me that Lindsay's depression was genuine, although not for the reasons he gave. Always combative, by now he'd acquired a reputation for crabbiness. It could be "a risky experience," Anthony Page remembered, to go to the theatre with him: "At the opening night of a play called *Call It Love,* Lindsay said loudly during the first act, 'Call it off!' He was asked to leave, but refused. Funny, of course, and deserved, but his disparaging comments on Richard Eyre's production of *Hamlet* at the National were overheard, and soured his relationship with the theatre."

He seemed driven, in fact, to court unpopularity and isolate himself; and at the same time, as I learned many years later from David

Storey, his relationship with Frank had begun to change. Instead of repressing its eroticism, Lindsay expunged it—not just from the relationship, but from his life. "I find the idea of sexual intercourse physically disgusting," he told David; and the father figure transformed Frank into his favorite son.

Lindsay was only sixty-two, so I doubt that his sexual drive died of old age. Soon after realizing the "awful" direction of that drive, he had tried and failed to block it, and advised himself to "beware of *emotional* attachments." But in fact the attachments became more passionate, the frustration more intense, and his remark to David suggests that he'd finally practiced some kind of aversion therapy on himself. Whatever it involved, the experience can't have been easy and must have been bitter.

Another clue to his emotional situation: after the Washington *Hamlet,* Lindsay accepted an invitation to lecture at Rice University, and during his stay in Houston was driven around by an American friend, Gary Sweet. Sweet later told David Sherwin that Lindsay kept asking him to stop so he could give a dollar to each of the city's numerous beggars holding a "WILL WORK FOR FOOD" sign. "You can't change the world," Sweet finally said. "I suppose you're right," Lindsay answered, and looked so sad that Sweet wondered if "that was his tragedy." An oversimplification, of course, although perhaps by this time Lindsay blamed the human race as well as himself for his failure to change the world.

But disappointment in his personal life and the human race never stopped him from caring deeply about his friends and increasingly dysfunctional "family." When Sandy wanted to give up photography and study Latin American music in Brazil, Lindsay once more agreed to help. A few months later his nephew landed in a mental hospital in Rio, after burning his passport, clothes, and return plane ticket. The British consul informed the Foreign Office, who informed Lindsay, who immediately telexed the necessary money to rescue him, then arranged for Sandy's hospitalization and therapy on his return. "Where was his father?" I asked. "On a trip to India," Lindsay said. "But they haven't been on speaking terms for years. And Jenny cut herself off from all of us a long time ago."

Patsy Healey, he wrote me, had left Stirling Mansions for a while, to stay in her agent's flat, but came back because she felt "homesick." And Jill Bennett's divorce from John Osborne struck him as "lastingly traumatic." She had begun an affair with an architect, forty-four years old to Jill's fifty-five, and was badly shaken when he broke it off: "He seemed to be everything she needed, but of course he proved unstable and she really does need someone to be with." As her only offer of work was another unrewarding movie role, he decided to form a company called Reductio ad Absurdum Productions, and direct "an Agatha Christie play with all the nice and talented friends who can't get work elsewhere. Jill is at the moment wading through Agatha's output to see if we can find a novel suitable for adaptation."

A month later, a postcard mailed from Hong Kong informed me of a change of plan:

> *Shooting a documentary on the epoch-making*
> *visit to China of the phenomenal Pop Duo*
> *WHAM!—and which I find myself mysteriously*
> *"directing." Actually the pop world is much*
> *too determinedly chaotic, wasteful, shallow etc.,*
> *to allow the shooting of any such documentary*
> *to be effectively organized.*

George Michael and Andrew Ridgeley, the phenomenal Pop Duo, were at the height of their popularity when the People's Republic invited them to tour China in May 1985. The country had temporarily relaxed its hard isolationist line, and under a new policy of cultural exchange, WHAM! became the first rock band to play there, and Martin Lewis, producer of the documentary, wanted a "prestige" director, with experience in location shooting, to record the event.

But WHAM!, of course, were basically interested in publicizing themselves, and Lindsay's interest was in recording the impact of one culture on another. In the opening scene of *WHAM! in China,* Michael and Ridgeley acknowledge wild applause from hundreds of fans at the end of a concert in Britain, then tell them, "See you after we get back from China." Cut to a Chinese girl playing traditional music on a zither, followed by shots of pagodas, teahouses, and incense sticks, with a soundtrack also featuring bronze bells, stone chimes, and ocarinas.

Although Lewis and the Pop Duo approved Lindsay's idea of cultural cross-cutting throughout the movie, when they viewed his cut of the material, "they wanted less China and more WHAM! And when I say 'they,' " Lindsay wrote me, "I mean particularly George Michael. An inflated ego with no interest in anything except his own reality." Martin Lewis supervised the re-edited version, which Lindsay did not approve. It lopped off about twenty minutes of the People's Republic, added ten minutes of the Pop Duo, and ran just over an hour. But even in modified form, its original idea survives, along with many distinctly personal scenes.

While Lindsay treats the Pop Duo objectively, as an undeniable phenomenon, he's clearly charmed by their young Chinese fans, eager for a taste of foreign honey and as naive in their own way as the musical theatre students of *The Singing Lesson*. Even though the Chinese students can't understand the words of the songs, they sense "something new, something foreign," as one of them explains, find pop music "romantic" and "exciting," and are fascinated by the Duo's extensive wardrobe. As the film was shot during May 1985, their excitement seems at once ironic and touching in retrospect. And one brief scene has acquired a subtext that no one could have predicted: a group of students watching Michael and Ridgeley as they walk across a peaceful, uncrowded Tiananmen Square with a huge banner-portrait of Mao on one wall.

Even the very old, although not particularly excited, are friendly and curious. Only the police and the bureaucrats remain warily impassive. "Anything outside their regulations completely baffles them," as Michael comments to Ridgeley. Discreet but alert, they shadow the band during its promotional tour of the Great Wall, with press cameras clicking; they watch Ridgeley explore a street market, where he tries on a Chinese jacket and comments that "it reeks of camphor"; they hover in the background as a group of Chinese musicians demonstrate their panpipes, bamboo oboes, gourds, and drums; and they're not quite able to conceal disapproval of the rapturous applause that greets the band's concert in Beijing.

Another kind of cultural cross-cutting occurs at the British embassy's garden party for WHAM! Behind these high walls, where the waiters provide the only clue that we're in China, and only the women's dresses and hairstyles betray the fact that we're not in Britain some time before World War II, Lindsay's candid camera eye focuses on an extraordinary display of upper-class condescension and insularity. The ambassador and his wife do their best not to appear stuffed shirts as they greet the Duo with dutiful patronizing smiles, basically disinterested but forced to acknowledge that they matter, like the Queen when she honored the Beatles. Pretty and androgynous Michael with blonded bouffant hair and one earring, Ridgeley in his tartan jacket, a wave of long dark hair teased "casually" over one eye, seem no less startling to this time-warped enclave than to the Chinese. Members of the embassy staff turn politely away after being introduced, and resume their tight, superior huddles. "Are you going to be a groupie?" a young man asks a girl. "But of course!" she replies in the same impeccable yuppie accent, and they both titter.

After Beijing, the band moves to Guangzhou (Canton), where the longest concert sequence concludes the film. It seems even more enthusiastically received, perhaps because the police are less evident. The concert begins with a Chinese-inflected introduction by the band's black trumpeter, who gets a standing ovation. Then the Duo parade their wares: standard rock noise and gaudy lighting, but Michael has an effective line in coquettish struts and wiggles.

Lindsay's atmospheric images of Guangzhou, the river port with its busy water traffic, the narrow slanting streets with ancient wooden houses, reflect a city that looks like a real place, built on a human scale, unlike the "new" rebuilt Beijing, with its grandiose and oppressive Soviet-style architecture. But it's the Chinese students who haunt the film. You wonder how many of them were in Tiananmen Square two years later, when the police opened fire on demonstrators.

Back in London, Lindsay began discussions with David Sherwin on *If 2*, about the young rebels of *If . . .* twenty-five years later. Their main problem, never satisfactorily resolved, was to decide how Mick Travis and his friends on the rooftop escaped death from "the massed fire power of the establishment." Although Lindsay met with two producers who expressed interest in the project, he found "both of them, though wishing to be agreeable, repulsive," and *If 2* was relegated to the shelf for a while.

With no movie or theatre offers in the wings, Lindsay accepted an invitation to serve on the jury of the Berlin Film Festival, a mainly dreary affair, he wrote me on March 6, 1986, enlivened by the jury's president, Gina Lollobrigida:

An authentic monstre, *devotedly self-obsessed:*
apart from the inevitable thickening, she
manages to look quite indistinguishable from
the Star of twenty (thirty?) years ago. Her
great moment came when she discovered that
the German film Stammheim, *a pretty valuable*
dramatized documentary about the trial of the
Baader Meinhoff terrorists, had actually,
without her noticing it, won the Golden Bear.
She burst into wonderful Neapolitan fishwife
tears, proclaiming that if she returned to
Italy, having awarded a prize to a film which
"glorified terrorism," she would be spat upon
and very probably herself assassinated.

And one afternoon he crossed to East Berlin to look at the Brecht Theatre, "a bit mouldy now and typically drab," then to visit the cemetery behind the house where Brecht and Helene Weigel used to live in separate apartments. Brecht's grave stood next to Weigel's, identically plain, bleak headstones with a light coating of snow and neglect. Lindsay found the scene "strangely affecting in a poetic-ironic way," and wondered as he stared at the playwright's grave with just the two words of his name on it: "What would the wily, brilliant Brecht, who at least had the luck to live most of his life in a climate where belief in a socialist ideal was possible, think of the disabused, wicked, lunatic world of today? How could he function? And would he be able to function at all?"

Questions that Lindsay, of course, had begun to ask himself.

And questions that I also began to ask myself, each time I left Morocco to work for a few months in the increasingly lunatic world of Hollywood. By the late 1970s, industrial conglomerates had taken over most of the studios, and the industry had started to recover from its economic slump. But the frightened committees in charge of it, as John Schlesinger commented, were proving more tyrannical than the confident personal despots of the past. Since the hugely profitable *Jaws,* high-tech blockbusters had become the genre of commercial choice, followed (after the success of *Halloween* and *Superman*) by slasher and comic-book sagas. The decade had begun promisingly, with Scorsese's *Taxi Driver,* Coppola's two *Godfather* movies and *The Conversation,* Robert Altman's *McCabe and Mrs. Miller* and *Nashville,* but it ended in a false dawn, and their directors would find it increasingly difficult to make movies of creative choice.

I spent my first few months in the post-*Jaws* world, from November 1976 to May 1977, working on two movie scripts. The first was a Roger Corman production set in a Colorado ski resort, which I knew would earn me some money and hoped would do me no harm, but it was so bungled and rewritten by the director that I had my name removed from the credits. Meanwhile, Anthony Page, who was already in Hollywood directing a TV movie, had signed a contract to follow it with a low-budget production for the big screen: *I Never Promised You a Rose Garden,* from Joanne Greenberg's autobiographical novel about a young schizophrenic. A script already existed, but Anthony convinced the producers (four of them, including Corman) that it needed a total "page one" rewrite.

For the usual complex financial reasons, the start of shooting on *I Never Promised You a Rose Garden* couldn't be delayed, and I had only three weeks to work out a new approach to the material with Anthony, then write the screenplay. I passed it to him in installments of around twenty pages, and we met at night to discuss them, as he was busy during the day casting actors and choosing locations, exterior and interior, for a movie with no studio sets.

Principally on account of Anthony, whose work in TV had accustomed him to an atmosphere of crisis, the pressures were creatively stimulating. His flair for casting was reflected in the choice of the very talented semi-unknown Kathleen Quinlan for the leading role, Bibi Andersson (from *Persona* and several other Ingmar Bergman films) as her psychiatrist, and two indomitable Hollywood veterans, Sylvia Sidney and Signe Hasso, among the patients at the hospital. The confederacy of producers on *I Never Promised You a Rose Garden* was a welcome exception to Schlesinger's rule. They never interfered at any stage, and agreed to Anthony's request that I work with him throughout production, to make final adjustments to the script.

Shooting began early in April 1977 and was completed in twenty-eight days. Before going back to Morocco I saw the first cut, and was impressed by the way Anthony had either overcome the limitations of a

low budget or turned them to advantage. Although he opted for directness and immediacy, photography that gave the movie a raw semidocumentary surface, the performances were detailed and complex,
Kathleen sometimes pathetic and sometimes violently unnerving, Bibi
subtly patient and watchful, Sylvia defiant yet fragile, Signe mon-
strously sad.

Ten months after I returned to Tangier, my agent phoned with the
news that the screenplay for *I Never Promised You a Rose Garden* had been
nominated for an Academy Award. My main surprise was that Kathleen's performance hadn't been nominated, my least that the screenplay
for *Julia* won. But as well as making a small profit, the film had a critical success unusual for such a modest work, and was one of the first
"alternative" off-Hollywood productions with no money to spare or
flaunt, and human beings instead of special effects.

In 1986 Anthony offered me another chance to work with him under
similar conditions, on a movie for TV. *Second Serve* was based on the autobiography of Renée Richards, a successful male eye surgeon and amateur
tennis champion who became a professional female tennis player after
undergoing transsexual surgery. Once again the existing script needed a
"page one" rewrite, but this time I had four instead of three weeks before
shooting was unalterably scheduled to start. Enough time for a quick
trip to New York with producer Linda Yellen to interview Richards herself, who had given up tennis to resume practice as an eye surgeon. Low-
key, with an aura of loneliness, she almost disguised the masculine depth
that her voice had never lost by speaking very quietly. Because she'd disliked the first script, she was guarded at first, but after a while decided
she could trust us. She showed me the modest apartment where she
lived, back of her Park Avenue office, and confided as we stood in the
doorway to her little bedroom, with its single bed, that her romantic life
was over. Richards also told us about the son she'd first fathered and then
mothered, who still sometimes forgot to call her Mom instead of Dad,
and it gave me an idea for the movie's closing scene.

Back in California, at a hall belonging to an Episcopal church in
Santa Monica, I attended a meeting of a support group for transsexuals in
various stages, "pre-op" (emotionally but not yet technically feminine),
"intermediate" (androgynous, with hormone-induced female breasts
but male organs still intact), and "post-op." They all dressed as women,
some more convincingly than others, and worked in "ordinary" profes-

sions, as plumbers, electricians, dry cleaners, telephone repairmen. Some hadn't yet saved enough money for post-op, but they were all touchingly, even fanatically, determined to reach their goal.

Although only pre-op, the telephone repairman was already a totally convincing girl whose unisex clothes, boyish figure, and cropped hair reminded me of Jean Seberg in *Breathless*. But an intermediate plumber, in blond wig and emerald-green evening gown, was more like a female impersonator's Mae West. After the meeting ended, I walked along a corridor to the men's room, and heard a low but anguished sobbing on the other side of the door. I opened it quietly and saw that the plumber had removed his wig and makeup and changed into jeans and sweatshirt. With tears running down his cheeks to the five o'clock shadow on his chin, he mourned his lost identity as he stood in front of a mirror, gazing at his dark crew-cut hair grown thin on top and the outline of breasts under his sweatshirt. The moment was far too poignant to be grotesque, and I tried but failed to find a moment for it in the film. It was "wrong" for Richards him-/herself, and to create the "right" minor character would have taken too much time.

The serial life of Renée Richards—from husband and father to pre-op to intermediate to post-op with a lover to single mother with a son—was portrayed by Vanessa Redgrave. She had attended the same support group meeting, but the truth of her performance(s) owed more to imagination and instinct than research. Two days before it was due to be shot, she made a mysterious objection to a scene in the script where Richards wakes up in great pain after the operation. Vanessa insisted it was "unnecessary," and refused my point that it was important to show the pain because only someone with an intense need for self-transformation, as a post-op had told me, would willingly endure it. Anthony also failed to persuade Vanessa to change her mind, and the night before the scene was due to be shot, she was still refusing to play the scene. But next morning she arrived on the hospital set in a hospital gown, told Anthony she was ready, lay down on the bed, and acted "pain" with a bloodcurdling reality.

Perhaps Vanessa herself didn't know until the last moment whether she would play the scene, and perhaps she needed to work herself into a highly emotional state before she *could* play it. I never asked, partly because I wasn't sure that she would or could tell me, partly out of respect for the creative privacy of an extraordinary actress.

Between the two films with Anthony, I was in Los Angeles again, working on a script that was never produced. Rachel Roberts was there, living with Darren, and during the fall of 1980 I saw her alone several times. Each time, she talked about wanting to die. Like her other friends, I tried all the usual arguments—you're a wonderful person, a wonderful actress, you have many friends who love you—but each time the person and the actress seemed further away. A few days before I went back to Tangier, Rachel arrived unexpectedly at my apartment hotel. She made an effort, as usual, to be good company, and to look good, but although she wore a rakish cap, form-fitting sweater, and pants, there was no glimmer of light in her eyes. And she said without any preamble: "I've lost the will to live." Hoping to make her laugh, I suggested that she place an ad in the *Los Angeles Times*. " 'Lost, Rachel Roberts's will to live,' " I said. "Specify place and time, and offer a reward." She laughed, kissed me, and said goodbye. Two days later, she was found dead on her kitchen floor.

In Tangier I started work on my longest and most ambitious "Hollywood" novel. *Running Time,* published in 1983 and dedicated to Lindsay, was structured as a series of alternating and sometimes contradictory monologues by an epic stage mother and the daughter she's determined to make Hollywood's greatest, most long-running child star. The story begins in 1919, when Elva and Baby arrive in the promised land from Chicago, with no friends or connections and $575 in the bank. It ends shortly after Elva's death, when the seventy-year-old former Baby Jewel has inherited $250,000,000 from her mother's huge and secretly criminal business empire, and Los Angeles has developed from a string of small hick towns to a swarming city-state.

The book appeared first in England, where "serious" literary critics declined to consider Hollywood a worthy subject for a "serious" novel, and unserious ones found *Running Time* "amusing fare" for movie buffs. "I guess, for all its wit, it is too humanistic, too fond and even too positive for the smart-sophisticates who have taken over the media," Lindsay wrote me, citing a recent BBC program as typical: "*Tootsie* was discussed, dissected and dismissed by a very truculent lesbian in collar and tie, and a very weedly [*sic*] male homosexual, both indignant about the film's insulting attitude to Women and the Sexual Question generally."

The American reviews were on the whole "good," I wrote Lindsay a few weeks later. "They should have been brilliant," he replied in a char-

Faces of old age in *The Whales of August:* Lillian Gish and Bette Davis

The Whales of August. Ann Sothern

acteristically supportive letter. And enclosed a generous and astute review of *Running Time* that he'd written for *The Guardian:* "Fortunately nobody [on the editorial staff] spotted the dedication, which might raise a liberal eyebrow or two."

For more than a year after *WHAM! in China,* Lindsay worked on two film projects: *If 2,* taken off the shelf and then returned to it after long but inconclusive discussions with David Sherwin, and *The Cherry Orchard.* Frank Grimes, he wrote me, had collaborated on the Chekhov adaptation, Maggie Smith had agreed to play Ranevskaya and Alan Bates her brother Gayev, but no British company was interested. His letters also kept me informed of movies he'd liked, notably *Libeled Lady* and *Wife Versus Secretary,* revived on TV ("what friendly fun they had in those days"); those he'd disliked, notably the current British success *A Room with a View* ("spineless mush"); and the National Film Theatre's program during February 1986 to mark the thirtieth anniversary of Free Cinema. "The 'critics' and columnists reluctantly praised but more obviously resented it. I enclose some reviews just to remind you of This England." One of them referred to Lindsay as "headmaster-like," another called him "a cold-eyed intellectual." The persona, it seemed, was continuing to overshadow the person.

But as Lindsay grew older, the contradictions in the nature of the person became more extreme, and the next film he made reflected them. Its producer, Mike Kaplan, was a friend and admirer of Lillian Gish. During a visit to his family in Rhode Island in 1978, he had seen a play at the Trinity Square Repertory in Providence about two elderly sisters who shared a summerhouse on the coast of Maine. When *The Whales of August* was produced a few months later off-Broadway, Mike took Gish to see it; he explained that he hoped to secure Bette Davis for the other sister, and Gish agreed to do the film "if you can set it up."

But by the late 1970s the movie career of Bette Davis was winding down—she could only get work on TV—and no Hollywood studio expressed interest in Gish, with or without Davis. It was only in the mid-eighties, when a modestly budgeted movie could recoup its costs on the expanding TV and video market, that a company called Alive Films was willing to back the project. Mike, who began his movie career as a publicity director and oversaw the campaigns for *2001* and

A Clockwork Orange, had met Lindsay through Malcolm McDowell. In late 1985 he asked him to direct *The Whales of August.* Lindsay agreed, then had an unusually long and intense attack of self-doubt, even refusing to take Mike's phone calls for two weeks. Finally, Lindsay's agent, "so keen on making DEALS," Lindsay wrote me on June 5, 1986, persuaded him to sign the contract. "Now it looks HORRIBLY as though I am going to have to direct it."

In the meantime, Bette Davis had turned down the other leading role, which was also rejected by Barbara Stanwyck and Katharine Hepburn. Then Davis changed her mind—and Gish withdrew. Seven years had passed since she'd seen the play with Mike, and she feared she no longer had the energy for another movie. Fortunately Mike persuaded her otherwise. "I'm affirmative," she finally said, and so was Ann Sothern, cast in the important role of a neighbor.

At the start of shooting, Gish was ninety-two, Bette Davis seventy-eight, Ann Sothern seventy-seven, and Vincent Price (replacing John Gielgud, who had originally agreed to play the most substantial male role, but proved unavailable) the baby of the company at seventy-two. Their combined ages prompted Coral Browne, Price's wife, to suggest that Alive Films should change its name to Barely Alive. In fact, the authentically "golden" years of the three actresses heightened the movie's reality, as well as creating technical problems. Gish was fairly deaf, and had moments of vagueness; Davis had endured a mastectomy, two strokes, and an operation for hip replacement; and Ann Sothern had difficulty walking, the result of an accident many years earlier. She was playing in a summer stock theatre when a property tree fell on her, fracturing her spinal column and severely damaging the nerves in her legs.

In *The Whales of August,* the pace is adjusted to the slowed down, restricted movements of senior citizenry, and the dialogue scenes have a few hesitantly timed moments; but the result is a painstakingly and sometimes painfully truthful record of the resilience as well as the infirmities of old age. None of the actors attempts any kind of disguise or wears makeup to look younger or older, and in the last act of their careers, Gish and Ann Sothern in particular give performances of extraordinary vitality as well as skill.

Lindsay recognized from the start that the material was "weak," and needed a stronger ending. In David Berry's play, the younger sister

(Gish, actually fourteen years older than Bette) decides to leave her dependent but testy blind sibling and "live her own life." He found this "too reminiscent of the current American cliché of women finding their own way," and asked Berry to write a new scene that he described as "the only possible solution." After years of quarreling and mutual resentment, Sarah and Libby finally reach a kind of accommodation, and begin to understand each other's needs.

Shot entirely on location in and around a house on an island off the coast of Maine, during September and October 1986, the movie opens with a prologue in black and white. A long shot of the ocean beyond the house is followed by a medium shot of a buoy with a clanging bell, and another of three adolescent girls in long white summer dresses as they run from the house to the edge of the promontory. While they wait for a glimpse of the whales that traditionally surface during August, the camera never moves close enough for their faces to become clearly recognizable. Another shot of the buoy is followed by a shot of it in color, then of Sarah, Libby, and their neighbor Tisha, sixty years later, standing exactly where we first saw them as young girls in the monochrome past.

For all three, it soon becomes apparent, old age means physical decline and a sense of being marginalized. But although both sisters are widowed, Sarah (Gish) finds a degree of consolation and peace in the memory of her dead husband's telling her, "Passion and truth, that's all we need," while Libby (Davis) withdraws into bitterness with "Life fools you, it always does." At the heart of the film is a relationship between someone who's come to terms with loneliness, and someone whose loneliness is all the greater because she resents it so fiercely. Tisha, also a widow, and able to walk only a short distance with the aid of a cane, is deeply humiliated when she's no longer allowed to drive her car. But although fearful of the prospect of a housebound future, she refuses to despair, like the impoverished Russian exile (Vincent Price), who has nowhere to go when his hostess of many years suddenly dies.

The same love that Lindsay brought to Gielgud and Ralph Richardson in *Home* is evident in his handling of Gish, Ann Sothern, and (as an actress, if not as a person) Bette Davis. He also brought a similar ironic-elegiac mood to *The Whales of August,* especially in two almost silent scenes where the sisters are alone with themselves and their past. Sarah has kept the telegram informing her of her husband's death in action during World War II, and she likes to reread it aloud, then gaze at his photograph on her dressing table. Libby clings to a very different memento, and reacts very differently to it. She's preserved a lock of her hair, cut when she was a young girl, which she passes longingly across her cheek. The touch of lost youth brings a look of terrible rancor to her face, and explains why Sarah, as she tells Trisha, is afraid that Libby has "given up on life."

One of their recurrent disputes is over a picture window that Sarah wants to add to the living room. It will make the view even more spectacular, she says, but Libby insists that "we're too old to be considering new things." In a final scene, she unexpectedly changes her mind. She'll never be able to see the view, but by imagining the pleasure it will give Sarah, she can break out of her self-imposed isolation. Although performances and direction avoid sentimentality here, they can't quite achieve conviction in an underwritten scene.

But the closing shots are consciously and effectively Fordian, a nod to the end of *My Darling Clementine* with its two solitary figures in an empty landscape, the schoolteacher watching Wyatt Earp ride off into the West. Arm in arm, the two sisters slowly cross the veranda, and the camera holds on an empty rocking chair after they leave the frame. It picks them up on their way through the overgrown garden to the edge of the promontory, where they stand gazing at the ocean, as we first saw them. The island location of the movie, coincidentally, is less than fifty miles offshore from Portland, the birthplace of John Ford.

Gish dominates *The Whales of August* with a performance of "passion and truth," Ann Sothern is richly humorous and touching in a supporting role, but Bette Davis seems more studied and external in contrast, and did herself no favor by choosing to wear a profoundly unconvincing wig. Its long, silvery white hair, as Jocelyn Herbert commented, "looked as if it was made of nylon." Ironically, the silent-movie star seems more contemporary in style than the star whose career began in talkies. In one of his postcards from Maine, Lindsay described Gish as "mysteriously spellbinding," and part of the mystery is that, unlike Bette, she never allows you to see the actress at work.

Lindsay and Ann Sothern also saw the actress at work in other ways. Bette brought her own hairdresser and makeup man, whom she refused to share with Gish or Ann. "In fact poor Bette, who wasn't well, was a holy terror, crabby and irascible," Ann remembered. "She was terribly jealous of Lillian because she wanted to play her part." And their relationship in the movie had its counterpart in Gish's reaction to Bette's meanness. "Lillian just shakes her head," Lindsay noted. " 'Poor Bette,' she says. 'How she must be suffering. What an unhappy life she's led.' " He also recorded another parallel with their roles:

> *Lillian likes to repeat her mother's advice on how best to make one's way through life. 'You can get on by being rude to people, but you'll find things a good deal easier if you treat people well, with kindness and courtesy.' Bette's mother surely gave her no such counsel. Bette's impulse is to treat the world and everyone in it with hostility.*

"For all her trials and conflicts with Warner Brothers," Lindsay's diary continued, "Bette had no relish for freedom and yearned continually for Burbank." She was not used to going out on location, as she reminded anyone who would listen, because "locations always used to come to *me*," and seemed indifferent to "the beautiful seascapes visible without benefit of back projection" beyond the windows. Her most frequent response to any suggestion that Lindsay made was an emphatic "Rubbish!" Occasionally she agreed with a grudging nod, and once announced to the crew: "That's twice I've given in to the director today. I must be slipping." Finally she provoked Lindsay to say, "You're not taking over this picture, Bette," which provoked her to walk off the set and refuse to come back until he apologized. Work stopped for half an hour until, at Mike's insistence, Lindsay made peace with her.

By the sixth week of shooting, another postcard from Maine informed me, "Bette has gone full circle, from suspicion and hostility to paranoia to (proclaimed) friendship and admiration. I think she is essentially MAD." Gish, by contrast, he found "simple and saintly," their disagreements few and "unfailingly pleasant." When they rehearsed her scene with the telegram, she noticed that Lindsay had angled the camera behind the dressing table, leaving her face in three-quarter profile. "You won't catch the expression in my eyes," she said. "Mr. Griffith always told me, you have to show everything through the eyes." Then Lindsay asked if she remembered Whistler's portrait of his mother, and Gish nodded. "Well," he explained, "Whistler painted her from exactly the same angle as I'm photographing you. And you can tell exactly what she's feeling."

Gish thought this over. "Maybe," she said finally. "But the Mona Lisa's more popular than Whistler's Mother." Then she played the scene as Lindsay directed, and in spite of Mr. Griffith, managed to show "everything."

Deafness was Gish's major problem, as Ann Sothern recalled: "Lillian could remember lines okay, but she couldn't hear. She worked with some hearing aid, could read lips, and Lindsay communicated with some kind of walkie-talkie mike, feeding her lines. It was difficult, as there was often a long space, which had to be fixed later in the cutting, before she picked up her cue." And Jocelyn Herbert recalled that she sometimes confused a character in the movie with a character from her own life: "When I showed her the various photos we were going to put on her dressing table, Lillian looked at the face that was supposed to represent a sister who'd died many years earlier, and shook her head. 'That's not Dorothy,' she said."

On and off the set, the least problematic of the trio was Ann Sothern. Lindsay had always admired her, and wrote me that she was "great good fun as well." They evidently relaxed each other, and when Ann discovered that Lindsay knew "just about every popular song ever written, we used to sing together a lot of the time. I'd brought my own cook to the location and he loved to come over and have dinner at my cottage." She also found him "patient, kind and inspirational with actors. He thought of good things to give you to do."

"Good or bad, I feel we are making movie history!" Lindsay wrote on his final postcard from Maine. He also fulfilled Mike Kaplan's hope of producing a final tribute to Gish's unique talent, and in various ways *The Whales of August* proved a landmark in the career of all three actresses. For Bette, "giving in" to Lindsay was an exercise in self-restraint after years of self-indulgence, and her last completed movie did much to restore a declining reputation. (In 1988 she began filming *Wicked Stepmother,* but illness forced her to withdraw after two weeks. As she played a witch, a plot twist was added to turn her into either Barbara Carrera or a black cat for the rest of the story, and the film was eventually released on video.) But Ann Sothern's talent was exceptionally unselfish as well as exceptional. In *The Whales of August* she had one of her best roles, and was as deservedly Oscar-nominated as Gish was undeservedly overlooked.

Realizing that Berry's play was almost totally actor-dependent, and as a movie would need as much visual expressiveness as he could devise, Lindsay turned to two valued colleagues for help. Mike Fash, who gave *Britannia Hospital* its hard, primary-colored, TV-commercial look, photographed *The Whales of August* in muted and mellow tones, while Jocelyn Herbert's art direction created an unobtrusively lived-in look for every room in the sisters' house. She chose furniture and knickknacks that seemed to have been there for years, rugs that were subtly faded, and in a secondhand store she found an old cardigan sweater that Gish loved, wearing it for several scenes and wrapping herself in it like an element of her character.

Bette, of course, refused to accept any suggestion from Jocelyn about her costumes.

In spite of his admiration and fondness for Gish, according to Jocelyn, "in a way Lindsay found Bette more intriguing." As she pointed out, they were both confrontational; and from another angle, Lindsay and Bette, like Lindsay and Gish, were mirror images of each other. At sixty-three, although looking older, Lindsay was on the cusp of old age when he directed a movie about old age, represented at its most generous and tolerant by Gish, at its most cantankerous by Bette. But from his diary notes on the filming and the postcards he wrote me, he never realized that they also represented two sides of himself. He invariably portrayed himself as Gish-like, a model of patience and equanimity, although Mike Kaplan recalled quite a few Bette Davis moments.

Apart from the two weeks when Lindsay had refused to take Mike's calls, their relationship had been friendly. But when Lindsay arrived on the location, he "bristled with hostility. 'This is *your* movie, not *my* movie,' he said." Bette, as Jocelyn remembered, "wanted it to be *her* film," and to Mike it seemed that the same grudge affected them in the same way:

> *Lindsay was usually thoughtful and kind with*
> *the actors. But although Bette was fractious,*
> *he seemed to enjoy provoking her, and she*
> *threatened to quit several times. And with the*
> *others he was occasionally ruthless. He rewrote*
> *dialogue at the last moment, which he knew*
> *created difficulties for Gish, he kept Vincent*
> *Price waiting for several days to play his first*
> *scene, and he even upset the wonderfully genial*
> *Ann Sothern by refusing to block her first major*
> *scene with Gish. Then, typically, he relented and*
> *staged it brilliantly.*

Tension on the small, isolated island, Mike added, was often "extreme," and seeing the dailies "provided the only relief from the hell of it." Bette, "still the consummate if egomaniac professional," was the only actor who came to see them, "and for all her animosity toward Gish as well as Lindsay, had to admit they were good."

But Lindsay was partly right when he told Mike Kaplan that *The Whales of August* wasn't "his" movie. There's a good deal of Lindsay in it, but also a good deal of Lindsay that's not in it: the dynamic vision and outrageous humor of his most personal work, and the fact, as Vincent Price said later, that "it's a dear little story, but not really about anything."

The movie was well received when it opened in New York in February 1988; and in the same week Lindsay's production of Philip Barry's *Holiday* opened (February 15) at the Old Vic in London. Another project that was not "his," it offered Frank Grimes a promising role, that of the alcoholic brother created by Lew Ayres in Cukor's classic 1938 film. Mary Steenburgen and Malcolm McDowell, who were married at the time, played the Katharine Hepburn and Cary Grant roles, but only Steenburgen was well cast. And in spite of her humor and lightness, the production seemed heavy-handed, with Frank competent in the Lew

Ayres part but lacking his charm, Malcolm not at his best, Lindsay no more at ease with the Park Avenue rich than with Chekhov's landed gentry.

At a time when Stallone and Schwarzenegger spelled commercial success, it was sad but not surprising that Lillian Gish and Bette Davis in *The Whales of August* spelled commercial failure. And not surprising that Lindsay had begun to feel time running out when he accepted an offer to direct a miniseries for Home Box Office in Toronto. "I honestly don't know if I can do it—not my speed at all—and ever since *Whales* I have felt profoundly alienated from the whole business," he wrote me. "So this is a real last crazy venture."

PART FOUR

New Times

~ Lindsay on Lindsay ~

I've never been an extreme left-winger, but I think that in the fifties and sixties there was reason to hope there might be a social democratic solution. But the English rejected radicalism. They've stuck by the Queen.

I don't think one can regret anything really, do you? I mean, everything that's happened is fated, is what we are. Could one ever have been different? "We know what we are but we know not what we may be."

11

By the time Lindsay left for Toronto, he had opened a new door for me as a writer, although when I reread his letters to me, I realized that one of them had opened the door a subliminal crack five years earlier, on June 14, 1983:

> *A sad day—when I open my* Daily Telegraph *and find that Norma {Shearer} has gone. She remains (for me) the most romantic myth of all. The purest Star. She wasn't a great actress, like Garbo; not as witty or skillful as Lombard or Loy; not as brutish and implacable as Crawford; certainly never as brilliant as Davis. But she was unashamedly a Star—with a sometimes outrageous, always captivating domination of and seduction by the camera that was surely unique.*

On a visit to London from Tangier four years later, I spent an evening with Lindsay at Stirling Mansions, and after dinner he took down a videocassette from the collection that occupied almost one entire wall of the living room. As well as complete movies, it included sequences from others that he particularly liked or found memorably absurd. The reel he chose that night began with a musical number from *Good News,* continued with a mink-coated Joan Crawford cowering in *Sudden Fear,* and climaxed with two intense confrontation scenes, between Norma Shearer and Charles Laughton in *The Barretts of Wimpole Street* and between Norma and Conrad Veidt in *Escape.*

The last time I saw a Shearer movie, I told Lindsay, was in 1973, when she invited me to a screening of *Idiot's Delight* at her alma mater, MGM. I described her mixture of glittering star persona and strange disorientation, like the moment when we arrived at the studio and she gazed at the MGM sign above the moonlit Thalberg Building, suddenly uncertain where she was; the intense self-absorption of seventy-one-year-old Norma as she confronted thirty-seven-year-old Norma in a white satin Adrian gown and blond Sydney Guilaroff wig, affecting a languid foreign accent and waving a long cigarette holder; and the way she clutched my hand and said "You understand!" when I told her that I realized she was parodying Garbo.

This reminded Lindsay how much he'd enjoyed Norma's performance in *Idiot's Delight,* and he remarked on the contrast between its high artifice and the emotional tension of the scenes we'd just watched. He was also very interested in my account of the way Norma's psyche drifted sadly and helplessly into a twilight zone, although it made him feel glad that he'd never met her. "But I'm glad *you* did," he added, "because there's obviously an extraordinary life to tell, and I think you should tell it. Why don't you write her biography?"

Although I had never written a biography, I had read and admired a great many, especially Stefan Zweig's *Mary, Queen of Scotland and the Isles,* A. J. A. Symons's *The Quest for Corvo,* Henri Troyat's *Catherine the Great* and *Turgenev,* Suetonius' *The Twelve Caesars* and its remote descendant, Lytton Strachey's *Eminent Victorians.* They all read like novels, and with no novel in my head at the time, it occurred to me that writing a biography would be like writing a novel with the plot already laid out. You couldn't depart from it, but you could always write as well as read a good plot between the lines. And Norma's life, from what I'd heard and what she'd told me about it, had a very good plot.

As well as opening this door, Lindsay was partly responsible for reopening another. To research a biography of Norma, I would have to spend at least a year in Los Angeles, long enough to decide whether or not I wanted to live there again. In any case I had already decided to leave Tangier fairly soon. As Paul Bowles had predicted, it was slowly running down: a thicker film of neglect over everything, more buckles in the sidewalks, more potholes in the streets, many of the younger and livelier expatriates leaving, buckles and potholes apparent in many who remained and had begun to resemble the characters in the last volume of Proust.

I still loved Morocco (always would), especially the magical south beyond the Atlas Mountains, with its succession of battlemented casbahs, its pastoral valleys, salt lakes, dark petrified steppes, and finally the Sahara dunes, overwhelmingly still and silent. But on the cusp of sixty-three, I was old enough to start wondering where I wanted or didn't want to die. As England had never really felt like home, there was no question of trying to go home again, and I suspected that Los Angeles would be preferable to Tangier for living as well as dying.

And there was even less to hold me in Tangier after my relationship with Cherrat ended. Over the years he'd failed in one enterprise or job after another, and most recently the owner of the restaurant where he worked as a waiter had fired him, after an enormous row during which they hurled accusations at each other, then went outside for a fistfight on the beach. I never discovered what the row was about, and it didn't really matter. What mattered was something I could no longer deny to myself: in spite of his ebullience, charm, and sexual power, Cherrat was a beautiful incurable loser. Of course I never told him so, but on my side the relationship was beginning to cool, and I couldn't entirely disguise the fact. Cherrat never spoke of it, but finally surprised me with a marvelous display of dramatic flair and genuine pride. You no longer love me, he said, so it's better that I leave you.

Relieved, sad, and a little ashamed that Cherrat had the courage to make the first move, I didn't object when he blamed me for ending the affair. In fact I apologized, because he was right. It was my feelings that had changed, after all, not Cherrat's. I gave him enough money to live on for a few months, told him to be sure and get in touch if he was ever in need, and was rewarded with a smoldering look and a promise that he would never forget me. A few days before I left Tangier, he arrived unexpectedly at the house, wanting to say goodbye. We made love, I drove him back into town, dropped him off at the entrance to the medina, and he walked away without looking back. Then he disappeared into a crowded alley, and I never saw him again. Although I asked for news of Cherrat whenever I went back to Tangier on a visit, no one could tell me anything, and that last glimpse of him is another indelible, unfaded photograph in the mind's eye.

.   .   .

"The crazy ones often turn out surprisingly well," I wrote Lindsay about the miniseries he'd described as his "last crazy venture." His reply:

> I shall be repeating that to myself quite
> often during the months to come—though I
> also have a nasty suspicion that old dogs
> shouldn't try new tricks. At least I know
> better, whatever happens, than to resign. I
> am right, am I not, that if they fire you,
> they've got to pay you? I remember warning
> John Gielgud, when he set out for the US to
> direct Debbie Reynolds in Irene, on no account
> to resign. Well, he didn't; they fired him;
> and he did get paid.

But the old dog wasn't really being asked to perform new tricks. After reading Stan Daniels's script of *Glory! Glory!*, a satire on American TV evangelism, Lindsay noted in his diary that although there were "too many long, actionless scenes in the second half," he was struck by "its sharpness, unusually frank in its language, its openness about sex and drugs." And its central character, journeying from *Candide*-like innocence to corruption, reminded him of Mick Travis in *O Lucky Man!* But Lindsay's habitual stage fright was intensified by the project's rigorous schedule: only six weeks to prepare and thirty-five days to shoot three hours and twenty minutes of film.

Because production costs were lower there, *Glory! Glory!* was shot in Canada with a Canadian cast, apart from the three American leads, and a Canadian crew, apart from Mike Fash, the fast, dependable, and inventive cinematographer of *Britannia Hospital* and *The Whales of August*. When Lindsay left London for Toronto on March 16, he noted in his diary that "the comparative failure of *Whales* and *Holiday*" was all he had to show for the past year, "and in a month's time I shall be 65." And the in-flight movie aggravated his self-doubt: "*Suspect*, with the glum but powerfully egotistical Cher. I reflect on the contemporary made-for-TV look, all cuts and close shots. And I think—God!—is that what I'm supposed to be doing?"

In fact, as long as he stayed on schedule, Lindsay was given a stylistically free hand. But although (at first) he found the producer, Bonny Dore, "pleasant" and "respectful," the HBO executives confirmed his mistrust of authority figures when they insisted that the sequences of Sister Ruth's rock 'n' roll evangelism "must make the men in the audience want to cream in their pants." Their "cheapness of sensibility," he noted, "makes even more nightmarish the pseudo-'tasteful,' huge glass-and-concrete palaces in which the Devil's work is conducted." He left the concrete palace in a fractious mood that lasted throughout the shoot, and found Bonny Dore guilty by association.

On the day before shooting started, a phone call from Murray compounded his anxiety. "In his usual measured tone," Lindsay wrote me, his brother told him that Sandy had taken the train to a town on the Devonshire coast and "walked into the sea. By some God-given chance he was seen by the coastguard watch, who sent out a rescue boat. They found him floating face down in the water, pulled him in and applied respiration *just in time.*"

As shooting progressed, Lindsay's dispatches from the front reported "daily tension" with Bonny Dore, whom he accused of "obsessive ill-judgment," daily rows with the costume designer that ended with her resignation, and furious disputes with the "inexperienced hysteric" Ellen Greene, who played Sister Ruth. Inexperienced Greene was not, having recently starred in *The Little Shop of Horrors,* but like Lindsay she translated insecurity into aggression. In her own case, the traumas probably contributed to a brilliant, nervy performance. In Lindsay's, they had no visible effect on his professionalism (in contrast to his disposition), and a final postcard informed me that he completed his last major work "at 3.50 a.m.—ten minutes ahead of schedule."

Under the main credits, a sepia-tinted photograph of the modest Church of the Companions of Christ in Waco, Texas, with a car parked nearby to establish the period as 1960s. A choir sings the church's theme song, "Call Jesus up and tell him what you want / The line is never busy," until the last credit, then color and motion seep into the

photograph. Inside the church, Reverend Dan preaches a fundamental-
ist sermon. A shameless grandstander, he alternately cajoles, threatens,
and spellbinds the congregation, while his six-year-old son, Bobby Joe,
listens and parrots "Praise Jesus" on cue.

Twenty years later, the church operates from a much larger, more
ostentatious building, and syndicated TV airs the "miracles" performed
by Reverend Dan on the incurably ill and disabled. But Bobby Joe
(Richard Thomas) has to take over the business when his father suffers a
stroke after praying Jesus to heal a wheelchair case. (In the confusion
that follows, the wheelchair case gets up and makes a quick exit.)
Unlike Reverend Dan, his son is not a cunning spiritual bully but a
sincere believer. Sincerity proves far less effective than manipulation,
and the church's followers fail to respond to his sermons with the same
hugely profitable mixture of fear and hysteria. Soon Bobby Joe is
preaching to almost empty houses; the ladies in an underground vault,
who used to count the dollar bills pouring in as expertly as bank tellers,
and murmur "Praise Jesus" at the same time, suddenly have nothing to
do; and Lester (James Whitmore), the money-laundering accountant of
a "complex, sophisticated, multi-million-dollar organization," warns
Bobby Joe that it's headed for bankruptcy.

Hoping for "inspiration," Bobby Joe crosses to the other side of
town to visit the original church that he attended as a child. It's now a
rock joint, with a singer (Ellen Greene) who provokes an audience
response that strikes him as uncannily close to the frenzy of Reverend
Dan's followers. When Bobby Joe begs her to become the church's
gospel singer and revive its fortunes, she turns him down with "God
and me, we don't hang out," but changes her mind when she learns that
the church's meetings are syndicated on one hundred TV stations across
the country.

Onstage, backed by her rock group and a glittering cross, Sister
Ruth's evangelical vocals bring in more dollar bills than ever before, and
the ladies in the underground vault praise Jesus as they count them at
record speed. Offstage, the church's savior is a foul-mouthed drug
addict, supplied with packets of cocaine between the pages of a Bible by
the organization's undercover operator. When Bobby Joe confesses that
he's fallen in love with her, she drops her guitarist-lover to accommodate
him, partly out of expediency, partly because his innocence touches her.
(Bobby Joe, very shyly: "I've never been with a woman before." Sister

Glory! Glory! Directing the ladies who count dollar bills (in background, James Whitmore as Lester, and Richard Thomas as Bobby Joe)

Glory! Glory! Onstage, Ellen Greene as Sister Ruth the healer

Ruth: "Don't worry. I have.") And Lester, the accountant, relieves Bobby
Joe's guilt about sins of the flesh by revealing that his father committed
them "with many sopranos and maybe a couple of tenors."

Meanwhile Sister Ruth's single, "Satan Sucks," goes platinum, she
makes the cover of *Time* magazine, tells the press that her favorite drink
is "grape juice with a dash of Christ," and the *Sister Ruth Show* gradu-
ates to major-network TV. Like Paula Corbin Jones with the Christian
Coalition, she projects a manufactured image so convincingly that we
can't be sure who is manipulating whom. Neither can Bobby Joe.
Morally anesthetized by infatuation and his reborn church, he's at first
horrified when Ruth insists on an abortion after discovering she's pregnant. "I planted my seed in you and I want it to grow," he tells her.
"Your seed's not the only one that's been planted in me," Ruth answers,
and once again he has to live with it or lose her.

But the price of stardom is vulnerability to the media, in Sister
Ruth's case a plausible and unscrupulous TV "investigative reporter." A
married man and self-proclaimed believer in family values, he seduces
her, then threatens to expose her abortion, even though he also believes
in a woman's right to choose. There's a further satirical twist when the
media person is defeated by the superior corrupting power of politics.
With the help of a right-wing senator whose campaign for reelection
the church has promised to fund, and the network chief who's angling
for a "major" appointment from the senator if he's reelected, Lester and
his undercover operator succeed in killing the story.

In yet another twist, Sister Ruth confounds everyone by breaking
the story herself on her TV show. As befits a star, her show has moved to
Los Angeles, and in an act of public repentance, she confesses her
cocaine habit as well as her abortion to a live audience of trusting fans.
But she sinned *before* finding Christ, she tells them, and humbly begs
for forgiveness. Bobby Joe is so moved that he confesses his own sins of
the flesh, and even the infinitely venal Lester breaks down to admit that
he's stashed millions of dollars away in a secret Swiss bank account.
Although Ruth's audience is deeply stirred by this orgy of repentance,
it terrifies the network executives—until they learn that the show has
broken all rating records.

Stan Daniels's script ended on this high point of cynicism, but
Lindsay added an epilogue that moved beyond it. In a direct reference
to *O Lucky Man!,* the audience joins Sister Ruth, Bobby Joe, and Lester

onstage. The rock band strikes up, the rest of the cast appears from the wings, and everyone starts dancing, including the statue of Christ on the cross. The figure in a loincloth, bloodstains painted on his arms and thighs, comes nimbly to life and skips down to earth to join the celebration.

Britannia Hospital marked a change in the angle at which Lindsay stood to the universe, its tilt from skepticism to satire. Like the earlier film, *Glory! Glory!* is satirical but not, as he commented later, "in any way sour. The film is never as unpleasant as the evangelists are in reality." Although they have grown even more unpleasant and more powerful since 1988, the reality of *Glory! Glory!* is still acutely topical, fundamentalism in unholy alliance with right-wing politics, Christian rock and money laundering, the hypocrisy and opportunism of the media, the sexual inquisition of celebrities and the striptease of public repentance. But cynicism reflects the death of feeling, whereas satire is a weapon of self-defense as well as attack, and the satirist inflicts wounds in retaliation for his own wounds of outrage and pain.

A less imaginative director would have turned Stan Daniels's script into a merely cynical movie and Ruth into a one-dimensional, coke-snorting, scurrilous monster. True to his belief that comic characters, however extreme, had to be played with total conviction, Lindsay told Ellen Greene that only someone driven and tormented would lose herself so completely in the role of Sister Ruth, and by finding this subtext she created an appalling, touching, absurd original. Belief in her own image leads Ruth to belief in God, and in a knife-edged scene she tells Bobby Joe that she feels "sorry" for God because he's stuck with the imperfect world he created. Then, with total conviction, she adds: "He *needs* me." To Bobby Joe as well as Ruth, it seems that she's finally "become" Sister Ruth, and arrived at a kind of peace. But neither of them picks up the scent, in that last line, of the profound egomania of the star.

Lindsay saw both Bobby Joe and Ruth as self-deceivers in their different ways, and Richard Thomas found a different kind of subtext in Bobby Joe, charmingly innocent but fatally lacking in self-knowledge. When Reverend Dan told his congregation that no matter what happened, God made it happen and God always had his reasons, it was manipulation. When Bobby Joe says the same thing, convinced that God sent Ruth to save his church, it's not only the true believer but the sublime dupe speaking, unaware that he's been corrupted into serving God and Mammon. And Christ leaps from his cross to join the dance of life when he finally realizes that it's a fool's game to take the world's sins on your shoulders. If you can't lick them, join them.

Although made for American TV, *Glory! Glory!* was shot on film, then transferred to video for editing, and most of it looks like a real movie. In a few scenes the visual texture is relatively thin, in part because of a very demanding shooting schedule, but in greater part because the movie was shot in and around Toronto. The early Bible Belt scenes lack a sense of place, the extras are not quite uninhibited enough to convey revivalist mania, the "bad part of town," where Bobby Joe discovers Ruth in a rock joint, looks too respectable (is there no bad part of Toronto?), and the Los Angeles studio audience in the final scene is not tanned or picturesque enough. But these are minor flaws in a movie that never aims at naturalism, and reaches a satiric peak with the Christian rock numbers, lit with deliberately over-the-top garishness by Mike Fash, and staged by Lindsay with a knowing nod to his experience of the music world on *WHAM! in China.*

"*Glory! Glory!* was well received," Lindsay told Karel Reisz, "but although HBO were very pleased by its success, and congratulated me for bringing it in on budget, they never asked me back." He'd hoped the film would "shake off this reputation for integrity, the myth that if it's commercial, I won't touch it. We all want to be commercial on our own terms." But he seemed unaware, Karel recalled, that his behavior on the set had earned him a reputation for being "difficult." Two more years passed, in fact, before he fully understood why producers had grown wary of employing him, and meanwhile (in December 1988) he wrote me a disconsolate letter:

> It seems I'm not one of those people who can
> create their own worlds—their working worlds,
> I mean. But then how many directors have been
> able to do such a thing? Welles wasted years and
> years. Ford became exiled and excluded in the
> last years of his life. Sternberg and Sturges
> were lost without Paramount.

In a way, this is too simple. It takes no account of Ford's self-exile by heavy drinking during the last ten years of his life; or of whether Sternberg was "lost" without Paramount, or without Dietrich (his work declined sharply after they stopped making films together); or of how Welles, in fact, *did* create a working world for each of his later movies by improvising financing from various sources when no studio in Hollywood would back him. But the letter is also very revealing. In America and Britain, the obliging journeymen are allowed to keep busy until they drop, because they carry out orders and ask no questions. The industry always feels more comfortable with a Mervyn LeRoy or a Richard Donner than with an Orson Welles or a Martin Scorsese, and any filmmaker with a strong personal signature eventually faces exile. He has offended by subverting the movies he was expected to make, and/or by making too many movies that failed at the box office, usually because they failed to reassure audiences that they lived in the best of all possible worlds. Additionally, when this kind of filmmaker reaches sixty, he's considered "out of touch" with younger audiences, and if he's personally "difficult," the industry finds yet another reason to exile him.

In Europe, Buñuel directed his last film at seventy-seven; Bresson, Dreyer, and Renoir all at seventy-five; and Eric Rohmer, in his late seventies, was still managing to work on his own terms, because his very modestly budgeted films were accessible enough to show a modest profit. But even in Europe, it's unimaginable that an artist as uncompromisingly "difficult" as Samuel Beckett or Patrick White could make a career for himself in movies. For a filmmaker, as George Cukor remarked, "there's no such thing as absolute freedom. You have freedom within the context of what you're doing and what you're able to do." In the United States and Britain, it has always taken phenomenal energy and zest to survive the physical demands of moviemaking and to maintain, in old age, the struggle against commercial pressures. Apart from John Huston, the most notable survivors (Hitchcock, Ford, Cukor, Hawks, Wilder, Michael Powell) did their best work by the time they reached sixty-five.

During the last years of his life, Lindsay often wrote and spoke about the problem of survival. Among his posthumous papers I found a 1992 diary note, for an article he planned to write on Japanese cinema, that summed up his thoughts: "Incredible that films of such quality

[by Mizoguchi, Ozu, and Kurosawa] can be produced within the framework of a commercial industry—and apparently make money. Too
often the supposed limitations of the cinema are not limitations of the
medium itself, but of the cultures within which western film-makers
are obliged to work."

As the culture of market research increasingly dominated the
Hollywood studios during the 1980s, box-office performance became
the only measure of success, and corporate greed measured success in
terms of an increasingly higher margin of profit. But although box-
office success in America also became the British dream, a few talented
directors managed to create their own working worlds on the edge of
a shrinking, commercially unstable industry, and writer-painter–gay
activist–filmmaker Derek Jarman created a one-man show outside it,
like Andy Warhol in New York during the sixties. Lindsay, however, so
often proclaimed that "nothing was happening" in British cinema that
I finally asked if he'd seen Ken Loach's *Riff-Raff,* or Terence Davies'
Distant Voices, Still Lives, or Peter Medak's *Let Him Have It,* or Stephen
Frears' *The Hit* and *My Beautiful Laundrette,* or Jarman's *The Last of
England.* His reply: "I can't help feeling those British films you've seen
and liked mean more to you because you live in LA. Or do they mean
less to me because I can't find anyone to back any of my own projects?"

As well as *If 2,* these projects included two further collaborations
with David Sherwin. *When the Garden Gnomes Began to Bleed* (defiantly
uninviting title) was a comedy based on Sherwin's domestic crises and
experiences on the dole. More promisingly, the idea for *The Monster
Butler* came from the biography of a criminal butler who served the rich
and famous, including the Queen Mother. As well as charming all his
employers, he murdered his boyfriend, his brother, and the last couple
he worked for, an elderly member of Parliament and his wife. Finally
arrested and tried, he was declared insane. "I'm sure it would make an
absolutely horrible and quite successful movie," Lindsay wrote me, but
although Malcolm McDowell agreed to play the butler, and Gary Old-
man his boyfriend, it never found a producer. Only *The Cherry Orchard*
almost did, in the improbable person of Menahem Golan.

Golan's Cannon Group had prospered with soft porn (*The Last
American Virgin, Hot Chili*) and *Death Wish 2, 3,* and 6 starring Charles
Bronson, then floundered in the world of "art" with Norman Mailer's
Tough Guys Don't Dance and Godard's postmodern *King Lear* starring

Burgess Meredith and Molly Ringwald. Still hoping to combine prestige and box office, Golan negotiated a deal with the Soviet state production company Lenfilm for *The Cherry Orchard,* to be shot entirely in
Russia, but alarmed Lindsay by demanding "a big emotional opportunity for Maggie Smith as Ranevskaya in the last act, something
Chekhov neglected to write," then by offering Dustin Hoffman the role
of Lopakhin, the businessman who buys her estate and chops down her
orchard.

"Incapable of leaping into a movie project on Golan's scale, with all
the inevitable arguments about 'international stars,' location trips to
Russia etc.," Lindsay broke off negotiations. "Working as a loner
'against all systems' suddenly has become too exhausting," he wrote
me. "Is it autobiography time?"

It was certainly a turning point. During the early nineties he tried,
sporadically and unsuccessfully, to interest other producers in *The
Cherry Orchard,* and often quoted the response from a TV executive:
"Dear Mr. Chekhov, I am afraid this isn't quite the kind of thing we
like to make, but if you do write anything in the future, please let us
see it." And the tone of his letters reflected diminishing expectations:

> *A mad friend of David Sherwin's, who had a*
> *breakdown three or four years ago, has been*
> *trying to set up* Garden Gnomes. *Another friend*
> *has flown off to Prague to meet the people at*
> *Barrandov Studios and see what the prospects*
> *are of making* The Cherry Orchard *there. A crazy*
> *and very elderly millionaire keeps telephoning*
> *me from New York saying that he owns the rights*
> *to a play by Pirandello, {and} is supposed to*
> *have sent me the script, but it's never*
> *arrived. Get the picture?*

With so many doors closing on the future, his thoughts inevitably
turned toward the past. In 1990, after accepting a London publisher's
offer to reprint *Sequence,* he asked me to write an introduction.
Although I warned him that "it's a part of my life that seems a bit
remote to me now," he liked the result: "Personal, authoritative, with
just the right touch of disdain." But he was soon at odds with the pub-

lisher, who decided it would be too expensive to reprint every issue of the magazine in its entirety. "Please settle for a selection," I wrote. "So much of what I wrote forty years ago, I would like to stay buried deep in the earth." He refused, and the *Sequence* reprint became another unrealized project.

But during 1991 Lindsay had a relatively good year in the United States. He attended a retrospective of his feature films at the Cleveland Film Society; lectured on John Ford and screened *Wagonmaster* at the Telluride Festival, where Helen Mirren was a guest and remembered "a wonderful evening, with Lindsay at his very best—warm, incredibly knowledgeable"; and in September the Cincinnati Film Society advertised "The Most Complete Retrospective of His [Lindsay's] Films Ever Shown," from *Wakefield Express* to *Glory! Glory!* Audience reaction was pleasingly enthusiastic, but a brief visit to Los Angeles at the end of the month, in the hope of raising American money for *The Monster Butler,* proved disappointing. Although Lindsay's agent advised him that cable TV would be more receptive than a movie studio, the script was turned down everywhere. "So I suppose it's either autobiography time or Retrospective time," he said. "And I suppose they're really the same thing."

Back in London, Lindsay soon found himself without a resident "family." Sandy decided to live in Portugal ("God knows what will happen to him"), Patsy Healey was finally granted a suitable Council flat, and his own flat seemed even emptier after the loss, a year earlier, of his most important "family" friend.

When Jill Bennett committed suicide on October 5, 1990, it stunned both of us. Rachel Roberts had tried and threatened to kill herself so often that when she finally succeeded, the agonizing method she chose was more shocking than the act itself. But Jill was far more private, and although we knew that she was involved in a troubling love affair, she never made it seem a matter of life and death. And the quick, sharp humor that masked her deepest feelings was never more effective than on the last evening we met in London, only two weeks before she died.

Since her divorce from John Osborne, she'd had several brief affairs, and was now seriously involved with a Swiss businessman whom she hoped to marry. "It's either third time lucky, or I've missed the bus," she said. But Thomas was married and refused to divorce his wife: "He wants me to play the Margaret Sullavan role in *Back Street,* but I'm too old [she was fifty-nine] and not *noble* enough for it. And *he's* not really as charming as Charles Boyer." Then Jill wondered what movie role she could play to convince Thomas to marry her. I suggested Mary Astor in *Dodsworth,* and she saw the point at once. "Of course! Calm, patient, loving—and irresistible. I shall start rehearsing tonight."

But the scene didn't play and there was no happy ending. "Jill's lovers were always drawn to her strength and glamour," Lindsay wrote me, "and always proved unable to cope with her high-powered quality." (Although Thomas could cope with it in a mistress, he needed a more conventional, less demanding wife.) "So many other things, I'm sure, went to make up her mind," Lindsay's letter continued. "Age, and also a lack of work. Although different and seemingly less obsessive, Jill did have many things in common with Rachel. I can't help feeling that if both of them had been more acceptable to the English establishment theatre and cinema, they'd still be with us."

In a loving obituary that he wrote for *The Independent,* Lindsay mourned the loss of Jill's "disrespectful laughter," and seemed to make an oblique reference to their mutual empathy when he pointed out that for all her apparent self-control, she was "tremendously emotional. Life, other people, could hurt her. In the end unbearably. It is terrible to think of."

Soon after Jill died, I wrote Lindsay that Tony Richardson had contracted AIDS:

> *The immediate visible symptom is Kaposi's sarcoma.*
> *I think he's been covering up the lesions on his*
> *body for some time, but now they're on his hands*
> *and just starting on the face. He doesn't refer to*
> *them and his whole attitude is one of heroic denial.*
> *His energy is undiminished, as far as I can see.*
> *He plays tennis, talks about his next picture, and*
> *by silent mutual understanding his friends (at least*
> *the ones I know) make no reference to it. Well, if*
> *anyone can beat it, Tony can. Triumph of the Will*
> *has always been his specialty.*

If the new drugs had been developed a few years earlier, Tony might not have died on November 14, 1991. By an ironic coincidence Lindsay heard the news when he was in Turin for the Festival of Free Cinema. In a letter to me, he recalled Tony's part in the original National Film Theatre program of 1956, and the creation of the Royal Court Theatre: "If it hadn't been for Tony, I'd probably never have directed a play." He also saw *Hotel New Hampshire* again on video, and found it "tremendously redolent of Tony's wilful, extravagant personality. In other words, much better than it was taken to be. If only he had not had those ambitions to write his own scripts. But there was a strange arrogance in him, which preferred to fail on his own terms rather than succeed on anyone else's. A paradoxical kind of chap, always fascinating, and I can understand why you miss him."

By the time Tony died I was living in Los Angeles again, and he wasn't the only person I missed. One by one, Natalie Wood, Cukor, Krishnamurti, and Isherwood had died while I was living in Tangier, and I missed them one by one, but didn't feel a collective loss until Los Angeles had once more become, in the language of passport and visa, my "permanent domicile."

Although Nick Ray had died in 1979, before any of the others, he hadn't lived in Los Angeles for twenty years and I hadn't seen him in almost as long. But from our occasional talks on the phone, I knew he'd lost his sight in one eye; had lectured at various universities in the Midwest and East; had directed a movie (his first in over ten years) with a crew of film students; had married one of them and was living very happily with her in a New York loft. I also heard that he was fairly heavily into amphetamines and moderately into cocaine. But even though Nick had told me, the last time we talked, that he was under treatment for lung cancer, I wasn't prepared for the poignant human ruin on display in *Lightning over Water*.

I went to a screening of Wim Wenders' film about the last weeks of Nick's life with a mutual friend, John Houseman, who had produced *They Live by Night*. At first sight of Nick, the word "afflicted" flashed through my mind, a sudden memory of that Hollywood psychic's reaction to his astrological signs. Sitting close to the screen, as I always do, to see Nick skeletal, exhausted, and almost bald from chemotherapy was like shock treatment. But the opening scene of *Lightning over Water* became a kind of aversion therapy to Wenders.

He arrives at Nick's loft when Nick has just woken up in bed. The cancer has started to metastasize and is obviously causing him a great deal of pain, but Wenders in his voice-over commentary seems far more concerned with how painful *he* finds the experience of making the film, and the "pressure" *he* feels. "It reminded me of Miriam Hopkins trying to upstage Bette Davis in *Old Acquaintance*," I said to Houseman afterward. "Wenders wants us to believe his role is just as important as Nick's, even though Nick is the bigger star."

Only one scene, when Nick leads a group discussion among film students at Vassar, is relatively free of Wenders' intrusiveness. Although he appears in it, self-importantly giving directions to the camera crew, he at least allows the camera to stay mainly on Nick. At moments Nick stumbles over words and thoughts, but for the most part talks lucidly about his disagreements with Horace McCoy over the screenplay of *The Lusty Men,* and how he improvised on the set with Robert Mitchum. But shortly after Wenders filmed him at Vassar, Nick underwent more chemotherapy, this time for a brain tumor, and most of the rest of *Lightning over Water* takes place in a hospital ward.

Its lowest point occurs when Wenders stages an improvised scene costarring Wenders' current girlfriend, Ronee Blakley, as Cordelia to Nick's King Lear. Visibly in pain, his mind going in and out of focus, Nick somehow finds the will and the energy to complete it. Later he agrees to improvise another scene, even more bizarre although equally pointless, in which he and Wenders exchange roles. But toward the end of it he suddenly breaks off. "I'm sick," he says, then makes a last desperate effort to continue and tells Wenders, "Don't cut!" Less than a minute later, when he changes his mind, Nick speaks a final word in the last visually recorded moment of his life: "Cut!"

When we came out of the screening room, Houseman conferred his favorite word of dismissal on *Lightning over Water:* "Repulsive." But he supposed that the idea of dying on film must have made Nick happy. In fact, as we learned later, Nick had not only suggested it to Wenders, but wanted to die in a fictional movie, and cast himself as a painter stricken with terminal cancer. Characteristically, he changed his mind soon after shooting began and decided to play Nick Ray. He even agreed to take part in his own staged funeral before he died, then died before the scene could be shot, obliging Wenders to film the real thing. But if Nick was at least partly responsible for the uneasy mixture of improvised "drama" and documentary, Wenders was guilty of indulging and exploiting someone no longer entirely responsible for himself.

The screening took place, I remember, in a bleakly anonymous building in the stretch of bleakly anonymous suburbia known as Culver City. After Houseman said goodbye and drove off, I sat in my car for a while thinking about Nick, recalling various images of the man who changed my life, and of our life together. One moment from the past brought tears to my eyes: Nick standing in the arena of a Roman amphitheatre on the Libyan coast, empty except for the two of us, his arms outstretched as he declaimed, "Call no man happy till he is dead."

In 1988 Houseman himself died. "Apart from the loss of him," I wrote Lindsay, "his death was very moving because he went out with such dignity and cool":

> *"I'm not afraid of death, only of being undignified*
> *about it," he told Norman Lloyd. Well, he needn't*
> *have worried. Fortunately, after the cancer spread*
> *from prostate to spine, he was paralyzed below the*
> *waist and felt no pain. He read, listened to music,*
> *did a couple of TV interviews propped up in bed,*
> *until the cancer spread further. And then he faded*
> *away. A wonderful friend and a great intelligence.*
> *And will always be remembered, like Krishnamurti,*
> *Cukor and Christopher {Isherwood}, as part of the*
> *best part of my life here.*

This sounds as if I believed the best part of my life in Los Angeles was over, and for a while I probably did. The sense of collective loss made me aware of how much the place had changed in the fifteen years since I left, and at first I was more aware of changes for the worse. In the movie industry, corporate greed had increased alongside fear of failure, and made the formulaic search for commercial success even more desperate. Cash-flow anxiety and obsession with demographics and merchandise tie-in potential left the new ruling class no time for pleasure. There was more than a whiff of neo-Puritanism in the air, and of computer-cloned movies on the screen. And another industry, officially known as "neighborhood revival," seemed equally joyless. Conceived in the same spirit as New York's Disneyfication of Times Square, it was an homage to mall culture, the architectural equivalent of fast food. The lobby of Grauman's Chinese Theater had been "restored" in drugstore-Oriental, and a civic project was under way to "revitalize" three blocks of Hollywood Boulevard with a combined shopping center and "theme walk" for tourists, its centerpiece a reconstruction of the set for the Babylonian Court in Griffith's *Intolerance.*

Driving toward the hills one day, with the HOLLYWOOD sign in my line of vision, I thought of a more appropriate centerpiece: a continuous video performance of Mack Sennett's Keystone Comedies. The sign was originally a promotional gimmick for a real estate venture by the creator of movie comedy, whose wildly speeded-up chases were filmed on location in the Los Angeles of 1912–18, and anticipated the city of the future. In the reckless, disorderly, and exhilarating Keystone world, people sometimes forgot whether they were pursued or pursuers, criminals and cops seemed equally demented, vehicles collided and raced backward as well as forward, and doors struck back when pushed open. Sennett once said that he enjoyed "whaling the daylights" out of authority and convention, and it made him a natural child of the twentieth century, just as Griffith's sermonizing made him a man of the nineteenth.

Apart from the sweet, airheaded Bathing Beauties, Sennett's actors came from vaudeville and the circus, a few were cocaine addicts, others allegedly on the lam from mental institutions, and many were freaks who delighted in their freakishness, giants and midgets, the spectacularly obese and cross-eyed. Seventy years later they'd mutated to tattooed and ponytailed bikers roaring along Sunset Strip, drag queens blowing kisses from Gay Parade floats, starlets looking like drag queens as they posed for photographers on Oscar night, musclemen in tank tops walking miniature poodles, and Hare Krishna followers, white-robed, shaven-headed, tinkling their bells like lepers.

And seventy years later, "impermanence" had become the visitor's Pavlovian reflex to the Los Angeles cityscape, the random makeshift look of suburban development, houses here yesterday and gone tomorrow, and the unreliable topography, earthquakes with lingering aftershocks, cliffs, beachfront and hillside homes tumbling or sliding after winter storms. But although the place has always been overconcerned with the next twenty-four hours, and has always undervalued the last hundred years, when I returned to Los Angeles I found its impermanence reassuringly true to life.

It was still a city of the continuous present, with a precarious future and a mythical past, reckless commercial growth aboveground, animal relics from the Jurassic era below (a camel's tooth and horse's toe were discovered by workmen excavating a section of Hollywood for the new Red Line subway). And I could still replay my first experience of the land's original wildness by driving from seedy Hollywood Boulevard to an uninhabited area of the San Gabriel Mountains in thirty-five minutes. Two remote horizons, sky and the Pacific to the west, sky and the Mojave Desert to the east, created two views of the edge of the world. The sense of space was overwhelming, and there was a sense of outer space as well. Something alien and inhospitable in the whole region made it hard to believe that a mini-civilization had developed and overdeveloped there so quickly.

Without the movies, of course, it would never have happened. By 1915, when Sennett was making his Keystone Comedies, the leading production companies had moved west from New York and New Jersey. Ten years later, a string of dull and prudish suburbs had acquired a sophisticated and cosmopolitan cultural center, headed by Chaplin, von Stroheim, von Sternberg, Lubitsch, and Rex Ingram and the set designers William Cameron Menzies, Anton Grot, and Hans Dreier. The new look of Los Angeles and the movies evolved synchronously, residential areas and studio sets like mirror images of each other. Within the space of a few blocks you could pass a hacienda, a Tudor cottage, a French farmhouse, a driveway with an Art Deco gate. But in the beginning was not the word. It was only after the talkies arrived that the "writers' table" at the MGM commissary became the Algonquin Round Table West; and in another synchronous moment, Raymond Chandler with his first Philip Marlowe story and James M. Cain with *The Postman Always Rings Twice* became the first writers to grasp the fictional possibilities of Los Angeles in the same year, 1934.

In a sense, biography is history reflected in one person's life, and I began researching this mini-civilization because Norma Shearer became part of it soon after she arrived in Los Angeles in 1923. As an

MGM contract star she was directed by Lubitsch and Cukor, acted with Lon Chaney, John Gilbert, Clark Gable, Charles Laughton, John Barrymore, and Nazimova. As the wife of Irving Thalberg she knew "everybody" in the movie colony, from Chaplin to William Randolph Hearst and Marion Davies, King Vidor to Douglas Fairbanks and Mary Pickford, Gloria Swanson to David and Irene Selznick, Garbo to Scott Fitzgerald. Fortunately MGM was the one studio with a long-standing policy of preserving its films. The others had routinely consigned much of their old product to the junk heap, just as Los Angeles had destroyed or terminally defiled much of its natural environment and architecture. Then video made the past newly profitable, and studio executives ordered their vaults ransacked. Meanwhile, independent archivists had rescued many films thought to be lost, and historians had begun to tape interviews with retired directors, writers, and actors before their memories, like nitrate film, disintegrated with age.

But lost films and lost time could never be wholly recovered. Prints of five silent Shearers were missing from the MGM library, eight of the ten she made in New York had disappeared, and although almost everyone who had known her agreed to be interviewed, from a high school friend in Montreal to colleagues who visited an old, blind, deranged woman in the Motion Picture Country Home, I discovered the existence of others too late. Either their memory had failed, or they'd died the previous week.

In another sense, biography is detective work. On the personal level, Norma was extraordinarily conflicted—ambitious and insecure, calculating and passionate, selfish and generous, resolute and unstable; and she aroused conflicting personal reactions. Sifting the evidence and looking for a point of departure, I found it in Stefan Zweig's preface to *Mary, Queen of Scotland and the Isles:* "The clear, the manifest, is self-explanatory; but mystery is a spur to creative imagination. [It] stimulates the ingenuity of the artistic mind." He followed this with some basic guidelines: "When the sources do not run clear, he [the biographer] will endeavor to clarify; when contemporary reports give one another the lie, he will choose between accusations and exonerations; [and sometimes] he will find his canons of personal honesty best satisfied by leaving questions open."

The past, in fact, is only relatively more secure than the present, the biographer who believes in "objective truth" is deceiving himself, and the existence of so many biographies of one person, from the Virgin Queen to Hitler, is an index of that person's complexity.

Novelist as well as biographer, Zweig also provided a narrative key. Chronological and subjective time, he suggested, run on different clocks, "a human being is not fully alive except when his best energies are at work," and the two years of Mary of Scotland's "tragical passions" occupied more pages in his biography than all the rest of her life, her twenty-three years of youth and nineteen of imprisonment. In the same way, Norma was most "fully alive" during her twelve years as a star, which demanded three times more pages than her slow forty-year fade-out.

Reviews of *Norma Shearer* were generally favorable, but it was Lindsay's reaction that meant the most:

> *You've researched the book wonderfully and this,*
> *apart from anything else, makes it continuously*
> *fascinating—and, of course, the portrait of an*
> *era and a whole tradition of "movie culture" more*
> *vivid and understandable than any I've seen before.*
> *I feel I understand Norma in a way I never have*
> *before. And what a price God made her pay for the*
> *implacable ambition and determination he planted*
> *in her.*

In the New Hollywood (*Terminator 2, Home Alone 2, Rocky V,* etc.) I felt as much an outsider as Lindsay in Britain. But for a few more years TV continued to produce movies in the genre tradition of Old Hollywood and I wrote a few of them. The NBC production of Tennessee's 1959 play, *Sweet Bird of Youth,* came about because Elizabeth Taylor wanted to play Alexandra del Lago. Although I loved many things about the original, I knew it had a structural problem. As Tennessee himself realized later, he'd failed to dovetail Boss Finley's scenes with the central situation of Alexandra and Chance Wayne; but probably because several critics at the time had dismissed the portrait of Finley as "unreal" and "exaggerated," he also came to believe that his Southern demagogue lacked conviction. Thirty years later, glimpses of Jesse Helms and Strom Thurmond on TV were all I needed to realize that the portrait of Finley was not in the least exaggerated, and totally convincing.

Elizabeth had the authentic star aura and personal baggage that Geraldine Page (in the original movie) lacked; but she herself lacked, and frankly admitted it, Page's bravura and vocal range. So I shortened or interrupted Alexandra's great arias, as well as restructuring the second act, and was rebuked on both counts by the critics. In poor health during filming, Elizabeth gave a performance whose energy level was sometimes low, but I thought her Alexandra, a stingray to Page's flamboyant shark, notably successful in the hotel bedroom scenes with Chance Wayne. Under Nic Roeg's direction they played more intimately and reflectively than usual, and Mark Harmon made an arresting Chance, not the familiar tarnished golden boy but a troubled, reluctant animal, simple at heart, cunning by necessity.

"I'm glad you like Nic Roeg," Lindsay wrote me shortly before *Sweet Bird* began shooting. "I never told you, but my agent here got very excited at the possibility of *my* scooping this assignment. But the producer had been told that I was 'difficult.' " In fact Lindsay minded more about the reputation he'd earned than the opportunity he'd lost. Although he admired Tennessee's plays, he never felt he was the right director for them, and he'd just directed a new play by David Storey, for which of course he felt emphatically right.

The March on Russia, like *In Celebration,* centered on an uneasy and conflicted family reunion, but from the point of view of parents rather than children. (And to emphasize a continuity in the two plays, Lindsay cast the same actors, Bill Owen and Constance Chapman, as the parents in both.) The day after it opened at the National Theatre on April 6, 1989, there was another family reunion at Stirling Mansions. Sandy returned from Portugal, "started going 'high' again," Lindsay wrote me, "and ended up back in the Royal Free [Hospital]—with all the attendant nightmares of our decaying National Health Service. Sandy himself keeps quoting from *Britannia Hospital,* which seems to become more and more apposite as the years pass."

In his next letter Lindsay wrote that a British film producer had approached him to direct a film of Noël Coward's *Hay Fever,* to star

Maggie Smith. The project was "definitely" set up several times over the next eighteen months, but by the end of 1991 it became clear that the producer had "quite failed to get the money. And the scripts I'd like to make don't attract finance at all. There's no doubt that here I am regarded, as I often and no doubt foolishly say, as one of 'Yesterday's Men.' "

And then, early in January 1992, I had a note from our friend Daphne Hunter telling me that Lindsay had been hospitalized with heart trouble, but was now back home and apparently all right. He confirmed this when I called, and at the end of the month wrote to explain in detail what had happened. After suffering from shortness of breath for a few days, he thought he had "some sort of bronchial infection" and consulted his doctor, who sent him to the Royal Free Hospital for a heart examination. The doctor there ordered an EKG test, checked the result, and sent him to Emergency:

> *I was deposited on one of those mobile stretchers, where I lay quite agreeably for five and a half hours. Finally they wheeled me upstairs to the Cardiac Unit, where I was told that my heart was beating too fast and also erratically. I was put into a ward with three other people and three days later sent down to Cardiac again for "Cardioversion," which consists in putting an electric shock through the heart (under anaesthetic) which is supposed to restore it to its natural rhythm. All seemed to be O.K. with the heart afterward, but unfortunately it reverted the next day. I left hospital and since then have been eating a lot of pills which seem to be beneficial.*

When I called Lindsay again, planning to suggest that what had happened was a warning signal, he anticipated me: "I'm sure you remember that terrible British-middle-class expression, 'Don't take it to heart.' Well, *I* always do and no doubt I'm paying for it." In that case, I said, he could surely afford to consult a private heart specialist, instead of relying on a National Health Service he'd recently described as "decaying." But he found this "very American" of me, and insisted he felt much better.

From his next letter, dated March 18:

> *I went up to the Royal Free last week for an*
> *appointment with my Consultant. I don't need to*
> *tell you, do I?, that he failed to turn up. The*
> *Registrar who had been in charge of me has*
> *departed, and my own National Health doctor tells*
> *me he will be leaving for Australia soon. But*
> *my previous EKG at the Royal Free found me in*
> *"Sinus Rhythm," which means O.K.*

In the same letter he wrote that he'd just received two commissions from BBC TV, one for a documentary on John Ford (in two parts of fifty minutes each), the other for a documentary on himself, as part of a series called "The Director's Place." A month later he arrived in Los Angeles to film interviews with some of Ford's surviving colleagues. I noticed that he walked more slowly than usual, but he assured me it was because of an arthritic knee. And although he'd settled firmly into the "Brechtian" look of his final years, with its deliberately proletarian statement of worn leather jacket and cloth cap, his imperial nose contradicted it.

Mentally energized by being at work again, Lindsay was on fine sharpshooting form. On our first evening together his targets ranged from the "sickeningly awful" *The Fisher King* to the (pre–Tony Blair) Labour Party, more "grotesque" than ever: "If Glenda Jackson wasn't my Labour candidate, I might even vote Tory in the next election." He also aimed a broadside at the National Theatre, where he was due to direct David Storey's *Stages* later in the year. Among its "fatuous promotional gimmicks," he told me, was a series of tea-time discussions with theatrical celebrities. "You pay three pounds fifty for tea, scone (not 'scones,' please note), cream, jam—and Dame Judi Dench talking about her brilliant career. I am *not* making this up."

Before leaving for Monument Valley to film background material for his Ford documentary, Lindsay showed me a list of actors, writers, and cinematographers he planned to interview, and asked if I could think of any important omissions. I mentioned actress Gloria Stuart, from *The Prisoner of Shark Island*. "Do you know her?" Lindsay asked. I said that I'd met her once. "Did you talk about Ford? Did she like him?" Yes, I said, but she had more rapport with James Whale on *The Old Dark House* and *The Invisible Man*. A quizzical look informed me that Gloria Stuart would not be added to the list.

"Some of the interviews were not a great deal of fun," Lindsay wrote from London in September. William Clothier, who photographed *The Man Who Shot Liberty Valance*, had grown very deaf, and his memory was faulty. "Specimen: '*Liberty Valance?* Did John Ford shoot that?' " Roddy McDowall was "one of the few who could talk clearly and precisely and intelligently [about *How Green Was My Valley*]," and Maureen O'Hara was "sparky. It was most touching when, at the end of our interview, she read a piece she had written the night before about Ford as a friend and human being. When she came to the end of it, she stopped and put her head down and her hand to her eyes, and wept."

The BBC aired *John Ford* in January 1993, and a considerably shortened version was shown on PBS in the United States several months later. But the film had originated forty years earlier, in a monograph on Ford that I commissioned Lindsay to write in 1953. It was planned as the first in a series for the British Film Institute, to be followed by myself on Pabst, others on Buñuel, von Stroheim, Hitchcock, and Ophüls. Soon after I left England, the BFI canceled the series for lack of funds, although Lindsay's monograph eventually appeared in 1971 in the Los Angeles magazine *Cinema,* edited by Paul Schrader. And it reappeared in 1982 as the basis for his biography-memoir *About John Ford.*

By this time prints of several of Ford's early silent movies, missing and presumed lost, had been discovered in studio vaults and private collections. For *About John Ford,* Lindsay expanded his monograph to include them as well the later work, from *The Searchers* to *Seven Women.* He also interviewed several of the director's colleagues and described his own encounters with Ford, from the 1950 interview for *Sequence,* when Ford was making *The Quiet Man,* to their last conversation in 1973, when Lindsay had come to Los Angeles for the opening of *O Lucky Man!* and Ford was dying of cancer:

> *His hand lay on the bedcover, freckled with age. I*
> *held it for a moment, then kissed it goodbye. "Thanks*
> *for coming," said Ford. I turned at the door. "Is*
> *there anything you want?" I said. "Only your friendship."*
> *"You have that."*

John Ford

With an undercurrent of emotion, Lindsay recalls this farewell scene in the documentary. Wearing his signature leather jacket, he also introduces the film clips and some fascinating archival material, notably of Ford the notorious interviewer-tease dealing with an aggressive French critic who speaks uncertain English. (Critic: "How did you come to the motion picture?" Ford: "By train." Critic: "Why are women in your films always beaten? Always punished?" Ford: "That's an influence I get from the French. The *Apaches*.") The documentary, like the book, approaches Ford as "a poet of faith in an age of unbelief," with a deep nostalgia for America's pioneering past and its traditional values of "comradeship and the shared struggle for survival." Both recognize *They Were Expendable* as one of Ford's finest and most underrated works, and both are surprisingly indulgent to the "late-Shakespearean expansiveness" in *Donovan's Reef,* and the "emotional simplicity" of *The Sun Shines Bright.*

When Lindsay began writing about him, Ford was out of critical fashion. He was back in fashion by the time Lindsay made the documentary, but a new generation of critics found Lindsay's view of him unfashionable. *The Searchers* (1957) formed the great divide. Ford's younger admirers considered it a masterpiece that dramatically rejected his earlier view of the heroic West. But Lindsay's documentary repeated his earlier verdict in *About John Ford:* Although impressively crafted, *The Searchers* lacked "the humane idealism" of its director's greatest work, and "Ford's heart wasn't in it."

Earlier in the documentary he insists that "Ford was not a man to change." But nor was Lindsay a man to change his view of Ford. *The Searchers,* undeniably darker than Ford's previous movies, didn't fit this view; and Lindsay compared it unfavorably to a movie that did. *John Ford* ends with a tribute to the "graceful nostalgia" of *The Sun Shines Bright* (1954), a mawkish and racially patronizing account of the Old South, where happy pickaninnies play the harmonica, black mammies burst into song, and Stepin Fetchit repeats his 1930s comic stereotype.

How to explain the satirist of *Britannia Hospital* who embraces the sentimental never-never land of *The Sun Shines Bright,* "where justice is dispensed without regard to creed or color," and the director of *The Sun Shines Bright* who creates the somber world of *The Searchers* only three years later?

In *About John Ford,* Lindsay wrote that Ford's greatest movies were full of losses and partings, but "their sense of man's ultimate isolation [is] made clear and joyous by the bulwarks we erect, bulwarks of comradeship, family, love." In a moment of unconscious autobiography, he attributed this to something "buried deep no doubt in the artist's childhood, in some experience of community early on, lost and longed for." And as compensation, Lindsay suggested, Ford made films that emphasized "comradeship." But in *The Searchers,* of course, the bulwarks crumble, losses and partings are bitter and final, and the film's closing image is of a door closing on John Wayne's loner-outsider walking away toward the desert and terminal exile.

Rather than accept such a change of heart, Lindsay apparently convinced himself that Ford "never really believed" in *The Searchers* and his heart wasn't in it. But although flawed by a conventional romantic subplot, the movie has a power that could only have come from a director whose heart *was* in it, just as his heart had also been in *The Sun Shines Bright,* a last mistily nostalgic attempt to capture "the experience of community." And the change that intervened isn't entirely unexpected.

Ford had profiled his dark side before, notably with the ruthless pitch-black comedy that interrupted the touching scenes of backwoods poverty in *Tobacco Road,* and the sense of impending defeat that shadowed the heroism of *They Were Expendable.* Only three years separate

The Sun Shines Bright and *The Searchers,* where the dark side finally appeared full face, but during that time Ford had witnessed Martin Luther King, Jr., organize nonviolent protests against segregation in the South, and Anthony Mann's *The Naked Spur* and *The Man from Laramie* had introduced movie audiences to a West cruel and unheroic, very different from Ford's own.

Welcomed or feared, change involves leaving a part of yourself behind, and this is surely what Ford did in *The Searchers,* and the sadly inferior films that followed it. In *Sergeant Rutledge,* the story of a black cavalry officer accused of rape, he made Woody Strode a mysterious, dignified figure, light-years away from Stepin Fetchit. *Two Rode Together* and *The Man Who Shot Liberty Valance* were westerns that echoed the dark and ironic tone of *The Searchers,* and in *Cheyenne Autumn* Ford reversed himself again. "After killing off so many Indians in my pictures," he announced, "I felt it was right to tell *their* side of the story." (But he told it with a "Native American" cast that included Dolores del Rio, Sal Mineo, and Ricardo Montalban.) And his last, strange movie, the story of *Seven Women* missionaries in China during the 1930s, was soap-operatic but extraordinarily bleak.

Did Lindsay admire Ford, first and last, for a quality that he himself lacked? Although they had both endured the loss of "some experience of community early on," he was too skeptical by nature to compensate for it by making films that emphasized "comradeship, family, love." Unlike Ford, who became a "poet of faith," he became a poet of doubt; and later on, hindsight suggests, Lindsay refused to face the possibility that Ford had lost his faith, the doubter insisting that the dying man whose hand he kissed never "surrendered" to disillusion.

The only time I met John Ford, in 1965, he was visibly tired and unexpectedly benign. When I heard that he was preparing *Seven Women* at MGM, where I was working on that abortive script for Pandro S. Berman, curiosity proved stronger than trepidation. I called his office to introduce myself, mentioning Lindsay, and he asked me to "come over right away." Eye patch over one eye, dark glasses over both, Ford explained that he was about to screen a documentary on the Civil War. "Making pictures is only my avocation," he said as we entered the projection room. "My real vocation is studying history, particularly the

Civil War." The lights dimmed, and I didn't have to answer this deliberately perverse remark. Ford watched the documentary in silence, without removing his dark glasses. When it was over, he asked what I thought of it. "Not much," I said, and he nodded: "Nothing there."

Back in his office, Ford asked what I was doing in Hollywood. I explained how I came to work for Nick Ray, and Ford said: "Never heard of him. Who are you working for now?" I told him. "Enjoying it?" Not at all, I said, and he wanted to know why. "Because *he's* not enjoying it. He's too anxious," I said. Ford told me that Pandro Berman was "too anxious" thirty years ago, when he was the producer assigned to *Mary of Scotland.* "Now they're all like him. You should have come out here earlier." Then we talked of Lindsay, and Ford said how much he'd admired *This Sporting Life.* I mentioned this to Lindsay next time we met, and the reaction was a raised eyebrow. "With Ford, you never know. He told me the same thing a couple of years ago, but I'm not sure he ever saw the picture." I feel sure he did, and meant what he said. Like *The Searchers,* Lindsay's movie was about "man's ultimate isolation," and Ford seemed very isolated that day.

As *About John Ford* and the documentary reveal, Lindsay and Ford always had more in common than they realized. Several of Ford's colleagues and friends mention the disconcerting split in his personality, his acts of extraordinary kindness and extraordinary meanness. Henry Fonda (in an archival clip) comments on his "poet's eye," and Maureen O'Hara says that "with all his faults and virtues, you had to love him." In life, Lindsay's colleagues and friends often talked about him in exactly the same terms; and as Lindsay once said of himself, and as Ford more than once showed himself in his movies, they could both be "disastrously sentimental."

Lindsay on Ford, in fact, is the record of a profound affair of the spirit. Like all profound affairs it was a mixture of love, respect, insight, indulgence, and misunderstanding. And the final misunderstanding was ironic. In his next and last film, aired on BBC TV three weeks after his death, Lindsay portrayed himself as the kind of character he criticized as "un-Fordian" and "unconvincing" in *The Searchers:* the alienated loner-outsider, headed for exile.

12

Lindsay shot his second film for BBC TV during the last two weeks of September 1992, and a week later began rehearsing *Stages*, the last David Storey play he would direct: "Alan Bates in the lead of what is really a sort-of-one-man, poetic, subjective show." Rehearsals were "sticky," he wrote me, because "I have to say, in all honesty, that I (sometimes) don't understand what the characters are saying. As you can imagine, this doesn't go down awfully well with the author."

But what really disturbed Storey, as he told me after Lindsay died, were "the signs of mental as well as physical deterioration." Storey had noticed the physical signs three years earlier, when Lindsay sometimes fell asleep during rehearsals of *The March on Russia:*

> *"Are you okay?" I'd ask, and he'd wake up at once, totally in control again as he gave the actors moves and so on. But on* Stages *he was sometimes just not with it. Lighting changes were very important in the play, but until I pointed it out, he never suggested a single change. Then we'd devise one together, and the play was really "directed" that way.*

Lindsay had written me at the time, in fact, that he was beginning to feel "vaguely unwell," and pondered the cause of his "general fatigue." Was he overdoing it? "I start rehearsing at 10.30 in the morning, which isn't too bad, and finish between 5.30 and 6.0. But then I have to go, most evenings, into the cutting-room to supervise progress on the fifty-minute film for BBC Scotland." After the doctor at the

Royal Free Hospital checked his heart and pronounced it "okay," he consulted two other doctors, who found "nothing wrong," then a Chinese herbalist recommended by Eleanor Fazan. "According to her my 'Yin' and my 'Yang' are in imbalance. She said she was going to send me some herbs which have to be boiled up and one drinks the liquid which, it seems, tastes vile."

So vile, according to his next letter, that he soon gave up the treatment. Meanwhile *Stages* had opened at the National Theatre on November 12, and I had begun to research another biography, of Alla Nazimova. In January 1993 I went to London to view the National Film Archive's print of a short film that she had made in 1919, and also saw *Stages* on closing night.

A play in Storey's later style, spare, elliptical, antinaturalistic, it reminded me of *Early Days,* which was also structured around a central figure at crisis point, trying to settle accounts with himself by piecing together remembered fragments of his past. But unlike the politician of *Early Days,* Fenchurch in *Stages* is an alter ego, with a working-class background and family history very similar to Storey's. A well-known writer and painter, married with children, he's living alone after a nervous breakdown: "The self disintegrates at night. When I wake in the morning my state of mind is indistinguishable from that of a man falling off a cliff." The location is unspecified, but presumably a low-income, rundown London suburb: "I've intervened in two muggings since I came down here. And escorted a lady to her home whom I found one evening lying in the gutter."

As in *Early Days,* characters don't enter or exit on cue, but arrive unexpectedly in the present, or haunt Fenchurch from the past. ("I see ghosts here every night.") All the obsessive themes of Storey's work recur: the coal miner's son who becomes an artist, the splintered family, the failed marriage, the passionate affair with an older woman who died (a widow in *This Sporting Life,* Fenchurch's own mother-in-law here), the generational divide between parents and children.

Watching *Stages,* I remember, was like being taken on a journey inside a dreamer's mind. Jocelyn Herbert's set, with its geometric, almost abstract design, muted colors, and minimal furnishing, subtly evoked a nowhere place, next door to limbo, and Alan Bates, with his powerful stage presence, skill, and conviction, was a "poetic one-man show" in himself. I also remember that Lindsay's direction seemed rather slack. "Because you never really came to terms with the play?" I asked, and he agreed. Then he said: "But I'm getting old. Retirement beckons." Although only sixty-nine, he had visibly slowed down since we'd met in Los Angeles earlier that year, and his arthritic left knee made "walking a not very agreeable experience, like having all your movie projects turned down." He also felt very unsure about the film he'd agreed to make for BBC TV: "I wonder if anyone will understand it. *You* will, I think, but that doesn't mean you'll *like* it."

Soon after accepting the commission, Lindsay had written me a letter outlining the kind of film he hoped to make: a documentary about his daily life, centered on his flat and conversations with visitors around the kitchen table:

> *My title is "Is That All There Is?," a song which*
> *I remember Rachel {Roberts} singing, years ago,*
> *after a peculiarly horrible evening {in Los*
> *Angeles}, eating Mexican food and getting drunk*
> *in or round a swimming pool. I thought a good*
> *last sequence would be the distribution of*
> *Rachel's ashes into the Thames from a pleasure*
> *steamer. I also thought I would like to have a*
> *sequence of shopping in Waitrose {supermarket}*
> *and seeing all the heavily laden trolleys piloted*
> *by old ladies and Yuppies. The soundtrack to be*
> *provided by myself singing "Casey Junior" from*
> Dumbo.

Later he decided not to sing "Casey Junior" over the supermarket scene, but to intercut newsreel shots of starving Somalian children with shelves and shopping carts laden with food. And for the riverboat scene he decided to scatter the ashes of Jill Bennett as well as Rachel, while mutual friends watched from the deck, "gossiping (as theatre people will) and drinking and eating sandwiches," and Alan Price sang the title song.

Before I left for Los Angeles, Lindsay arranged a screening of *Is That All There Is?* and asked me, "for auld lang syne," to write about it for *Sight and Sound,* "provided of course that you like it." I liked it very much, and wrote about it, but presumably the BBC, as Lindsay feared, didn't understand it. They delayed its showing until shortly after his death; and then it seemed as if Lindsay had unconsciously filmed his own obituary.

Its "Day in the Life of . . ." framework manages to touch on almost every aspect of Lindsay's career, without any self-important attempt to explain his "creative methods." Scenes of "the director at work," in fact, are the briefest in the film. Only about five minutes of the total fifty are taken up with Lindsay discussing the set of *Stages* with Jocelyn Herbert and David Storey, listening to a fragment of Alan Price's incidental music, and dictating a biographical note for the theatre program to his secretary, Kathy Burke. The documentary is basically a portrait of the artist as an old man, and the world as he sees it: quirky, funny, sadder perhaps than he realized, and as nakedly personal as he intended.

After the main title, a quotation from his 1956 Free Cinema manifesto, "Perfection is not an aim," appears on the screen. It serves partly as a reminder of Lindsay's attitude to making movies, and partly (he told me later) as a coded excuse for some lapses in technical quality. Cinematographers Miroslav Ondriček and Mike Fash were both unavailable at the time, "and the one I ended up with was *not* first-class." Although the exteriors are competent, a bluish light that seeps into the first interior shot warns of color-control problems ahead.

After an opening shot of Stirling Mansions, the moderately ugly late Victorian block of flats where Lindsay lives, the characteristic device of an intertitle: "EVERY DAY." Lindsay wakes up with a few heavy sighs and one faint groan, then switches on the radio on his bedside table. The first of the media bombardments that punctuate the film is relatively mild, a refined female newsreader announcing that "one thousand businesses are failing in Britain every month." But TV will soon provide sight and sound bites of natural and man-made disasters (floods in Kashmir, civil wars across the globe), absurdities (film director Richard Donner expounding with great seriousness his belief in "provoking" an audience), and mindless gratuitous violence (a clip from Donner's *Lethal Weapon 3*). Alternating with clips from TV commercials, they reflect the media-dominated world in which Lindsay feels he's living.

In the kitchen he swallows a handful of prescription pills, and after a quick cut to the Queen Mother, still smiling relentlessly on the notice-board, he's lying in a bubble bath and gazing up at posters of his film and theatre productions on the walls. Later, in cloth cap and leather jacket, he walks up the street to leave a bundle of clothes for dry cleaning, buy a bottle of wine, and contrast the supermarket of plenty with famine in Somalia. In these scenes, as I wrote in *Sight and Sound:*

> *He is beginning to "play" himself, very much
> a "character," ironic and crusty, in his
> exchanges with the shop people. This is clearly
> a ritual; they expect it, Lindsay enjoys it, and
> there's an affectionately programmed Beckett-
> like futility to the whole thing.*

He also walks slowly, at moments uncertainly, and although still chunky seems somehow diminished. But the doctor who checks his EKG at the Royal Free Hospital once again says he's "fine."

Back at the flat for the next section, "INTERVIEWS," he receives a series of visitors. When a young producer of TV documentaries says that he wants "to make people think about what's going on in the world," Lindsay gives him a sympathetic but skeptical look. "You really think people *want* to think?" To Andrew Eaton, producer of *John Ford,* he remarks that movie directors fall into two categories, professionals who handle all kinds of subjects with style and assurance, and poets who work best with material that reflects their own personal values. "Ford," he concludes, "was a professional *and* a poet." To David Sherwin he reads from a batch of letters rejecting *The Monster Butler* and *The Cherry Orchard,* reacting each time with the ghost of a sardonic smile.

Two members of the Anderson family also appear. Lindsay discusses the state of the nation with his brother Murray, and they agree that it's deeply unpromising. But Murray takes the long view, gravely peeling a pear as he points out that civilizations rise and fall. "Britain is slowly going down the drain and *maybe* we'll make a comeback in three or four hundred years." Cut to a photograph on the wall: Mum peering over her spectacles, which have slipped to the end of her nose. In another scene, Lindsay serves lunch in the kitchen to an actor friend (who played one of the schoolboys in *If . . .*). Sandy joins them, leans back too far in his chair, loses his balance, and tumbles to the floor. Lindsay and the actor burst out laughing. Infuriated, Sandy gets to his feet,

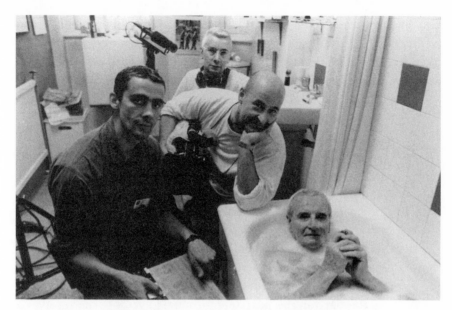

Is That All There Is? Lining up Lindsay in his bathtub

picks up a bottle of wine from the table, and pours the contents over his uncle's head. Cut to another TV news flash: the Queen (seen in her gold coronation coach) has agreed to consider a cut in her pay, currently "seven point nine million pounds a year." A non sequitur? Not really. Compared with the royal salary, Sandy's outburst seems far less extreme.

In dramatic movies, improvised scenes are always less convincing than scripted ones, because the actors lack a clear sense of direction and seldom avoid the risk of stepping out of character. But when people are playing themselves, like Lindsay and friends, they're automatically in character, as well as being familiar with each other's characters. In Sandy's case, so familiar that Lindsay could ask him to replay an incident that had actually occurred a few months earlier, and Sandy could willingly agree. The others were asked to talk about what they usually talk about, the world and the nation, the National Theatre, the movie industry, the BBC, and of course themselves. The scenes around the kitchen table suggest that it was all the direction they needed. Everyone has sat there before, with the same hopes and doubts that they reenact for the camera like a series of ironic routines, while Lindsay presides like everyone's favorite wise-but-testy father figure.

Is That All There Is? Anthony Page and Jocelyn Herbert on the riverboat

Is That All There Is? The lost, Rachel
Roberts and Jill Bennett

The final section, "Envoi, to Jill Bennett and Rachel Roberts," takes place on a small, crowded riverboat as it moves along the dingy, greenish Thames under a grayish sky. Until the camera moves closer, the passengers might be a group on a pleasure trip, buoyant in spite of cheerless weather. Then Alan Price starts to sing "Is That All There Is?," accompanying himself on an electric piano, backed by a combo of trumpet and sax, his voice as sure and vibrant as when he sang "Everyone's goin' through changes" twenty years earlier in *O Lucky Man!* Among others on board the Ship of Friends, we glimpse Alan Bates, Alan Bennett, Betsy Blair, Graham Crowden, Frank Grimes, Eleanor Fazan, Jocelyn Herbert, Anthony Page, Richard Eyre, David Storey, and Lindsay himself. The riverboat passes the Houses of Parliament, then a dreary shoreline of office blocks, and a couple dance as the song drifts across the water. It fades, and Lindsay proposes a toast to Jill and Rachel: "Friends of ours, friends of each other—and life is not the same without them."

Rachel's ashes are scattered first, from a plain white cardboard box, followed by Jill's, from an elegant wooden coffer. Lindsay and others throw white chrysanthemums after them, the flowers intercut with shots of Jill in *The Old Crowd,* saying "Thank-you very much" to the young waiter who takes her fur coat, of Rachel silent and withdrawn in *This Sporting Life,* of the two actresses photographed side by side in a London street. Then more flowers float away in the riverboat's wake, accompanied by Alan Price's music with its slow, dying fall. In the silence that follows, a black-and-white photograph fills the screen: Lindsay aged nine or ten at the seashore, gazing into the distance and waving. Farewell or greeting? We don't know, but it makes an eloquent conclusion to a film that's emphatically both.

"No, Lindsay, you *can't* throw the ashes of two of your dearest friends in that awful, cold, dirty Thames." This was her first reaction, Eleanor Fazan remembered, when Lindsay invited her to take part in the ceremony. But once on board, she changed her mind: "He was right. The whole scene was extraordinarily joyous and warm." The sense of loss in the final images of white chrysanthemums borne away by the muddied flow of the river is deeply poignant; and yet the film has an afterglow of celebration, of undying love for the dead.

· · ·

It was not coincidental, of course, that Lindsay chose to celebrate two generous and troubled outsiders, admired and loved for their irreverence, humor, and talent. In *Is That All There Is?* he emerges as a member of the same club, battling on in spite of physical decline and professional rejection. But there's no self-pity in his self-portrait, and there was none in his conversation on my last evening in London.

The last evening, as it turned out, that we would spend together. The setting, of course, was the kitchen table at Stirling Mansions. Lindsay cooked dinner, we polished off a bottle of wine under the eyes of HRH the Queen Mother and John Wayne, he asked me about the people I'd interviewed so far for my biography of Nazimova, and savored a morsel of serious movie trivia: Patsy Ruth Miller, who played a small role in the 1921 *Camille,* was the sister of Winston Miller, who scripted *My Darling Clementine.* Some time later he gave me a very direct look and quoted from the final chapter of *About John Ford:* " 'Ford saw the world going in a way he could neither approve nor wholly understand, and this made him sad.' " This was spoken very matter-of-factly, like the comment that followed: "I don't approve the way it's going any more than Ford did, but I think I understand it better—which makes me even sadder."

Then he changed the subject and interrupted my attempts to return to it. I've forgotten the rest of our conversation that evening, only remember Lindsay singing the refrain of a hymn before I left, "Lord, dismiss us with thy blessing," and his wanting to know if it brought back any memories. Of course, I said. At Cheltenham College, on the last day before the holidays, we always sang it in chapel.

Two weeks later, I sent him the piece I'd written about *Is That All There Is?* Toward the end of it, I remarked that the price Lindsay paid for being "an opposition party of one" and "remaining faithful to his pungently original, shit-kicking talent," was to have made only six feature films in thirty years:

> *From time to time, over the years, I've heard the comment, "Lindsay doesn't make it easy for himself." This, of course, is only a way of asking why he doesn't compromise, and overlooks a basic point. If compromise were in his nature, Lindsay would never have made the films he has succeeded in making.*

"Exactly the kind of piece I hoped you'd write," he wrote back:

> *You're quite right when you say that I've been*
> *reproached for "not compromising." But of course*
> *it hasn't been a decision. I just haven't been*
> *able to compromise. I suppose that's the meaning*
> *of the word "Free" in "Free Cinema." If I'd not*
> *felt the Liberty that comes from freedom, I just*
> *haven't been any good. Inconvenient, but*
> *inescapable.*

On April 17, 1993, Lindsay rented a church hall to celebrate his seventieth birthday in defiantly unfashionable style. "The food was appropriately church hall, fish paste sandwiches and so on," Alan Bennett remembered. "At one point Lindsay noticed someone's wheelchair. He appropriated it for a while, and played the crippled old fogey."

He had hoped I would come over for the party, but I was busy with *Nazimova* and called next day instead. How did it feel, I asked, to reach three score years and ten? It took him a long while to get to sleep that night, he said, because he couldn't stop thinking about the past, and how far away the days of *Sequence* and *Sight and Sound* seemed: "With you in California, Peter Ericsson living another life in the country, and Karel giving up films for the theatre."

Having seen Karel Reisz on my last visit to London, I knew he was about to direct a revival of Terence Rattigan's *The Deep Blue Sea,* and asked Lindsay if it had opened already. Yes, he said, and was a great success. "Very intelligently done, I thought, although not tremendously moving." Then his voice sounded a familiar battle cry. "But is it possible to be moved by a *totally* English-upper-middle-class play?"

This was our last conversation. A year later, shortly before his seventy-first birthday, it was Retrospective Time again. Lindsay flew to the Czech Republic to be honored at the Karlovy Vary Festival, and his old friend Vladimir Pucholt, now a doctor in Toronto, flew over for it. Although sad to see that Lindsay clearly "wasn't well," he was cheered by the "tremendous standing ovation" from an audience composed mainly of students: "They recognized him, as I had, as a man you could trust."

Soon after his return, Lindsay wrote me (May 8, 1994) that Sandy had gone "high" again, saying he felt low and depressed and suicidal, then exploding with incoherent manic anger and moving out of Stirling Mansions again. Living alone once more, Lindsay felt "a greatly diminished vitality," which he attributed to "a virus infection" that was sweeping the country: "Do you think it's the English disease?" In his last letter to me (June 8), he wrote that he'd finally "squeezed" a first-draft script for *If 2* out of David Sherwin, who was drinking heavily, but Paramount had rejected it:

> *I've been trying to get it put into "Turnaround,"*
> *but Sherry Lansing {head of production} has*
> *apparently replied that "she never puts things into*
> *Turnaround." And anyway the sequel couldn't be made*
> *unless Paramount gave us the authority to use*
> *material from the original film, which certainly*
> *won't happen.*

"Things seem to be winding down," he commented, and as I discovered after his death, Lindsay's diary was among them. After his notes on *The Whales of August* in 1987, it contains only a few brief entries. None refers to his personal life, as if he felt there was nothing more to say about it, and most are undated, as if chronological and subjective time had started to run on different clocks.

Among the undated entries is a note on Lindsay's final visit to Warsaw, where he met Krysztof Kieslowski, evidently before the international success of *Three Colors: Blue.* "He [Kieslowski] tells me, 'I talk about the world, not about myself.' A healthy philosophy for a young film-maker." Kieslowski also invited him to a screening of *A Short Film About Killing,* which Lindsay found "continually gripping [but] not quite satisfactory. There is something missing in the arbitrary fatality which is all it can offer as a comment on life."

Another entry records a posthumous encounter with Bette Davis, on a rerun of the *David Letterman Show:* "She looked painfully grotesque in a huge crownlike hat with large medallions of different colors stuck round it, and a big tinsel heart on her little black dress: wizened, gaunt, like an old witch. Letterman fawning skilfully. All she said about *The Whales of August* was 'There isn't a whale in it! I implored the director, the producer, but . . .' Not a mention of Lillian, of course."

Included with that last letter was a copy of *Sixty Voices,* a collection of interviews with British directors, writers, stars, and producers of the 1940s and '50s, "compiled by a friend of mine from Australia, strangely obsessed with the British cinema of those years. Pretty depressing, but it may bring back memories of the Old Days." The book was inscribed "with love and thanks," and a footnote: "Is That All There Was?"

A friend from the Old Days whom Lindsay saw whenever she came to London was Lois Smith. Formerly Lois Sutcliffe, she had launched his career as a director by persuading him to make his first documentary, *Meet the Pioneers.* Widowed, remarried, and divorced since then, she had continued to live in Yorkshire while becoming joint owner of a second home in the southwest of France with her friend Alice ("Al") Woodcock. Lindsay had stayed at their house in 1991, and in the summer of 1994 Lois invited him for a return visit.

Neither Lois nor Al, who later wrote separate accounts of Lindsay's visit, knew beforehand that during the previous few months he'd grown severely depressed, and was taking Prozac. And as neither of them had seen Lindsay since his previous visit, they were unprepared for the "frail old man" who got off the train on the afternoon of August 24. "His weakness tore at our hearts," Al wrote, although his eyes were sharp and still "suggested fight."

Before dinner at the house, he took a bath and reappeared in a handsome robe that "he proudly told us was a Christmas present from Frank Grimes and his family." After dinner he opened a plastic bag full of medications, and seemed "ruefully serious" as he explained the reason for each capsule and tablet. Then, Al remembered, Lindsay "told us how much he liked the house, considered our partnership a great success, and stated: 'It works, this place, it really works.' A quick embrace and good-night and off he went to bed."

Next morning they visited a neighboring French couple who owned a farm, then drove to Angoulême, where Lindsay bought postcards and took photographs. "He liked taking photos of us doing things," Lois wrote, "getting petrol at the grocer's shop, coming out of the butcher's." In the late afternoon they drove to a place that Lindsay particularly liked, a lake almost entirely surrounded by tall trees, pine, chestnut, and silver birch. And as he seemed happy and relaxed at dinner that night, Lois tried (not for the first time) to get Lindsay to talk about his early life. She had often wondered how his childhood in India, his parents' divorce, and his mother's remarriage had affected him; but as usual, "nothing was revealed. I was to remain in the dark about his personal feelings."

During the next few days Lindsay followed the same routine. As if needing to escape into other people's lives, he watched and photographed the neighboring couple at work on their farm, Lois and Al at their household chores, going to market, swimming in the lake. But on the evening of August 28 he began talking about the Christian belief in life after death. Although he dismissed it as "nonsense," and declared himself an agnostic, he confessed that on a few "difficult" occasions he had prayed and felt "comforted." Later they all sang hymns remembered from their school days, then Lindsay sang his favorite theme tunes from movies, among them a John Ford favorite, "Red River Valley."

Next morning, when Lois had gone out, he suddenly asked Al if she thought he was going to die. "I feel so very, very tired, you see." Maybe he had cancer, or was his lack of energy psychosomatic, the result of depression, itself the result of professional exile? "He became bitter and angry when we discussed his work situation," Al wrote. "He spoke of the futility of his plans and his own sense of loss. 'We're all washed up,' he said. 'The whole bloody country is finished.' Then he said, 'But they'll all be talking about me again after I'm dead.' As if for a brief moment he had looked through a glass darkly."

Tuesday, August 30, Lois wrote, was "a beautiful nearly-autumn day," and in the late afternoon the three of them set off for the lake. It was almost deserted, just a few people further along the shore. Lois and Al went for a swim, and Lindsay photographed them while they dried themselves off on the bank. Then he decided to go in the water himself, and they watched him "moving at a steady speed with his strong breast stroke." He swam back, clambered up the bank, and they turned discreetly away while he removed his swimming trunks and changed back into his clothes.

Then Lois heard "a strange rustle." They both turned around in time to see Lindsay plummet into the shallows of the lake. He lay very still, and at first they thought he must have tripped on a stone and been knocked unconscious by the fall. Al: "Eyes closed, and that extraordinary regal nose, conveyed the impression that he was simply having a nap." Lois: "We tried to drag him out but he was too heavy for us. All we could do was to raise his trunk out of the water, supporting him with our knees." He was bleeding from a cut on his forehead, and Al managed to hold him while Lois ran for a towel and mopped up the blood on his red jersey. The bleeding stopped very quickly, and she realized "it wasn't concussion":

> *Just at that moment, as we were looking around desperately, two fishermen were approaching. We shouted out and they pulled Lindsay up the bank. None of us could give first aid in such a condition. He was lying on his left side and becoming a dreadful purple colour. Al and I were speechless, but we looked at each other and somehow knew what we were facing together.*

Summoned from a nearby emergency phone, a doctor arrived in the fading light. He gave Lindsay oxygen, heart massage, and an Adrenalin injection, then listened to his heart. Finally he turned to Lois with an expression that told her Lindsay was dead. *"Crise de coeur, massive,"* he wrote on the death certificate after Lois explained that Lindsay had a history of heart trouble. Shortly afterward, two gendarmes arrived. They took down a statement from Lois, and as darkness fell an ambulance left to take Lindsay's body to the morgue at Périgueux.

Back at their house, Lois and Al went upstairs to Lindsay's bedroom, where his clothes and belongings were strewn around. ("It was so poignant, this fresh evidence that he was dead.") They found his address book, and Lois called Kathy Burke, Lindsay's devoted secretary for seventeen years. "Before I explained to her about Lindsay's death, I suggested that she sit down. Then I asked her to contact his nearest friends."

Later that evening Lois called Murray, who was too stunned to make any immediate decision about Lindsay's funeral arrangements.

But in the morning a friend offered to consult the nearest British consulate on the options available when a British subject dies in France. Shipping Lindsay back to England, it turned out, would involve a series of complex bureaucratic procedures, and his body would have to be sealed in a lead-lined coffin in the presence of port officials. But a local cremation would be relatively simple.

Although Murray agreed with Lois that cremation was preferable, he wanted no publicity, and explained how strongly he'd disapproved of the "flamboyant" ceremony for Jill Bennett and Rachel Roberts in *Is That All There Is?*

A macabre but unavoidable duty for Lois and Al was to choose the clothes for Lindsay to be cremated in. They settled on a dark-blue blazer, gray trousers, black shoes, and a second red jersey they found in the wardrobe. Later, in an antechapel at the crematorium, Lois watched an attendant wheel in Lindsay's body on a trolley. Surrounded by a display of Bibles and prayerbooks in glass cases, he lay dressed for cremation in an open coffin. Skin no longer purple, he looked pale and calm. Lois touched him and said a private goodbye. Then the attendant handed her a plastic bag containing the clothes taken off Lindsay's body after his heart stopped.

Lindsay once remarked that David Storey's plays "derived from his family experience in a Eugene O'Neill kind of way." And during the two days that preceded his cremation, Lindsay's own family history seemed to echo Mary Tyrone in *Long Day's Journey into Night:* "The past *is* the present, isn't it? It's the future, too. We try to live our way out of it, and can't." Lindsay's niece, Jenny, stayed away, maintaining her complete break from father, brother, and uncle. Murray and Sandy arrived separately, and although they hadn't spoken to each other for a long time, were obliged to share a guest bedroom. They didn't reconcile, but agreed on a truce for the duration. Frank Grimes, who had arrived earlier, occupied the other guest bedroom. At first, Lois recalled, he was uneasy at the thought of sleeping in the bed that Lindsay had used. But next morning he told her that he'd slept very well, disturbed only by cockcrow from the neighboring farm.

"A strange house party," as Lois commented later, and the atmosphere became even more emotionally charged when Al drove Frank, Murray, and Sandy to the lake, to show them where Lindsay had keeled over and died. Meanwhile Malcolm McDowell, who had been making a film in Italy, arrived with his wife, Kelley, and checked into a hotel. Lois drove them to the lake, which the others had just left, and they also took photographs. Later she drove them to the morgue, as they wanted to photograph Lindsay in his coffin.

A few close friends, David Sherwin among them, were unable to make the journey. He'd recently joined Alcoholics Anonymous, and his wife feared the occasion would prove too much for him to handle. But on the day of the funeral, September 5, three longtime friends arrived at the crematorium by taxi from Bordeaux airport: Jocelyn Herbert, Eleanor Fazan, and Miriam Clore, whose husband, Leon, had coproduced *Every Day Except Christmas.*

There was no English minister in the area, which Lois decided was "probably just as well," as Lindsay was not a believer. And there was no funeral service in the chapel, just a period of silence while his friends sat in a semicircle around the bier covered with red roses. Then Lois was the first to speak:

> *All I could say was that I felt we represented*
> *all of Lindsay's friends, not just us; all those*
> *who might have wanted to be there. Murray spoke*
> *as his brother and remembered their shared past.*
> *Sandy moved around the edge, unable to keep still*
> *and full of emotion. Lastly, Frank took up his*
> *guitar and sang "Red River Valley."*

Then it was over, and everyone started to leave. Except Sandy, who reached in his pocket for a handful of gravel that he'd collected at the lakeside. He walked slowly around the bier, scattering the little stones among the roses.

As Lindsay had predicted, there was a good deal of talk about him after he died. In general it was more appreciative than during his lifetime. *The Independent* even suggested that "he may well have been the single most important individual in the postwar British cinema," but drew the line at *Britannia Hospital,* whose "dyspeptic view of Britain made it a total failure." *The Times* went almost as far ("If one of the most imaginative film directors, he was also one of the least understood"), and *The Guardian* noted that "the failure of the British film industry to support him was lamentable." His work in the theatre was also praised, although the writer for *The Times* felt that Lindsay's collaboration with David Storey eventually began to look "a bit oldfashioned."

But fashions are temporary and style is perennial, as personal tributes from Lindsay's friends and colleagues implied. Jocelyn Herbert: "He was not a stager of sensational productions, he hated gimmicks and 'concepts.' His capacity to help an actor find the truth in his performance was a very rare ability." Anthony Page: "Lindsay as a [theatre] director was largely taken up with David Storey's plays. He brought out a beautiful Buddhistic kind of poetry in them, restrained but very passionate." David Storey: "Unique among British film-makers, he sustained an artistic vision from his first films to his last. The subjects he put up were not fashionable, and it was singularly difficult for him to get films together because of his integrity of perception in an industry constantly looking for novelty." Graham Crowden: "*Britannia Hospital* is a powerful vision of the state of the country, and very prophetic. It's a hard film but it has great compassion, and was absolutely Lindsay's view of things." Karel Reisz: "There was an absoluteness of stance about him. He was a conscience for us."

Karel was the first to call me in Los Angeles with the news of Lindsay's death. A few minutes later, Sandy called. Between the two calls, there was only time for shock and desolation, the feeling that a major lifeline had been abruptly and unexpectedly cut. After Sandy's call, I remembered a story about Lindsay that went the rounds for many years. He'd often attended the Cannes Film Festival, first as a critic, then as a director, and after the screening of a controversial movie, the same question could be heard in bars, restaurants, the press room, and hotel lobbies: *"What does Lindsay think?"* It was a question I'd asked myself in many different situations, and would never be able to ask again.

During the last year of his life, according to several mutual friends, Lindsay looked not only physically frail but "defeated," and Malcolm McDowell believed that the doctor at the Royal Free had underestimated the seriousness of his heart condition, then aggravated it by prescribing Prozac. I asked two Los Angeles doctors whether a person with heart disease should take Prozac, and received conflicting answers. In any case, the drug was a symptom, not a cause; and what caused Lindsay, I wondered, to fall into a depression so profound that he virtually self-destructed?

Although several of his friends also remarked how lonely he seemed toward the end, I doubt that anyone except Lindsay could have perceived the depth of that loneliness. Professional exile was only part of it. Directing movies and plays had always compensated, to some extent at least, for the pain of never having been loved as he wished to be loved. But without work, without love, without even his resident "family," he was isolated on every front.

As a movie director, Lindsay never achieved the major commercial success that would have given him what the industry calls "clout." The script that he "squeezed" out of David Sherwin for *The Monster Butler*, the most promising and potentially commercial of his later projects, was inadequate; and after alcoholism put their partnership on hold, it seems unlikely that Lindsay, at this stage in his career, could have found another equally talented writer to work with, or willing to work with him.

But Lindsay's professional isolation, as Alan Bates came to realize, was partly self-created: "His abrasiveness with critics was definitely one reason for their hostility, and the same abrasiveness with producers probably lost him the opportunity to make more films." In Malcolm McDowell's view, the abrasiveness was finally a mask for loss of self-confidence: "He deliberately created difficulties over *The Cherry Orchard* because he didn't feel well enough or sure enough to take it on."

At a severely depressive period in his life, Tennessee Williams rejected the idea of psychoanalysis: "If they take away my demons, what happens to my angels?" In the last year of his life, it seems that Lindsay's angels deserted him, and he was left to struggle alone with his demons. "By nature," he had confided to his diary at the age of twenty-eight, "I am strongly possessed by the vision of what might be, what should be." In other words, he was an idealist, and idealists seldom die happy.

The movie industry is particularly hard on them, which is one reason why Lindsay felt particularly close, among his contemporaries, to Satyajit Ray. Among the occasional pieces he wrote during his final years was a review for *The Spectator* (April 7, 1990) of *Satyajit Ray: The Inner Eye,* by Andrew Robinson. It quoted from a letter by Ray to a fellow director on the state of Western moviemaking in the 1970s:

> *The exterior of a film is beginning to count for more than ever before. People don't seem to bother about what you say, so long as you say it in a sufficiently oblique and unconventional manner. As if being modern for a film-maker consisted solely in how he juggles with his visuals and not in his attitude to life as he expresses it through the film.*

"This has only become truer as the years have passed," Lindsay commented, "and it is a trend that has affected critics as well as artists. But it has never affected Ray." And it never affected Lindsay. The Outer Eye may create a brilliant surface, but the Inner Eye sees further. Or, as Lindsay the critic wrote: "An attitude means a style. A style means an attitude." Lindsay the artist, of course, proved his own point with *The White Bus, If . . . , O Lucky Man!, The Old Crowd,* and *Britannia Hospital,* his unique Human Comedy of life in Britain during the second half of the twentieth century.

Afterword:

In Celebration

Helen Mirren
After he directed me in *The Seagull,* I always wanted Lindsay to see me in other plays. One night when I was doing *The Duchess of Malfi* I was convinced I saw him in the second or third row of the stalls. "I've got to be really good tonight," I thought, and felt I was—but he didn't come around afterward and I was devastated. Later he denied that he'd ever seen the production, and I realized that *hoping* he'd be there made me hallucinate him. He was so intelligent and articulate and talented that I longed, like many others, for his approval.

Alan Bates
Lindsay was a great friend. If I really needed advice, professional or otherwise, I consulted him. He was so clearheaded. I remember him saying once, "Remember, no offer is an insult."

Alan Bennett
Anyone who was his friend will miss those instantly recognizable postcards with their capitals, underlinings and exclamation marks, like the one he sent me from Moscow in 1987. "I have been standing for PEACE and MR. GORBACHEV with Gregory Peck and Yoko Ono and Gore Vidal and Fay Weldon. Where were you?"

Malcolm McDowell
I was having lunch one day with Lindsay and Ben Travers, and they discussed the epitaph they'd like on their tombstones. Ben: "NOW THE FUN BEGINS." Lindsay: "SURROUNDED BY FUCKING IDIOTS."

Is That All There Is? The parting shot

Karel Reisz

One day a man came up to Lindsay and myself in the street and congratulated us on *This Sporting Life.* He praised it effusively and called it the most important British film in years, etc., etc. We thanked him, and then he said, "But there's a scene near the end that I don't think—" and got no further. "Fuck off!" Lindsay said, and walked on.

Richard Harris

At a dinner party one evening I heard a story about John Huston. When he was dying, [his daughter] Anjelica asked him: "Dad, is there anything you want?" And John answered: "A good script." I told this story to Lindsay a few weeks before he died. And he said: "My dear Richard, that has been the story of my life for the last seven years."

Ann Sothern

I really miss the old boy.

Acknowledgments

There were many more friends and colleagues of Lindsay's that I could have asked to talk about him, but as I never planned to write a "definitive" life, I limited myself to the following, and am deeply grateful for their information and insights:

Alan Bates, Alan Bennett, Eleanor Fazan, Stephen Frears, Jocelyn Herbert, Daphne Hunter, Mike Kaplan, Malcolm McDowell, Michael Medwin, Helen Mirren, Anthony Page, Karel Reisz, David Sherwin, Ann Sothern, David Storey.

Many thanks also to others who helped me in different ways:

Murray Anderson, who contributed family history and photos; Kathy Burke, formerly Lindsay's secretary, a wellspring of practical information; John Haynes, who provided several prints of his photos of Lindsay's stage productions; Paul Howson and Sean Lewis, current and former directors of the Films, TV and Video Department of the British Council, who performed various acts of kindness; film historians David Robinson and Joseph McBride, likewise; Lois (Sutcliffe) Smith and Alice Woodcock, who allowed me to quote from their unpublished accounts of Lindsay's final days; and Monty White, Lindsay's executor, who granted access to Lindsay's private papers.

Finally, special thanks to my astute and supportive editors: Victoria Wilson and her assistant Lee Buttala at Alfred A. Knopf in New York, and Walter Donohue at Faber & Faber in London.

The quotations from Ben Travers on Lindsay and the production of *The Bed Before Yesterday* are from Travers's autobiography, *A-Sitting on a Gate* (London: W. H. Allen, 1978).

Index

Photographic Credits

Photographs in this work are used by permission and courtesy of the following:

Academy of Motion Picture Arts and Sciences: pages 42, 68, 158

Alive Productions / Circle Associates: page 288 (both)

Collection of the Anderson family: pages 4, 17, 22, 32, 155, 156, 158, 244, 327

BBC Scotland: pages 336, 337 (both), 352

John Cowan: page 103

Dominic Photographers: page 241

John Haynes: pages 180, 185, 236, 238, 255 (both)

HBO/Orion: page 307 (both)

Kobal Collection: pages 71, 102, 116, 119, 167, 169, 170 (both), 178, 198, 199, 203

London Weekend Television: page 252 (both)

Lumiere Pictures: pages 261, 262, 263

Tom Murray: page 181

Lois Smith: page 55

Warner Brothers: pages 200, 207

A NOTE ON THE TYPE

The text of this book was set in Garamond No. 3. It is not a true copy of any of the designs of Claude Garamond (ca. 1480–1561), but an adaptation of his types, which set the European standard for two centuries. It probably owes as much to the designs of Jean Jannon, a Protestant printer working in Sedan in the early seventeenth century, who had worked with Garamond's romans earlier, in Paris, but who was denied their use because of Catholic censorship. Jannon's matrices came into the possession of the Imprimerie Nationale, where they were thought to be by Garamond himself, and were so described when the Imprimerie revived the type in 1900. This particular version is based on an adaptation by Morris Fuller Benton.

Composed by North Market Street Graphics,
Lancaster, Pennsylvania

Printed and bound by Quebecor Printing,
Fairfield, Pennsylvania

Designed by Soonyoung Kwon